The Dragon and the Crescent

In memory of my father

The Dragon and the Crescent

Welsh encounters with Islam

Grahame Davies

SEREN

Seren is the book imprint of
Poetry Wales Press Ltd
Nolton Street, Bridgend, Wales
www.serenbooks.com

ISBN 978-1-85411-556-0

A CIP record for this title is available from the British Library

The publisher works with the financial assistance of the Welsh Books Council

Cover Image: Dragon and Crescent on Cardiff City Hall, by Pat Aithie/ffotograff www.ffotograff.com

Printed by The Berforts Group Ltd, Stevenage

CONTENTS

The Dragon and the Crescent: Introduction and a Note on the Text

To involve oneself with the study of Islam and a Western society in the early twenty-first century is to enter a field charged with tension, preconception and unease. Many times, during the years I have been researching this book, when asked that old conversational standby question: 'What are you working on at the moment?' I have answered: 'A study of the relationship between Wales and Islam.' Almost always, polite inquiry becomes keen interest, and, usually with a note of confidential gravity, I am asked the supplementary question: 'So, you're interviewing radicals?'

I have to explain that this study is rather different. It is not political fieldwork, but a study of attitudes towards Islam from the Crusades up to and including the present day as displayed in the literatures of Wales. Its aim is to show that, for all the intensity of current concerns, the relationship between Wales and Islam is not actually something new, not just the product of recent political events, population movements or media coverage, but rather something much more extensive and deep-rooted, much more complex and intriguing. In examining material from nine centuries of literature, it is hoped the study will illuminate areas of current social and political discourse including interfaith relations, prejudice, immigration, imperialism, community cohesion and, yes, radicalisation.

This study has several aims. It seeks to inform the wider contemporary debate about Islam and the West by taking as its field the literature of one small European nation, one whose own relationship with the dominant culture and language of the West has itself been complex and ambivalent. In showing that contact with Islam has been mediated not merely via major cultures, but via minority ones too, it is hoped this work will help contribute to a fuller understanding of how multi-faceted have been the relationships Western cultures have conducted with Islam through the centuries.

It is also hoped this study will help enable those in Wales who follow the Islamic faith to locate themselves within a continuum of Welsh relationship with Islam, which, while not always comfortable, is real, extensive and significant. Further, it is hoped the wide range of material gathered here for the first time – nearly 200 items from many centuries and very varied contexts – together with the contextual information and analysis, will provide other researchers and commentators with the opportunity to develop the study of Wales and Islam more fully in the future.

An additional aim is to contribute to the debate about identity within Wales itself, a nation where, due to the pervasive influence of a stronger neighbouring power for close on fifteen hundred years, the default mode of negotiating questions of history, belonging, and national consciousness has often been a binary narrative in which the Welsh are defined by an oppositional, subordinate relationship with England. In fact, the testimony of Welsh portrayals of Islam gathered here disturbs that simplistic dualism and shows that many Welsh people give evidence of a much broader relational repertoire.

It is my hope that in all these ways, this study will contribute to a candid assessment of Welsh intercultural attitudes through the ages, and will inform and aid cross-cultural relationships in the future.

As with my 2002 book, *The Chosen People*, a literary anthology examining the relationship of the Welsh and the Jewish people as reflected in literature, this study uses the extant literary materials of the Welsh and English-language cultures of Wales as a guide to cross-cultural attitudes through the ages. In the interests of capturing a wide range of Welsh responses to the Islamic world, 'literature' has been interpreted broadly, and as well as creative writing, the study includes genres such as biography, autobiography, theology, travelogues, travel guides and journalism, always with the proviso that the writing contains some flavour of personal opinion. I have accordingly excluded a smaller category of simply factual treatments, and translations into Welsh where the original material has not been modified. To avoid the observer effect, whereby evidence is distorted by the act of acquiring it, nothing has been solicited or commissioned.

However, while the net has been cast very widely indeed, some caveats are nonetheless necessary. As a selection of literature, this material is primarily the product of a class of articulate cultural practitioners, and while it can be taken as indicative of attitudes existing in a particular society or period, it may not necessarily be strictly representative of the totality of the opinions of that period or society. It is possible, for instance, that the more recent material, in common with the output of British artists and intellectuals of the period generally, may be more liberal than is public opinion generally. This is true in the case of Welsh-language material of the last 40 years or so, where the custodians of the written culture tend to be more committed and politicised than the society from which they are drawn. Such possible divergences are noted in the text where appropriate. For earlier periods, as the literary survivals collected here represent the main, if not the only, source of evidence for societal attitudes, any such divergences can only be conjecture, although the possibility of their existence should be noted.

The material is grouped in categories according to historical periods and mechanisms of contact, for example, the Crusades or Seafaring. In each case, the material is examined largely in chronological order to help trace the progression of thought, although in the interests of clarity some material is also grouped thematically within the chapters. There is, of course, considerable overlap; for instance, a missionary's account of a seaborne encounter with Muslims could be relevant to the 'Seafaring' category as much as to the category 'Pilgrims and Missionaries'. So, although I have tried to locate the material where it will best illustrate the mechanisms of contact and the attitudes associated with that theme, these are guidelines, not rules, and the categories are permeable; 43, the reader will readily see where a passage discussed in one chapter is also relevant to material dealt with elsewhere.

As this book seeks to mediate two cultures, knowledge of Welsh and Islamic references is not assumed, and attempts are made to indicate the significance and context of authors, places, events and institutions mentioned in the text.

Current practice is followed in transliteration of Arabic names, so in the main text, for instance, the spellings '*Qur'an*',

'Muhammad', and 'Muslim' are used. However, in quotations, the terms and spellings used by the original author are used, even when these differ from current practice. So, within quoted passages, variants such as 'Mahomet', 'Mohammed', 'Mahommed', 'Moslem', 'Mahommedan' and 'Mohammedan' are all found. Punctuation, italicisation and spellings are given in the quotations as they appear in the original. In the case of material translated from Welsh, transliterations are rendered as closely as possible to how they appeared in the Welsh.

More than two thirds of the items examined were originally written in Welsh and appear here in my own English translation, or, in a few cases, all of which are noted and credited, in extant translations by others. As far as possible, my translations try to reflect the literary quality of the original, whether that be accomplished or amateurish. In the case of poetry, the translations try to replicate the rhyme and metre of the original, except when the original poems are in *cynghanedd*, the intricate and ancient strict-metres of Welsh poetry, whose internal alliterative consonantal symmetry defies translation. In those cases, I have attempted to reproduce rhyme, metre and some alliteration, but not the complexity of the *cynghanedd* itself. As is said of the *Qur'an*, some things can only be fully appreciated in the original.

'Gone to Jerusalem': Wales and the Crusades

The relationship between the West and Islam has long lived in the shadow of the antagonism and warfare that characterised the early centuries of contact between the two cultures. Wales is no exception. The first records of contact with the Muslim world in Welsh literature date from the Crusades, which began in the late eleventh century, some four centuries after the birth of Islam.

However, it would be wrong to assume there would have been no awareness of the religion in Wales prior to those first literary references. Certainly, in the eighth century, there was a degree of contact with Islam in the neighbouring Saxon kingdom of Mercia, whose king, Offa (*d.*796), commissioned the earthwork barrier between Wales and England which still largely defines the borders of the two countries to this day. The British Museum displays a gold dinar coin dated 774, which depicts Offa on one side and the Islamic profession of faith, in faulty Arabic, on the other. The exact reasons for the use of the Islamic inscription are unknown, although theories abound. They include the unlikely, such as the claim that Offa was a secret Muslim convert, a notion whose credibility is hampered by the fact that putting the profession of faith on his coinage would hardly have concealed his conversion; the inventive, which suggest that the coinage was designed as an insulting means of paying a resented papal tax; the prosaic, which say that the coin-maker simply copied the intriguing foreign pattern without knowing its significance, and finally the pragmatic, and most likely, which supposes the coin was designed for trade with Muslim Spain.

Whatever the truth may be, it shows contact between the Islamic world and that of western Britain. The Harvard scholar Matthieu Boyd has shown that Viking trade in goods and slaves between Ireland, Britain and Islamic Spain and North Africa, was responsible for an exchange of material and of ideas between

Islam and Christian Britain.[1] And, writing in 1968, the great American mythologist, Joseph Campbell, in an extended analysis of the Tristan myth, speculated that at least by the late eleventh century, Islamic stories had reached the Celtic west:

> It is possible that even earlier than this date a flow of ideas may already have been set in motion from Moorish Spain to the north, and in particular by sea to Celtic Ireland, Wales, Cornwall, and Brittany (the lands of the romance of Tristan and Isolt), where a golden age of amalgamated pagan and Christian poetry and learning had glowed with a strange light of its own throughout the long grim night of the early Christian Middle Ages.[2]

Certainly, Wales participated in the general European celebration of the campaigns of the Frankish king Charlemagne (*c.*742-814) against the Muslim presence in Spain later in the eighth century. Later medieval Welsh translations and adaptations of the *Deeds of Charlemagne*[3] show that interest in the conflict was widespread, even if the surviving records are not contemporary with Charlemagne or the Crusades. In later Welsh praise poems, it was customary to attribute the characteristics of Charlemagne, or his most famous paladins, Roland and Oliver, among many other heroes, to the person being eulogised. At the time of its first contact with Islam, Wales was therefore not isolated from knowledge of the major events of the period, and there had been a long tradition of interest in, and contact with, the Holy Land. Wales had been part of the Roman Empire, had adopted Christianity long before the English had arrived in Britain, and its people had long taken part enthusiastically in the pilgrim movement which saw people forsaking their homes in all parts of the Christian world to visit the sites in Palestine where their faith had been born. As early as 386, St Jerome, the main translator of the Bible into Latin, writing from his home in Bethlehem, urged friends to visit the Holy Land, pointing out that pilgrims from as far away as Britain were doing so: 'The Briton, "sundered from our world,"[4] no sooner makes progress in religion than he leaves the setting sun in quest of a spot of which he knows only through Scripture and common report.'[5]

While some Welsh people had therefore visited the real territory of Palestine, the Holy Land was also part of the mental and mythical landscape for many more. The major Welsh saints

Padarn and Teilo, and the country's patron saint Dewi himself were all reputed to have undertaken pilgrimages to the Holy Land.[6] Dewi was even claimed to have been consecrated bishop in Jerusalem. Even King Arthur was said to have visited Jerusalem, and in one of the most valuable of Welsh texts, *The Black Book of Carmarthen*, copied in the thirteenth century, the enigmatic shape-shifting figure of Taliesin is depicted as claiming to have returned from 'Caer Seon', the Fortress of Zion – Jerusalem – where he has been 'contending with Jews'. Whether the reference was the original author's intent or, as has been suggested, a mistake by a later scribe working at the time of the Crusades, it nonetheless indicates the use of the Holy Land as a significant location.[7]

In addition, the Welsh felt a particular interest in the fate of the Holy Places, due to the widespread belief that the Empress Helena of Constantinople (*c*.246-50-*c*.330), discoverer of the True Cross and mother of the first Christian Roman Emperor, Constantine the Great (272-337), was Welsh. Helena was actually from Asia Minor, but popular legend in Wales confused her with Elen, or St Elen, of Caernarfon, a Romano-British woman living more than half a century later, who was traditionally supposed to have married the British-based Roman general, Magnus Maximus (*c*.335-88), who later became Emperor of the western portion of the empire. That Constantine the Great had himself been stationed in Britain at the time he was proclaimed emperor and that one of Elen's children was called Constantine simply added to the combination of confusion and wishful thinking that made Welsh people believe that one of their countrywomen was the 'Helen' who, with the encouragement of her emperor son, had excavated the holy places in Jerusalem and brought back to the West the very cross on which Jesus had been crucified.[8]

The sense of involvement was intensified by the fact that the holiest relic of the Gwynedd dynasty, whose power-base in north-west Wales was the mainstay of Welsh resistance to English expansion, was a piece of that very same True Cross, known as 'Y Groes Naid'. The Anglican priest, historian and Latinist Griffith Hartwell Jones (1858-1944), in his extensive 1912 study, *Celtic Britain and the Pilgrim Movement*,[9] says of 'Y Groes Naid' that it was reputed to have been brought from the Holy Land by

St Neotus. He adds: 'Among the Welsh relics none was more precious than the Groes Naid ... adorned with gold, silver and jewels, which was regarded by the Welsh as a national palladium and carried before the princes of Wales.' People would swear by the Groes Naid, and its possession was believed to keep the kingdom safe.

Therefore, with the Holy Land as a long-established place of Welsh pilgrimage, as the source of Wales's most potent national talisman, and as the location of some of its most cherished legends, it is understandable to suppose the Welsh would take more than a passing interest in the fate of the holy places as Crusading fever swept Christendom in the late eleventh century, sparked by the widespread sense of resentment and threat European Christians felt at perceived Muslim usurpation of Christian privileges in the Holy Land.

However, when it came to supporting the Crusading enterprise with actual military force, any general or particular sympathy the Welsh may have felt in favour of the project had to contend with a contrary consideration: that any resource directed to Palestine was a resource lost to the constant struggle to maintain Welsh independence in the face of Anglo-Norman encroachment. The Welsh had been waging a periodic defensive battle with expansionist English power for five hundred years, ever since the Anglo-Saxons had first landed in Britain following the withdrawal of the Roman legions in 410. The arrival of the land-hungry Norman barons on the Welsh borders following the Norman conquest of Saxon England in 1066 was only the latest, albeit the most threatening, in a series of invasions. The Welsh may have shared with the English and the Normans the general concern about Christian rights in the Holy Land, but in practical terms, the Saracens were not threatening to conquer Wales; the Anglo-Normans were. Under such circumstances, it is understandable if the Welsh should have prioritised a local war of survival over a distant war of religion. There is evidence that these priorities were indeed at work. In the historical and literary records, references to Welsh military presence in Palestine are very scarce, while there is strong evidence that the Welsh exploited Anglo-Norman preoccupation with the Crusades to regain or consolidate their own territories at home.

Among the most important sources for the period are the

Welsh annalistic chronicles, seven manuscripts produced by monasteries in Wales, probably the most significant of which is *Brut y Tywysogion*, the *Chronicle of the Welsh Princes*, a record of Welsh history from the seventh to the fourteenth centuries.[10] Much of the material from the Crusading period, in the eleventh, twelfth and thirteenth centuries, records the dynastic battles, deaths, annexations, feuds and rebellions within Wales itself. But major events in England and France and beyond were recorded too, including some major events of the Crusades. Quotations and translations below are taken from Thomas Jones's 1952 edition of the *Brut*, except for occasional references to other annals of the period, which are mentioned specifically. The first relevant entry from the *Brut* records how the son of William the Conqueror was drawn into the First Crusade, creating a power vacuum the Welsh were quick to exploit.

> 1092-94 A year after that, king William, son of William the Elder, who first defeated the Saxons in glorious war, went to Normandy to defend the kingdom of Robert, his brother, who had gone to Jerusalem to fight against the Saracens and to defend Christendom. And while he stayed there, the Britons, being unable to bear the tyranny and injustice of the French, threw off the rule of the French, and they destroyed their castles in Gwynedd and inflicted slaughters upon them.[11]

Alison Elizabeth Barnes, who has studied Welsh involvement in the Crusades from 1095-1200, notes 'The Britons (as they are referred to in the account) [the *Brut*] saw in England a "kingless kingdom", an opportunity to overthrow the Norman rule in Wales at the time.'[12] She adds that the domestic opportunities afforded by Anglo-Norman distraction may have deterred the Welsh themselves from participating wholeheartedly in the Crusades: '... with their fighting forces for once loosely united against the common enemy of the French, it seems unsurprising they would not be looking to commit themselves elsewhere, regardless of the gravity of the movement.'[13] We will return shortly to consider the wider implications for Welsh independence of the fact that Norman power had been distracted from the project of conquering Wales by the larger enterprise of the Crusades. But for the moment, as a means of sketching the progress of the Crusades themselves, let us examine some of the other main references to them which are contained in the *Brut.*

Some of the entries for the Crusading period give considerable detail about campaigns in the Holy Land, although for the purposes of this study, the extracts quoted have been restricted to ones which involve figures important to Welsh history. The entry, from 1125-28, shows the only reference in any of the Welsh annals to a named Welsh person reaching the Holy Land. In this case, however, it is unclear if the journey was specifically one of military Crusade, or penance, or a mixture of the two:

> Towards the end of that year, Morgan ap Cadwgan went to Jerusalem because of the murder of his brother, and as he was returning he died in the island of Cyprus in the Tyrrhene Sea.[14]

As the *Brut*'s authors display no scepticism about the Crusades or their aims *per se,* and seem to share the attitudes one would have expected of any Christian nation of the period, it seems clear the near-total absence of references to named Welsh presence in Palestine cannot be attributed to ideological reasons. Other entries in the Welsh annals record the departure on pilgrimage or campaign of named border barons[15] and kings of England (whose absence, it is fair to speculate, might have allowed the hard-pressed defenders a welcome respite). The more numerous Anglo-Norman chronicles of the period are equally detailed in references to Anglo-Norman named participants in the Crusades, and equally lacking in references to Welsh ones.

Morgan ap Cadwgan's journey was undertaken at a time of comparative stability in Palestine.[16] It should be remembered that during the two centuries of the Crusading enterprise, large-scale open warfare was very much the exception, and most of the period was characterised by varying degrees of peace, truce or stalemate. It was during a similar period that the following incident occurred:

> 1143-44: In that year Welsh pilgrims were drowned on their way to Jerusalem.[17]

By 1147, hostilities in Palestine were once more intense, and after the Christians lost the city of Edessa, the Second Crusade was proclaimed. The *Brut* records:

> 1146-47 ... the king of France, who was called Louis, and the Emperor of Germany, and a vast multitude of earls and barons along with them, went to Jerusalem.[18]

This venture, which lasted until 1149, was unsuccessful; the campaign's legacy of disunity among the Christian forces, and distrust among neighbouring powers, left the Crusader states isolated as Muslim power became stronger and more unified. It was clear a further conflict was coming, as this entry from 1185 shows:

> ... the Patriarch came from Jerusalem to England to seek help from the king of England lest the Saracens and the Jews should harry all the land of Jerusalem. And he went back with a multitude of knights and foot-soldiers among them.[19]

The Christian preparations were in vain, however, as the Muslim forces, under the inspirational leadership of Salah ad-Din Yusuf ibn Ayyub, (1138-93) known as Saladin, retook Jerusalem in 1187, extinguishing nearly all the Crusader possessions in Palestine. The *Brut* records the fall, and the response of Christian Europe: another Crusade, the Third.

> 1188 A year after that the Pagans and the Saracens came to Jerusalem and they took the whole city on the first assault on Ash Wednesday, and carried off the Holy Cross with them. And the Christians they found in the city, some of them they killed and others they carried off with them into bondage. And for that reason, Philip, King of France, and Henry, King of England, and Baldwin, archbishop of Canterbury, and a multitude beyond number of Christians took the Cross.[20]

> 1190 ... One thousand one hundred and ninety was the year of Christ when Philip, King of France, and Richard, King of England, and Baldwin, archbishop of Canterbury, and earls and barons beyond number and a multitude of others, went as Crusaders to Jerusalem.[21]

It was in preparation for this Crusade that Baldwin (*c.*1125-90) the Archbishop of Canterbury, had conducted a preaching tour in Wales in 1188. He was accompanied by the Norman-Welsh churchman and chronicler Giraldus Cambrensis (*c.*1146-*c.*1223), whose 1191 record of the journey, *Itinerarium*

Cambriae (*Journey through Wales*) is a document of outstanding value to Welsh history, and to medieval history generally, as it is the most complete account of a Crusade preaching tour from anywhere in Europe. Professor Peter Edbury of Cardiff University, an expert in the Crusades, has observed that the tour, which had no equivalents in England, was a response to the particular governance arrangements of Wales at the time. Marcher Lordships and Wales were not subject to the 'Saladin Tithe' which was used in England to fund the campaign, so support would have to come in the form of fighting men, a measure which would not only mean that the Crusade would gain a supply of reliable soldiers – companies of skilled Welsh archers in particular had long served in English kings' armies – but would mean that numbers of fighting men would be removed from a troublesome region into the bargain.[22] Giraldus's account of the tour can be examined more closely now before we return to the final references to the Crusades in the *Brut*, and to an assessment of the larger significance of the Crusades for Wales.

Giraldus was himself a Norman with some Welsh heritage, and he held an ambivalent position between the two parties, serving the Anglo-Norman crown on the one hand, while, on the other, seeking to emphasise Welsh distinctiveness, particularly in the ecclesiastical realm, in the interests of persuading the Anglo-Norman and Papal establishments to realise his personal long-cherished ambition of being made Archbishop of St David's, a project which placed him at the heart of a struggle with Canterbury over the independence of the Welsh church. He was ultimately unsuccessful in his quest for the Archbishopric, but when he wrote the *Journey*, his dream was very much alive, and his account has something of the character of an extended job application. His journey would have been an uneasy enterprise, as the Welsh were suspicious of the claims of the Norman-dominated Archbishopric of Canterbury to jurisdiction in Wales, and the native Welsh princes and the recently-arrived Norman barons and English settlers lived in a state of mutual suspicion and tension punctuated by open warfare. Giraldus, however, was nothing if not optimistic. His record of his journey is enlivened by his disarmingly self-aggrandising descriptions of his own abilities, for instance, in this extract from Chapter 11 of the first volume of his book where he reviews his own preaching performance at Haverfordwest:

> In Haverfordwest first the Archbishop himself gave a sermon, and then the word of God was preached with some eloquence by the Archdeacon of St David's, the man whose name appears on the title-page of this book, in short by me. A great crowd of people assembled, some of them soldiers, others civilians. Many found it odd and some, indeed, thought it little short of miraculous, that when I, the Archdeacon, preached the word of God, speaking first in Latin and then in French, those who could not understand a word of either language were just as much moved to tears as the others, rushing forward in equal numbers to receive the sign of the Cross.[23]

It should be noted, however, that these people were not necessarily native Welsh, but Flemings, settlers with whom the Welsh were periodically involved in bitter conflict, as Giraldus himself notes a few lines later:

> The folk who lived in the neighbourhood came from Flanders, for they had been sent there by king Henry I to colonize the districts. They are a brave and robust people, but very hostile to the Welsh.[24]

In Chapter 5, he had recorded an earlier preaching success, this time explicitly including the Welsh:

> In Usk Castle a large group of men was signed with the Cross. This was the result of the Archbishop's sermon and of an address by that good and honest man, William, Bishop of Llandaff, who remained constantly at our side as long as we were in his diocese. Alexander, Archdeacon of Bangor, acted as interpreter for the Welsh. To the great astonishment of everyone present, and it was, indeed, an extraordinary circumstance, some of the most notorious criminals of those parts were among those converted, robbers, highwaymen and murderers.[25]

In Llandaff near Cardiff, the divided nature of society in Wales was apparent even as the churchmen appealed for common cause in the interests of Christendom:

> The next morning the Cross was preached in Llandaff. The English stood on one side and the Welsh on the other; and from each nation many took the Cross.[26]

At Cardigan in west Wales, among the Welsh, Giraldus again

records that 'the word of God was preached with great effect, first by the archbishop and then by me, the Archdeacon of St David's'[27]. He then gives one of the spectacular retributive legends with which his chronicle is filled[28], telling how a woman physically prevented her husband from going to the Archbishop, and was punished three days later by a voice from heaven and by the death of her infant son, after which she repented and sewed the symbolic cross on her husband's garment herself.[29]

Giraldus reports further recruitment success in north Wales. However, it is clear that the Crusading message was not universally welcome. Peter Edbury has pointed out that Giraldus's tour took its time through the Anglo-Norman districts of the south, but passed very quickly through the native Welsh areas of the north.[30] On that part of the tour, Giraldus tells of three young noblemen brothers, Gruffydd, Maelgwn and Cynwrig, disputing about taking the cross, with Maelgwn eventually promising to go only if the king himself advised him to. And in Oswestry, Giraldus tells of a young Welsh nobleman who had wanted to impose conditions of a different kind: when spoken to by a previous visitor, Bishop Reiner, also preaching the Crusade, the youth promised he would take the cross only if he could avenge a local blood-feud first. However, Giraldus says, no sooner had he said this than the lance he was brandishing shattered in his hand: 'He was alarmed and terrified by this omen, which he accepted as a sign that he must indeed take the cross, and this he did without further argument.'[31] In Shrewsbury, Giraldus says 'by the Archbishop's preaching and by the elegant sermons delivered by me, Gerald, Archdeacon of St David's, we persuaded many folk to take the Cross.'[32] However, Giraldus and Baldwin were forced to excommunicate the Welsh prince Owain Cyfeiliog (c.1130-97), '... because he alone, of all the Welsh princes, had made no move to come with his people to meet the Archbishop. This Owain was much more fluent in speech than the other Welsh princes, and he was well-known for the sensible way in which he managed his land.'[33]

Giraldus concludes his account with a predictably optimistic assessment of the recruitment exercise, although it is possible to gather that while securing the promised enlistments was one thing, delivering the forces to the Holy Land was quite another.

> We worked very hard to make a success of our mission. About three thousand men were signed with the Cross, all of them highly skilled in the use of the spear and the arrow, most experienced in military affairs and only too keen to attack the enemies of our faith at the first opportunity. They were all sincerely and warmly committed to Christ's service. If only the Crusade itself had been prosecuted with an urgency and forethought on a par with the enthusiasm and devotion of these men whom we collected![34]

Giraldus blames internal Christian dissent, and a dilatory leadership for the failure to follow through with the campaign successfully. The Third Crusade, when it did eventually reach Palestine, saw a few Christian victories, and some diplomatic successes, but was ultimately a strategic failure, leaving Baldwin – 'that most saintly man', the *Brut* for 1191 called him[35] – dead at the siege of Acre, and King Richard, returning from the uneasy truce which was the result of the expedition, imprisoned for over a year by a hostile rival. How many of Gerald's estimated 3,000 men were actually among the 8,000 who accompanied King Richard's expedition is difficult to say, but the note of regret in Giraldus's retrospective conclusion to his *Journey*, suggests that it was not as many as he would have hoped. After all, Giraldus himself had taken the Cross, had vowed to go to the Holy Land, but, being absolved from his vow a year later, had not actually gone at all. There may, in fact, have been very few Welsh participants in the expedition. In her 2009 study, *Crusades and Crusading in the Welsh Annalistic Chronicles*, the historian Kathryn Hurlock notes that the important native Welsh leader, Lord Rhys of Deheubarth, had also taken the Cross but had not actually gone on Crusade either, and that he 'instead spent the early 1190s recapturing castles which had previously fallen to the marcher lords.' In her 2002 study of the 1095-1200 period, Alison Elizabeth Barnes could find no references to named Welsh participants in the Third Crusade, whether in the few Welsh or many Anglo-Norman records.[36]

That expedition did, however, produce one legend of anonymous Welsh enterprise in the Holy Land, as recorded, among other chronicles, by Richard of Devizes in 1190 in an entry entitled: 'How a Parthian bowman was shot by a Welch bowman, for not keeping to his agreement.'

> It chanced, moreover, one day that the slingers and bowmen, and all who were skilled in throwing missiles, frequently challenged one another on both sides, and discharged their weapons for exercise. When the rest had departed from the field in their turns, a Parthian and a Welchman began to aim their arrows at each other in a hostile manner, and discharge them so as to strike with all their might. But the Welchman, aware of his foe's intention, repaid like for like; on which the Parthian, making a truce, approached him, and when within hearing, began a parley. 'Of what country are you?' said he, 'and by what name may I be pleased to know you? I see you are a good bowman, and in order that you may be more inclined to tell me, I am a Parthian by nation, brought up from childhood in the art of shooting, and my name is Grammatyr, of good reputation amongst my people for my deeds of renown, and well known for my victories.' The Welchman told his name and nation. 'Let us prove', said the Parthian, 'which is the best bowman, by each taking an arrow, and aiming them against one another from our bows. You shall stand still first, and I will aim an arrow at you, and afterwards you shall shoot in like manner at me.' The Welchman agreed. The Parthian having fitted his arrow, and parting his feet as the art requires, with his hands stretched asunder, and his eyes fixed on the mark,
>
> 'Lets fly the arrow, failing of its aim.'
>
> The Welchman, unhurt, demanded the fulfilment of the aforesaid condition. 'I will not agree', said the Parthian; 'but you must stand another shot, and then have two at me.' The Welchman replied, 'You do not stand by your agreement, nor observe the condition you yourself dictated; and if you will not stand, although I may delay it for a time, as I may best be able, God will take revenge on you according to His will, for your treachery;' and he had scarce finished speaking, when in the twinkling of an eye he smote the Turk with his arrow in the breast, as he was selecting an arrow from his quiver to suit his purpose, and the weapon, meeting with no obstacle, came out at the back, having pierced the Turk's body; upon which he said to the Turk, 'You stood not by your agreement, nor I by my word.' Animated by these and the like successes, the Christians thought they should preserve themselves for good fortune by bearing all their misfortunes with more cheerful faith, and more fervent hope.[37]

Legends aside, the harder facts of the contemporary chronicles seem to indicate that the Welsh generally found their enemies closer to home. From the time of Richard I's capture, the *Brut* contains extensive accounts of Welsh attacks on the castles of

Anglo-Normans and Welsh rivals.[38] Kathryn Hurlock notes that during this period, until Richard's return in 1194: 'It appears that the Welsh princes were taking advantage of the English king's extended stay in Austria to regain some control in Wales.'[39]

In the thirteenth century, the *Brut* records later efforts to re-establish Christian supremacy in Palestine. These two entries, written in the final decades of Welsh freedom, refer to the Fifth and Eighth Crusades respectively, and one can imagine the hard-pressed native Welsh princes would have welcomed these costly overseas expeditions by figures whose presence would otherwise have been felt with greater weight in Wales:

> 1218 In that year many Crusaders went to Jerusalem, along with whom went the earl of Chester and Earl Ferrars and Brian de L'Ile and many others of the leading men of England.[40]

> 1270 In that year Louis, king of France, died while his son and the Pope's legate were on their way going to Jerusalem. And Edward, son of King Henry, went to Jerusalem.[41]

There are legends of a few named Welsh travellers to the Holy Land during this later period. Ednyfed Fychan (*c.*1170-1246), seneschal to the Kingdom of Gwynedd, serving Llywelyn ap Iorwerth ('Llywelyn the Great') (1172-1240) and his son Dafydd ap Llywelyn (1215-46), is reported to have received a gift of a silver cup in London from Henry III when leaving on Crusade in 1235.[42] A later apocryphal folk tale has Ednyfed composing a farewell song to his wife before leaving for Crusade, and then returning disguised as a beggar years later after he had long been thought dead, and revealing his identity by singing the same song at the court of his wife, who had remarried; he then leaves her to her new husband and departs.[43] Lowe also recounts the story of how Ednyfed's coat of arms, a Saracen's head, inherited from his ninth-century ancestor Marchudd ap Cynan, was changed by Llywelyn to three Saxons' heads after his notable victory over the forces of the Earl of Chester in 1209.[44]

The lack of references to the Crusades in the copious Welsh-language poetry of the period is notable. Although this was the age of 'Beirdd y Tywysogion', the 'Poets of the Princes', when some of the greatest names of medieval Welsh literature were writing in a thriving economy of courtly praise, elegy and patronage, events in Palestine are scarcely reflected in the surviving material. In the work of Elidir Sais, (1160-1220), who was writing a century after the beginning of the Crusades, we find the following:

> Respecting the grave of Christ, the creator of heaven, there is sorrow,
> the infidels have taken possession of it
> and ravaged the land,
> the Saracen oppressor under Saladin.[45]

It is significant that in the context of the poem, while the reference to the Saracens assumes that the poem's audience had a common attitude towards the Crusades, the indignation that Elidir expresses at perceived Saracen perfidy is actually in service to a domestic Welsh agenda. It is a rhetorical device intended to intensify the effect of his condemnation of a recent event in the dynastic politics of Gwynedd in the last years of the twelfth century, namely the fact that Dafydd ab Owain Gwynedd (*d.*1203) had been forced to seek refuge in England by his nephew, Llywelyn the Great. Elidir is saying the iniquity of Dafydd's exile is second only to that perpetrated by Saladin. Here can be seen what will become a common theme in the material collected in this book: many references to Muslims are actually not primarily about Muslims at all; they are much more about the preoccupations of the author's own society. D. Myrddin Lloyd (1909-81) notes in a paper on the range of references used by the Poets of the Princes that references to events outside Britain are very scarce, and that the isolated example of this reference by Elidir Sais is itself a case of the author 'turning the water from a distant stream to his own mill.'[46]

Another poem generally attributed to the early thirteenth century contains a reference to contemporary Palestine. 'Cwyn y Pererin' ('The Pilgrim's Lament') found in *The Red Book of Hergest*, and probably the work of Einion ap Gwalchmai, is a unique example of a Welsh poet displaying apparent first-hand knowledge of the geography of the Holy Land, although it makes no mention of the Crusades or of Islam.[47] From late in the century comes a legend that Gruffydd ap Llywelyn ap Ynyr of Iâl in north east Wales was killed while storming a city in Palestine. What is known about Gruffydd's dates indicates that the

Crusade was presumably the Ninth and last, in 1271-2.[48] That expedition's failure to recapture territory for the Christians signalled the end of the Crusading enterprise.

That Crusade was jointly led by the future Edward the First of England. As Edward was returning from the Crusade, his father, King Henry III, died in England. The *Brut* for 1274 records: 'In that year Edward came from the land of Jerusalem'.[49] He came back a king and a seasoned campaigner with no intention of countenancing anything but total submission from Wales. Three years after his return, Edward defeated Llywelyn ap Gruffudd in the war of 1277, and although the peace terms allowed Llywelyn to keep Snowdonia and the title of Prince of Wales, the deal was, in reality, unsustainable. For the Welsh, it gave too little freedom. For the Anglo-Normans, that little was still too much.

In 1282, in the last tense weeks of preparation for what was to prove the final campaign in Wales, Edward and Llywelyn traded letters, mainly through the mediation of John Peckham, Archbishop of Canterbury, as the King sought to force Welsh surrender, and Llywelyn sought to avoid it. As they edged inexorably towards conflict, each used the Crusading ideal in their arguments. Writing to Peckham in November 1282, Llywelyn said:

> We fight because we are forced to fight, for we, and all Wales, are oppressed, subjugated, despoiled, reduced to servitude by the royal officers and bailiffs, in defiance of the form of the peace and of all justice, more maliciously than if we were Saracens or Jews, so that we feel, and have often so protested to the king, that we are left without any remedy.[50]

In return, Peckham, a man unsympathetic towards Welsh national aspirations, proposed that Llywelyn's hot-headed brother Dafydd should 'go to the Holy Land'. The King would equip him for the journey on condition that he did not return unless pardoned. Dafydd, however, was not to be sidelined that easily. Nor, despite the precariousness of the Welsh position, was he to be intimidated. Dafydd replied:

> When he desires to visit the Holy Land, he will do so of his own accord and in fulfilment of a vow for God and not for man; he will

> not go on pilgrimage against his will. But if in future he should happen to visit the Holy Land, prompted by a good impulse, he failed to see why he and his heirs should on that account be disinherited; rather they should be rewarded. Nor will he accept land in England.[51]

That defiance turned into open conflict only weeks later, when Dafydd precipitated a rebellion that quickly pulled his brother into a full-scale, but doomed, war of independence. On 11 December, 1282, Llywelyn was killed in a skirmish with English forces. The independence of the native Welsh dynasties was at an end, and Edward, using techniques of military architecture he had observed while on Crusade, began plans for a chain of impregnable castles to consolidate his conquest of Wales. The sacred Croes Naid, possibly found on Llywelyn's body itself, was put on display in London. Its capture was, according to Griffith Hartwell Jones, a loss that '... proved the Ichabod of Welsh liberties, and struck dismay into the hearts of the Welsh race.'[52]

The Crusades had begun in 1095, some twenty years after the Normans had completed their conquest of England.[53] They ended in 1272. Welsh freedom effectively ended five years later, in 1277, and was finally destroyed in 1282. Wales had retained its independence after the Norman Conquest of England for as long as the Crusades lasted, and a bare decade beyond. The chronology is suggestive, and it is tempting to speculate as to whether the Crusades may actually have delayed the conquest of Wales. Certainly, the campaigns in Palestine were a drain on the military resources of Wales's expansionist neighbour. And while it would be gratifying to think that the conquest was postponed solely because of Welsh tenacity, given the disparity of resources of material and manpower, it is worth considering whether Anglo-Norman distraction with the Crusades might not have been a factor too. Certainly, the swiftness with which Welsh independence was extinguished once the full power of the Anglo-Norman state was brought to bear, suggests the aim might have been achieved much earlier had not that power been directed elsewhere. Of course, if both Welsh and Anglo-Normans had left for the Crusades in equal proportions, then all would have been even and no advantage would have been afforded to the defender. But from the evidence shown earlier, there is reason to believe the Welsh were more reluctant than the Anglo-Normans to enlist. Alison Elizabeth Barnes concludes her study of the period: 'With the evidence for the Crusade in Wales laid out and evaluated, it is clear there was not the same degree of participation by the Welsh in the Crusades of the eleventh and twelfth centuries as from neighbouring Western countries.'[54]

Griffith Hartwell Jones certainly believed the Welsh were singularly reluctant to participate in the Crusades due to the pressure they faced domestically from the Normans. Referring to Owain Cyfeiliog's excommunication, he says:

> The probability is that the Celtic imagination would have been still further fired but for the social and ecclesiastical conditions of Wales at that time. There were valid reasons to explain Owain Cyfeiliog's refusal and the hesitation of other princes to enrol themselves or to start. Owain was a brave soldier, and a patron renowned for his hospitality, and his influence would have been invaluable. It did not, however, require unusual penetration to see through the hollow pretensions of the emissary, and Owain determined, therefore, that his first duty and wisdom lay in protecting his countrymen, though he braved the Church's ban. Nor did he stand alone. The Lord Rhys had also thought of going to Palestine, but his lady dissuaded him from fulfilling his purpose, and in consequence drew down upon her head the fulminations of Canterbury. To such anathemas they turned a deaf ear. Admittedly, the Welsh chiefs did not make a prominent figure at this juncture of supreme interest to Christendom. Several assumed the badge of the Holy War, and stayed at home. But they were not exceptional. Elsewhere, men talked of the Crusades, but did not engage in them. The reason why the undertaking languished lay not in any fear of Moslem scimitars, but in the state of chronic disorder into which Wales had fallen. The narratives of Crusaders who had spent blood and treasure in objects remote from the original aims, and returned crestfallen, and accounts of men who pined and died in Saracen prisons, were little calculated to intensify their ardour. Then there were evils which pressed them more nearly, the presence of the hostile Lord Marchers hanging on their borders, a constant menace to the safety of their persons and their property, steadily invading their privileges, and stealthily encroaching on their territory; the thought of leaving their families for an unknown number of years to the tender mercies of unscrupulous neighbours, with the whole continent of Europe interposed between themselves and those whom they left behind; and the fatalities which so often changed the laurel wreath into cypress. These were the arguments that gave them pause. Their sadly-reduced acres would be in alien

> hands long before their return, and their kinsmen driven out from hearth and home.[55]

Jones and the other commentators quoted do not speculate as to the possible consequences for Welsh independence of the Welsh prioritising the defence of their homeland over that of the Holy Land. However, if it is true that the Welsh on the whole put domestic security before pan-Christian solidarity, then it is certainly worth considering how that might have created a crucial change in the tense balance of power between the two nations for the period under consideration. The protracted warfare and contact with Muslims in the east may have produced little curiosity or comment about Islam in Welsh literature. However, as shown, it is certain that Wales is indebted, indirectly, to Islam for one of its most important historical documents, Giraldus Cambrensis's *Journey Through Wales*, and it is possible that, also indirectly, Wales also owes to Islam some two centuries of continued freedom.

The Crusades left other legacies too. There was the physical presence in Wales of the ecclesiastical properties of the Crusading orders of knights, such as the Hospitallers, who had a commandery at Slebech in Pembrokeshire. There were also the cultural legacies in terms of the language, legends and mindset of the nations which took part in the conflict. For instance, the Anglo-Norman *Geste de Boeve de Haumtone*, the story of an English hero whose exploits include fighting villainous Saracens (although not specifically in a crusading setting), was available in Welsh translation by the mid thirteenth century as *Ystorya Bown o Hamtwn*. In the fourteenth century, a hundred years after the end of the Crusades, we find crusading language active within Welsh poetry. Iolo Goch (1320-98), the great praise-poet of Owain Glyndŵr's court, satirises a colleague, Madog ap Hywel, by saying that he has 'calon Mahumed',[56] the heart of Mohammed, a comment which, as it is contained within a string of abuse, is undoubtedly intended as an insult. Elsewhere, Iolo urges Edward III (1327-77) to 'take the cross' and conquer the Holy Land.[57] In doing this, Iolo was acting in a flourishing tradition of Welsh prophetic poetry which gained particular strength in the mid fourteenth century and which foretold the coming of a heroic leader, 'Y Mab Darogan', the 'Son of Prophecy', who was seen as fulfilling Welsh national aspirations for the recovery of liberty and often Christian ambitions for the recovery of Jerusalem.[58]

Conquering the Holy Land was a common and important motif in the prophetic poetry which flourished during this period not only in Wales but also, with some different emphases, in England, where, for instance, the propagandists of Edward IV (1442-1483) also foretold his conquest of the Holy Land, an enterprise he did not in fact attempt. In the fifteenth century, Lewys Glyn Cothi, (1447-86), praising a patron, Sir Rhisiart Herbert, wishes that Edward IV might add the territories of the Sultan and Babylon to his conquests, and that he will be the man who will 'come to the grave of Christ with true vengeance'.[59] The convention continued, with more than one homeloving country nobleman being urged to heroic exploits in Palestine. Lewys Môn (1485-1527) promised Robert ap Rhys of Ysbyty Ifan that the Turk would flee in terror from him,[60] and elsewhere urged Edwart Grae of Chirk to pursue military glory overseas, concluding with the promise: 'You shall, unless I be decieved, cut the Turk's ear by hand.'[61] Dafydd Gorlech (1410-*c.*1490), in his prophetic poem, 'Ymddiddan rhwng y bardd a'r Wyddfa' ('Converse between the bard and Snowdon'), foresees the Son of Prophecy restoring the Welsh to their rightful inheritance before going on to take:

> The path a second time to Jerusalem
> To carry the Cross of Christ, a fair-dawned journey.[63]

The fifteenth-century *Life of St David* tells the story of how a Welsh Crusader from St David's was saved miraculously from a Saracen prison by the repeated use of the invocation 'Dewi, wareth!' ('David, deliver [me]!)'. A German fellow-prisoner, suspecting there was special virtue in the words the Welshman used, began to use the same invocation, resulting in his own miraculous deliverance. Later, trying to find out the meaning of the prayer, he met Welsh clergy in Paris who directed him to St David's where he made a pilgrimage in gratitude.[64] Griffith Hartwell Jones, recounting the history, notes that the inclusion of the anecdote 'sheds a sidelight on the ecclesiastical rivalries of the Middle Ages', the suggestion being that it was intended to aggrandise the claims to primacy of a particular diocese.[65] If that is the case, it would not be the first, and would certainly not be the last example of a conflict with Muslims being used as a means of scoring points in Wales.

A poem to St Margaret of Llanfaches by Tomas Derllys from the fifteenth or sixteenth century portrays the eponymous saint resisting the advances of 'A certain prince of Antioch', called Olaibrys. The poem refers to him as a 'pagan' and to his God as 'false' and criticises Muhammad roundly. The following couplet is from a translation of Tomas Derllys's poem by Dr Barry Lewis of the Centre for Advanced Welsh and Celtic Studies at Aberystwyth, for a forthcoming volume:

> An evil oppression, the name of some ancient wandering minstrel
> fit to destroy himself, was Mohammed.[66]

In the sixteenth century, we find some bloodthirsty condemnations of the Turks in the poem 'Pe bai'r Twrc Rhwng pawb a'r Tân' ('Were the Turk between everyone and the fire'), by Harri ap Rhys ap Gwilym,[67] and a pejorative reference to supposed Turkish facial characteristics in 'Ateb' ('Answer')[68] by Gruffudd Hiraethog (*d.*1564), author of one of the first ever Welsh-language books to be printed. Meanwhile, his contemporary, Lewis Morgannwg (1520-65) one of the century's foremost Welsh-language poets, praising William, Lord Herbert, congratulates him for 'striking the Turk'[69], while in his praise-poem for Henry VIII, he has a peroration anticipating Henry's exploits in the Holy Land, where he relishes the thought of him burning Turkish flesh, and concludes by urging him: 'light thou the fire.'[70]

As for later treatments of Welsh involvement in the Crusades, the attitude of hostility towards Islam and Muslims continues for centuries. In the early nineteenth century, we find the Flintshire poet John Blackwell (1797-1840), known by his *nom de plume* of 'Alun', imagining Edward I drawing on his Crusader past as a motivation for his Welsh conquests. Alun's poem 'Genedigaeth Iorwerth II' ('The Birth of Edward II'), written in *cynghanedd*, depicts Edward I, father of Edward II, returning from the Crusades and contemplating the continued defiance of Wales, which he plans to subdue by naming his son Prince of Wales; he attributes to the conqueror this speech:

What should it profit me, the praise,
that I subdued Sudan in former days,
or shattered the shields of Palestine,
vanquished the vile Turks, the vulpine,
that I hurled the hero's heart to earth,
yes, worsted the men of most worth,
If Wales, undefiled, undefended,
its champions in chains, surrounded,
with no ramparts, no barred door,
no legions to summon, no succour,
should defy my dominion,
should not count me as their king?[71]

And in the same volume, in the long poem, 'Awdl ar fuddugoliaethau diweddar y Groegiaid ar y Tyrciaid,' ('Ode on the recent victories of the Greeks over the Turks') we find Alun expressing unabashed antagonism to Islam. Wishing success to the banner of Greece in the war of independence against Turkey, Alun says:

... may it see only success,
may its freedom flourish:
let not the Crescent Moon be blessed
with light on the sea's darkness,
But let it low, low be laid,
and to the Cross subject be made.[72]

The Greek War of Independence, which began in 1821, and which eventually ended in victory for the Greeks thanks to the aid of Western powers, inspired numerous Western sympathisers, most notably, of course, Lord Byron (1788-1824), who died while aiding the Greek cause. Byron, while opposing aspects of Islam both in practice and in principle, nonetheless was often generous and humane towards Muslims both in his writings and in his actions while campaigning in Greece. This was due partly to an orientalism fostered by his boyhood immersion in tales of the east and of the Ottoman Empire, and reinforced by his later travels in that empire. Alun, however, without the benefit of having encountered Turks either as companions or adversaries, had a much less nuanced approach to the conflict. As a promising scholar in his mid twenties, and destined for the Anglican priesthood, he saw the war in Greece not merely as one of national liberation, but as part of a cosmic war with the

Antichrist, a war which would lead to the Christian reconquest of Jerusalem from Islam. In his apocalyptic ode, written from the depths of rural Montgomeryshire where he was studying at the time, we find the spirit of the Crusades still burning, and this devout would-be priest appears much more bloodthirsty than the sceptical libertine Byron who had actually risked his life in opposition to the Turks:

> Angels, white heralds in hundreds thronging,
> to guide the greatest of armies are flying,
> the walls they are shattering, storms they are freeing,
> the thunder fearless, the sea-waves heaving,
> the hosts of the Prophet are trembling – when they see,
> and so they flee to their place of hiding.
>
> And now, (may God bring this fate)
> we look to a future state
> when he, the armed antichrist,
> abhorrent, black, down is cast,
> and when, so fair its face,
> a fortress of truth takes his place,
> through the means of the muse's glass,
> I see peace come to pass,
> when hosts shall, in Jesu's name,
> their ancient kingdom reclaim,
> the perfect land of prophecy,
> from pain and oppression free.
>
> The icy East and the lands of freezing
> snow their fearless hosts are sending;
> the South, of every tongue, is marching,
> the West's most puissant legions striding;
> with one accord they are coming – a great parade,
> of new Crusaders, and overwhelming.
>
> In Salem's city, on every citadel,
> freedom's flag will summon hither
> the scattered tribes, a splendid signal,
> to their fathers' land again to gather;
> and on the Mosques of the routed rabble – shall be raised
> the Cross in praise and power forever.[73]

With the mention of 'tongues', it is possible Alun is thinking of the Crusader practice of grouping armies according to their common language into various commands known as '*langues*'. The reference to the 'scattered tribes' seems to indicate the Jewish people, whom evangelical Christians had long believed, as a precondition of the Second Coming, must return to their ancestral homeland from their dispersion. Alun's poem is an example of the kind of evangelical Protestant sympathy for the Jewish return which, beginning in the late nineteenth century, underpinned Christian support for the political Zionist movement and also for the Allied military campaign which, during the First World War, would see Christian armies capture Jerusalem from the Turks in 1917 and create the conditions for a 'Jewish National Home'.

The Greek victories were a popular theme with Welsh poets, and not just with those who were religious professionals. In 1828, David Rice, of Llan-sant-ffraid, a brewer by profession, published a pamphlet poem *Hanes Brwydr Naverino* ('The Story of the Battle of Navarino')[74] in vigorous rhyming couplets. Its introduction describes the villain of the piece in terms which show scant acquaintance with Islamic theology: 'Ibrahim Pasha is the beast the song mentions, he who is high-priest of the church of Mecca, and is one of the ministers of the God Mahomet.' At one point, the poet has the angry British admiral vow that 'no wrathful Turk or black Egyptian who pisses on a wall tonight shall see the dawn arise.' In due course the defeated Turks cry for divine aid

> But deaf to them was Mahomet, for all their wailings drear.
> and had no way to save them, and had no ear to hear.

The poem describes the Allied victory, and, considering what has gone before, ends on an oddly conciliatory note, with the wish:

> ... that Britain's hosts and banner shall rule o'er all again,
> and that the Turks will love the Greeks, and all can say Amen.

During the First World War, Crusading imagery was invoked, without irony, by Welsh poets, as will be seen in Chapter Six of this book.[75] And the 'Dewi Wareth' story was versified for children in 1931 by Edgar Phillips in *Trysor o Gân i'r Plant* ('A Treasury of Children's Song') as 'Dewi, Gwared!', with the explicitly Muslim enemies portrayed as one-dimensional villains:

The Muslim tyrant, Saladin, destruction had unleashed
to shatter into fragments all the churches of the East,
the Cross of Christ for many years was held in honour there
and young and old would seek the shrines to bow their heads in
prayer.
But now the towers of Salem, the sad old Jew's abode,
are in the hands of men who show no care for Jesu's God.
So there came a call for warriors to go on the Crusade,
and many Welshmen came to join the gallant host they made.
And with them travelled Ifan, with his arrows and his bow
to save the town where Jesus lived a thousand years ago.[76]

Later, Ifan is shown 'driving the Muslim from many a tower and town' before being captured and imprisoned. There, after making the invocation his mother had urged him to remember, his chains are broken miraculously, and the castle where he is being kept is destroyed by an earthquake – 'The defiant Muslim's tower was shattered on the floor' – and Ifan goes free, to return to Wales, to make a thankful pilgrimage to St David's and to tell others of the power of David's name.

It would be a mistake to think that the cheerfully simplistic attitude displayed towards Muslims in this poem is the product of a sequestered, aged author who had spent longer in the nineteenth century than he had in the twentieth. In fact, Edgar Phillips (1889-1962) had served, and been badly wounded, as an artilleryman in the First World War, and when he published 'Dewi, Gwared!' he was still only 42. Known by his bardic name of 'Trefin', he became Archdruid of Wales in 1960.

Only after the Second World War does a more nuanced perspective in the treatment of the Crusades by Welsh authors become common. For instance, in 1969, Vivian Griffiths (*b.*1935) recreating the fall of Byzantium in his poem 'Pray Wolf', has the following:

Was this the one time when miracles
couldn't happen?
Or was it that the Muezzin's cry ringing
clear, carried further
Than the mumbled enchantments of the monks.
Perhaps, the dark invaders, better understood
That mosaic of a living man.[77]

Sheenagh Pugh (*b.*1950) in her poem 'Crusaders', from a 1987 collection, has a Crusader protagonist recount his experiences in the war:

> ... Guy took a girl
> from a town we sacked, and learned some Moorish;
> he told me once he wasn't sure the Church
> had the right of it.[78]

The American historical novelist Sharon Penman (*b.*1945), who moved to Wales and wrote a series of novels about the Welsh princes, is a further example. Her 1988 novel, *Falls the Shadow*, set in the thirteenth century, depicts Welsh participants in the Crusades. In the following passage, the Crusaders' female camp followers are sojourning in Brindisi, Sicily, an embarkation port for the campaigns in 'Death's favourite hunting ground ... the blood-soaked soil where Christ once walked.' Her depiction of the period is characteristic of a late–twentieth-century perspective in which idealism is suspect, in which scepticism as to the purity of Christian motives is universal, and in which the necessity to attempt a rendition of the true complexity of the historical situation is unquestioned. In this scene, Rhonwen, a Welsh governess working for Nell, the Countess of Pembroke and youngest daughter of King John of England, is talking with an attendant of Nell's late sister Isabella, who had married the Holy Roman Emperor:

> Rhonwen leaned forward. 'Are the tales told of him true? Does he really keep a harem of Saracen harlots?'
>
> 'Indeed he does, and cares not a whit who knows it! Whilst my poor lady, may God assoil her, was kept sequestered, verily like a nun. The day after the wedding, he sent all her English maids away, save only Dame Margaret, her old nurse, and me, and then he handed her over to his Saracen eunuchs, who watched her like hungry hawks!'[79]

Compared to the uncritical accounts of the Crusades which pertained up until the mid twentieth century, the work of Penman is an example of the more recent artistic response in which an attempt is being made to give a balanced, objective depiction of the true conditions of the period. The final work considered in this chapter shows the pendulum having swung further still, beyond objectivity, and to a position where the Crusades and their aftermath are conceived as a nightmarish collision of irrational belief and violence, a vision implicitly critical of some of the basic assumptions of the Western world-view.

The highly successful and much-translated 1987 Welsh-language novel *Y Pla*, ('Pestilence'), by Wiliam Owen Roberts (*b.*1960), is set during the Black Death, around seventy years after the Crusades, but still in the long shadow of that conflict. Its sympathetic protagonist, Salah ibn al Khatib, is a Muslim assassin sent 'into the very heart of the dark continent, to the cradle of the infidel, there to kill the King of France, Philip of Valois, who lived in a far-off city called Paris. This man's grandfather had been responsible for killing Salah ibn al Khatib's grandfather in one of those impious campaigns the infidels called Crusades.'[80]

This post-modern novel's inversion of the common perception of Europe as enlightened and the East as benighted seems designed to challenge European preconceptions, an impression strengthened as the book shows Christian conventions as hollow, corrupt and hypocritical while Salah is humane and steadfast. However, while one of the main methods of this work seems to be to demythologise and revise romantic conceptions of the European Middle Ages, particularly as relating to Wales, and while Salah undoubtedly serves the purpose of allowing that society to be viewed from outside and to be compared, unfavourably, to a different civilisation, it would be wrong to think he is a mere cipher, a noble savage whose role is simply to provide a perspective on the society which is the audience's, and the author's, main interest. The opening passage of the novel shows the care with which his world is evoked:

> Far away, the sun shone steadily on the delicate arcades, the marble courts, the musical fountains of the Madrasa, Sultan Hasan's renowned academy in Cairo. A century earlier, Baghdad had fallen to the Mongol hordes, and now Cairo was the capital of the Muslim world. The building of the Madrasa was not yet quite complete, but the heart of the academy, its lofty central hall, stood in all its austere beauty. The roof soared heavenward, almost it seemed to infinity, above the groups of students, the *ulmas*, gathered round their teachers. Here the chosen scholars came as children, to spend their youth in studying the Holy Koran and its traditions, learning it by heart, and learning too the complex laws of the *fiqh*. Only after years of

> dedicated study would they qualify as missionaries, to be sent to every corner of the Muslim world and beyond.
>
> And here the young student Salah Ibn al Khatib was coming to an important stage of his studies. For ten years, from the age of seven, he had heard and learned daily about the Law of the Prophet as it is revealed in the Holy Koran. He had been taught of the need for a rational understanding of the universe created through Allah's Divine Will, of man's requirement to discover and create a just social system in accordance with that Divine Will, the injunctions to curb covetous impulses and worldly desires, and the greatness of the Eternal Wisdom compared with the pettiness and irrelevance of mankind's earthly existence. Salah could not remember a time when he had not heard the *muqri* reading aloud from the Book, a time when he had not daily immersed himself in its sacred truths. He had read it six times from beginning to end: one hundred and twenty thousand words, a hundred and fourteen *suras* and six thousand *ayas*. The Madrasa's reputation was founded on learning by heart, and some of the *muqris* had become rich and respected for the beauty of their voices and their eloquence in reciting the scriptures. And Salah, sentence by sentence, episode by episode, and through constant repetition, had made the Holy Book a part of himself, weaving him, with its fine web, into the rich tapestry which patterned and comprehended every part of the universe. Almost everything he knew, about his fellow men and about the world outside the Madrasa's high walls, had come from the pronouncements of his teachers. Salah hoped the end of his long pupillage would bring some of the answers to the eternal questions, about the origin and destiny of the human race, the relationship between humanity and the Divine Order, and about the Will of the All-Merciful.[81]

Salah may still be an example of that common figure in this study, the Muslim as mirror for the West, but he is an unusually sophisticated one; sympathetic and credible. Roberts's work shares with that of his late-twentieth-century colleagues a basic scepticism regarding the medieval Christian values that had inspired the Crusades. And if Roberts is more critical of that milieu than is his contemporary Sharon Penman, the difference is of degree not of essence.

Roberts's phantasmagorical, chaotic Middle Ages is a long way from the simple dichotomies of the writers of the Crusading period and a long way even from the work of Edgar Phillips, who, as late as 1931, could depict gallant Christian opposition to 'the

Muslim tyrant' without irony or qualification. In that year, 1931, when the Empire State Building was completed, when Ramsay MacDonald formed a National Government to combat Britain's economic crisis, and when British authorities began negotiations with Mahatma Gandhi regarding Indian independence, it was still possible for Phillips to write in an attitude towards Islam unchanged from the Middle Ages. That confident, combative attitude had survived the horror of the First World War. It could not survive the Second. Only fourteen years after that poem was written, the attitudes it contained were fatally discredited.

The writers quoted from the post-Second World War period, share the disillusion with previous religious and societal certainties, and the revulsion from stereotypical portrayal of other groups, that is the common inheritance of the Western intellectual in the wake of that conflict, which, in the Holocaust, had exposed the evils of racial and religious prejudice as never before. As will be seen in subsequent chapters, if there is a watershed in attitudes to Islam and to Muslims among Welsh writers, after which prejudice becomes the exception rather than the rule, it can be located most readily in the immediate post-war period, and it occurs not primarily for reasons directly associated with Western contact with the Islamic world itself, but for reasons related to the West's own sense of complicity in permitting the growth of genocidal prejudice, and in its consequent recoil from any conscious assumptions of supremacy. It could be argued that if the Crusades themselves ended in the late thirteenth century, the Crusading ideal only finally died in 1945, although it was tragedy, not tolerance, that brought about the change.

Notes

1. Matthieu Boyd, 'Celts seen as Muslims and Muslims seen as Celts', Jerold C. Frakes (ed.), *Contextualizing the Muslim Other in Medieval Judeo-Christian Discourse* New York, (forthcoming).
2. Joseph Campbell, *The Masks of God: Creative Mythology* (London, 1977 edition) 62.
3. A.O.H. Jarman (ed.), *Chwedlau Cymraeg Canol* (Cardiff, 1957) which reproduces some of the Welsh translations of the legends of 'Siarl Fawr'. See also Stephen J. Williams (ed.) *Ystorya de Carolo Magno* (Cardiff, 1930).

4. A quotation from Virgil's Second Eclogue.
5. St Jerome, 'Letter XLVI. Paula and Eustochium to Marcella', Philip Schaff and Henry Wace (eds.) *The Principal Works of St. Jerome* (Grand Rapids, 1889) 65.
6. For instance, Ieuan ap Rhydderch has a poem 'I Ddewi Sant' ('To Saint David') which depicts Dewi's visit to Jerusalem. *Gwaith Ieuan ap Rhydderch*, K. Iestyn Daniel (ed.), (Aberystwyth, 2003) 95.
7. The Dialogue of Taliesin and Ugnach', *The Black Book of Carmarthen*, XXXV. J. Gwenogvryn Evans (1852-1930), in his 1906 edition of *The Black Book*, argues that 'Caer Seon' is actually a placename near Caernarfon, and that the copyist, working at the time of the Crusades in another part of Wales, mistook it for the Welsh name for Jerusalem, subsequently mistaking 'cerddorion' ('musicians') for 'Iddewon' ('Jews'). J. Gwenogvryn Evans (ed.) *The Black Book of Carmarthen* (Pwllheli, 1896) xvi-xviii. Graham R. Isaac questions this interpretation, saying Taliesin's statement should be taken as an example of the conflation between Muslims and Jews which was common in Christian literature of the period, and suggesting that Taliesin is presented as the spirit of a Crusader killed defending the faith, who is travelling to his heavenly reward: 'Ymddiddan Taliesin ac Ugnach: Propaganda Cymreig yn Oes y Croesgadau?' *Llên Cymru,* 25 (2002) 12-20.
8. This legend is responsible for a 160-mile Roman road through Wales being known as 'Sarn Helen'. The legend is mentioned in the late fifteenth-century poet Huw Cae Llwyd's poem,'Y Creiriau yn Rhufain' ('The Relics in Rome'), in Leslie Harries (ed), *Gwaith Huw Cae Llwyd ac Eraill* (Cardiff, 1953) 85.
9. Griffith Hartwell Jones, *Celtic Britain and the Pilgrim Movement,* (London, 1912).
10. Surviving in several variant translated Welsh versions of a lost Latin original, probably the product of the Welsh monastic houses of Llanbadarn and Strata Florida.
11. Thomas Jones (ed.) *Brut y Tywysogion or The Chronicle of the Princes*, Peniarth MS 20 Version (Cardiff, 1952) 19.
12. Alison Elizabeth Barnes, 'Welsh Involvement in the Crusades, 1095-1200', MA thesis, (Cardiff University, 2002) 11.
13. *Ibid.* 17.
14. *Brut y Tywysogion* 50.
15. It is likely these barons would have recruited from their Welsh lands, ensuring some Welsh people became Crusaders via that route.
16. Giraldus Cambrensis records at least one other Welsh Crusader penitent, albeit from the reign of Henry I, earlier in the century. In Chapter I of his *Journey Through Wales* he recounts a story of the lord of the castle of Radnor, struck blind after impiously spending the night in Llanafan church with his dogs. The lord is conveyed to Jerusalem where he made 'a spirited attack upon the enemies of the faith, and, being mortally wounded, closed his life with honour.'
17. *Brut y Tywysogion*, 53. In contemporary terminology, 'pilgrim' could

have meant a military Crusader: see Kathryn Hurlock, *Crusades and Crusading in the Welsh Annalistic Chronicles* (Lampeter, 2009) 9.
18. *Ibid.* 55.
19. *Ibid.* 72.
20. *Ibid.* 73. Peter Edbury points out (correspondence with author) that the Chronicle entry conflates and confuses several events. The Holy Cross was lost at Hattin in July 1187, and Jerusalem fell in October 1187, but through surrender, not assault. Ash Wednesday 1188 was the approximate date of the council of Geddington (Northamptonshire) where the Cross was formally preached in England at the king's council and it was agreed Archbishop Baldwin should go on his tour of Wales.
21. *Brut y Tywysogion, op. cit.* 74.
22. Peter Edbury 'Preaching the Crusade in Wales', *England and Germany in the High Middle Ages,* Alfred Haverkamp and Hanna Vollrath (eds.) (Oxford, 1996) 221-23.
23. Giraldus Cambrensis, *The Journey Through Wales/The Description of Wales,* trans. Lewis Thorpe (Harmondsworth, 1978) 141).
24. *Ibid.* 141.
25. *Ibid.* 114
26. *Ibid.* 126.
27. *Ibid.* 171.
28. See, for example, *ibid.* 77, 83.
29. *Ibid.* 172.
30. Correspondence with the author.
31. Giraldus Cambrensis, *op. cit.* 201.
32. *Ibid.* 202.
33. *Ibid.* 202.
34. *Ibid.* 204.
35. *Op. cit.* 29.
36. *Op. cit.* 31. Arthur Collins, in *The English Baronetage,* (London, 1741) 459 says Sir Aaron ap Rhys ap Bledri, was made a Knight of the Sepulchre by Richard I in 1190, because he had 'behaved himself so gallantly, against the Saracens'. However, Alison Elizabeth Barnes believes Aaron may have joined the order but not necessarily gone to Palestine, *op. cit.* 26-27.
37. Richard of Devizes, *Chronicles of the Crusades: Itinerary of Richard the First,* (1190) Chapter 58), quoted in Griffith Hartwell Jones, *op. cit.* 121. See also *Richard of Holy Trinity Itinerary of Richard I and others to the Holy Land* (Ontario, 2001) 70.
38. *Brut y Tywysogion, op. cit.* 74-5.
39. Kathryn Hurlock, *op. cit.* 13.
40. *Brut y Tywysogion,* 96. Kathryn Hurlock (*op. cit.* 25) notes that the Earl and Llywelyn ap Iorwerth, 'Llywelyn the Great', were firm allies, and that Llywelyn personally met the Earl at Chester on his return from Crusade. She notes that in the court poetry of Gwynedd the use of Crusader imagery, such as the example by Elidir Sais, and other references to the Charlemagne histories can be dated after the time of this alliance between Gwynedd and

Chester.
41. *Ibid.* 115.
42. David Walker, *Medieval Wales* (Cambridge, 1990) 108.
43. Walter Bezant Lowe, *The Heart of Northern Wales, I* (Llanfairfechan, 1912) 357.
44. *Ibid.* 354-5. That victory took place prior to the alliance, mentioned above (n. 40) which saw Llywelyn welcome the Earl back from the Crusades. The Saracen's Head coat of arms survives as the symbol of Abergele Town Council.
45. Elidir Sais, 'Awdl i Dduw', *The poetry of the Gogynfeirdd from the Myvyrian archaiology of Wales. With an introd. to the study of Old Welsh poetry* Edward Anwyl (ed.) (Denbigh, 1909) 133.
46. D. Myrddin Lloyd, *Rhai Agweddau ar Ddysg y Gogynfeirdd*, (Cardiff, 1977) 15.
47. Morfydd E. Owen, 'Cwyn y Pererin', in R. Geraint Gruffydd (ed.) *Gwaith Dafydd Benfras ac Eraill* (Cardiff, 1995) 561. Research by Rhian M. Andrews makes the case for the attribution of this poem to the early thirteenth-century poet Einion ap Gwalchmai, 'Ar Drywydd Pererin: *Gwaith Dafydd Benfras*, Cerdd 36', in *Llên Cymru,* 32 (2009) 1-31.
48. Despite suffering a mortal wound in his stomach, Gruffydd is reported to have fought on until a dog seized his protruding bowels. He is buried at Valle Crucis abbey near Llangollen, and his monumental effigy, dated to 1320, was later transferred to the church at Llanarmon yn Iâl, where it remains. The detail about the bowels and the dog is actually recorded about other Crusaders too, and is probably apocryphal, possibly occasioned by the fact that there is a small carving of a dog gnawing a branch at the foot of the figure on the tomb. Griffith Hartwell Jones *op. cit.* 130.
49. *Brut y Tywysogion, op. cit.* 116.
50. Griffith Hartwell Jones, *op. cit.* 128.
51. *Ibid.* 128. Dafydd's reply was delivered verbally, and the Archbishop summarised it for the King's council. C.T. Martin (ed.) *Registrum Epistolarum Johannis Peckham* 2: 359 (London, 1884).
52. *Ibid.* 103. The Groes Naid, which appears to have been kept in a gold reliquary in the shape of a Celtic cross, became part of the riches of the English royal family. It was last known to have been kept at St George's Chapel in Windsor, in the late sixteenth century, after which it vanishes from history, possibly as a result of iconoclasm either at the Reformation or during the Cromwellian period. See also T.H. Parry-Williams, 'Y Groes Naid', *Y Llinyn Arian* (Aberystwyth, 1947) 91-3.
53. The Normans had conquered Saxon England in 1066, and had completely crushed all attempts at resistance in England, even those aided by foreign powers, by 1071.
54. *Op. cit.* 33
55. Griffith Hartwell Jones, *op. cit.* 118.
56. Iolo Goch, 'Dychan i Fadog ap Hywel', Dafydd Johnston (ed.), *Gwaith Iolo Goch* (Cardiff, 1988) 170.

57. Iolo Goch, in Dafydd Johnston (ed.) *Iolo Goch: Poems* (Llandysul, 1993) Poem I, line 55.
58. I am indebted to Dr Barry Lewis of the University of Wales Centre for Advanced Welsh & Celtic Studies at Aberystwyth, for guidance with this subject.
59. Lewys Glyn Cothi, 'Syr Rhisiart Herbert ap Syr Wiliam ap Tomas,' in Dafydd Johnston (ed.), *Gwaith Lewys Glyn Cothi* (Cardiff, 1995) 257.
60. Lewys Môn, 'Moliant Robert ap Rhys' in Eurys I. Rowlands (ed.), *Gwaith Lewys Môn* (Cardiff, 1975) 178.
61. Lewys Môn, 'Moliant Edwart Grae', *ibid.* 303.
62. Dafydd Gorlech, 'Ymddiddan rhwng y bardd a'r Wyddfa' in Erwain R. Rheinallt (ed.), *Gwaith Dafydd Gorlech* (Aberystwyth, 1997) 51.
63. *The Welsh Life of St. David*, D. Simon Evans (ed.) (Cardiff, 1988).
64. See Michael J. Curley, 'The Miracles of St David: A New Text and its Context', *Traditio*, 62 (2007) 135-205.
65. Griffith Hartwell Jones, *op. cit.* 133.
66. See Barry Lewis, 'St Margaret of Llanfaches' in *Poems for Saints and Shrines* (Dublin, forthcoming).
67. From the Llansteffan Manuscript in the National Library of Wales. See The Index to Welsh Poetry in Manuscript: http://maldwyn.llgc.org.uk/chwilio.php?BRN=7234 Griffith Hartwell Jones, (*op cit.* 130) attributes the poem to Morys Mawddwy.
68. Gruffudd Hiraethog, 'Ateb', in D.J. Bowen (ed.), *Gwaith Gruffudd Hiraethog* (Cardiff, 1990) 407.
69. Lewys Morgannwg, 'Moliant Wiliam, Arglwydd Herbert', in A. Cynfael Lake (ed.) *Gwaith Lewys Morgannwg I* (Aberystwyth, 2004) 176.
70. Lewys Morgannwg, 'Moliant Harri'r Wythfed', *ibid.* 487.
71. John Blackwell, 'Genedigaeth Iorwerth II' in Owen Morgan Edwards (ed), *Gwaith Alun*, (Llanuwchllyn, 1909) 13.
72. *Ibid.* 33.
73. *Ibid.* 36.
74. David Rice, *Hanes Brwydr Naverino* (Swansea, 1828).
75. In the inter-war period, Iorwerth Cyfeiliog Peate (1901–82) could write nostalgically about Roncesvalles, where the rearguard of Charlemagne's retreating Frankish army was defeated by Iberian Saracen forces in 778 and where the hero, Roland, was killed. In his poem 'Roncesvalles', from the collection *Plu'r Gweunydd* (Liverpool, 1933), Peate gives a lyrical portrayal of 'All the greatness of France, all the pride of Spain, / Roland and his men, and the Suleiman' who are depicted as sharing now in the forgiving, forgetful embrace of nature. Although this legend predates the medieval Crusades, it is nonetheless part of the legacy of Muslim-Christian antagonism that fed the later conflict, and Peate represents it merely as a romantic historical event, with no questioning its rights or wrongs.
76. Edgar Phillips, 'Dewi, Gwared!', *Trysor o Gân i'r Plant* (Cardiff, 1931) 39.
77. Vivian Griffiths, 'Pray Wolf,' *Sinews from Salt* (Llandybïe, 1969) 36.

78. Sheenagh Pugh, 'Crusaders', *Beware Falling Tortoises* (Bridgend, 1987) 52.
79. Sharon Penman, *Falls the Shadow* (London, 1988) 175.
80. William Owen Roberts, *Pestilence*, trans. Elisabeth Roberts (London 1991) 14.
81. *Ibid.* 7.

'Was there not in him something I do not understand?': Welsh Ccommentators on Islam

All travellers take with them the values and assumptions of their own culture. In the case of attitudes towards Islam, the religious beliefs of the traveller's own society have a crucial formative role. This chapter attempts to survey specifically religious views about Islam articulated by Welsh commentators over the centuries. In so doing, it is hoped to show what ideological baggage was being carried by the travellers whose first-hand accounts of meetings with Muslims form a major element of other chapters.

As shown in the previous chapter, the Crusades created a level of awareness of Islam in Welsh society. This awareness was augmented by material from other sources which was in circulation in Wales, such as a sixteenth-century Welsh translation of the fourteenth-century descriptive work *Travels of Sir John Mandeville*, which had extensive, and to a degree sympathetic, descriptions of Muslim belief and practice.[1] Further early references come from the two surviving medieval Welsh religious verse dramas, *Y Tri Brenin o Gwlen* ('The Three Kings of Cologne') and *Y Dioddefaint a'r Atgyfodiad* ('The Passion and the Resurrection'), themselves indebted to English originals, which survive in manuscripts from the sixteenth century, but which are possibly of slightly earlier composition. The first depicts a dialogue between the Three Kings and Herod, together with the story of the visit to Bethlehem, the Flight into Egypt and the Slaughter of the Innocents.[2] It is notable for the use of the word 'Mahound', a derogatory form of the name 'Muhammad', and commonly used in Europe at the time. *Y Tri Brenin o Gwlen* shares with other contemporary British religious dramas the use of this word as a name invoked by villains in their oaths and promises – invocations which are, of course, anachronistic, as the drama is set six hundred years before the birth of Muhammad himself. In *Y Tri Brenin o Gwlen*, a Messenger says:

> Lord king, I will go there,
> may mahount amen keep me.[3]

Herod himself makes a similar invocation, crying 'Mahownt Mahownt' as he prepares to 'break heads'.[4] In *Y Dioddefaint a'r Atgyfodiad*, 'Syr Peilad' ('Sir Pilate') for his part, takes the confusion even further, conflating 'Mahound' with the Jewish deity: 'myn Mahownd yr Iddewon',[5] 'By Mahound of the Jews'.

In Wales as elsewhere in Britain at the time, and even centuries later, the popular imagination was often unsure as to whether the entity known by names such as 'Mahound' or 'Mahomet' was a deity, a demon, or simply a deceitful human being. Neither was it sure to what historical period, or to what non-Christian religion the name belonged, hence its frequent use in depictions of the events of Jesus's time.

Against such a background, it would be a daring man who would use a favourable reference to Muslims in a heated religious argument. The seventeenth-century radical preacher William Erbery (1604-54)[6] was such a man. In the fevered sectarian atmosphere of mid-seventeenth-century Britain, Erbery, who came from Roath-Dogfield, Cardiff, was forced to defend himself against accusations that he had 'turned Turk' and had actually become a Muslim.

Erbery was no stranger to controversy. In 1635, during the tensions that preceded the English Civil War, as an Anglican clergyman of Puritan tendencies, he was forced out of his parish of St Mary's, Cardiff, by the Bishop of Llandaff for refusing to read a message from James I clarifying which sports were lawful to be played on Sundays. During the war, he became a chaplain with the Parliamentary forces, and afterwards returned to Cardiff as a minister. He was an influential figure in his day, and the renowned Puritan theologian and mystic Morgan Llwyd (1619-59), a fellow chaplain during the war, regarded him as his teacher. But Erbery fell foul of the new regime too, being hauled before the Committee for Plundered Ministers[7] in 1652 to explain his views, which, under the influence of the German radical theologian Jacob Böhme, tended towards allowing mysticism to subordinate long-established theological distinctions. As a millenarian, Erbery believed the turmoil of his age would soon be resolved by the Second Coming of Jesus, and a thousand-year reign of peace. Confident that post-millennial posterity would vindicate him and would also find the disputes in which he had been engaged of minute interest, he wrote a copious account of his defence to the charges he faced: 'An Answer to the Articles and Charge Exhibited Against Mr William Erbery before the Honourable Committee for Plundered Ministers, March the 9th, 1652',[8] which included his answers to the allegation of converting to Islam.

He begins by pointing out that he has '... been a Sufferer from the beginning; first, by the *Prelates* in the *High Commission*: next, by the *Royall Party* for my affection to the *Parliament*, being the first *Plundered Minister* in *Wales*.'[9] He then addresses the charges in turn, eventually reaching the allegation of preaching Islam.

> To the 10th, *that I saw no evil in the Turkish Alkoran and wished liberty to the Popish religion &c.* Truly, the *Turkish Alkoron* I never saw, therefore knew not the evil of it: but (not to repeat what I spake last to your Honours) I shall onely add that as the three chief Religions in the World are the Christians, Jews, and Turks; so this Christian Common-wealth appearing so favourable to the Jews, why not to the Turks? Who more honour *Christ Jesus*, than the Jews do, who curse and blaspheme him, yet Liberty of Conscience was once highly moved in *Councel of War* by the General Officers to Petition the *Parliament* for Liberty of Conscience for the Jews: And if for unbelieving *Jews*, why not for misbelieving Christians, who to their utmost knowledge love the Truth and Peace? Secondly, as the Calling of the Jews is a Mystery which most Christians understand not (for Mr *Calvin* interprets that *Israel of God* in the Spirit which our Divines do of the Jews in the letter) so, though the Turks are turned away from the *Son* to the *Father*, because the Spirit of Christ did not commonly appear in Christians; yet the *Teutonic Theosopher* Faith, that the Turks do (in their righteous ways) worship the Son in the Father, though not naming Christ as Christians do. The same author adds, that the Turks shall yet turn to be true Christian, and that Christians shall all know the Truth as it is in Jesus... *If Christians, with us, turn to be Turks, why should not Turks turn to be Christians?*[10]

It is clear that Erbery is very far from preaching Islam itself, of which it is evident he knows little. The logic of his argument, however, is strong: the Puritan Commonwealth had extended religious toleration to Jews, who openly rejected the Christian faith, so why should it not extend that tolerance to Muslims, who at least held Jesus Christ in great honour? And if to them, then why not to Christians – implicitly, ones like Erbery – from whom the theological distance was even less? It should be noted, however, that despite the impeccable logic, this is essentially another example of Islam being used as a debating pawn in a domestic dispute.[11] Erbery's tolerance towards Islam was theoretical rather than based on any real experience. One of his Welsh Puritan contemporaries, however, Charles Edwards (*c.*1628-91), *had* taken the trouble to acquaint himself with the 'Alcoran'. His reading, however, did not lead to greater tolerance.

Edwards, born to a gentry family in Denbighshire, became a scholar of All Souls, and later of Jesus College, Oxford, and was a minister following the Civil War, experiencing the kind of turbulent career that was common for religious ministers in that age. His main legacy is his first book, *Hanes y Ffydd Ddi-Ffuant*,[12] ('A History of the True Faith'), whose first edition appeared in 1667. It is a masterpiece of prose style which tells the story of the Christian faith, specifically with reference to Wales, but also with an eye to the larger context, which is why it contains an extended section, around thirty pages, on Islam, and entitled 'Ynghylch crefydd Mahomet' ('Concerning the religion of Mahomet').

> Around the year of the Lord six hundred and sixty six, the religion of Mahomet began to spread through the power of the Saracens, those who had fallen out with the empire of the Christians which in that age had been sorrily divided in their opinions, with human imaginings being welcomed into religious matters. Whereupon, the charismatic Mahomet (through the help of the excommunicated Monk, Sergius[13]) devised the Alcoran, which is the book of the false religion of the Turks. And because he often fell into faints, he maintained that it was his converse with the Angel Gabriel that caused him to swoon. And as the world came to accept his doctrine more readily, he moderated it in order to please everyone somewhat. Christ is acknowledged as a faithful prophet in order to satisfy the true Christian. Circumcision was ordered in order to please the Jews. The divinity of Christ was denied in order to satisfy the Arians who were numerous in that region. A multiplicity of wives were allowed for one man, and freedom of the flesh, in order to attract those who loved Sin, that which is natural to all the world, and that not only in this life, but in paradise he promised feasts and wives to those who would follow his faith, and he would kill everyone who refused.[14]

Edwards goes on to provide a hostile summary of the life of Muhammad as he had received it, saying his deliberate deceptions, and his fainting fits, created the impression of sanctity, while his shrewd offer of liberation to slaves and his politic alliance with the Saracens, 'who joined this false prophet and took him as their chief-villain', allowed him to create an army which swept all before it 'through the power of the sword ... as happened too truly to the woe of many a country'.[15]

Y Ffydd Ddi-Ffuant presents extensive summaries from the *Qur'an*, prefaced as follows:

> Because it sometimes mentions Christianity, I chose and translated the best things in it, because an enemy's testimony is strong in his own condemnation. And the mistaken things which are in it should urge us to love our saving faith more warmly, because the pure is seen more affectionately when compared to the vile. And the prodigal children when they come to themselves will prefer the homely sustenance after eating the husks which are in the distant country.[16]

Edwards summarises 20 of the 114 suras, or chapters, of the *Qur'an* (Suras 1-13, 16-18, 22, 27, 33 and 35.). To begin with, each of his summaries runs to hundreds of words, but by Sura 11, this has reduced to a short sentence or two for each, and beyond Sura 35, no further summaries are attempted at all. Often, only one of many points in the original sura is given, and an entire sura is reduced to the briefest of outlines. For instance, Sura 11, which contains 123 verses, many of them running to several lines, is represented as follows: 'Worship God alone. Give fair weights and measures. Do not withhold anything from your neighbour'. Edwards's choice of material to précis seems somewhat arbitrary, and while he cannot be accused in all cases of selecting only the parts most likely to induce prejudice in his readers, some of the selections do certainly have this effect. An example is when he summarises Sura 22, as follows: 'He who is indignant at the succouring of Mahomet, let him tie a rope to the ceiling of his house and hang himself to see if that cools his bile,' before adding the non sequitur: 'We have set a law for sacrifice offerings'.[17] In fact, Sura 22 contains 78 verses, most of which would have provided a much more positive portrayal of Islam than the very brief extract Edwards has chosen to cite.

In his introduction to his 1936 edition of *Y Ffydd Ddi-Ffuant*,

Griffith John Williams (1892-1963) showed that Edwards's translation was not from the Arabic but from a 1649 English version. In 1968, Cyril Glyndŵr Williams, in an article 'The Unfeigned Faith and an Eighteenth Century Pantheologia', further noted that Edwards's account is 'less charitable' than the original.[18] The 'best parts' of the *Qur'an* as provided by Edwards seem to be largely the best parts for advancing his argument that Islam and its prophet, although they may have had some commendable characteristics, are fundamentally false. He concludes his account of the life and work of Muhammad by saying:

> And now, reader, you can see that the true religion was among men long before this bungler stitched together his patchwork of deception and led himself astray in many of his principles. It is easy to believe that plenty of people in his day found him charismatic and asked him for wondrous signs to make them believe his prophecies, and that he could not provide any, and that his other methods of shutting the mouths of those who opposed him were merely bondage and massacre. And that his lust and his greed for plunder, and for blood are clear signs of the nature of his spirit.[19]

In subsequent chapters, he makes passing reference to Islam, equating the *Alcoran* and the Catholic mass as instruments of error[20] and then, before he concludes with a short factual portrayal of contemporary Muslim worship, he gives an account of the conquest of Constantinople by the 'Cruel Turks'. He blames the conquest on the corruption of the Christian powers, who had put their trust in saints rather than in Jesus, and who had, on one occasion, opportunistically broken the terms of a treaty with the Turks in order to recover lost territory, only to be defeated when the Turkish commander reproached God about the fact that the Christians were dishonouring the agreement. He says of the Turks:

> God allowed them to be a constant scourge to his disobedient people. Scarcely is there a city or town in Asia, Africa and a large part of Europe that these rough infidels have not made flow with the blood of the Christians. And those who are spared the sword are sold like animals from market to market, to pull in place of oxen, or to carry out some other hardship. And now the Christians, who are under the heavy tax of the Turks, can only gather in secret, cannot hold office, cannot bear arms, nor wear clothes of the same kind as

> them, nor oppose any blasphemy against Christ, and if they say anything against Mahomet, they are burned. And the most pitiable thing of all is that they have to let their children go into the hands of the enemies of Christ to be brought up as though in monasteries in the false religion, and to be trained so that they come to forget their parents (for they are not allowed to know them once they are separated) and to then fight skillfully against the gospel.[21]

The importance of Edwards's work should be stressed. *Y Ffydd Ddi-Ffuant* was a seminal work of religious history for Welsh readers, and its influence persisted for centuries. The extensive and hostile portrayal of Islam that it contains cannot have been without effect in the mindset of a country which continued to be profoundly affected by Protestant piety and which treated religious ideas with great seriousness.

Just under forty years after the publication of *Y Ffydd Ddi-Ffuant*, another of the canonical works of Welsh literature was published, and again, it contained extensive denunciations of Islam. *Gweledigaetheu y Bardd Cwsc* ('The Visions of the Sleeping Bard') was published in 1703 by Ellis Wynne (1671-1734) of Lasynys. Wynne was an Anglican clergyman who combined Royalist and Tory sympathies with reforming tendencies, and who was possessed of a gift for rollicking satire and withering invective, a gift to which he gave full expression in his most famous work, which takes the form of a phantasmagoric vision of the world, the flesh and the devil. As he traverses his dream landscape, Wynne's sleeping bard takes every opportunity to ridicule those whom Wynne regarded as worthy of contempt, and he does so in an exuberant style which is regarded as a masterpiece of Welsh prose and which is still stylistically influential today.

The Tory Royalism which Wynne represented was facing, in his view, two main threats: from Catholicism and from Puritanism. He regarded both with equal loathing. At one point in his fantasy, he depicts Rome as the home of three malign forces: the Pope, 'the Turk' and Louis XIV of France. The sleeping bard asks his guiding angel why these three should be in league, and receives the classic conspiracy theorist's response: '"Oh, there is many a dark reason," said the Angel'.[22]

Throughout the book, the 'Turk', while portrayed in a hostile manner, does not seem to be the main focus of Wynne's distaste. For instance, in one episode of his vision, he depicts various religions, including the Quakers, whom he despises, before portraying Muslim worshippers, who, by comparison, escape quite lightly:

> From these dumb dogs [the Quakers] we chanced to turn into an immense, roofless church, with thousands of shoes lying at the porch, whereby I learnt it was a Turkish mosque. These had but very dark and misty spectacles called the Alcoran; yet through these they gazed intently from the summit of their church for their prophet, who falsely promised to return and visit them long ago, but has left his promise unfulfilled.[23]

In this as in the numerous other references to Islam in Wynne's vision, the author's enmities begin at home, and the 'Turk' is largely only introduced as an exotic rhetorical intensifier in a local conflict. It is worth comparing this usage to the way references to the Nazis are invoked in arguments in our age as a shorthand for evil and prejudice. Just as someone today might seek to discredit an opponent by associating them with Nazism, Wynne puts his enemies in company with the 'Turk' knowing that, given his audience's preconceptions, this juxtaposition will bypass logic and will produce a damaging guilt by association. This can be seen most clearly in a late section of the book, where the bard finds himself in Hell, a place of continual turmoil, just at the point where Catholics, Muslims and Puritans escape from their prisons, and engage in a three-way battle: '...the Turks, the Papists and the murderous Roundheads in three armies, filling the whole plain of Darkness, committing every outrage and turning everything topsy-turvy'.

> 'How came they out?' demanded the Evil One, frowning more terribly than Demigorgon. 'The Papists', said the messenger, 'somehow or other broke out of their purgatory, and then, to pay off old scores, went to unhinge the portals of Mahomet's paradise, and let loose the Turks from their prison, and afterwards in the confusion, through some ill chance, Cromwell's crew escaped from their cells'. Then Lucifer turned and peered beneath his throne, where every damned king lay, and commanded that Cromwell himself should be kept secure in his kennel, and that all the sultans should be guarded.
>
> Accordingly, Lucifer and his host hurried across the sombre wilds of darkness, each one's own person furnishing light and heat; guided

> by the tumultuous clangour he marched fearlessly upon them. Silence was proclaimed in the King's name, and Lucifer demanded the cause of such uproar in his realm. 'May it please your infernal majesty', said Mahomet, 'a quarrel arose between myself and Pope Leo as to which had done you the better service – my Alcoran or the Romish religion; and when this was going on a pack of Roundheads, who had broken out of their prison during the disorder, joined in and clamoured that their Solemn League and Covenant[24] deserved more respect at your hands than either; so, from striving to striking from words to blows. But now, since your majesty hath returned from Hell, I lay the matter for your decision'.
>
> 'Stay, we've not done with you yet', cried Pope Julius, and madly they engaged once more, tooth and nail, until the strokes clashed like earthquakes; the three armies of the damned tore each other piecemeal, and like snakes became whole again, and spread far and wide over the jagged, burning crags, until Lucifer bade his veterans, the giants of Hell, separate them, which indeed was no easy task.
>
> When the conflict ceased, Pope Clement spake: 'Thou Emperor of Horrors, no throne has ever performed more faithful and universal service to the infernal crown than have the bishops of Rome, throughout a large portion of the world, for eleven centuries, and I hope you will allow none to vie with them for your favour'. 'Well,' said a Scotch-man of Cromwell's gang, 'however great has been the service of the Alcoran for these eight hundred years, and of popish superstitions for a longer period, yet the Covenant has done far more since its appearance, and everyone begins to doubt the others and be weary of them, but we are still increasing, the wide world over, and have much power in the island of your foes, that is, in Britain and in London, the happiest city under the sun'. 'Ha ha', exclaimed Lucifer, 'if I hear rightly ye too are about to suffer disgrace there. But whatever ye may have done in other kingdoms, I will have none of your rioting in mine. Wherefore make your peace forthwith under the penalty of more woes, bodily and spiritual'. And at the word I could see many of the fiends and all the damned, with their tails between their hoofs, steal away to their holes in fear of a change for the worse.[25]

It is hardly an indication of tolerance on Wynne's part that he should portray Muslims in this context less negatively than he does Catholics or, especially, Puritans. There can be little doubt of the disdain with which he regards Islam; if Muslims are shown as less contemptible than certain Christians in his work, it is merely because Wynne hates some of his fellow Christians more than he does Muslims. However, even if the role of Muslims is merely to serve as foreign conscripts in Wynne's religious civil wars, it is certainly significant for the image of Islam in Welsh literature that the religion, its prophet and its holy book should have figured so prominently in one of the most enduring volumes of Welsh literature.

Another of the most prominent writers in Welsh history also wrote extensively on Islam. William Williams (1717-91), from Llanfair-ar-y-bryn in Carmarthenshire, was one of the leaders of the Methodist movement in Wales in the eighteenth century. Known as 'Williams Pantycelyn' after the name of his family farmhouse, he was a tireless worker in promoting Methodist ideals and in establishing the small confessional groups of believers which were the backbone of the movement in Wales. He also made it his business to give the movement the literature it needed, most notably in the prodigious number of hymns he wrote in both Welsh and English, a work which made him undoubtedly Wales's most important hymn writer. But his prolific output also included prose works, including *Pantheologia*, his 1762-79 encyclopaedic survey of all the world's religions. It is from this book that his comments on Islam are taken.

Williams devotes a 58-page chapter to Islam, which, in the custom of the day he refers to as 'Mahommetanism'.[26] Written in a question-and-answer format with an imaginary interlocutor, it is a detailed description which takes the trouble to explain the location of Arabia, its geography, climate and economy. Williams's account of the religion is equally detailed, although it is also frequently impatient, as when he describes the legends surrounding Muhammad's birth, including signs in the heavens and the toppling of pagan idols, '...and all kinds of lies of that sort which it is of no value to recount'. He does, nonetheless, go on to recount many more until his interlocutor responds: 'Leave these empty stories and proceed to tell us the things that are most likely to be true'.[27]

Williams duly proceeds to give the familiar version of Muhammad's life in which the prophet is portrayed as having seized upon the dissension and immorality of the Christians and the Jews as a chance to promote a new religion of his own invention, and that he retreated to a cave in order to give the impression of holiness: '... after he had lived an austere and self-denying life for over two years, he took upon himself the title of the apostle of God, and under that name he spread the deception he had throughout all that time been practising'.[28] Williams's rendition of the prophet's life and of Muslim practices such as pilgrimage continues in the same vein, with large tracts of factual material accompanied by occasional derogatory comments. He finds very little positive to say until his interlocutor comments: 'Enough now, I am amazed how many public sessions of worship they have. Do they not put Christians to shame in this?' Williams replies: 'You would feel even more shame if you knew how punctilious they were about being present in their temples at these times; because keeping the prayer times is greatly praised among the Mahommetans, and the more wealthy a man is the sooner he will be accounted a Pagan, an unbeliever, or ungodly, if he were to neglect prayer once or twice; and the people of low estate are thrown out of their parishes by their priests, if they do not go to public prayer in their temples; because they say that prayer is a pillar of religion, and whoever hates prayer destroys religion'.[29] But such sentiments of grudging admiration are rare; more common is the kind of condemnation with which Williams concludes his chapter on Islam: 'Such words and such prayers show the extreme darkness of that mistaken faith'.[30]

In the main body of the chapter, Williams keeps to a style which suggests objectivity and a reliance on facts rather than opinion, an impression aided by the interlocutory format, which creates the appearance of open intellectual inquiry. His expressions of opinion in the main text are therefore marginal, although, as shown above, the subjective interventions are almost all negative, and very little positive material is presented. In his footnotes, however, Williams allows himself greater freedom to express opinion. In his account of the beginning of Muhammad's ministry, Williams attaches a long and revealing footnote, which gives some indication of the rhetorical ability that made him such an influential preacher:

> I would not set out for the Welshman such false principles, such empty stories, and such lying blasphemies if it were not that such an inexpressibly large part of the world, yes close to half the old world, is of this false religion. Will the monoglot Welshman blame me for trying to enlighten just a little for those who would hear and understand what superstitious religions there are in the world. It is pitiful to think that there are legions of people in Wales, who suspect

nothing less than that the gospel prevails from one corner of the world to the other, and that it is preached either by priests in surplices, or Presbyterian ministers in bands, or Quakers with hats on their heads or by a counsellor on a stool, and from the days of Adam until now. And supposing that there were no religion, form or passion of any kind, other than that which is in Wales. Scarcely anyone of our nation will inquire into the root of things, but will only accept them on the surface, and will suppose that things are throughout the world as they are at home. A host of people have not considered that the sun that set last night over Cardigan had risen that morning over Gloucester – But despite all this, let those who would know no more know that I am going to show more to those who would read; and that it is not to draw anyone to the Mahommetan religion or the Alcoran that I venture this but to move people to wonder at the blindness and pride of the human heart, and for every true Christian to prostrate themselves and ask for infinite grace that we should never be in the state of those dark wretches, those who have, as I said, conquered more than half the world.

The old government of Rome, when it was in its greatest power, and had stretched its bounds across all the kingdoms of Europe (those which are today around 12 or 15 extensive kingdoms) and a large part of Asia and Africa, and as far as India, is nothing in comparison with the length and breadth of the land won Mohammetanism from its beginning to now; for Turkey in Europe itself, which is at least nine times bigger than Wales and England, is entirely Mahommetan; and Turkey in Asia is as large again, and of the same religion, and so is Turkey in Africa, such as Egypt, and other places there which have been conquered by this religion. From the expanse of great Persia, not to mention the Moghul empire in India, which is almost twice as large, and Arabia which is not much less, all have been won by the Mahommetan religion; let alone hundreds of islands here and there across the seas that cannot easily be enumerated without spending a long time. And now, the monoglot Welshman can be told that, believe it or not, this superstitious religion that I have described, has won a hundred times as much territory as Wales and England; should the children of Gomer[31] be ignorant of this; and shall we not love God the more that his great sun has risen upon us when we consider how many parts of the world lie in extreme darkness?[32]

The fact that writers as important as William Williams, Charles Edwards and Ellis Wynne had engaged so extensively with Islam shows that a knowledge of the religion – albeit a partial and hostile knowledge – was widespread among Welsh people throughout the centuries in question.

Widespread, but not universal. As many strands of evangelical eighteenth-century Protestantism were fighting bitter battles with rival parts of the Christian church for the allegiance of worshippers and for influence in public life, and decrying the hold which other religions had over other parts of the world, another strand of thought, under the influence of the Enlightenment, was becoming ever more liberal and deistic, ever more removed from the enmities of the engaged, and therefore ever more prepared to look at Islam objectively.

To this strand belonged Sir William Jones (1746-94). The son of the distinguished mathematician William Jones of Llanfihangel Tre'r Beirdd, Anglesey, he was a man of immense erudition, and was the most prominent orientalist of his day. A gifted polyglot and translator, he was widely-travelled in Asia, and spoke Arabic, among many other languages. He opened up the literature of India to English-language scholarship, made a huge contribution to the discipline of comparative religion, and founded the Asiatic Society. By his mid twenties, he 'had simply become the greatest Oriental scholar in Europe'.[33] While much of the work of 'Oriental Jones', or 'Persian Jones' as he was sometimes known, dealt with Hindu, Sanskrit and pre-Islamic culture, it did encompass Muslim material as well. For instance, in his masterly monograph 'Essay on the Poetry of the Eastern Nations' he refers to a story of the Arabic poet Lebid, a contemporary and opponent of the prophet Muhammad, who, following a local custom of hanging up verses in the temple as challenges to fellow poets, displayed a couplet satirising the new religion of Islam. In Jones's translation, the couplet reads: 'Are not all things vain, which come not from God? and will not all honours decay, but those, which he confers?' Jones continues the story:

> These lines appeared so sublime, that none of the poets ventured to answer them; till Mahomed, who was himself a poet, having composed a new chapter of his Alcoran (the second, I think,) placed the opening of it by the side of Lebid's poem, who no sooner read it, than he declared it to be something divine, confessed his own inferiority, tore his verses from the gate, and embraced the religion of his rival; to whom he was afterwards extremely useful in replying to the satires of Amralkeis, who was continually attacking the doctrine of Mahomed: the Asiaticks add, that their lawgiver acknowledged some

> time after, that no heathen poet had ever produced a nobler distich than that of Lebid just quoted.[34]

Less typical of Jones's scholarly work, but indicative of the breadth of his scholarship, the liberal nature of his religious ideas, and the lively interest he felt in his own Celtic heritage, is the irreverent poem 'Kneel to the Goddess whom all Men Adore'. It was written in 1780, apparently in the space of an hour, for a dinner at Cardigan of a Welsh society, The Druids, of which Jones was the founder.[35] Garland Cannon and Michael J. Franklin described the poem as: 'the exasperated response of his Enlightened deism to the anti-Catholic Gordon riots of early June 1780.[36] It playfully urges his fellow Druids to teach Muslims, Christians, Hindus, Parsis, pagan Greeks and Romans that they all in reality worshipped one goddess – be she called Diana, Mary, Astarte, or Gangã. The impassioned syncretism of this lyrical *jeu d'esprit* prefigures the universalizing tendencies of his ground-breaking discourse 'On the Gods of Greece, Italy, and India'.[37]

Syncretistic the poem certainly is, although its universalism is of a reductive kind, in the sense that all religions seem to be equally fallible, and equally the products of human aspiration and invention, and in the sense that the followers of all the religions are shown as being flawed, and their claims to exclusivity are implicitly undermined. Islam is not exempted, and the poem's first stanza makes reference to the legend, quoted earlier in the work of Charles Edwards, that Muhammad had a trained pigeon to help him create an impression of divine inspiration:

> What means all this frenzy, what mad men are they
> Who broil and are broil'd for a shade in religion?
> Since all sage inspirers one doctrine convey
> From Numa's wild nymph to sly Mohamed's pigeon.
> Then Druids arise,
> Teach the world to be wise,
> And the grape's rosy blood for your sacrifice pour,
> Th'immortals invoke,
> And under this oak
> Kneel, kneel to the Goddess whom all men adore.

Subsequent stanzas are devoted to particular religions such as those of the 'sallow Parsees' and the 'dark-visag'd Bramins', and in each case the devotees are cheerfully urged to forego their accustomed rites and acknowledge the universal Mother; the poem's humour deriving from the very incongruity of the suggestion that these millennia-old beliefs and practices, many of them severely ascetic, could be abandoned lightly in favour of bibulous frivolity. The stanza on Islam provides what might well be a juxtaposition unique in literature, of the Prophet Muhammad and the shape-shifting Celtic poet-shaman, Taliesin:

> Say why to sweet Araby pilgrims repair,
> And troop in full caravans yearly to Mecca?
> Their mosque is like ours, and no altar is there
> Save that which the Patriarch bless'd in Rebecca;
> The Koran for you,
> Ye Mussulmen true,
> Has of nymphs with black eyes and black tresses a store:
> Then sink to the ground,
> Tho' turban'd and gown'd,
> And kneel to the Goddess whom all men adore.
> See, Teifi, with joy see our mystical rite
> On steep woody marge after ages renewed;
> Here once Taliesin thou heard'st with delight,
> But what was his voice to the voice of our Druid?

Jones's poem, which, it must be remembered, was an ironic throwaway piece for the amusement of sophisticated friends, is not so much a plea that all religions be treated with equal reverence as a suggestion that they may all be treated with equal scepticism. In more sober mood, such detachment from a commitment to any particular faith position permitted Jones to have a clear-sighted assessment of the characteristics of different faiths, making him a pioneer in the field of comparative religion. He asserted that if the doctrines of the various faiths could be represented objectively, then it would be possible to achieve widespread agreement as to their essentials. Michael J. Franklin notes that, seven years after writing 'Kneel to the Goddess', Jones, who was by then living in India, wrote, referring to the sermons of his friend the prominent radical Welsh nonconformist minister and philosopher, Dr Richard Price (1723-91): '...if Price's book were accurately and perspicuously translated into Persian, [the Mohammadans] would certainly not be shocked by the Christian doctrine'.[38]

In return, Jones hoped that a fair representation of Muslim beliefs to Christians would be equally reassuring. Jones's instinct was to seek connections and areas of commonality. In his 1788 essay, 'On the Gods of Greece, Italy, and India', he wrote:

> The Mussulmans are already a sort of heterodox Christians: they are Christians, if Locke reasons justly, because they firmly believe the immaculate conception, divine character, and miracles of the Messiah: but they are heterodox in denying vehemently his character of Son, and his equality as God, with the Father, of whose unity and attributes they entertain and express the most awful ideas, while they consider our doctrines as perfect blasphemy, and insist that our copies of the Scriptures have been corrupted both by Jews and Christians.[39]

As a mediator between religions and cultures, Jones's monumental importance can hardly be overstressed. Of all the religions dealt with by this great Welsh scholar, Islam might not have been the one which received most attention, but Sir William Jones is without doubt the greatest Welsh scholar to have given attention to Islam. Jones's detached and scholarly attitude towards other religions has a very modern feel. However, the liberalism of his religious views was rare during his age.

That references to Islam were common currency in Welsh discourse of the time can be seen from the life of one of the greatest of all Welsh religious figures, the mystic and hymn writer Ann Griffiths (1776-1805) of Dolwar Fach in Montgomeryshire.[40] In her short life, under the influence of the devout Methodist movement which was sweeping the rural communities where she lived, Ann Griffiths wrote a body of religious verses remarkable for their sensual appreciation of the presence of God, and for the striking originality of their incarnational imagery. But before she was swept up by the religious fervour herself, Ann Griffiths was a conventional Anglican who shared the common disdain for the Methodists. Her mentor, John Hughes (1755-1854), in a memoir of his protégée written over forty years after her death, said that before her conversion she had been contemptuous of the Methodists who would travel together over the hills to regular meetings at Bala, one of the main centres of the movement.

> She would say scornfully of the people who would go to the

> [Methodist] Association [meetings] in Bala, 'There go the pilgrims on their way to Mecca', referring to the pilgrimage of the Mohametans.[41]

Only a short while after making that remark, she was to join that very pilgrimage to Bala herself. Once again, Griffiths's comment is a case of a writer using Islam as a debating device in a local religious rivalry. However, that a young woman of modest origins and limited education, living all her short life within a few miles of her isolated inland mountain parish, should use such a term casually is an indication that understanding of at least some of the basic features of Islam was widespread.

That understanding was, of course, not necessarily a sympathetic one. The pilgrims on their way to Bala were attending the meetings convened by the Methodist leader Thomas Charles (1755-1814), the founder of the British and Foreign Bible Society.[42] A tireless provider of religious reading matter for the scripture-hungry masses of Wales, and a preacher so charismatic that his town had become, as Ann Griffiths said, a 'Mecca', he was not, however, conciliatory towards the believers who regarded the real Mecca as their spiritual home. Writing in his four-volume *Geiriadur Ysgrythurol* ('Scriptural Dictionary'), published between 1805 and 1811, he referred to Muhammad:

> In the year 626 when this cruel and destructive false prophet arose, it is said that there was an unusual darkness on the sun from June to October. Through weapons of war he spread his errors, and succeeded amazingly across very many of the lands of the east, and so it remains to this day. It was the corruption, the immorality and the errors of the Christians in those regions that gave them over to this heavy judgement. For the same reason, and around the same time, the Antichrist and his fearful errors arose in the western lands of the world. The two shall go to destruction together, and may God speed the day! See Rev. xx.

Such was the picture of Islam in one of the most widely-read and most influential books of nineteenth-century Wales. It was not an isolated view. Hugh Jones (1749-1825) of Maesglasau, a Methodist poet, translator and hymn writer, and a contemporary of Thomas Charles, was equally keen to see the end of Islam. In the wake of the Anglo-French War in 1802, he wrote an essay on current events, calling for 'The Fall of Antichrist or the

Destruction of Popery – the Extinction of Mahometanism and Idolatry – the Conversion of the Jews, and the general success of the Gospel in the Last Days'.[43] As has been well documented in the work of the scholars of Welsh Nonconformity, E. Wyn James and Derec Llwyd Morgan, it was an article of faith of evangelical Protestantism that Biblical prophecy required that the Second Coming must be preceded by the return of the Jewish people to their homeland, and their conversion.[44] The fact that the Turkish Empire was occupying that homeland meant that the supplanting of Islam was implicit in this millenarian worldview, and signs that this could be imminent were greeted enthusiastically.

In 1799, the land surveyor, author, and almanac-maker Mathew Williams (1732-1819), in his *Hanes Holl Grefyddau'r Byd* ('History of all the World's Religions'), which devotes a long chapter to Islam, begins by portraying Muhammad as one who had cynically decided to exploit religious schisms and credulity by posing as a prophet. Williams goes on to give a summary of Muslim belief and practice which, while not comprehensive, is nonetheless largely accurate and without obvious animus. But his summary of the faith is ultimately dismissive:

> The Mahometans are not Pagans, Jews or Christians; not Pagans because they do not worship idols; not Jews, because they do not follow the laws of Moses; and not Christians, because they do not believe the gospel. So what can they be called? The answer is obvious enough, men who are the object of pity, misled from the path by a crafty deceiver, in whom, to this day, they still believe.[45]

In 1817, a close friend of Thomas Charles, the influential Methodist Reverend Simon Lloyd (1756-1836), in his *Amseryddiaeth Ysgrythurol* ('Scriptural Chronology'), refers to other world chronologies, and, discussing the Islamic system, beginning in 622 of the Christian era, dismisses it as follows:

> What brought about this era was the conversion of the deceiver Mahomet of Mecca, a city in Arabia; for when the governors of that city had understood that his errors were tending to disturb the general peace, they decided to cut off the author of them, so that his evil would not spread further: but Mahomet, having been warned of their intention, fled by night to Medina, another city in Arabia, in the year mentioned above.[46]

The extent to which Islam was regarded, in much of Welsh society, as a false and manufactured religion can be seen from the relevant entries in *An English and Welsh Dictionary* published between 1770 and 1794 by John Walters (1721-97), the Rector of Llandough in the Vale of Glamorgan:

> *Mahometan*: (one who professes the religion of Mahomet) Mahomed, or Mahommed, a famous Arabian impostor in the beginning of the seventh century, whose tenets are contained in an Arabic book called the Koran. One of the followers or disciples of the deceiver Mahomed, 1; *Mahometans*, Mahometaniaid.
>
> *The Mahometan religion*, Crefydd Mahomet. Mahometanism: (the religion fabricated by Mahomet) Crefydd Mahomet.[47]

The frequent use of Islam to inflame enmity against Roman Catholicism can be seen in the work of the religious poet and hymn-writer, Edward Jones (1761-1836), of Maes-y-Plwm. In the poem given below, Jones, a popular preacher and Sunday school teacher in north east Wales, uses repeated references to 'Mahomet' as a means of producing guilt by association for the 'Papists' who seem to be the real focus of the hymn's vengeful eschatology. The following selected translated stanzas, published posthumously in 1839, give an idea of the author's enmities, as well as of the poem's literary merits, which are slight:

> **Hymn XII. –**
> Destruction of the kingdom of the enemy
>
> Mahomet's kingdom is trembling,
> the time is come when from his throne
> the devil will at last be toppled
> down the hillside like a stone;
>
> . . .
>
> Mahomet's throne is trembling,
> The false prophet will one day fall
> And the beast will lose the dominion
> That once made him king over all.
>
> . . .

Mahomet's kingdom is trembling,
The false prophet will one day fall
The Antichrist's league will be broken,
No Papists continue at all.[48]

This equation of Rome and Islam can also be seen in the short anonymous book *Y Twrc wedi ei Glwyfo* ('The Turk Wounded') occasioned by the victory of the Allied navies over those of Ottoman Turkey and Egypt in 1827 in the Greek War of Independence. It describes the Turks' earlier conquest of Constantinople as 'merciless', and the Turks themselves as 'diabolical Barbarians'.

> There are cruelties belonging to the Mahometan religion greater than any which have been formed by the imagination of man, and although it is the sister of Rome, she excels in every open atrocity, although the Pope can be equal to it in the secret workings of the hellish inquisition. The Path of the False Prophet, has been coloured with human blood, and his followers have travelled in his accursed footsteps, through spilling the blood of their contemporaries, and making the most delectable regions entirely uninhabitable ... so this Empire has been a scourge in the almighty hand of the Ruler of the Nations, to punish many kingdoms in different parts of the world for their many sins against him.

The author goes on to describe the battle and concludes with the hope that these 'excitements will be sovereignly ordered by the King of Kings to open the way for the Gospel to be proclaimed'. The work concludes with a series of verses contemplating the overthrow of Islam:

The angry stubborn Mahometan,
Is the oppressor, enemy of men,
Though he raves insanely
Soon he will be cast down again.

. . .

When the *Beast* abominable
And the *Prophet False* are thrown
Alive into the lake of fire
Where they shall forever moan.[49]

Pejorative references to 'Y Twrc' were common in Welsh-language hymnody and religious poetry. The seventeenth-century Puritan theologian Morgan Llwyd, mentioned earlier, believed the dominion of 'the Turk' must be overthrown before the Second Coming could take place: 'The Pope shall be despoiled, the Jew shall be called / and the Turk shall be cast down cruelly'.[50] The belief persisted for centuries. In 1856, the Congregationalist minister William Williams (1801-69), known as 'Caledfryn', wrote 'Awdl ar yr Adgyfodiad' ('Ode on the Resurrection') and referred to 'y Twrc aflan', 'the filthy Turk' being given the chance to discover heaven and leave his darkness behind.[51]

In 1834, the Calvinistic Methodist minister Owen Jones (1806-89), known as 'Meudwy Môn' ('The Hermit of Anglesey') published *Y Cyniweirydd* ('The Wayfarer, or a Magazine of Profitable Knowledge, and a Sunday School Companion'). The entry on Islam forms part of a comparative discussion of the various forms of religion:

> The Pagan, the Mahometan or Natural religion. As for the pagan, a glance at it is enough to make every reasonable man abominate it; the same is true of the Mahometan religion. As for Mahomet, it is enough to observe that there are in his writings abundant evidence to prove that he was a shameless deceiver... Let the two religions be set next to one another, and let reason decide which is the true one. Behold Mahomet and his disciples in their bloody war-garb riding in pomp, and killing thousands, and tens of thousands, and taking their possessions as plunder for themselves: behold the cities burned by Mahomet, the lands he destroyed and ravaged, and the oppression he brought upon the dwellers of the earth; having beheld him so, let us go with him to the secret places; we see the prophet's chamber, his wives and concubines; we behold his abominable adultery, and we hear him claiming divine inspiration to justify his lust and oppression. Having tired of looking there, let us behold the blessed Jesus, humble and meek, doing good to all the sons of men, patient in teaching the ignorant and the stubborn.[52]

In 1849, Evan Lewis published a Welsh-language work in which Muhammad was included in a study of six 'religious hotheads' including the founder of Mormonism, Joseph Smith, and the English 'prophetess' Joanna Southcott.[53] In 1855, the draper and trade unionist Morgan Richards (d.1901), known as 'Morgrugyn Machno' ('The Ant of Machno') published a history of the 'false prophet Mahomet'.[54] Also in 1855, the Wesleyan Methodist minister from Llantrisant, John Jones (1818–69), known as 'Humilis', published a detailed 80-page essay on Turkey, entitled *Traethawd ar Dwrci*, which was casually scathing about Islam:

> Every nation that has not known God, or which has departed from him and his ways, has been in a pagan condition until someone should come to them once again with knowledge about God. We have now to deal with a nation which jumped straight from paganism to superstition, in the darkness of which it has been living for seven or eight hundred years, without showing any sign, *of itself*, or on the part of its government, of owning the religion of Christ – the only religion which exalts a nation, as well as a man personally. The night of Mahommetanism has for ages enveloped millions of the residents of Turkey, even though the Holy Land is in their possession, and all those places that were the scenes of the labour and success of Christ and his apostles
>
> . . .
>
> It appears that Turkey now occupies more space in the minds and concerns of the great, the wealthy and the godly in our land than ever. The continuance and fate of this dark land depends on the use it makes of its opportunities to improve itself and to come from darkness to light. Only the Reformation of the country can keep it from destruction. The religion of the Greek church is not much of an improvement on Mahommetanism. Turkey must be planted with the best vine – and with the gospel, before it will bear fruit in national greatness and in holiness to the Lord.[55]

He says slaves can still be traded in the market at Constantinople, and that women are merely 'instruments of the lust, fickleness, profiteering and idleness of the Turk'.

> Asia Minor is overflowing with memories which are interesting and sacred to the students of the Bible. Here were the Seven Churches of Revelation; here the apostles and their fellow-labourers planted Christianity, and from here the gospel went forth to the lands of the west. But oh! oh! the lamentable change that has come across this region, as well as the holy land. Villages and towns are now ruins, the land is neglected and parties of nomads and their flocks wander here and there; but there is nothing to say that Christians had once dwelt here, apart from the odd carving on old stones that have escaped the destruction of time, and the frown of the conquerors. Spiritual and moral darkness cover the people.[56]

Later, he goes into greater detail about Islam itself, which he refers to as 'this enormous heresy'. Explaining the early days of the religion, he says that Mahomet, who was 'notable for his mental abilities', resolved to reform religion and institute the worship of the one true god.[57] To that end, he retired to a cave with a renegade Christian and Jew who helped him compose the *Qur'an*. He then killed them in order to keep the deception a secret. The 'false prophet' then began to preach, gradually winning adherents. Jones reports that learned Arabists say the Arabic of the *Qur'an* is excellent. However, his own opinion of the content of the holy book of Islam is not high:

> Regarding the divine inspiration of the Koran, it is, of course, out of the question. It has about as much *divinity* as the Book of Mormon or Robinson Crusoe.[58]

In the mid nineteenth century, we find another extended depiction of Islam in the publisher Thomas Gee's *Gwyddoniadur*, an encyclopaedia published from 1854 in 10 volumes and edited by Gee's brother in law, John Parry (1812-74), a lecturer at the Calvinistic Methodists' training college at Bala. The *Gwyddoniadur* was regarded as the century's most ambitious publishing enterprise in Welsh, and the entries on Muhammad and Islam are therefore close to being the official consensus on the subject at the time.

The entries are extensive: that on 'Mahomet' is 3,500 words; that on 'Mahometiaeth' ('Mahommetism'), some 8,000. Most of the material is simply factual, dealing with the events of the prophet's life, with Islamic history and with the details of Islamic theology and practices. It is the parts which express opinion that are of most interest to the present study. For instance, the entry on 'Mahomet' gives a highly-detailed account of the prophet's birth and family, but says of the tales of miracles told of his childhood: 'although they are believed unshakeably by his followers, they are, of course, completely baseless'.[59] A little later, after much discussion of Muhammad's beliefs, the entry says: 'It is next to impossible to free Mahomet from the accusation of being guilty of deliberate deceit when he claimed to have had the privilege of visiting the Highest in heaven'.[60] The author goes on to quote at length the Lutheran historian, Johann Lorenz von

Mosheim, who speculated that Muhammad had been led astray by his own zeal for reform to believe that he was divinely inspired, and that he became gradually prone to deliberate deceit as he saw how readily people accepted his claims.

The author compares Islamic doctrines unfavourably with those of Christianity, saying: 'Mahomet's teachings, contrary to those of the gospel, tended to satisfy, not to crucify, the flesh, and its desires. Those who spread the religion were not poor, defenceless, patronless fishermen, but the soldiers of a victorious chieftain, whom to disobey was death'.[61] He compares the prophet's curses on the Jews during his last days with Jesus's prayers on behalf of his own people.[62] He sums up the prophet of Islam as follows:

> In judging a man of the abilities and talents of Mahomet, we should of course, take into account the morals and the standards of the age and country in which he lived. We do not have the slightest tendency to exalt his character. He was at times deceitful, scheming and even vengeful and cruel, and tended to lead a life of fleshly pleasure. But in his personal character, it appears he was a pleasant man – faithful to his friends, gentle to his family, and often ready to forgive his enemies: besides that he was particularly simple in his family life, lived, when he was at the height of his power and authority, in a poor cottage, and was in the habit of mending his own clothes. His mind was, we suppose, composed of the most extraordinary mixture of good and bad, of truth and deceit.[63]

The entry on 'Mohametanism' itself is much longer, and slightly less opinionated, although its conclusions are ultimately the same. It begins by describing the religion as one 'which is now professed by around a hundred and fifty million of the human race, and which is such an effective barrier across the path of the spread of the Christian faith – a barrier, however, that will be removed'.[64] On occasions during his long discussion of Islamic theology the author permits himself some comparisons, such as when he says that the principle of divine love that 'breathes through every page of the Gospels' simply 'has no place in the doctrine of the *Koran*'.[65] He does, however, praise Muslim alms-giving: 'It is expressed that the Mohametans excel greatly in this. They provide particular sums to help poor travellers. And their compassion is shown even to senseless creatures; as they behave towards them with great gentleness'.[66] He also quotes approvingly a commentator who praises the devotion of Muslim pilgrims to Mecca. But his conclusion is generally negative. Considering the reasons for the success of the religion, he says this is due to the fact that its laws were few and easy and had been designed 'in a deceitful and shrewd manner to suit corrupt human nature', and particularly 'the evils and corruptions' that were characteristic of 'eastern nations'.[67]

Among this class of educated Nonconformist ministers, aversion to Islam was almost universal. Sheer ignorance of the basic facts of the religion was, however, rare. One such example comes from the preface to a guidebook of Christian sects, *Crefyddau y Byd Cristionogaidd* ('Religions of the Christian World'), published in Scranton, Pennsylvania, in 1868, at a time when the north-eastern United States was home to a thriving Welsh-language publishing industry among the flourishing community of emigrants and their descendants. The author, the Rev. J.E. Davies, of Hyde Park, Pennsylvania, a Calvinistic Methodist minister, said he intended his book 'to fill a little of the void among the monoglot Welsh' in their knowledge of the distinctions of the Christian sects, of which it lists 43 as orthodox and 91 as unorthodox.

The book's preface is by an anonymous 'Minister of the Calvinistic Methodists in America'. In it, he criticises Islam, primarily, it seems, to intensify his distaste for Roman Catholicism. In so doing, however, he betrays the fact that he thinks that Islam and Hinduism are the same:

> The propensity to worship, under the influence of ignorance and superstition, gives existence to the power of Mahomet among the Hindoos, of Confucius among the Chinese, the Pope of Rome in the Christian world, and priestcraft in every part of the world...
>
> The elements of superstition can also be discerned in different forms in the religious systems of the world. It is this that causes the Heathen to kneel before the idol, the Mahomet[an] to believe the fancies of the Koran, and drives him on processions to the Ark of the Founder in Mecca. It causes the Papist to worship through the mediation of false miracles, penances, purgatory, &c. Superstition is a powerful spirit in the world. Its sceptre reigns over the Heathen world, and it is emperor over more than half the Christian world.[68]

But such crassness was unusual. On the whole, these were not uncultured men. Simon Lloyd, for instance, who came from a gentry family, and who was a substantial landowner in his home town of Bala, was Oxford-educated. All were at least bilingual, and most were acquainted with a wide range of literature and thought and had struggled for their own brand of dissenting Christianity to be granted tolerance and respect by an Anglican establishment. However, while the theological interests of these authors, and others like them, extended beyond the contending forms of Protestantism among which they lived, their sympathies seem to have been largely coterminous with the boundaries of that strand of Christianity.

There were, however, exceptions. Towards the end of the nineteenth century, it is possible to find another Welsh commentator interpreting Islam to his countrymen in an objective and evidence-based manner which William Jones would have found commendable. By 1890, the British Empire was at its height, and controlled a quarter of the world's surface, including large parts of the Muslim world. Within that empire, the attitudes of the British towards the native peoples and their religions inevitably ranged from the most dismissive racism through paternalism to enlightened interest and empathy. The next commentator, Samuel Evans, (1859-1935) was on the liberal end of that scale.

Evans, from Ruabon near Wrexham, was chief of the coastal service in the khedival government of Egypt, a country which had a substantial ex-patriate British population. He later became inspector general of the Ottoman Bank, and was made a member of the Ottoman orders of Osmanie and Mejidie. He was a cousin of the Davies-Bryan family, who founded Cairo's most famous department store, and whose writings we will examine in Chapter 10. He lived in Alexandria, and involved himself heavily in local affairs, becoming a camel trader in his spare time.[69] He also took a great interest in Islam, as can be seen from a long article, 'Y Gwr o Fecca a'i Grefydd' ('The Man from Mecca and his Religion'), which he wrote in 1890 for *Y Traethodydd*, a magazine published by the Welsh Calvinistic Methodist Church. Evans is keen to correct the prejudices he feels Christians cherish towards Islam and its prophet. 'Virtually everything vile and unpleasant that Christian writers could devise has been said about him [Muhammad]',[70] he says, and he goes on to list insults and libels of Muhammad from writers as diverse as Martin Luther (who called Muhammad 'first-born of Satan'), Philip Melanchthon (who called him 'Gog or Magog, or perhaps both'), and Charles Wesley (who called him 'that Arab thief'), as well as the Welsh authors Ellis Wynne and Thomas Charles, whose views were mentioned above.

For Evans, this is simply not good enough. 'Is it not now time for the Christian world to grasp the fact that Mahommed was not some kind of Joseph Smith, and that the Coran is not something on the level of "the Book of Mormon"?' he asks. Writing for his Christian audience back in Wales, Evans's own portrayal of Muhammad is presented in stirring terms:

> Since the day of Jesus of Nazareth no-one greater has arisen among the children of men than Mahommed, the founder of Islam. Christianity took over three hundred years to make itself a power in the world; Mahommed and his disciples conquered in a hundred years a greater part of the earth than the Roman Empire at its height.... Only serious men, full of faith in their apostle and in his religion could have done this; people will not sacrifice their lives for a cause about which there is even the suspicion of fraud or hypocrisy.

Evans accuses Christian critics of repeating one another's views of Islam without examining primary sources: Ellis Wynne, for instance, incorrectly says Muslims are awaiting Muhammad's second coming. Evans says he has heard Methodist ministers in Wales preaching against the 'grave errors of the Mahometans', and saying that Muslims believe the coffin of their prophet is suspended between earth and heaven. Evans seeks to correct these wrong assumptions, refuting one after another.[71] On the question of polygamy, he says: 'There is much less unchastity in the lands of Islam than in the cities of England or the Continent. In the East, the Moslems are much more moral than the Christians – or rather those who call themselves Christians. Moslems never get drunk or gamble; which could scarcely be said for those who call themselves Christians even in London, or, as far as I know, in Caernarfon'.[72] In enumerating Muslim practices a little later, he says of alms-giving: 'The Moslems beat the whole world in this, without any exception. There is no such thing as a Poorhouse in the lands of Islam, nor is there any need for them. No-one has died of hunger in Egypt in the present age, and there is no danger of that happening while one of the children of Islam has corn in his barn'.[73]

As for the accusation of cruelty and intolerance, he is equally robust. The charge is, he says; 'totally wrong'. He goes on: 'The laws of Christian Russia are bitterer and harsher towards Judaism and Protestantism than the laws of any Moslem kingdom in the world. The Moslems were never, even in their worst days, as harsh and as inconsiderate in their dealings with other religions as the Church of Rome was until very recently and as the Orthodox Church still is today. There is not, in all the history of Islam, anything half as bloody as the Inquisition'. He notes the mercy shown by Muslim conquerors to their defeated enemies, and says that if there are cruelties committed by Turks in the present age, 'that has nothing to do with their religion. The Turks have corrupted Islam more than any other nation, and I believe that the Greek Christians are responsible to a very large extent for corrupting the Turks. It would be as fair to set the Spanish Catholics as an example of Christianity as it would be to count the Turks an example of Moslems'.[74]

Having dealt with some of the 'thorns and brambles that hide Mahommed and his religion from the writers and readers of the Christian world', Evans turns his attention to the life of the prophet himself, concluding:

> He was not without his faults, and it would be difficult to justify some of his actions; it would be just as difficult to justify many of the actions of David, king of Israel, a man after God's own heart. Taking all in all, I believe that Mahommed was one of the most splendid and honourable personalities our earth has seen. He swept away every kind of idolatry in Arabia, Persia and a large part of India; he taught his followers to practise a brotherly love that is far beyond what is known in Europe for all the preaching about love; he created a temperance movement more effective and more lasting than anything Sir Wilfred Lawson [(1829-1906) an English temperance leader] would have wished at his best. And he did more – he gave the world the Koran.[75]

Evans avoids the question of whether or not the *Qur'an* is the inspired word of God, but he praises the authenticity and accuracy of the text, and quotes Goethe as to its style and influence. He concludes by summarising Muslim belief, finding a shrewd and homely theological comparison for the benefit of his audience: 'It would be possible, with a great deal of justification, to call the Moslems Unitarian Calvinists'.[76] Evans's essay stands out in the nineteenth century as an example of a Welsh author discussing Islam not as a straw man to dismiss in order to confirm Christians in the certainty of their belief, but as a religious system worthy of the greatest respect.

The respect, however, was not accorded by John Jones (1837-1906) of Pwllheli, also writing in *Y Traethodydd* in 1905. His article on 'Mynydd Sinai' ('Mount Sinai') concludes: 'It must be admitted that there are good parts to the Mahometan religion, such as the Unity of God, moderation in food and drink, respect for women, kindness to animals. And yet, along with these excellent things, are found filthy and diabolical things such as the sword, vengeance, fatalism, lying and polygamy... No coexistence is possible between Christ and the false prophet, nor between Christianity and Mahometanism, any more than could be between light and darkness'.[77]

In 1907, one of the greatest of all Welsh authors, Sir John Morris-Jones (1864-1929), brought the work of a Muslim author before the Welsh-speaking public. Morris-Jones, Professor of Welsh at Bangor for more than 30 years, was a grammarian, an academic, and a poet. He was also an able translator, and in his 1907 volume, *Caniadau* ('Songs'), he published an extensive selection of translations from the work of the Persian poet Omar Khayyám (1048-1131). Although the project was undoubtedly inspired by the hugely popular English translations published in 1859 by Edward Fitzgerald (1809-83), Morris-Jones made his own translations directly from the original language. He accompanied his version with extensive contextual notes,[78] some of which seem to suggest that his interpretation of the mysterious original author was being quietly enlisted to challenge some of the orthodoxies of the translator's own day. Morris-Jones describes Khayyám as 'a daring rebel against the established religion' and suggests that he was a mystical Sufi at variance with stricter interpretations of Islam, sceptical about divine judgement, tolerant about drinking wine, and trustful about God's ultimate mercy to all creatures. Morris-Jones remarks: 'Here's a religion which has reached higher ground than most of the experience of the Seiat'. In a Wales which had just experienced the fervour of the 1904-5 religious revival in which the 'Seiat'[79] – an often intensely confessional prayer and fellowship group – was a central feature, it was a provocative statement to suggest that an Islamic poet understood God better than most Welsh Christians. It is tempting to speculate whether, in publishing these sensual, lyrical verses, which were in stark contrast to the dutifully virtuous and didactic poetry which had dominated much of the preceding decades in Wales, this most influential Welsh author might have been using the figure of the medieval Muslim mystic to challenge his own twentieth-century society to countenance greater artistic, religious, intellectual and social freedom.[80]

The year after the publication of John Morris-Jones's translations, *Y Traethodydd* printed another assessment of the character of Muhammad, this time in an essay, 'Cymeriadau Mawrion' ('Great Characters')[81] by John John Roberts (1840-1914), known as 'Iolo Caernarfon'. Roberts, a minister with the Calvinistic Methodists in north west Wales all his life, had not benefited from the first-hand experience of Islam available to Samuel Evans. His picture of Muhammad is mixed and ultimately negative, although the confidence which had characterised previous denunciations seems, here at the beginning of the twentieth century, to be faltering, at least judging by the way accusations are posed as questions rather than statements, and in the author's uneasy admission: 'Was there not in him something I do not understand?'

> The greatness of his genius and the breadth of his influence are generally acknowledged. What about his character? It appears he was a powerful and handsome man, dignified and amiable, of strong passions and honourable feelings, full of love and of vengeance, sensible and extremely determined. Was he also honest and faithful and pure? We find that he was a notably poor and simple man, living in a cold and bare lodging on barley bread and water, and completing daily the most ordinary tasks, such as patching his clothes and soling his shoes; which persisted after he had reached the highest fame – as the only Prophet of Jehovah, until the end, so simple was his greatest self-effacement. But was he at the same time crafty and fleshly, malicious and cruel? That is how he has been portrayed until recently – as the false Prophet – as the greatest deceiver mankind has

> ever produced – as the greatest adulterer of all Time – as the chief of all oppressors and murderers – as the Apostle of Satan. Christians no longer speak about him using such terms, because they started to think, and to ask themselves. How could such a villain initiate one of the most successful religions of History? It appears to me, after quite some consideration (1) that he was deceiving himself or deceiving others. He would retreat at certain times to a cave near his home, and would receive there, as he believed, or as he claimed, heavenly directions and instructions. He was also open to faints and swoons of all kinds, in which he saw wondrous visions, and heard divine revelations. He turned his imaginings into credos, and he turned his credos, regardless of who may be opposing him, into actions. (2.) He practised deception and trickery to a greater or lesser extent; no doubt he believed his aims justified his means. (3.) While we should not judge him according to the standards of this age, and although the behaviour of some of the godly ones of the Bible mitigates somewhat his own falsehood, we cannot do less than condemn his extreme intercourse with women. And when we remember that when he felt like having a new wife, he would receive, without exception, a message from the Lord to legitimise his desire, then his practices seem all the more repugnant. (4). I cannot at all defend his work in oppressing nations and despoiling countries. So, although Mahomet does not conform very much to my idea of a great personality, we cannot shut him out from among the Founders of Religions. I could easily refuse a place among them to Comte, Joseph Smith &c; he stands on higher ground. Was there not in him something I do not understand? Who am I to condemn a man whose words are believed by more people than the words of anyone else? So many millions of them joyfully proclaim his infallibility as a Prophet and the divinity of his Apostleship![82]

The next year, *Y Traethodydd* published a detailed article by R. Roberts of Trefnant, 'Dysgeidiaeth Muhammed am Grist' ('Muhammad's teaching about Christ') which after examining the subject in detail, is finally sceptical as to the claims of the *Qur'an* ('this strange book') to embody revelation, and the claims of Muhammad to speak in the name of the divine. Evans says that while 'the prophet of Islam did much good in his day', his teachings are so inconsistent and incredible as to render 'hollow' his claim to speak in the name of God.[83]

Owen Morgan Edwards (1858-1920), the educationalist, historian and author, and one of the fathers of modern Welsh nationalism, wrote about Islam in warmer terms. His article,

'Arabia', which appeared in his own magazine, *Cymru*, in 1916 was occasioned by the new focus on the Middle East brought about by the First World War. Its specific comments about Muslims and the war are examined in more detail in Chapter 6, but for now, it is worth noting Edwards's comments about Islam as a whole:

> The Mahometan religion is the child of the desert. The genius of the Arab brought it into being. The energy of desert horsemen sent its flame across western Asia, north Africa, and ancient Greece and Spain. And today more than two hundred million people look on Mecca as the most important place in the world.[84]

He goes on to summarise Islamic history and practices, acknowledging the orientalist Richard F. Burton (1821-90) as the source of his information, and the Welsh author J.Davies Bryan of Egypt – whose life we shall examine further in Chapter 10 – as the source of the photograph of Mecca used to illustrate the article.

In his mission to provide Welsh-language reading material on all kinds of subjects for his audience as a means of resisting anglicisation, Edwards was a prolific writer, whose work was characterised by warmth, appreciation and broad sympathies. He was not, however, immune from the prejudices of his age, and on one now-notorious occasion, in an 1889 travel book, *O'r Bala i Geneva* ('From Bala to Geneva'),[85] he produced the worst and most sustained piece of anti-semitic writing in Welsh literature, credulously reproducing the conspiracy theories contained in the Russian anti-semitic tracts later incorporated into *The Protocols of the Elders of Zion.* The views Edwards expressed there were uncharacteristic of general Welsh attitudes to the Jews, which, under the influence of evangelical Protestantism had tended to be *philo*-semitic. Paradoxically, in his treatment of Islam, despite the history of general hostility to that religion in his religious community, Edwards actually takes a positive line, first describing the great days of Islamic learning, and later the pilgrimage to Mecca:

> To these Arabs belonged a love of learning and invention. From them came governors like Harun al Raschid, the patron of science, and the learned Al Mamun. It was they who preserved the learning

> of Ancient Greece for the new world; it was they who were the teachers of the new dawn of science, mathematics and geometry.
>
> . . .
>
> To this wondrous temple come millions of people from all over the world. Once they arrive, they feast their eyes upon it. They spend the days of their pilgrimage in it, they sleep in it if they can, they feel every stone in it with hand and lip; the Black Stone has almost been kissed smooth. They swoon from fervour; they see visions; they lose themselves in trances; some dance; some are immovable. Wonderful is the grip which Mohammetanism has on the child of the desert, and on the many millions who have accepted his religion.[86]

Of course, one must be cautious in attributing such a view to a settled attitude on Edwards's part. As with many prolific journalistic generalists, his judgements were inevitably sometimes inconsistent and superficial. For instance, he was not an ideological or consistent anti-semite, as can be seen from the fact that he later published warmly philo-semitic articles in his magazine, and that he himself wrote religious stories drawing on examples from post-Biblical Jewish piety. His positive comments about Islam should be understood in the same way. They were not the product of prolonged engagement or study, but were occasioned by the priorities of current events and are therefore best understood as indicative of some of the conflicting attitudes towards Islam circulating in Welsh society and popular publications at the time.

There is much more substantial thought and engagement behind the assessment of Islam produced by D. Miall Edwards (1873-1941) in his 1923 book *Cristionogaeth a Chrefyddau Eraill* ('Christianity and Other Religions'). Edwards was an Oxford-educated theologian of international status and liberal views, and he wrote extensively on religious matters in both Welsh and English. His survey of world religions goes into detail about 'Islam or Mohametanism', noting that it spread swiftly 'partly through lawful missionary efforts aided by hot-headed zeal, but, to a degree greater than with any other religion, by the power of the sword. It was not founded on the sword, as is sometimes said, but rather on the spoken and written word of the prophet Mohamet. But it was through the sword more than any other way that it spread, and one must hold Mohamet himself responsible for the idea of a 'holy war' as a means of spreading his religion'.

In summarising 'the complex personality of this strange man, one of the creators of history', Edwards agrees with Thomas Carlyle[87] (1795-1881) that the accusation that Muhammad was a 'false deceiver' should be cast aside, although he finds the admiring portrait painted by Carlyle in his chapter on Muhammad in his 1841 book *On Heroes, Hero Worship, and the Heroic in History*, too positive. Miall's own opinion was rather different: 'Mohamet was a man of undoubted religious genius and strength of character, and the authenticity of his intentions when he was at his best cannot be doubted. But he was also a man who was illiterate and half-barbaric, and mixed with his sincerity and his passionate zeal for what he regarded as the true religion were elements less worthy of admiration, and inconsistencies difficult to explain'. As for the *Qur'an*, Edwards reports that most Westerners find it repetitive, long-winded and confused. He goes on to list the main points of Islamic theology and practice, noting that Jesus and the Old Testament prophets are accorded honour, although less than that of Muhammad himself, and that Muhammad and his followers are unsparingly condemnatory of Judaism and Christianity, of which he, and they, have only an imperfect understanding.[88] He concludes with a comparison of Christianity and Islam. He approves its testimony to monotheism, its condemnation of idolatry, and its idea of God's exalted being.

> Compared with his predecessors in Arabia, Mahomet stands before us as a man of undoubted religious genius and as a benefactor to his country and to the world. The religion he founded has been a means to raise many degraded tribes of the East to a higher territory of civilisation and morality. But, after all, it is little more than a corruption of Judaism and Christianity, even though it is more uncompromisingly hostile to Christianity than is any other religion. One could argue that this is because its comparative simplicity is more suitable for barbaric people than the religion of Christ, but it needs more audacity than knowledge to argue that it excels over Christianity or is equal to it as a spiritual and intellectual system and as a stimulus for moral and social progress. If the God of Islam is great and exalted, he is also as distant as he is glorious, and as harsh as he is powerful. He is looked upon by His worshippers as some kind of eastern Chieftain, or 'Sultan of Heaven'. His overlordship is stressed, but not his fatherhood. The complete and blind submission

> of his subjects is what he demands (that is the meaning of the word 'Islam'), rather than the moral obedience of rational and free beings who share his nature. His authority is founded on His despotic and arbitrary will rather than on His moral nature. His smile is life and his frown is death to his subjects; and who is man to withstand his fate? Islam can be seen to exalt God, but at the expense of belittling and degrading man, and in so doing, in the end, degrading God and depriving him of morality. The same thing is done with the portrait of God which is given in some theological systems within Christianity – in High Calvinism, for instance. But although Calvinism over-worked that one vein in the mine of Christian theology until it reached the bare, hard rock, and neglected other veins which were just as rich, even so, it was impossible for it to lose sight completely of the tenderness and grace of the Jesus of the Gospels as a revelation of the divine love, and that meant that its gospel was greater than its theology. If the logic of Calvinism was often Mohametan, its heart was Christian.
>
> But it is not my role to defend every Christian theological system. Suffice it to say that the picture of God which is given in the Scriptures, especially in the New Testament, is incomparably richer than the one given in the Koran. It is true that our God too is a consuming fire, an almighty Emperor, a just Judge. But he is also Christlike, and most of all we know Him as 'the one who shone in our hearts in the face of Jesus Christ'. 'For God so loved the world, that he gave his only begotten Son, that whosoever believeth in him should not perish, but have everlasting life' – that is a verse that is worth the whole of the Koran. Scarcely is it necessary to add that the figure of Mahomet, the passionate but inconsistent prophet, the one who spread his teaching by means of warfare and statesmanship, is not one who can be compared to the Christ of the Gospels, the teacher of the publicans and sinners, the sufferer of Gethsemane and Calvary, the gentle Lamb, 'the strong Son of God', the One who was Himself a perfect incarnation of the teaching he gave to others. Further, Islam does not have any stimulus to intellectual or social progress. In the Koran, the last word has been uttered, and what more has man to do than to explain that?[89]

Few of the attitudes contained in the remaining items collected in this chapter engage with Islam with the same degree of detail and seriousness as D. Miall Edwards. As Christian faith waned during the twentieth century, so too did a readiness to grapple with the claims of any religion. However, the subject still continued to attract the attention of important figures.

The first contact between Islam and the Byzantine Empire in

the seventh century was the subject of the final full-length play written by the artistocratic dramatist, librettist and patron of the arts, Lord Howard de Walden, Thomas Evelyn Scott-Ellis, (1880-1946), and produced in 1924. Howard de Walden, who had learned Welsh after taking up residence at his family's castle at Chirk near Wrexham, and who had become an influential figure in the Welsh artistic world, wrote the drama under his pen-name T.E. Ellis. It dealt with the emperor Heraclius (*c.*575- 641) and his relations with both Christianity and Islam, by whose followers he is generally viewed as a just and wise ruler and a friend of the Islamic faith.[90]

In 1947, we find passing reference to Islam in the work of the novelist John Cowper Powys (1872-1963), in his reflection on his Welsh identity in his book *Obstinate Cymric*, a collection of essays written between 1935 and 1947. He classes the Welsh with 'Jews, Arabs, Africans and Egyptians' as 'outside the pale of "Good Europeans",'[91] regards this fact as a source of pride, and notes how the defeat of the Byzantine empire by Islam 'scattered throughout the West, like the quickening drops of the cauldron of Ceridwen, the magic influence of Greek thought'.[92] He later expresses some regret that as 'a pseudo-philosophical bookworm', he lacks the religious practices of Hindus and Muslims 'as they go kneeling on their mats and tapping their skulls on the bricks and stones'.[93] Eclectic and idiosyncratic as Powys's comments are, it is notable that they are all positive. Coming as they do, however, among a torrent of arbitrary, contradictory and fanciful speculation, they cannot be said to be of any great significance or influence in Welsh public opinion.

Also in the late 1940s, we find one of the more extraordinary examples of a Welsh figure dealing with Islam, this time from a figure no-one could accuse of being fanciful. Rees Howells (1879-1950) was a miner from Brynaman who became one of the most prominent evangelists of his day. His ministry was characterised by the unusual depth and intensity with which he would intercede in prayer for people and situations. His biographer Norman Grubb tells of how, during the Second World War and afterwards, the members of the Bible College of Wales, an institution founded by Howells, would meet for days of prayer in the belief they were influencing world events. In the wake of the war, the focus of their intercession turned towards the ratification of the 1947 United Nations resolution to partition Palestine and create an Arab and a Jewish state. In supporting the creation of the State of Israel, Rees and his fellow members of the college stood in a long tradition of evangelical Christian Zionism. That strand, which continues to this day, flourishing now more in American than in British Christianity, has often been content to ignore or explain away the competing claims of the Arab peoples to the land of Palestine. Rees, however, was aware the Jewish people were not the only ones to see Palestine as their home. In his 1952 biography, *Rees Howells, Intercessor,* Norman Grubb records Howells's comments at the time of his prayer campaign relating to Palestine:

> He said: 'God put me aside for some days to reveal the position of the Arabs. In Genesis 16:12, God says of Ishmael that 'he shall dwell in the presence of all his brethren'. This is the problem. Does God mean the Arabs to dwell with the Jews? Abraham loved Ishmael and wanted him to have the inheritance; and God, who means what He says, declared: 'I have blessed him'. The Arabs only worship the One God. Did God mean them to be blessed as well as the Jews? They will afford shelter to the Jews (Isaiah 21:13-15), and will be the first to come to Jerusalem to pay homage to the King (Isaiah 60:7). Just as we were only burdened for the Jews when we had to make intercession for them, so the Lord wanted us to have a concern for the Arabs also. They also are the sons of Abraham. Can the Holy Ghost bring in something which will break down the barrier between the Jews and Arabs that there may be a home and a blessing for both? Certainly the Arabs are the people of God, if they are to shield the Jews and live in those countries which are to escape out of the hand of the Beast'. [Howells's name for Nazi Germany][94]

Howells's concern for the Muslims as fellow monotheists and children of Abraham is heartfelt, although it must be noted that the blessing desired for the Arabs is conditional on the prior claims of the Jewish people: the Arabs are the people of God *if* they shield the Jews.

If Howells was struggling with the reality of an almost irreconcilable political situation, another Welsh writer of the 1950s was contemplating the challenge of Islam from the more theoretical perspective of science fiction. Islwyn Ffowc Elis (1924-2004), author, broadcaster, lecturer and, briefly, Nonconformist minister, was also a popular Welsh-language novelist. His first novel, *Cysgod y Cryman* ('Shadow of the Sickle'), from 1953, which depicted Communist idealism in rural Wales, was a phenomenonal success, and with that book, and his subsequent ones, he was a major populariser of the novel in Welsh.

Elis was a committed Welsh nationalist, and one of his best-known works is *Wythnos yng Nghymru Fydd* ('A Week in Future Wales'), a 1957 novel telling the story of a Welshman from that year who time-travels to the Wales of 2033, finding an independent, economically thriving, ecological, pacifist, Welsh-speaking, Christian utopia. He returns to his own time, but, having fallen in love with a young woman in the Wales of 2033, goes – as it were – back to the future. On this visit, he discovers a Wales transformed into a nightmarish, depressed, violent, 'Western England' of endless caravan parks, gloomy conifer forests, army camps and deserted villages. In the Gwynedd town of Bala, the former spiritual home of Welsh Methodism, he finds the very last Welsh-speaker, an old woman who can, when prompted, haltingly recite the 23rd Psalm in her native tongue. The scene, for all its didactic motive, is nonetheless impossibly moving. The visitor learns that the future is not pre-determined: it can be utopia or dystopia, and it is decisions made in the present time that will decide which.

Elis's aim is unashamedly propagandistic – the novel itself was published by the Welsh nationalist party Plaid Cymru – and all the novel's action is subordinated to its political purpose. This is true of the passage dealing with Islam, which comes from the utopian part of the story, when the narrator, Powel, visits a church (the Wales of 2033 has undergone a religious revival, and churches are bursting at the seams) and finds that those who prefer an Anglican-style liturgical service and those who favour an unadorned Nonconformist style are cordially sharing the same purpose-built adaptable building. There he finds a lively and flourishing adult Sunday school made up of young men, under the guidance of their teacher, Doctor Llywarch, engaged in a deep discussion prompted by the fact that Jesus's miracle of walking on the water had just been repeated by 'an Arab called Ibrahim' in the port of Algiers. The long and earnest debate ends when the Nonconformists are visited by the Anglican priest, who is greeted with warmth and respect.[95]

This passage is notable for a number of reasons, not least the fact that the novelist clearly seems to regard the prospect of a Muslim repeating one of Jesus's more astounding miracles as infinitely less interesting – and possibly more unlikely – than the prospect of different strands of Welsh Christianity co-existing happily in the same building. The passage's truly radical suggestion – radical for its day in a Wales whose religious life was riven by sectarianism – was that Anglicanism and Nonconformity could be friends and allies. Today, those bitter denominational disputes are largely forgotten, dying along with the fervour of the faith which fuelled them, and the challenges of Christian ecumenism are now experienced mainly along other interfaces: between entire faiths rather than within individual ones, and between faith and unbelief.

The passage is notable also for the unintentional poignancy of its picture of a Wales where large groups of young men debate religion with earnestness and passion, an image which reveals of the author's own unfulfilled wishes – he had been a Christian minister for some six years prior to the publication of the book, but had quit in disillusion. It is also worth noting that this is another example of Islam being used as a means of reflecting the strengths and weaknesses of contemporary Christianity. The novelist could have had the miracle of walking on water performed by a Christian, an atheist or a follower of any other religion; it would not have affected the central point that the miracle had been repeated. But he chose to have it repeated by a Muslim. Why exactly that choice was made is unsure, although it is fair to imagine that long-held perceptions of Muslims as more committed than Christians would have played a part, and that the novelist, whether consciously or not, might have associated Islam with the idea of young men being earnest about their faith. Ibrahim might therefore be regarded as yet another case of a Muslim being used as a challenge to the piety of Christians – if not those of 2033, then certainly those of 1957. It is also worth noting that Elis chose Algiers as the location of this miracle, and that 1957, the year the novel was published, was the year of the Battle of Algiers, when fighting between French colonialist forces and those of Algerian freedom fighters reached a peak of brutal intensity. It may be that that most recent outbreak of the ancient antagonism between Muslim and Christian on the doorstep of

Europe had moved Elis to imagine a time when the shores of the Mediterranean might again be a place where ideas, not bullets, were traded, and where people of different faiths competed not in politics but in piety.

The remaining passages collected in this chapter are mostly of less significance, although they are still worth recording. By the 1960s, the dwindling current of Welsh-language theology could still produce some ripples of disquiet when it came to discussing Islam. In his 1965 book *Be Di Be Mewn Diwinyddiaeth* ('What's What In Theology'), R.R. Williams, has a two-page entry on Islam. Essentially, he reaches the same conclusions as D. Miall Edwards, mentioned above, albeit in a shorter format:

> Because of the emphasis on the power and sovereignty of Allah, life appears like a chess game, and every piece on the board is under his thumb, without anyone able to tell him how or where to move them, as he plays with no-one but himself. To the superficial thinker, who only sees the pieces moving from place to place on the board in the game at the time, it is fate not faith that is determining the course. To the Islamic theologian, Allah does not behave like blind fate. He knows how to govern and exercise sovereignty for his own purposes. The freedom that man has to break his commandments means next to nothing to his Master. Allah has the veto and the last word. He is too great and exalted for anything man can do to affect him.[96]

In its disposition of seemingly static elements of doctrine, Edwards's article could have been written at almost any time in the previous couple of centuries, although its lack of animus is possibly the result of the growing liberalism of the period in which it was written.

By the 1960s new expressions of Islam were coming to prominence, in the United States of America in particular, and these were attracting comment from Welsh writers too. In 1965, the same year that *Be Di Be Mewn Diwinyddiaeth* was published, the poet and Baptist minister Rhydwen Williams (1916-97) published a poem called 'Elias Muhammad', which depicted a very different form of Islam. The poem refers to Elijah Muhammad (1897-1975), the long-serving Supreme Minister of the Nation of Islam, an African-American group founded in 1930 by Wallace D. Fard Muhammad (*c.*1893 – date of death unknown). The Nation of Islam and its offshoots are highly controversial because of their theology, which differs very substantially from classical Islamic beliefs, and particularly because of their racial theories. The controversy, however, seems somewhat muted in Williams's poem; its central point seems to be that racism breeds racism, and that if the beliefs of Elijah Muhammad and his group are extreme, then they are the product of the extreme circumstances their ethnic community had suffered.

> When he was eleven, they say, this one saw
> A little black boy punished for a crime against a little white girl:
> The negro was hung on a cross exactly like Jesus was hung –
> When he was cut down, his body had been riddled.
> Today, the youth who saw that death in Georgia
> Is a saviour to two hundred thousand.
>
> * * *
>
> When he was twenty, he moved to Detroit:
> He went to chapel regularly, heard the preacher proclaiming the 'Word':
> But in nineteen thirty one a strange preacher came by,
> An Arab from Mecca, a pedlar of silks and goods of all kinds.
> He prophesied the end of the white man and the rule of the black man –
> The youth believed he had seen God.
>
> * * *
>
> When he prayed, he saw a black God before his eyes:
> When he dreamed, he saw mankind black – its skin and its belief!
> The white god had disappointed him – he wanted another one in his place:
> The white man had deceived him – he wanted to exterminate him:
> Old, old were the language and the passion and the ambition –
> This time it was the colour that was different.[97]

The spread of Islam among African Americans was also the subject of an article entitled 'Muhammad Ali' in the *Herald Cymraeg* weekly newspaper in 1980 by the columnist Robin Williams (1923-2003), a prominent broadcaster, television presenter and Presbyterian Methodist minister. Williams mentions, with irony, how he takes some comfort from the fact that the boxer Ali, at the age of nearly 40, is apparently human, having just lost a major title fight (presumably Ali's unsuccessful title challenge to Larry Holmes). He then goes on to say that whatever may become of Ali's sporting career, he is much more than a boxer and is a 'totally magnetic character and personality'. He mentions how, under his original name of Cassius Clay, the boxer had been brought up in the Baptist church, but had later taken a different religious path:

> In February 1964, Clay heard a preacher from the Muslim religion explaining that the black people were a people who had lost their roots. And that slavery had caused them to lose their language. On top of that, the forced exile had also been the means for them losing their names. 'Clay' was a name from the white man, the white man who had oppressed the slaves in America for so long.
>
> In that service, Cassius Clay discarded his old name, and chose for himself a brand new name, Muhammad Ali. From then on, he cast his lot with Allah, the god of the Muslim. By now, it can be said that Muhammad Ali is fighting not only in the ring, but outside it too, fighting for his new religion and his fellow dark-skinned man.[98]

Ali had converted to the Nation of Islam in 1964, later transferring to mainstream expressions of the faith. Robin Williams's article is not particularly trenchant, but, as with Rhydwen Williams's poem, it does show how, by the latter part of the twentieth century, conversion from Christianity to Islam could be viewed with something approaching complacency by certain Welsh commentators. It is possible to suggest some reasons for this: for instance, by the period concerned, the mainstream of Welsh-language literary opinion tended towards a nationalism which was naturally sympathetic to perceived underdogs, and which did not identify its own interests necessarily with those of white Christian Westerners; in addition, Christian belief, and particularly evangelical belief, itself was in decline in Wales, and the motivation for theological disagreement was therefore receding, as was the technical capacity to discern differences and to conduct disputations; in addition, conversion to Islam by African Americans was also an experience sufficiently removed from Wales for it to seem unthreatening.

Another Welsh writer who used Islamic material as a starting point for a reflection on his own faith was Selyf Roberts (1912-

95), a novelist and short-story writer of Christian convictions. In his 1982 collection of essays, *Hel Meddyliau* ('Gathering Thoughts'), he has a piece 'O Barch i'r Anffaeledig' ('Out of Respect to the Infallible'), in which he meditates upon a carpet in his home which was made in Belgium but which is patterned on 'one of those which are carried about by the people of the middle east to kneel upon when the voice calls from the minaret',[99] and which has a deliberate flaw in its pattern, in keeping with the Islamic tradition that man should not create anything perfect, out of respect for 'Allah, who alone is perfect'.[100] He commends the practice and concludes:

> I have no idea who made my carpet, but I have great respect for him, and when my eyes turn to the flaw at my feet I feel that he is related to me. And if I am feeling humble, no doubt I will be reminded of his humility, and will remember at the same time that it is a carpet to kneel upon that lies before my fire.[101]

Serious theological engagement with Islam in the last years of the twentieth century has often come from the evangelical wing of the church, the section most likely to disagree with Muslim beliefs, and yet, at the same time, in a society where familiarity with religious systems is fast eroding, the section most likely to take religion's claims seriously on their own terms. The Evangelical Movement of Wales's Welsh-language journal *Y Cylchgrawn Efengylaidd* ('The Evangelical Magazine') has been one of the most consistent locations of Welsh theological discussion of Islam. In 1980, D. Ioan Davies's article, 'Y Grefydd Islamaidd' ('The Islamic Religion') views with concern the growth of Islam in the West, and what Davies identifies as increasing persecution of Christians in Islamic countries. Islam, he says, is 'a religion of good works' which has no means of enabling its adherents to live up to their ideals.[102] In 1987, the magazine's cover carried a picture of an Islamic gathering in Singleton Park in Swansea, while the accompanying article by R. John Lewis, 'Iesu Grist: yr Unig Ffordd?' ('Jesus Christ: the Only Way?') sought to identify how evangelicals should approach the growth of Islam. Lewis dismisses the universalism of liberal Christians, and insists on the uniqueness of Christ. He concludes that courage, wisdom and sensitivity are all needed in order to take this message to 'our Asian neighbours'.[103]

In accordance with their serious evangelistic intent, many of the articles stress a commitment to being well-researched. In a further long article by Lewis in *Y Cylchgrawn Efengylaidd* in 1987, 'Islâm', Christians are urged to respond 'wisely and intelligently' to the growth of Islam, and are told 'clear understanding of Muslim beliefs' is essential. The article duly gives a detailed description of Muslim theology and practice, before listing advice as to how to evangelise Muslims: emphasising listening; then discussing the character of God ('But be careful not to get into a big argument about it'); the life and person of Christ ('The incomparable beauty of the life of Christ can melt the hardest heart ... and, for goodness sake, don't criticise Muhammad when talking about Christ'), and finally the Atonement. The author wishes for 'an overflowing spiritual harvest' of converts from Islam.[104]

In his 1991 article 'Islâm' in the same journal, Gwyddno Rowlands urges his readers to respond urgently to the challenge of a resurgent Islam, which is growing in fervour, growing in power thanks to the oil resources of the Gulf region, and growing in numbers in the UK through immigration. Rowlands says: 'In the mosque, the men hear and read that Islam is on a triumphant journey. There will be no rest until Britain, the West, and all the world has submitted at last to this religion'. He notes the concept of *jihad* as central to the Muslim's world view, and warns of growing hatred between British people and immigrants.[105] He goes on to say that Muslims have come to Britain 'as part of the strange providence of God', who 'sometimes uses foreign people to chastise his people', in this case because the church has poisoned its doctrines, and has weakened its faith in a supernatural God and in a saving gospel. 'The churches are declining – Islam is increasing. Indeed, in more than one case, church buildings have been sold and turned into Islamic centres. Is not this situation a rebuke to our churches? Perhaps we will see the churches repenting before God by admitting their weakness and their failure and their need, face to face with the challenge of Islam'.[106] The idea of Muslim success as a divine reproach to Christian laxity is identical to that found more than 300 years earlier in Charles Edwards's *Y Ffydd Ddi-Ffuant*, mentioned above, which says of the Muslims: 'God allowed them to be a constant scourge to his disobedient people'.

On the positive side, Rowlands says, the Muslims in Britain are a new mission field. To further that missionary aim, he explains some of Islam's beliefs, saying that the God of Islam is less accessible than that of Christianity: 'a distant God; a god to worship, to be sure; but not a god to love, nor a god who loves'.[107] Islam, he says, depends on 'works', not on faith. He concludes that this leaves a gap which Christianity can fill:

> Might not the Lord have many people of his own among the strangers who are now such a prominent part of British society? The Muslim faces a difficult situation in his new home: he does not expect – and he does not get – much respect, let alone love, from his fellow-citizens. Indeed, he does not know much about love in his own home. And certainly, he does not know much about love in his religion.
>
> Is there not a challenge to us here? Should we not be searching for an opportunity to express Christian love towards the Muslims in our midst? And is there not an obvious need for us to tell them about the love of God in Jesus Christ?
>
> The challenge of Islam is now at the door of the Christian Church, and it has to be faced seriously. We should repent at seeing its increase and its influence. But we should also take advantage of the opportunity to evangelise enthusiastically and faithfully in this new mission field which has come to us through the providence of God.[108]

While some evangelical critiques of Islam might be designed to find weaknesses for Christianity to exploit, other Christian perspectives, from the same period, have a less explicitly competitive agenda. For instance, the Methodist minister, Islwyn Blythin, a lecturer in comparative religion at Lampeter University, writing in the wake of the Rushdie affair in the ecumenical magazine *Cristion* ('Christian') in 1989, provides an analysis of the resurgence of Islam which is less utilitarian than Rowlands's, and more analytical of the place of Islam in the modern world, and in the secular West in particular.

> Christianity is long accustomed to secular powers, and has been badly bruised in the battle. But Islam has only had a few drops of the shower so far, and the Islamic world has not been torn by the processes of reformation and secularism to the same degree as the Christian world. One of the greatest mistakes that Western thinkers

> and politicians made this century was supposing that the pattern of relationship between secularism and religion in the West would be repeated also in the East. And if the authorities, who opened the doors to Muslims to come to this country in the fifties and sixties to live and work, were expecting to see Islam stumble in a new and strange land, then they were disappointed. It has been shown pretty clearly this year that Islam is a religion that can be transplanted without in any way impairing its energy or zeal.[109]

He concludes that Islam faces three choices: an emotional and irrational attempt to restore 'pure Islam'; a secularist break with the religious past, in the manner of modern Turkey; and an Islamic modernism taking a middle path between the two.

While Rowlands's and Blythin's different treatments show two aspects of the varying range of Welsh Christian theological response to Islam in the last two decades of the twentieth century, they do have in common the fact that they are both responses to tensions, and that the view of Islam is consequently problematised. As so often in the post-Second World War period, conflict rather than curiosity is the occasion for inquiry, and it is within the confines of competitive comparisons that the discourse is conducted.

If conflicts such as the Islamic Revolution and the Salman Rushdie *fatwa* had been the occasion for increasingly troubled reflection about Islam in Britain during the 1980s, then events of the next decade or so, such as the Gulf Wars, and the 9/11 attacks, were to intensify perceptions further. Other responses to those events will be examined in more detail in Chapter 9, but as the focus of this present chapter is on religious attitudes, a few final quotes will serve to show how a heightened awareness of Islamic assertiveness in the wider public context has been inevitably reflected even in responses which are primarily religious.

The Welsh-based Christian author Chris Bendon (*b.*1950), is a quarter Jewish and has travelled extensively in Muslim countries. In his poem, 'Insane', from his 1995 collection, *Jewry*, he finds himself contemplating Islam, but within the pressurised context of the First Gulf War, a conflict about which Bendon is deeply sceptical:

> We sold arms to our enemy...

> A land we helped raid and bomb
> just yesterday – 'Terrorist Syria', is now
> our friend.

As the war mobilises public sentiment and religious rhetoric in its own interests, he finds the protests of himself and Christians like him 'impotent', while his desire for peace leaves him in an uncomfortable no-man's land between his own culture's religion and that of the Muslim world he admires:

> How mnemonic, repetitive is the Koran!
> I shut my eyes and see *gold and rose and green*
> *fluorescent heavens.* A woman, a man a neon dove.
> *Amen.*
>
> O God I cannot praise you enough. But will not
> go to the confident and social church.
> The lone voice, Love, whose mood,
> unlike weather, does not change.[110]

Conflict too is what draws the veteran journalist and broadcaster John Roberts Williams (1914-2004), to reflect on Islam in one of his regular five-minute radio items, later collected and published as *Chwarter Canrif Fesul Pum Munud* ('A Quarter Century of Five Minutes'). Taking the occasion of Tony Blair's mission to the Middle East two months after the 9/11 attacks, he gives a brief history of the third Abrahamic religion – which, he adds, should not be called 'Mahometanism' – and of its prophet. He does not venture any strong opinions, but he does venture a Welsh translation (presumably from English) of some verses from Sura 2 (8-12) of the *Qur'an*, saying that he wonders what Osama Bin Laden would make of them. The quotation is revealing if only because of the content of the lines Williams has chosen to present – a condemnation of mischief-making – which seem to be an implicit rebuke to Bin Laden.[111]

By the twenty-first century, the simplicities that have characterised much of the history of Welsh religious writing about Islam are no longer tenable; new proximities defy generalisations; new challenges demand original thought. The circumstances invite a response which acknowledges the complexity of Islam, which recognises the multiplicity of Christian attitudes towards the faith, and which is conscious of the entanglement of spirituality and politics in perceptions of the religion. It is left to one of the most significant of contemporary Welsh poets, Gwyneth Lewis (*b.*1959) to find an artistic expression of the plurality of viewpoints and perceptions at the current interface of the West and Islam. Appropriately, as the location of this extended, eclectic tour through the tangled pathways of inter-cultural, inter-religious contact, Lewis chooses Istanbul – once the capital of a Christian empire, then conquered by Islam, and now part of an officially secular state, standing physically on the boundary of Europe and Asia. The poem is given in full:

Imaginary Walks in Istanbul

1

It's time I made my daily promenade
to nowhere special – round the footstool
and parlour. Just as Søren Kierkegaard

and father took imaginary strolls
inside looking out, not needing travel.
I apologise now to Istanbul –

never been there – but I find myself full
of mosques and ferries, crosses and crusades,
a journey that's purely fictional.

I've drunk cool sherbet and lemonade
in Bosphorus villas: quarters of mind.
Untaken photographs will never fade

because they're unreal. I want a dervish,
Neck broken, to spin like a radar dish.

2

Let's start with omphalos, the empire's O
In Haghia Sophia, a porphyry
Belly-button that was Justinian's throne.

(Ignore Anonymous of Banduri
On the marble columns, he's full of shit.)
Upstairs, Christ holds a digital TV

Like legal tablets. Notice that he squints,
One eye on me, one on eternity
And he won't stop looking, so that I split

Apart like an atom. From out the frieze
Birds fly, wings bladed, the doorways' veils
Are torn to shreds by the slasher breeze

A cathedral apocalypse: so vermeil
And glass chandeliers explode to shrapnel.

3

The hidden contents of the ottoman.
We could slide down its armrest, and we did,
Often, its dark brown Victorian oilskin

Was slippery enough – I'd bump my head
Each time. In other moods, I'd count and thumb
The rosary of upholstery studs

Along the edge. By now you know that I'm
A counter, and I do admire a square
With something in it. My buttocks would numb

If I read on it – no give in horsehair
So thin. But the syllables from the east
Intrigued me. I loved this backless chair,

A hard place, not designed for rest.
My whole life's secreted inside this chest.

4

The Great Ones left evidence everywhere:
Near where the Halberdiers-with-Tresses
Lodged is a casket containing the hair

Of the Prophet Muhammed. You may gaze
On his tooth, his footprint, admire the hem
Of the Holy Mantle. The guidebook says

That the delightful Circumcision Room
Is not to be missed – go back if it's full –
Check out the Saucepan of Ibrahim.

What's 'like the apple but not the apple?'
A pear? Ram's testicles. Look how the crease
Between sweetbreads is perfect, the pouches full

Of goodness. Each night leaves a cicatrice
On my face. By day, it heals without trace.

5

A language in which the point of the i
Is optional must be admired. I rate
Such subtlety – the disposed-of housefly,

The cauterized mole. I hallucinate
ts without crosses (not the same as l).
You can count me out of the caliphate

That's coming. Not because I'm infidel
But my fid is other and my style
Non-fanatic. My headquarters are smell,

Rotting melon. Goat shit's a spiritual
Discipline if your dogma's maggots,
From whose prophetic writhings one might tell

Who goes to hell, who doesn't. High carrots
And lilies ooze tea. I believe those dots.

6

Visitors can walk the top of these walls –
A cross-section of the Theodosian
Works shows moats and towers, and you may stroll

Between brick words, if you wish, just for fun
And look into courtyards through metal gates
For glimpses of fig trees, which a woman

Waters, jasmine that bees must pollinate
In purdah. Do you think that the works show
More than they hide? Or do I crenellate

Just for effect? To illustrate hollows
Of graveyards and cisterns? To imply minarets
In my voice? These may be virtuoso

Fortifications but enemies might
Say these defences have me by the throat.

7

Last turn's to the Church of Constantine Lips,
which had seven apses and three narthex
most unusual. Like the brain's lop-

sided map of the body: monstrous sex,
slight neck, a set of negligible limbs,
spatula fingertips – the practical codex

of how life feels. In the park by Taksim
Square: 'Madame, I am not a cannibal,
I merely wish to sell you a kilim

from my native province.' And, like a fool,
I let him. There are no silent letters
in Turkish, and he was so affable...

My tours, you'll note, have contained no errors.
Getting lost is what good guidebooks are for.[112]

By turns irreverent, erudite, intellectual, sensual, spiritual, sceptical, scientific, artistic, principled and playful, Lewis's poem presents a holistic, multi-faceted and authentic approach to a heterogeneous reality. Unwilling to shroud herself in dogma or delusion, this child of a Welsh chapel is a confident traveller through a fractured post-modern, and post-secular landscape of mosques and churches which could represent the past of two ancient faiths, but which could, just as easily, represent their future.

Notes

1. British Library MS. Add. 14921 (sixteenth century) unedited. Referenced in Matthieu Boyd, 'Celts seen as Muslims and Muslims seen as Celts', in Jerold C. Frakes (ed.), *Contextualizing the Muslim Other in Medieval Judeo-Christian Discourse* New York (forthcoming).
2. Meic Stephens (ed.) *The New Companion to the Literature of Wales* (Cardiff, 1998) 773.

3. *Tri Brenin o Gwlen* (MS. 1552) British Library Additional 14986, 37. Available online in the Cambridge University project *A Historical Corpus of the Welsh Language 1500-1850,* http://people.pwf.cam.ac.uk/dwew2/hcwl/menu.htm
4. *Ibid.* 38.
5. *Y Dioddefaint* (MS. 1552) British Library Additional 14986, 10v-33v., 13. *A Historical Corpus of the Welsh Language 1500-1850.*
6. For an account or Erbury's life, see Brian Ll. James, 'The evolution of a radical', *The Journal of Welsh Ecclesiastical History, 3* (1986) 31-48.
7. A Puritan body set up during the Civil War to depose ministers suspected of loyalty to the Crown.
8. William Erbery, *The testimony of William Erbery, left upon record for the saints of succeeding ages* (London, 1658).
10. *Ibid.* 333.
11. See also Nabil I Matar *Islam in Britain 1558-1685* (Cambridge, 1998) 47.
12. Charles Edwards, *Hanes y Ffydd Ddi-Ffuant.* References are to the University of Wales Press edition (Cardiff, 1936).
13. It was believed a Christian monk called Sergius had aided the composition of the *Qur'an.*
14. *Ibid.* 80.
15. *Ibid.* 83.
16. *Ibid.* 81.
17. *Ibid.* 95.
18. Cyril Glyndŵr Williams, 'The Unfeigned Faith and an Eighteenth Century Pantheologia' *Numen,* 15: 3 (Nov, 1968) 208-17.
19. Charles Edwards, *op. cit.* 96.
20. *Ibid.* 97.
21. Edwards refers to the Ottoman empire's corps of janissaries, many of whom were forcibly-recruited Christian youths.
22. Ellis Wynne, *Gweledigaetheu y bardd cwsc,* The Visions of the Sleeping Bard, trans. Robert Gwyneddon Davies (Caernarfon, 1897) 16.
23. *Ibid.* 32.
24. An agreement between Scottish and English Protestant reformers at the time of the English Civil War.
25. Ellis Wynne, *op. cit.* 114. The idea of Christian-Muslim antagonism continuing in the afterlife is dealt with briefly in the 2010 novel by Caryl Lewis, *Naw Mis* ('Nine Months'), which follows the experiences of a murdered teenager. The transitional otherworld where her departed spirit finds itself is shown to have been damaged by Christian-Muslim warfare, resulting in the banishment of the antogonists. *Naw Mis* (Talybont, 2010) 80.
26. For a discussion of Williams's sources see Alwyn Prosser, 'Diddordebau Lleyg Williams Pantycelyn', *Llên Cymru,* 4: 4 (1955) 200-14.
27. William Williams, *Pantheologia* (Carmarthen, 1762) 235.
28. *Ibid.* 237.
29. *Ibid.* 283.

30. *Ibid.* 286.
31. Williams is referring to a widely-believed assumption of his time, that the Welsh were descended from Gomer, grandson of Noah, and were therefore inheritors of the Biblical promises to the Hebrews, and possessors of a language directly descended from Hebrew. The assumption, which was based merely on the consonantal symmetry of the words 'Gomer' and 'Cymro' ('Welshman') and which was propounded in Theophilus Evans's (1693-1767) history of Wales, *Drych y Prif Oesoedd* ('Mirror of the Chief Ages') published in 1716, led to a substantial body of material which took the etymology as gospel. The belief persisted for centuries, and has contemporary echoes in the use of Gomer as a personal name and as the name of one of Wales's most prominent publishing houses. See E. Wyn James, '"The New Birth of a People": Welsh Language and Identity and the Welsh Methodists, c.1740-182' in Robert Pope (ed.) *Religion and National Identity: Wales and Scotland c.1700-2000* (Cardiff, 2001) 21, 35.
32. William Williams *op. cit.* 239-41n.
33. Michael J. Franklin, (ed.) *Sir William Jones. Selected Poetical and Prose Works* (Cardiff, 1995) xvi.
34. *Ibid.* 328.
35. The poem, never published in Jones's lifetime, was found as an incomplete manuscript in the papers of Mary Granville by the antiquarian, Lady Llanover. *Ibid.* 57.
36. Jones had witnessed the riots in London, in which Catholic churches were burned, *ibid.* 58n.
37. Garland Cannon and Michael J. Franklin 'A Cymmrodor claims kin in Calcutta: an assessment of Sir William Jones as philologer, polymath, and pluralist' *Transactions of the Honourable Society of Cymmrodorion*, ns, [11] (2004) 50-69.
38. Franklin, *Sir William Jones. Selected Poetical and Prose Works, op. cit.* 58n.
39. Lord Teignmouth, *The Work of Sir William Jones* (London, 1807) 395.
40. For an extensive, illustrated and annotated edition of Griffiths's hymns and letters, together with other relevant material see E. Wyn James (ed.), *Rhyfeddaf Fyth, Emynau a Llythyrau Ann Griffiths Ynghyd â'r Byrgofiant Iddi gan John Hughes, Pontrobert, a Rhai Llythyrau gan Gyfeillion* (Newtown, 1998).
41. John Hughes 'Cofiant a Llythyrau Ann Griffiths', *Y Traethodydd* (1846) 421. Quoted in Siân Megan, *Gwaith Ann Griffiths* (Llandybïe, 1982) 11.
42. He was inspired in his work by his encounter with Mary Jones (1784-1864) who, as a girl of 16, had walked 25 miles barefoot from her home at Llanfihangel-y-Pennant to Bala to buy one of the scarce Bibles available in her native tongue. The story of her journey became a worldwide classic of Christian piety.
43. Angharad Price, *'"O! Tyn y Gorchudd": Golwg ar fywyd a gwaith Hugh Jones, Maesglasau', Transactions of the Honourable Society of Cymmrodorion.* (London, 2003) 111. http://www.cymmrodorion1751.org.uk/pages/publications/maesglasau.html

44. See, for example: E. Wyn James, 'Williams Pantycelyn a Gwawr y Mudiad Cenhadol' *Cof Cenedl,* 17 (Llandysul, 2002) 81-2, and '"Seren Wib Olau"': Gweledigaeth a Chenhadaeth Morgan John Rhys (1760-1804)', *Trafodion Cymdeithas Hanes y Bedyddwyr,* 5 (2007) 23. See also: Derec Llwyd Morgan, 'Morgan Llwyd a'r Iddewon', *Ysgrifau Beirniadol* 21 (Denbigh, 1996) 90. See also the work of the Independent minister, Morgan Jones, *Gogoniant y Byd Hwn, neu ddesgrifiad o'r Dinasoedd mwyaf, godidocal, a rhyfeddaf yn y Byd* (Carmarthen, 1813) 20.
45. Mathew Williams, *Hanes Holl Grefyddau'r Byd* (Carmarthen, 1799) 55.
46. Simon Lloyd, *Amseryddiaeth Ysgrythurol,* reference from second edition (Bala, 1842) 17.
47. John Walters, *An English and Welsh Dictionary* (Denbigh, 1770-94) 56.
48. John and Daniel Jones (eds.) *Cofiant ynghyd a gweddillion caniadau Edward Jones o Faes y Plwm,* (Mold, 1839) 45.
49. Anon. *Y Twrc wedi ei Glwyfo* (Llanerchymedd, 1827) 20.
50. J. Graham Jones, Goronwy Wyn Owen (eds.) *Gweithiau Morgan Llwyd o Wynedd,* I (Cardiff 1993) 83, quoted in Derec Llwyd Morgan, *op. cit.* 90.
51. William Williams 'Caledfryn', *Caniadau Caledfryn* (Llanrwst, 1856) 99.
52. Owen Jones, *Y Cyniweirydd* (Mold, 1834) 35.
53. Evan Lewis, *Hanes chwech o benboethiaid crefyddol, sef Joseph Smith, Mahomet, Richard Brothers, Jemimah Wilson, Ann Lee, a Joanna Southcotte* (Merthyr Tydfil, 1849).
54. Morgan Richards, *Hanes bywyd a chrefydd y gau-brophwyd Mahomet, yn nghyda rhagdraith ar Arabia* (Bangor, 1855).
55. John Jones, *Traethawd ar Dwrci, a Hanes Bywyd Nicholas o Rwsia* (Llanidloes, 1855) 30.
56. *Ibid.* 37.
57. *Ibid.*
58. *Ibid.* 38.
59. John Parry, *Gwyddoniadur,* 10 (Denbigh, 1879) 178.
60. *Ibid.* 181.
61. *Ibid.* 182.
62. *Ibid.* 183.
63. *Ibid.* 183.
64. *Ibid.* 183.
65. *Ibid.* 188.
66. *Ibid.* 189.
67. *Ibid.* 192
68. J.E. Davies, *Crefyddau y Byd Cristionogaidd* (Scranton, 1868), trans. John Bear of Canberra, Australia. http://oldwelshbooks.net/
Translation by John Bear of Canberra, Australia. http://oldwelshbooks.net/
69. Samir Raafat, 'Four Welshmen Who Made Good In Egypt', *Egyptian Mail,* May 27, 1995. http://www.egy.com/landmarks/95-05-27.shtml See also Edward Morgan Humphreys , 'Evans, Samuel', in *Welsh Biography Online* http://yba.llgc.org.uk/en/s-EVAN-SAM-1859.html
70. Samuel Evans, 'Y Gwr o Fecca a'i Grefydd', *Y Traethodydd,* XLV

(1890), 280.
71. *Ibid.* 282.
72. *Ibid.* 283.
73. *Ibid.* 286.
74. *Ibid.* 283.
75. *Ibid.* 285.
76. *Ibid.* 286.
77. John Jones, 'Mynydd Sinai', *Y Traethodydd,* 60: 264 (1905) 218-225.
78. John Morris-Jones, *Caniadau* (Oxford, 1907) 183-195.
79. The word comes from the English 'society'.
80. See also J. Griffith Williams, *Omar* (Denbigh, 1981) a study of Omar Khayyám, John Morris-Jones and Edward Fitzgerald. An early review of Morris-Jones's work can be found in 'On Translating Omar', by W. Hughes Jones in *At the Foot of Eryri* (Bangor, 1912).
81. The other characters are: Charlemagne; Oliver Cromwell; George Washington; Constantine the Great; Zoroaster; Confucius and Gautama.
82. John John Roberts 'Cymeriadau Mawrion', *Y Traethodydd,* 63: 285 (1908) 434-5.
83. R. Roberts, 'Dysgeidiaeth Muhammed am Grist', *Y Traethodydd,* 64: 290 (1909) 417-26.
84. O.M. Edwards, 'Arabia', *Cymru* (September 1916) 129-31.
85. See *The Chosen People,* by the present author (Bridgend, 2002) 156, and Hazel Walford Davies, 'Boundaries: the early travel books and periodicals of O.M. Edwards', in Hywel Teifi Edwards (ed.) *A Guide to Welsh Literature c.1800-1900* (Cardiff, 2000) 186-209.
86. O.M. Edwards, *op. cit.* 129-31.
87. Thomas Carlyle, *On Heroes, Hero-Worship, and The Heroic in History* (London, 1841).
88. D. Miall Edwards, *Cristionogaeth a Chrefyddau Eraill* (Dolgellau, 1923) 62-65.
89. *Ibid.* 118-20.
90. T.E. Ellis (Thomas Evelyn Scott-Ellis, 8th Lord Howard de Walden), *The Byzantine Plays* (Windsor, 2006).
91. John Cowper Powys, *Obstinate Cymric* (Carmarthen, 1947) 10.
92. *Ibid.* 90.
93. *Ibid.* 169.
94. Norman Grubb, *Rees Howells, Intercessor* (Cambridge, 1952) 245.
95. Islwyn Ffowc Elis, *Wythnos yng Nghymru Fydd* (Cardiff, 1957) 64.
96. R.R. Williams, *Be Di Be Mewn Diwinyddiaeth* (Caernarfon, 1965) 38.
97. Rhydwen Williams, *Barddoniaeth Rhydwen Williams: Y Casgliad Cyflawn 1941-1991* (Llandybïe, 1991) 80.
98. Robin Williams, 'Muhammad Ali', *Colofn Bapur* (Llandysul, 1992) 41.
99. Selyf Roberts, *Hel Meddyliau* (Denbigh, 1982) 77.
100. *Ibid.* 78.
101. *Ibid.* 79.
102. *Y Cylchgrawn Efengylaidd,* 19: 2 (1980) 10-11.

103. *Ibid.* 24: 5 (1987) 6-7.
104. *Ibid.* 24: 6 (1987) 6-10.
105. *Ibid.* 28: 2 (1991) 6.
106. *Ibid.* 7.
107. *Ibid.* 7.
108. *Ibid.* 8.
109. Islwyn Blythin, 'Islam Ddoe a Heddiw' *Cristion* (September/October 1989) 17.
110. Chris Bendon, *Jewry* (Salzburg, 1995) 96.
111. John Roberts Williams, *Chwarter Canrif Fesul Pum Munud*, (Caernarfon, 2001) 155.
112. Gwyneth Lewis, 'Imaginary Walks in Istanbul,' *New Writing Partnership* website: http://www.newwritingpartnership.org.uk/nwp/site/page2-5.html

'One of the Family': Welsh Seafarers' Encounters with Islam

With the end of the Crusades, an important method of physical contact between Wales and Islam was brought to a close. Therefore, until the period of the British Empire, seafaring becomes the major method by which actual contact between Wales and the Islamic world was continued, so it is from maritime enterprise that we find the next source of evidence of Welsh attitudes to Islam and to Muslims.

As a country with a long coastline, Wales has always had an important relationship with the sea. In the days when sea travel was much faster, and sometimes safer, than travel by land, the coastal position of Wales meant goods and ideas could be readily trafficked between its shores and those of other countries, far and near. For instance, Celtic saints are shown making extensive use of the seaways surrounding the shores of western Britain for their missionary journeys to promote their faith.

However, if an extensive coast meant ample opportunity for profitable contact with the outside world, it also meant vulnerability to unwanted contact too. From the fourth century, Irish raiders founded extensive settlements in coastal areas of Wales, and from the eighth century, Wales experienced the depredations of the Vikings. While that latter period of coastal raiding particularly is still part of popular memory, a later period of piratical threat to the coasts of Wales is now largely forgotten. It is, however, particularly relevant to this study, because, although it seems to have left no direct mark in Welsh literature of the period, it is reasonable to suppose it would have affected attitudes displayed in later literary work. It is the period when Wales was subject to raids by Muslim corsairs seeking slaves for the markets of North Africa.

The story is told in Giles Milton's 2004 study *White Gold* which explains how, during the seventeenth and eighteenth centuries, fleets of corsairs, based in North Africa, terrorised surrounding European countries by attacking shipping and raiding coastal communities in search of people to be sold into slavery. In the way it shows European nations nearly helpless in the face of a more aggressive and technically superior adversary, it is an important corrective to common assumptions of European supremacy in the maritime and military fields of the period. It was 200 years before the British navy was sufficiently strong to bring the trade to an end. During the high point of the pirates' power, the extent of their activities is striking: they raided as far afield as Ireland and even Iceland, and in the seven years between 1609 and 1616 raiders operating from the single port of Algiers captured no fewer than 466 merchant ships from England alone.

Milton's account of a slaving raid in Cornwall in July 1625, gives a flavour of the fear felt at the corsairs' activities:

> Within days of their being sighted the corsairs began to wreak havoc, launching hit-and-run raids on the most vulnerable and unprotected seaports. They slipped ashore at Mount's Bay, on the south Cornish coast, while the villagers were at communal prayer. Dressed in Moorish djellabas and wielding damascene scimitars, they made a terrifying sight as they burst into the parish church. One later English captive would describe the corsairs as 'ugly onhumayne cretures' who struck the fear of God into all who saw them. 'With their heads shaved and their armes almost naked, [they] did teryfie me exceedingly.' They were merciless in their treatment of the hapless congregation of Mount's Bay. According to one eye-witness, sixty men, women and children were dragged from the church and carried back to the corsairs' ships.[1]

He goes on to say how the slaving fleet '...had achieved a most spectacular and disquieting coup: they had captured Lundy Island in the Bristol Channel, and raised the standard of Islam. It had now become their fortified base, from which they attacked the unprotected villages of northern Cornwall.' The number of villagers carried off from western England in that summer's raids numbered in the thousands. Milton notes 'Wales, too, was hit on several occasions'.[2]

With Welsh communities among the targets for slave raids, and with the raiders briefly maintaining an outpost off the coast of Wales itself, and with Welsh people providing a proportion of the crews on ships which were raided by the corsairs, it is, perhaps, unsurprising to find hostile depictions of Muslims as slave-owners in contemporary Welsh literature. However, the main exhibit in this respect comes from the pen of a man who apparently never left the shore, in fact, a man who spent his entire life as a farm labourer in one of the parts of Wales which are furthest from the sea.

Huw Jones (*c.*1700-82) from Llangwm in Denbighshire, was a prolific author of verse, much of it religious, some romantic, and some on the theme of current events.[3] He also edited some important anthologies and wrote several examples of the popular folk drama known as an *anterliwt*, an entertainment whose name is derived from the English word 'interlude', and whose action often involves stock characters in populist and moralistic scenarios played out by means of homely rhyming stanzas. It is in an *anterliwt* by Huw Jones, *Hanes y Capten Ffactor* ('The History of Captain Factor') and dating probably from 1762, that we find his portrayal of an encounter between Welsh seafarers and Muslims, a passage in which a Muslim character is shown to speak for himself, albeit in a highly unflattering context.

The drama, written in Huw Jones's Denbighshire dialect, tells the story of Welsh seafarers finding themselves in Smyrna in Turkey, and quickly encountering the Muslim locals, who send out a boat and a boarding party. A Welsh sailor comments:

> Look, the men are coming over
> Underneath the half-moon banner.
> With black colours above their store,
> That's for sure the Turk's coat-armour.[4]

The Turkish Consul greets the Welshmen with apparent courtesy.

> By all that's gracious, enter;
> We gather, by your colour
> And from your ship so fine of frame
> You came from England hither.[5]

The accompanying Turkish official, Supersul, adds his welcome:

> If you come to us with candour,
> You may walk with us in Smyrna;

By Mahomet, ruler of the globe,
We'll robe you with our honour.[6]

Captain Ffactor and his crew assure the Turks of their good intentions, and go ashore to begin trading, when they notice a body lying unburied in the street. Inquiring, they are told by Consul that this is a Christian, and a tax must be paid before any Christian can be buried. Captain Ffactor remarks:

Here they make no more distinction
For a pure departed Christian
Than if he were a rabid hound,
In the rubbish-mound they cast him.[7]

Unable to bear the sight, Ffactor himself pays the heavy fifty-pound fine, which is obsequiously accepted by the Turks. He and the crew then prepare to leave, when two more Turkish characters, Syltan and Sarasin, enter, with a Christian woman, Prudensia, who is to be stoned to death. Asked by the sailors why she is to be punished, she replies:

I was made a captive maiden
By the cruel Turkish seamen,
For three long summers now, I wait
On one of their great noblewomen.

I gave that one a little slapping
In return for many a thrashing.
And that's the reason – woe is me!
That they will see my death by stoning.[8]

Ffactor arranges to purchase her freedom from the 'worthless' Syltan and Sarasin, this time for a hundred pounds, and, after securing promises from Prudensia as to her virtue, allows her to become his housekeeper. As they leave Turkey, the Mate remarks:

Fie! these are the bloodiest vermin,
In the world, the most unwholesome;
Let us get away, for certain,
If we can escape still living.[9]

The Bosun replies:

Come, life and death are dreadful burdens
While we stay among these ravens.[10]

Whether Huw Jones based his stories on accounts of contemporary affairs, on popular beliefs or on the real or exaggerated accounts of returned mariners with experience of the still-extant 'white slave' trade, it is clear that his work reflects an assumption that Muslims are cruel, oppressive, greedy, prone to enslave and mistreat Christians, and given to covering their villainy with a cloak of insincere politeness. While the anterliwt as a form is not known for its subtle portrayals of any group, there is certainly no attempt made in *Hanes y Capten Ffactor* to portray Muslims as anything other than contemptible and threatening; they are presented for Huw Jones's landlocked audience as something close to literal pantomime villains.

However, not all portrayals of maritime encounters with Muslims were so negative. There is at least one brief example, from the mid seventeenth century, of a more positive attitude. It is found in the work of Rowland Watkyns (*d.*1664), a Welsh Anglican priest who produced most of his single volume, *Flamma sine Fumo: or Poems without Fictions*, published in 1662, when he was deprived of his living during the Cromwellian period.[11] His poem, 'The Blackamoors', given in full below, shows visitors to Britain from Mauritania, a country which was at that time, as now, almost entirely Muslim.

We many men from Mauritania see
To England come, as black as ravens be.
Into yourselves look with a curious eye
And you shall find you are more black than they.
Then wonder not at them so black in skin
But at yourselves so foul, so black by sin.[12]

Once again, as with *Hanes y Capten Ffactor*, the image of the raven is used to describe the ethnic characteristics of the foreigner. However, in this case, the image is deployed in order to subvert prejudice, albeit by simplistic and superficial means. While the poem can hardly be said to be a sophisticated view of its subjects – its portrayal is literally only skin-deep – it does at least accord them full moral stature. That said, it must be noted that the poem's primary interest is in the observer and his audience, not in the observed. The Muslim visitors are figures in a moralistic vignette intended to edify the reader. As such, they are further examples of the portrayal of Muslims as a mirror for Christian vice or virtue.

A further fictional account of Welsh-Muslim contact, this time from the sixteenth century, comes from *Heli yn y Gwaed* ('Salt Sea in the Blood'), a historical novel by William Philip Williams (1900-70).[13] Although written in 1969, and a product of its period, it attempts to recreate the attitudes of Elizabethan Britain, and depicts Muslim characters with considerable sympathy. The novel tells the story of how Dafydd and Ned, Welsh seamen in the British navy at the time of the wars with Spain, find themselves fugitives in Spain itself. While living in hiding, they find work with Amhed Ali, a native of Andalusia, who also has something to hide:

> As they worked together, he explained that his forefathers were Muslim, his grandfather a chief among his people, an owner of vineyards and orange groves and of thousands of merino sheep whose wool was more valuable than the gold of Peru. Mercifully he had died before the days of affliction had come upon them, when his estate was divided among the lazy peasants of Estremadura, who let the weeds choke the irrigation canals and let goats displace the sheep. His father was imprisoned for refusing to deny his faith: his own misfortune was having to become an outward Christian in order to protect for his family the little property that was left to them. If a priest accused a Morisco of backsliding, he would be burnt on the saints' days of his persecutors. Ned exclaimed that false religion corrupted everyone and everything.[14]

Ned, a devout Protestant in a hostile Catholic land at the time of the Inquisition, is inspired by Amhed's tales of martyrdom, and dreams of dying as a martyr for his own faith. However, following their departure from Amhed Ali, they later encounter an *auto da fe*, a public act of religious punishment, in which the Inquisition burns a Protestant, a Jew and a Muslim at the stake for their beliefs. This reduces Ned's fervour somewhat.[15]

Heli yn y Gwaed certainly provides an empathetic and respectful portrayal of a Muslim believer. At one point, the Welshmen consider naming their new mule 'Ali' in memory of their benefactor, but refrain as it would be 'an injustice to the learned Morisco'. They call the mule 'Aled' instead. However, in the case of this novel, produced by the Welsh Calvinistic Methodist Church's press, it could be argued that Amhed Ali and the moriscos – and some later Jewish characters – are not presented primarily out of inherent interest in their religion, but because they are a means of highlighting the oppressive and intolerant Roman Catholicism which provides the novel's main source of narrative jeopardy and of ideological opposition. It should also be remembered that British *realpolitik* of the Elizabethan period encouraged an Anglo-Turkish alliance against the Catholic countries of southern Europe, the danger of nearby Catholics being deemed greater than that of distant Muslims. The depiction of the followers of Islam in *Heli yn y Gwaed* is informed and sympathetic, although, given that Protestantism and Catholicism are the main contending religious forces in the book, it might be suspected that the Muslims are depicted more in order to condemn Catholicism by comparison than they are in order to depict Muslims *per se*.

In *Heli yn y Gwaed*, adversity, in the form of religious persecution, is shown to reduce the distance between followers of different faiths. This indicates another of the themes that emerges from this study: that shared experience, particularly shared hardship, can erode prejudice. Certainly, the danger of the sea itself seems productive of mutual respect between mariners, irrespective of their different religious backgrounds. It is in accounts of the shared enterprise and peril of life at sea that we find some of the most humane depictions of Muslims in Welsh literature.

There is no shortage of such accounts, as, for many years, Wales had a thriving maritime industry. As Britain became the world's first great industrial power, and as its empire grew across the globe, Wales found itself the source of the biggest single supply of the most important fuel in the world – coal.[16] Ports such as Cardiff and Barry exported coal to the fuelling stations of the empire to maintain its essential network of naval and merchant shipping. They also exported coal to serve developing industrial powers elsewhere. Meanwhile, another great Welsh extractive industry, slate, sent hundreds of vessels around the world to supply ever-growing markets for roofing materials. And all the while, Wales's coalmines, iron and steelworks needed to be fed with a constant stream of imports of materials such as timber and iron ore. This led to an immense amount of maritime activity, with coastal communities all across Wales such as Ceredigion and Anglesey accustomed to seeing large proportions of their male population becoming sailors. Well into the mid twentieth century, it was common for sizeable merchant ships to have crews made up entirely of Welsh-speakers. This activity also led to a steady flow of autobiography from the men who had gone to follow their fortune at sea, and an accompanying commentary on maritime experiences from those who had not. It is from that extensive genre of Welsh maritime writing that the following extracts recording experiences of Muslims are drawn. The British Empire included many predominantly Muslim lands, such as Egypt, and others, such as India, which had high numbers of Muslims among their population. That fact, together with the long-established British custom of employing foreign sailors, many of them Muslims, made the maritime world an important interface for encounters between Muslims and Welsh seafarers.

One of the more colourful Welsh mariners was Captain Jac Alun Jones (1908-82) a larger-than-life character and a member of Teulu'r Cilie, a famously cultured family of poets, farmers and seafarers from the Cilie farm near Llangrannog in Ceredigion, who exerted – and whose descendants exert – a widespread influence on Welsh-language culture, particularly in the eisteddfodic and political field. Jac Alun travelled the world as a merchant-navy captain, and his literary work became widely known. He was an accomplished poet, particularly in the *cynghanedd* strict metres. However, it is a prose article, entitled 'Arab', which gives his most extensive account of his experiences with Muslims. The article begins:

> Ever since I first went to sea as a youth of 17, the Arab, for many different reasons, has stirred my memories and attracted more of my attention than the natives of other countries with whom I sailed together during my 29 years of travelling the world.
>
> On the first ship out of Cardiff, when Welsh coal exporting was in its glory, and every ship was burning coal to drive the engines, most of the firemen were Arabs, and they were famous as men who were able to withstand the great heat of the stokehold.
>
> Between the sailors' cabins on the starboard side, and the

> firemen's on the port side, there was an important bulkhead, and the old hands would advise the greenhorns not to venture beyond that important partition, where the firemen spent their leisure hours and prayed to their god, Allah. If there were enough rooms to be had, they would set one of them aside especially for worship and would decorate the walls and the floor with special carpets, and the savour of the East would be strong there. When on their knees worshipping and kissing the floor, they would always make sure that their heads were towards Mecca, and it was amazing to me how they could know the direction in the middle of the sea and the bad weather, without sun or moon to guide them, and so, as I learned with time, it was no surprise that the old hands advised the nippers not to venture beyond that sacred partition.[17]

Jones goes on to describe the remarkable stamina and strength of the firemen at their work before describing an incident which proved the Muslims could be strong in other ways too.

> During the last war I was unfortunate enough to lose a new ship to a mine. In the crew of around 48 there were 16 Arabs. After realising that the ship was sinking, and everyone was scrambling for a boat or raft to save their lives, who appeared at my side on the bridge but one of the Arabs, a little man of around five feet, but possessed of a strong and deep voice, and he said, 'I stay with you, Sir', and refused to go to the boats with the rest of the crew. Between us, we were responsible for saving two of the crew who had been badly injured. It was a strange thing to see a black man carrying a white man on his back to safety. In my official report to the authorities about the disaster, I gave the little Arab his due, and it was to my great satisfaction that I found he had been rewarded by the king and had been given the B.E.M. – Ali Mohamed B.E.M.[18]

He concludes his article with a story about when Welsh-Muslim relations did not go quite so successfully. It happened after the war, in Basra in Iraq, when Jones was visiting the offices of his shipping agent: 'The officer staff were modern Arabs, quite a bit different to the firemen I talked about, but an Arab is an Arab on every continent.' While waiting for his appointment, Jones passed the time by reading Welsh-language newspapers and magazines from back home, to the curiosity of the staff, who had thought him an Englishman. The manager inquired politely whether this was not, in fact, the case. Jones replied:

> 'Calling me an Englishman is the same as calling you a Jew.' Well, if I ever ... he almost went on his knees asking for pardon, and then asked me to read some of the Welsh headlines aloud, which I did. By now the office staff were in a circle around us, and the agent's work had come to a stop. Then he asked me to greet him in Welsh by saying 'Bore da' and 'Dydd da', etc. and in a flash I remembered 'Tangnefedd' and 'Salaam' (Cynan) and translated the lot as well as I could into English. I remembered also what I had learned in Sunday School: 'Our Father, remember, The Arab out there; So thin is his garment, So biting Thy air!' And I did so in the most sermonical manner I could, and then translated it all into English. And that's where I put my foot in it; I saw a hostile flash in the manager's eye, and I thought he was going to throw me out of the office. And he said, 'We, Arabs, do not want you or any other nation to pray for us; you have insulted our nation.' I realised that the friendship was at an end, and that it would be as an Englishman that I would be treated from then on. The staff went back to their work, and I prepared to go back to my ship, while it was still daylight. I had offended unforgivably, and had raised the hackles of the Arab! As I left the office, he told me, 'Salaam, but no more greetings in Welsh inside this office.'[19]

The poem 'Salaam', by the Archdruid and highly-popular lyric poet, Albert Evans Jones (1895-1970), known by his bardic name Cynan, is an appreciative piece about the Muslim greeting which the poet learned during his First World War service as an army chaplain. It is easy to imagine that it would not have given offence. It is examined in greater detail in Chapter 6. The other quotation by Jones comes from a poem, 'Ora Pro Nobis', by another hugely popular lyric poet, Eifion Wyn (1867-1926), and published in his 1908 collection *Telynegion Maes a Môr* ('Lyrics of Field and Sea'). Although published not long before Cynan's work, it is the product of the sensibility of an earlier age. The poem depicts the author contemplating a storm from the safety of his cottage, and asking God to remember those who have no shelter from its fury, namely: the animals, the 'arabs', and the sailors. It is not certain from Eifion Wyn's poem whether he meant 'Arab' as in the ethnic group or 'arab' as in the then-current term for a street urchin. There is no other clue in the poem as to which meaning he had in mind, although it is notable that the word is not capitalised in Wyn's version, and elsewhere in the same collection he capitalises 'Welsh' and 'Welshman', so it is possible that he did not intend the word to refer to the ethnic group. Indeed, the suggestion that ethnic Arabs are peculiarly exposed to cold seems an unlikely one. However, the fact is that Jac Alun Jones chose to interpret the word in the ethnic sense (the quotation above uses Eifion Wyn's own English translation of his Welsh original, but the capital A of 'Arab' was added by Jones). It is not hard to imagine that to an office of suit-wearing, city-dwelling, modern Arab office workers, fluent in English, the well-meant but sentimental references to impoverished shelterless Arabs shivering in their thin garments might be a touch offensive, as Jones, who was sensitive enough about his own ethnic origins being respected, might have realised. Capable of recognising an Arab as his moral equal as they faced death on a sinking ship, he seems, on shore, not to have recognised them, at least in this instance, as being capable of equal cultural sensitivity.

Indeed, it is the sea in her harshest tempers that seems the best teacher of equality. The second example illustrating this is a contemporary account based closely on fact: the story of a widely-publicised shipwreck in June 1923, when the Hain Line steamer *Trevessa*,[20] on its way from Fremantle in Australia to Durban in South Africa, sank in the Indian Ocean during a storm. The 44 crew took to the ship's two lifeboats, and after 25 days on the open sea, with very meagre rations, with no compass, and in conditions which claimed the lives of ten of them, they managed to land at Mauritius some 1,700 miles away. This feat of seamanship inspired much comment at the time and considerable commemorative activity, which included hanging the ship's red ensign near the altar in St Paul's Church in Barry, the home town of its captain, Cecil Foster, and of one of the young apprentice crewmen, Arthur Phillips, credited with saving the flag from the sinking vessel.

Among the responses to the incident was a poem, *The 'Trevessa': An Epic of the Sea*, and subtitled 'Two Thousand Fathoms Deep!', published as a pamphlet by Ernest Forrest of Cardiff. A serviceable blank verse rendition of the story in a style which even in the 1920s might have seemed somewhat old-fashioned, it records the hardships endured by the survivors of the wreck. It is the poem's account of the death of two Arab seamen that is particularly relevant to this study.

Death

On the seventeenth day died Jacob Ali,
An Arab fireman, sable-skinned and spare,
– No more to urge the slice 'mid glaring heat,
Or cleanse the clotted clinker from the bars,
The rake and shovel ne'er to use again.
Nor will life's pricker stir that breathless flesh;
His fire is out; his body cold in death.
They could not weep – the threat of Ali's doom
Gazed at them with a fixity so cruel
That sent them searching in each other's eyes,
And from that moment all men understood!

On the next morning fireman Naji died,
Another Arab shipmate of the crew ;
No funeral rite; no bookwords for the dead.
– If prayer at all – 'twas voiceless in the void
And heard in silence by the silent God.
At once they buried death and turned to life,
Urging their fragile craft in anxious haste.

Merchant-navy historian Bernard Edwards, in a chapter on the *Trevessa* in his book *The Grey Widow-Maker*,[21] notes the likely cause of the men's deaths: 'Under the cover of darkness, in spite of Foster's warning, some began to drink salt water and suffered the inevitable consequences. On 20 June Fireman Jacob Ali died, to be followed next day on his long voyage to the unknown by his shipmate Mussim Nazi.' They were the only two to die on that boat. On the other lifeboat, four Arab firemen died from drinking seawater and four Europeans died: three from exposure and one by falling overboard.

It is likely the two seamen were Yemeni, as that country was, at the time, a major source of labour for stokers for the furnaces of coal-fired British merchant naval vessels, as well as being the major coal depot for British ships in the east. As Patricia Aithie has explored in her extensive study of the relationship between Wales and Yemen, *The Burning Ashes of Time*,[22] Yemeni firemen were greatly respected for their strength and their ability to withstand the oppressive heat of the ships' furnace rooms. The relationship between the Yemeni sailors and the British fleet was responsible for the creation of one of Britain's oldest Muslim communities, in Cardiff, then the world's greatest coal-exporting port. As early as 1900, the Yemeni community in the city numbered 5,000. Although the Welsh coal industry is at an end, Aithie's book shows that the family connections between Wales and Yemen continue strong, and the relationship has left a legacy of memory and folklore in Yemeni culture.

What is notable about the portrayal of the two firemen, who, if Yemenis, would almost certainly have been Muslim, given the country's near-total adherence to Islam, is the lack of condescension, and the clear implication of comradeship shown in the references to the desire to weep, to pray and to elegise. The way this passage emphasises common humanity over cultural differences makes it an early example of Muslims being treated as equals in the literature covered by this study. Indeed, the study seems to indicate that religious differences are more readily overcome when the people concerned have had shared experiences on a basis of equality. In the history of Welsh-Muslim contact, encounters have often been brought about through agencies such as warfare or missionary activity, or through unequal trading or governance relationships. Consequently, true commonality of experience has been rare. In Welsh-Muslim relationships, one of the few areas of contact in which unifying factors outweigh dividing ones has been in instances of danger on the sea; this may go some way towards explaining why seafarers' accounts of contact with Muslims are generally somewhat more humane and generous than those of other groups from similar historical periods. Many beliefs and ideologies enjoin understanding and tolerance on their adherents, but, in teaching the insignificance of external human differences, few things seem more effective than the shared experience of facing the immensity of the sea and the immediacy of death.

Indeed, death in particular seems to elicit the warmest portrayals of Muslims as fellow human beings. For instance, the ship's carpenter David Edmund Williams, who was born in Groeslon near Caernarfon in 1897 and who was one of the six founder members of Plaid Cymru, the Welsh Nationalist Party, gives an account of an Indian Muslim burial at sea in his 1945 memoir *Hwylio'r Moroedd* ('Sailing the Seas').[23]

> When one of them died, no white man could touch the body. The

> chief man of the sect would consecrate the part of the deck where the body was to lie. Then they made a kind of a tent over the spot, and the body was taken to it. Incense was burned inside the tent, and prayers were said outside. Then the body was left until sunset without anyone near it. I think it would have been death to a man to go near the body once it had been consecrated. They would sew the body into a new canvas, and would put a heavy iron either side of it so it would sink into the sea when it was dropped into the water. At sunset, the red Ensign would be raised to half mast, and the ship's engines would be stilled for two minutes while the body was dropped into the water, with the service once more conducted by the chief man.
>
> That two-minute silence is something to remember. The quiet feels overwhelming after being among the noise and racket of the machinery for days on end. The sound of the waves lapping lightly on the ship adds to the silence. And everyone stands during these two minutes – out of respect to the body that is committed to the sea.[24]

In the 1987 memoirs of O. Trevor Roberts, of Llanowain near Llan Ffestiniog in Gwynedd, *Ar Dir a Môr* ('On Land and Sea'), a further description is found, although the taboo of having the bodies touched by a non-Muslim seems not to have been practised in this case:

> I had quite an exceptional experience while sailing on the Agamemnon, which was calling in Jidda, the port of Mecca, and taking on board over two thousand Moslem pilgrims who had been fasting for many weeks in their holy city. That ship had two decks in its holds, and they had all been marked out to show where individuals and families were to live. The ship carried three doctors instead of the usual one, two or three interpreters, and a Priest or two. We were told at the beginning of the voyage that it would not be an easy one, and that, because of long fasting, the pilgrims would be in quite a pitiable state of health. We were given, therefore, a penny a head for every pilgrim, in addition to our wages. This was referred to by some as 'danger money'. The purpose of the voyage was to deliver these poor people to their own countries, and we had to call at ports in India, Malaysia, China and Japan. Dysentery was the main enemy, and we buried many of the passengers at sea. We would go around the decks with a torch at night to find if any deaths had taken place or not. It was we, in those cases, who would prepare the body when that happened – the metal bars and the cloths and so on. A brief and dignified service would be conducted by the Priest, and one of the ship's officers would always be present. At the end of the service, we would be given a sign by the officer to raise the trip-line, and then

> the body would slip from the cradle to the water. I had prepared many bodies in this manner before I was twenty one years old.[25]

Then in the Cricieth sea captain W.E. Williams's 1977 memoir, *Llyncu'r Angor* ('Swallowing the Anchor') we find an account of a 'Lascar' burial. As with the other accounts, the practicalities are discussed in some detail: the stopped engines, the best clothes, the silence. It is, however, the common humanity which is most salient for this study:

> This was a black man, one of the children of Mohammed. Losing him was a bereavement for us all, as the ship's family is a small and tight-knit one, and being close to death has a strange kind of effect on us.
>
> In this funeral the captain did not take the burial service. One of the Lascars was the religious leader for the others, and it is he who would always lead them in prayer and in recitation from the Koran. We could hardly understand a word, but the feeling was as clear as though it had been said in the first language of each of us. One of the family was gone.[26]

Williams explains that, while sailing to Calcutta and southeast Africa, ships of his Harrison Company would be officered by white men, but always had 'Lascars' among the crew, usually from Sylhet, in Assam, close to Lushai. Williams, who was, in his shore life, a leading member of his church, notes that Welsh missionaries were active in the Lascars' home area, a project examined in more detail in Chapter 5. He goes on to describe the Lascars' daily life aboard ship, such as their caste system, their cooking practices, and their religious beliefs, and he does so with a keen and sympathetic interest:

> I marvelled at how faithful was the Lascar to the high festivals of his religion. The most important to him was ramadan, the festival of the ninth month of his calendar; this lasts from the ninth of May to the ninth of June[27]. I remember how the Lascars would search the firmament for a sign of the new moon, and the excitement that would follow the shout of the first to find it.
>
> They would set a clean white tarpaulin on the fifth hatch, and everyone who was not working at the time would go to crouch on the hatch while facing Mecca. Their religious leader would sit in front of them to read the Koran and to lead them in prayer. Their midday meal was the most important to them, and was rather like our

> Christmas dinner. Shortly before dinner, the two Serangs [the most senior Lascar rank, equivalent to bosun] and the rest of his crew would go as one company to the captain's cabin. They would have a special curry on a tray, and they would present it to him. The Lascars would have an extra ration of fresh water that day too.
>
> Sunday was a special day for the Lascars aboard ship. Each of them would bring his chest out on to the deck and would clean his cabin. At eleven o'clock that morning, the captain, the mate, the chief engineer and the chief steward would come to inspect the rooms. Each Lascar would stand smartly by his chest while uttering his salaam as the captain came to him. When they left the ship at Calcutta, one of the officers would guard the chests in case something illegal should go ashore.
>
> . . .
>
> They were a strange crew, and sometimes the melancholy would drive them into the pit of despair. If a Lascar had decided he was to die, nothing and no-one could prevent him.[28]

The term 'Lascar', derived from the Arabic *al-askar*, meaning soldier or guard, and itself a loanword from the Persian lashkar, meaning an armed camp, was once widely used to describe seamen recruited from the Indian subcontinent. They comprised a substantial proportion of the crews of many British ships, and the system for recruiting and managing them was, by long custom, highly systematised. For instance, in 1955, M. Watkins-Thomas, in an article entitled 'Our Asian Crews' in the P&O company's magazine, *About Ourselves*, in September 1955, explained, primarily for the benefit of his land-bound colleagues, the way different ethnic and religious groups were employed: 'These crews are found in all three departments, Moslems and Hindus on deck, Moslems in the engineroom[29] and Goanese in the Purser's department. Only Moslems are found on deck in the P & O.' M. Watkins-Thomas goes into great detail about Muslim religious beliefs and practices, which he has observed with a shipmate's rather than a scholar's eye:

> The Moslems frequently read their Koran or Hindustani magazines. They may be seen regularly at prayers in approved Mohammedan fashion... In the Calendar of Islam, Ramadan is the ninth month and for all Moslems it is a time of fasting. Through the month, from sunrise to sunset, neither food nor drink may pass the lips of any Moslem, nor is he allowed to smoke. It is indeed a rigorous test and

> is strictly observed. They believe that it was during this month that God sent from the Seventh Heaven, by the Angel Gabriel, the Holy Koran to be revealed to the Prophet Mahommed. It is upon this Book that the Mahommedan religion is largely based. It is noteworthy that the Koran was sent by the hand of the Angel Gabriel, for the Angels, the Prophets and even Jesus Christ all figure in the Islamic faith... The last festival, though it is not celebrated by all Moslems, is in the month of Mohorram, usually on the tenth. It is connected with the murder of various of the early followers of Mohammed and especially with that of his grandson Hussein. Ashore, a religious procession often takes place on this day and, before the War, the crews of ships at Tilbury often staged one. The time of the year that these festivals take place is not constant. This is due to the fact that Moslems use the uncorrected lunar calendar so that their years are never the same length as ours.

He says that, having served with European and Asian crews, he sometimes misses what he calls 'a European *crowd*', but he finds non-European crews more tractable, and concludes 'from the point of view of a ship's officer, I must say that I prefer to sail with Asian crews.'[30]

However, if the sensibilities of men like M. Watkins-Thomas had been quickened by long familiarity with Muslim crews, not all of his colleagues in the company were as sympathetic. A fellow P&O officer, John Jones Williams, writing in his 1983 memoir, *Llongwr o Ros-Lan* ('A Seaman from Rhos-Lan') and recounting a voyage on a troopship en route from Australia to Egypt during the First World War, has the following comments:

> Port Said is a big town depending for its existence on the ships coming and going through the canal. The Arabs would swarm onto the ship to sell all kinds of things, and it was impossible to get rid of them, and they followed everyone on shore in the same way. The thing I hate most is seeing their dirty faces and their little red caps. My forefathers must have fought the Turk and the Arab and the hatred must be in the blood. I had rather spend a week in prison than be in Port Said for another week.[31]

Although such attitudes could be due to the kind of generalised prejudice towards non-European peoples common in the period, rather than as any particular reference to Muslims, they come within the scope of this study due to the reference to the Crusades. Seven centuries after they ended, the Crusades can still be found to provide convenient categories and excuses for ethnic and religious antagonism.

On shore too, the presence of 'Lascar' seaman in British ports, including in Wales, could still be a source of unease and suspicion for land-dwellers, as shown in the following poem by Peter Thomas (1939-2007), and referring to the Swansea of the immediate post-war period. As the poem, given in full, shows, the very word 'Lascar' carried an air of exoticism and danger:

The Lascars

When I was a boy they came in blackness
from black ships together, gripping an unseen circle
protected from the pack of the crowd.
Lascars, my father would say, *they'll empty the pubs tonight*,
and we'd see them in Wind Street by tailors' windows
huddled together, left alone.

One Monday, the *Evening Post* said blood had been found
on the pavement across the road from Sidney Heath's,
so *Lascars* my father said, and I stopped writing homework,
feeling the deft slit of the knife.

Then I was looking at coats in the window,
a man at the edge of means, indifferent to the town,
aching to be away. Quietly
they ringed me, staring into the same tailor's window,
dark in their quietness, unsure of the strange town,
nudging each other like schoolboys, they giggled
and fingered the frayed collars of loose shirts.
And *Lascars* I thought, as my dead father tugged,
but they smiled at me shyly, turning
to walk down Wind Street
to their ship.[32]

The 2007 autobiography of Raymond Hicks (*b.*1925), *An Odyssey: From Ebbw Vale to Tyneside*, is the most recent of the Welsh maritime memoirs examined here, and may well be one of the last wartime records to emerge. After lying about his age, Hicks, a teenage steelworker from the south Wales Valleys, served with the British and Dutch merchant navies for four years from 1942, experiencing the dangers of the Atlantic convoys. He says that sixty years later he is still haunted by an incident when, in obedience to an order forbidding attempts to rescue survivors of torpedoed ships lest they should lead to further sinkings by waiting U-boats, his vessel was forced to sail past a group of survivors he knew contained teenagers like himself, both Muslims and Christians. He repeatedly testifies to the egalitarian nature of shipboard life, and the role of shared peril in removing prejudice:

> In the whole of my four years at sea I cannot recall any instance of ethnic or religious intolerance.[33]
>
> . . .
>
> At sea the crew are united by one unchallengeable fact: that in war or peace they have to rely on one another in order to survive. This single fact overcomes all possible conflict over nationality, religion, colour, standard of education and so on. In my entire time at sea I cannot recall one incident in which any of these issues caused a problem worth mentioning.[34]

It is timely here to point out that as this book is a record of Welsh perceptions of Muslims as recorded in literature, all the depictions in this chapter are from the European perspective. This is in common with literary records of British maritime activity generally, as is shown in Tony Lane's 1991 study, *The Merchant Seaman's War*, which devotes a chapter, 'Sons of Empire' to the experience of non-European crews in the Second World War:

> In all the reports of Lascar seamen it is extremely hard to find any narrative where perceptions have not been filtered through the categories required by the racial hierarchy of empire. Judgments were made but ethnographies were excluded. On matters of Lascars' social and economic backgrounds, political allegiances, culture and attitudes there was simply a void.[35]

Lest that void should be filled by assumptions based only on the European voice, Lane shows that post-war social history projects, which collected the experiences of non-European sailors in the British Merchant Navy, revealed considerable dissatisfaction among many with the way they were treated. While complaints of racial prejudice were by no means absent, the men's grievances primarily related to the fact that they were paid less and had more unfavourable terms of employment than white colleagues. Indeed disputes and strikes relating to this inequality were not uncommon. Contemporary records of reports by wartime British officers, as collected by Lane, also reveal a picture in which racial stereotypes, whether positive or negative, were common currency in discussions of their non-European crews.

Therefore, while considering the Welsh authors' accounts of contact with Muslims, which, on the whole, tend to be comparatively positive and broad-minded according to the standards of the general society of the day, it must be borne in mind that in all cases these Welsh writers held a position of much greater economic and social power than their Muslim fellow-voyagers, whether passengers or crew. In their economic relations, whatever cordiality may have existed within the strict demarcations of shipboard hierarchies, the Europeans and their non-European crews were very far from being equal. For instance, in the next extract, D. Edmund Williams, whose description of a Muslim funeral was given a little earlier, recalls getting to know his Muslim crew while on a trip to India. While the goodwill is obvious, so are the hierarchies:

> The black Indians' way of life was now of great interest to me, and I wasn't afraid of them. I saw that most of them were kind men. There were exceptions among them like everyone else. But on the whole they were hard workers, and clean. They were Mohametans in their religion and on the whole they were much more faithful than the Christians I met. They worshipped every day without exception. They would come on deck first thing in the morning and at sunset, and that's when they would bow to pray. It was necessary to observe them from a distance, and that without appearing as though you were watching them, as they were angry towards others for watching them. On Sunday they would wear their best clothes, and those were very different to ours. Also, on the day they called something like 'Barro Dean,'[36] i.e. the big day, the best costume would come to light, and they would have coloured their beards, and some of them wore a turban (a kind of cap) of different colours. This was a sign that they had been on pilgrimage to Mecca, or somewhere else sacred to the Mohametan. They could tell by the colour where they had been. These pilgrimages also determined their social status, with 'Mecca' being the highest on their list, of course.

Williams describes the Muslims' dietary customs, particularly their methods of ritual slaughter and their abhorrence of pork. Then he continues:

> On their most important days, the first day of the year according to their calendar, we, the white men, had to be their guests. The dinner that day was a gift from them, and to fail to eat it would be the greatest dishonour to them. Indeed, none of us wished to fail to eat it either – they would make us a marvellous meal. Very often, they would work through the night preparing it, and you could tell from their faces that they got pleasure in giving it to us.[37]

Similar hierarchies appear in the following example, where the Muslim tradition of hospitality towards the Christian ships' officers took an unusual aspect. In his 1976 memoir *Blas y Môr* ('A Taste of the Sea'), Commander John Penri Davies says how, in the inter-war years, he sailed on the *Magic Star* from London to China, having been engaged for the voyage the night before the ship sailed, as a replacement for a young officer suddenly taken ill. His first encounter with the Muslim crewmen was puzzling:

> As I watched them going back and fore about their duties, a young man, tall and good-looking, raised both his arms as a sign for the others to stand, and suddenly, they all bowed, and with a smile went about their duties. They were Arabs, and of course I thought that this was their usual custom in greeting officers. But, strangely enough, this happened every day when I appeared on the bridge at eight in the morning. After seeing this ceremony, the captain asked me for an explanation, but I answered immediately that he should know better than me, as they were his crew, and perhaps he should ask them! The captain and the officers did not say anything further, but I knew they were discussing the matter behind my back, and yet doing nothing to solve the mystery.[38]

The mystery deepened as Davies returned to his cabin after leaving Port Said to find a basket of fruit on his table. The steward could not explain how it got there. The same thing happened in every port. At Colombo, the young Arab man approached Davies and asked him to read letters written to the crew from wives and lovers in South Shields and Cardiff. He also invited him to their feast to celebrate the end of Ramadan. After some hesitation, Davies accepted, on condition that they told no-one. The meal was held in a room the captain has set aside for them so that their songs and readings from the *Qur'an* do not disturb the rest of the crew.

> I was surprised how clean and tidy the room was, and how attractively it had been decorated ready for the ceremony. It was all administered by the young man who had first approached me, and all in a clear voice. And as I looked at him, I noticed his aristocratic bearing, and at the influence he had with his friends. They were all in white gowns, and I too, mercifully, was in my white rig, and suddenly I thought that this was the sight that had been seen in Sinai many centuries ago, when the old nation gave thanks for their salvation from the Egyptians. I learned that these were Arabs from the south west of the country, from the place where the quail come, which were blown northwards along the Red Sea as sustenance for the Israelites, after they had complained long about the manna. The explanation in the Koran is this, that the bones of quail from Yemen are so light, like sinews, that it is possible to eat them whole. I had the opportunity to ask the oldest of the Arabs why the young man had such influence, and the answer I was given was that he was a descendant of the prophet Mohamed.[39]

After four months, the ship returned to London, and was visited by the inspector-captain. Davies told him about his disagreement with the captain at the start of the voyage regarding the Arabs' behaviour towards him. The inspector-captain laughed as he explained what it was all about:

> 'You'll remember I asked a favour of you, which was to switch ships at short notice, and take the place of a young boy who had been taken ill? Well, the name of that young man was the Honourable Allison Winn, the eldest son and heir of Lord Headley,[40] the famous scholar and an authority on the culture and religion of the Mohametans, and one who has made three pilgrimages to the Holy City of Mecca. I'm sure', he said, 'that the Arabs knew that Allison Winn had been chosen especially as an officer for the ship because they were to be its crew. So now you know why they showed you honour and respect during the voyage. To them, you were Alison Winn, the heir of the honorary chief of British Mohametans.'[41]

If, due to the case of mistaken identity, the respect shown to John Penri Davies was, considerably more elaborate than was customary, it is nonetheless fair to note that mutual respect generally seems to have been the rule in Welsh seafarers' dealings with their Muslim fellow voyagers, at least according to the literary records they have left. Faced with such material, it is tempting to suppose the Welshmen's cultural sensitivities were heightened by the fact that they themselves belonged to a subordinated nation playing a junior part in a greater imperial project, and that their knowledge of a minority language had sensitised them to ethnic differences. But one must be cautious about projecting backwards into history the political sensibilities of a later age. None of the writers here claim a sense of Welsh national identity or a consciousness of minority status as a basis for their positive attitudes towards their non-European contacts. Only one, Jac Alun, seeks to make any contact based on his separate ethnicity, and that unsuccessfully. Indeed, their attitudes seem to be exactly what one would have expected from any other Briton of their class and period. Where they give a reason for their sense of fellowship with Muslims on board ship, they invariably cite their awareness of common humanity in the face of the challenge of the sea. If these authors' attitudes tend towards the enlightened, it seems reasonable to take them at their word and accept that their sympathy was promoted by the particular intensity of life at sea, where both the small necessities of human existence and the great questions of life and death, alike insist on an equality more fundamental than any external differences of colour, caste, nation or religion.

Notes

1. Giles Milton, *White Gold* (London, 2004) 10.
2. *Ibid.* 14.
3. Ernest Edward Wynne, 'Jones, Huw', *Welsh Biography Online,* National Library of Wales, http://yba.llgc.org.uk/en/s-JONE-HUW-1700.html
4. Huw Jones, *Hanes y Capten Ffactor* in A. Cynfael Lake (ed.), *Anterliwtiau Huw Jones o Langwm* (Swansea, 2000) 78.
5. *Ibid.* 79.
6. *Ibid.* 79.
7. *Ibid.* 80.
8. *Ibid.* 80.
9. *Ibid.* 82.
10. *Ibid.*
11. Meic Stephens (ed.), *The New Companion to the Literature of Wales*

(Cardiff, 1998) 768.
12. Raymond Garlick and Roland Mathias (eds.) *Anglo Welsh Poetry 1480-1990* (Bridgend, 1990) 84.
13. From Bethesda, a Bangor history graduate and MA, he taught at Leigh Grammar School near Manchester until retiring to Aberystwyth. Biographical information from his daughter, Dwynwen Kovacs.
14. William Philip Williams, *Heli yn y Gwaed* (Caernarfon, 1969) 130.
15. *Ibid.* 136.
16. The 1851 Census showed Wales was the first nation in the world to have the majority of its population employed in industry rather than agriculture.
17. Gerallt Jones (ed.) *Y Capten Jac Alun* (Llandysul, 1984) 87.
18. *Ibid.* 89. The B.E.M. is the British Empire Medal.
19. *Ibid.* 90.
20. The Hain company relocated to Cardiff from Cornwall in 1901, and its ships sailed from there and from Barry. For this information and for much of the material relating to the *Trevessa*, I am indebted to Keith Greenway, tireless researcher of the history of the *Trevessa*, its sister ships, and their crews.
21. Bernard Edwards, *The Grey Widow-Maker* (London, 1990) 72.
22. Patricia Aithie, *The Burning Ashes of Time* (Bridgend, 2005).
23. David Edmund Williams, *Hwylio'r Moroedd* (Denbigh, 1945) 22. See also Derec Llwyd Morgan, *Adnabod Deg* (Denbigh, 1977) 116-27.
24. *Ibid.* 24
25. O. Trevor Roberts, *Ar Dir a Môr* (Ruthin, 1987) 31.
26. W.E. Williams, *Llyncu'r Angor* (Denbigh, 1977) 127.
27. Williams incorrectly supposes that Ramadan has a fixed date.
28. *Ibid.* 129.
29. D. Edmund Williams, *op. cit.* 23, notes a caste system operating between the occupants of various shipboard roles.
30. M. Watkins-Thomas, 'Our Asian Crews', *About Ourselves*, (September 1955) http://www.lascars.co.uk/crew.html
31. John Jones Williams, *Llongwr o Ros-Lan* (Pen-y-groes, 1983) 91.
32. Garlick and Mathias, *op. cit.* 303
33. Raymond Hicks, *An Odyssey: From Ebbw Vale to Tyneside* (Newcastle upon Tyne, 2007) 116.
34. *Ibid*, 127.
35. Tony Lane, *The Merchant Seaman's War*, (Manchester, 1991) 183.
36. From the Hindi *burra din*, meaning 'great day'.
37. D. Edmund Williams *op. cit.* 22-23.
38. John Penri Davies, *Blas y Môr* (Denbigh, 1976) 75.
39. *Ibid.* 77,
40. Rt. Hon. Rowland George Allanson Allanson-Winn, 5th Baron Headley, also known as Lord Headley Al-Farooq, (1855–1935) was a prominent British convert to Islam.
41. John Penri Davies *op. cit.* 78.

'One of the most remarkable nations under the sun': Welsh Pilgrims and Missionaries in the Lands of Islam

It is one thing for writers to develop their religious ideas of Islam from the comfort of their own studies, as did many of the authors discussed in Chapter 3. It is quite another to encounter the religion and its practitioners in reality. This chapter will look at the experiences of the many Welsh people who travelled on religious journeys, whether as pilgrims refreshing their faith at its ancient sources in the Middle East, or as missionaries carrying their own brand of Christianity to foreign lands.

From at least the time of the Methodist Revival in the eighteenth century, there was a strong current of evangelical Protestantism in Wales, leading to a wide range of missionary activity directed both at domestic constituencies and at ones further afield. In 1897, Penar G. Griffith published an extensive study of Welsh mission work 'in pagan lands' up to that date, and found that from 1662 until 1895, he could identify a total of 171 Welsh overseas missionaries, all but three of them commissioned after 1813.[1] It is from some of these overseas missions, together with pilgrim journeys, that we find many portrayals of Muslims and of Islam.

In many of these encounters, nearly all of which took place under the aegis of the British Empire, we will find the complexity of the Welsh position within that enterprise, as both an internal colony of England and a core participant in an imperial project. In a 2003 essay 'The Welsh World and the British Empire, *c.*1851-1939: an Exploration', the historians Aled Jones and Bill Jones described the situation: 'Wales, like Ireland and Scotland, presents something of a paradox in having been regarded as both imperial and colonial, although the relationships between the two were perhaps more complex and diverse than a straightforward colonised/coloniser dichotomy might suggest.'[2] The passages of missionary and pilgrim encounter with the Muslim world collected here, give ample evidence of that complexity.

The first extract is the product of a Welsh missionary enterprise which was itself a response to a metropolitan English initiative. It comes from the work of John Mills (1812-73),[3] a prominent Calvinistic Methodist minister from Montgomeryshire, who, in 1846, was engaged by his church as a missionary to the Jewish people. It is a measure of the confidence of Welsh Calvinistic Methodism in the mid nineteenth century, that it should have felt that a church based in the Welsh-speaking community of Wales should play a role in the conversion of the Jewish people to Christianity. In supporting such a project, the Welsh Methodists were following a stream of evangelical Christian activity which had been gathering pace since early in the century when leading British Christians and social reformers such as William Wilberforce and Lord Shaftsbury established the Society for the Promotion of Christianity Amongst the Jews (now known as the C.M.J.) in 1809. The evangelical impulse was given impetus by the belief that the Second Coming of Jesus Christ would be hastened if the Jews were converted to Christianity and restored to their ancient homeland of Palestine. John Mills was employed as a missionary among the Jewish people of London, where he learned Hebrew and immersed himself in Jewish religion and history, becoming, over time, a leading interpreter between the Jewish community and the majority society, although without recording a single convert. It was not for want of trying, however. Twice, he even made the journey to Palestine to make contact with Jewish communities there. His 1858 book *Palestina* recorded his experience in the Holy Land, where, as well as the Jewish people, he also encountered Muslims. No account of a visit to Jerusalem was complete without a description of the Temple Mount and Dome of the Rock. Here is part of John Mills's version:

> It is paved with marble; and there are many Mahommetan prayer places – very beautiful ones too – which have been built here and there upon it. On the eastern side, next to the Mosque is an area rather like a font, with columns and a beautiful dome on it, as well as a prayer station facing Mecca – this, the Mahommetan tradition says, is the judgement seat of David. On this raised area, as can be seen, the Mosque of Omar stands, or, as it is called by the residents themselves, *Al Sachra*, i.e. the rock, after the holy rock that is there.[4]

The description, detailed, knowledgeable and appreciative, goes on for some pages. It must be remembered that Mills's mission was to make contact with the Jewish communities of Palestine, to make converts, and to report back to his denomination. As such, the focus of his book is primarily on the Jewish elements of the land and the community. However, he provides substantial descriptions of the Muslim communities of Palestine too, going to considerable trouble to explain the demarcations between nomadic Bedouin and settled Fellahin, and the Ottoman Turkish overlords, and even the sub-divisions within those groups.

Most of Mills's writing about the Arabs and Turks is factual information about their living arrangements, their government, costume, music and cuisine. However, when it comes to morality, Mills is roundly condemnatory of what he sees as greed and deceitfulness, by the Fellahin in particular:

> Some say that love of money only exists in lands of commerce. That is a great mistake. Mammon is a god worshipped in every country, and no-one under the sun serves him more warmly and heartily than the Arab. He will do anything for money – he will work (although not too hard), he will beg, he will lie, he will do almost anything, and never have the eyes of Jew or Gentile shone more than his while receiving this idol.[5]
>
> . . .
>
> The standard of morality among them is so low that one could think that neither master nor servant, parents or children, old or young, have the least feeling for justice and injustice. It is true that this characteristic, like the others I have mentioned, does not belong to the Arab alone, but it is like a leprosy that has sunk deep into the nature of all the orientals. Be that as it may, there is one peculiarity of the moral constitution of the Arab that adds hugely to his plague, and that is his amazing ability to conceal his deceit. Accuse one of dishonesty, and you will hear immediately the most fluent and persuasive speech being used, not just in self-defence, but also to condemn all kinds of dishonesty. And what is more, they can do all this, while concealing their feelings completely, if they have feelings at all.[6]

As is common among British portrayals of Arabs of the period, the shock and distaste felt at their apparent moral failings is offset by admiration of their hardiness and tenacity, particularly so in the case of the nomadic Bedouin. In a section entitled 'Their Independence', Mills praises them as having the stubborn unconquerable nature of the wild ass:

> That is what the Bedouin are like, they have never been subjected to any foreign country's yoke. Everyone has failed, from Alexander to Napoleon. They have been, through all the ages, free men, wandering like wild asses, the length and breadth of Arabia, and the neighbouring countries; and if Britain, or any other power, tried to oppress them under a yoke, they would laugh at the kingdoms of the world. But there is one king, the Messiah, whose government the Bedouin will one day come to acknowledge.[7]

In his bid to hasten the return of that Messiah by making His people Christians, Mills befriended Jewish communities, who lived in a state of what he called 'the cruellest enmity ... with their Mahommetan neighbours.'[8] On a visit to Hebron, he saw an example of this as he walked through a bazaar with his Jewish hosts: '... a host of children had surrounded the place, and one or two of them were full of Mahommetan zeal and started nicknaming us: Yehudi, Nozraani, Jew, Christian, Dog, &c., but surprisingly, they hid as they did so, as though they were half-expecting to be in danger from so doing.' However, despite this atmosphere of hostility, Mills, at his lodging at a Jewish home in the town that night, received a message from the local governor who said he would like to pay a call on him, if it is agreeable to Mills. The Welshman reflects:

> ...of course it was agreeable to me for him to come if only for the residents to see their governor paying so much respect to a Christian visiting Hebron, the most Mahommetan town in Palestine. Many of them were amazed at the fact, and I have no doubt that it will have been a means of reducing the prejudice of some of them against Christians. But I was inexpressibly pleased for the sake of the Jews. For the governor to come into their midst in a friendly manner was something very new – new to the Jews and new and incomprehensible to the Mahommetans. However, that is how it was – he and some of his chosen servants came, in one entourage, through the town, and into the Jewish neighbourhood, and straight to our room, where we were waiting for them...
>
> The governor stayed with me for around half an hour, and we conversed about many political and social matters. I took the opportunity to praise his magnanimity in visiting me, a Christian, and that

> in a Jewish house, and in the middle of the Jewish neighbourhood; and that he had shown an excellent example. I observed that this is how it should be between men – that it was right for the subjects to obey their governors whatever their religion may be – that a man's religion was something between him and his Creator. He often gave grunts of approbation, and when I made clear my confidence that such a thing would be of great blessing to the whole country, he said several times, with a special emphasis *anshala, anshala* – by the will of God.[9]

John Mills was tireless in his efforts, and never less than ambitious. In 1857, in his monthly newsletter to his denominational journal, *Y Drysorfa* ('The Treasury'), he advocated support for a railway to Jerusalem, which he believed would help develop the country as part of the Christian witness to Jews and Arabs. In the same letter, he said plans were well advanced for a Welsh colony in the north of the country which he said was 'the best place in the world for a Welsh colony' on the grounds of its Biblical past and its potential for hastening the Jewish return to the promised land, and so precipitating the Second Coming.[10] Mills was writing in a context in which there was growing support among the Welsh intelligentsia for political autonomy, for the preservation of the Welsh language and for the ability to worship as Nonconformists free from the interference of the Anglican Church. The establishment of a utopian overseas colony was seen as one means of securing those freedoms, and there was much debate in the middle of the nineteenth century as to where would be best for such a venture. Mills spoke to the National Eisteddfod of Wales in 1857 to promote his plans for a colony in Palestine. Michael D. Jones, an early advocate of Welsh political nationalism, also supported the planned colony in the 'Esdraelon' ('Jezreel') Valley.[11] However, the Palestine scheme came to nothing, and, Jones's plans for a utopian Welsh overseas community were eventually realised in Patagonia in Argentina in 1865. As the Welsh colonists in Argentina succeeded in the face of all hardships, and managed to retain their Nonconformist religion, their language and their communal identity to a remarkable degree into the twenty-first century, it is fascinating to speculate what might have happened if Mills's plan for a colony in Palestine had come to fruition and had attracted equally tenacious emigrants.[12]

Despite his ambition, however, John Mills's efforts to create Christian converts among the Jewish people were not to bear fruit, and he faced periodic questioning from the perplexed leaders of his denomination. Other missionary efforts to the Jewish people did, however, occasionally succeed. One Jewish convert to Christianity was the means for occasioning one of the more remarkable Welsh literary testimonies about Islam. The convert was the Rev. E.B. Frankel (*d.*1908), and the Welsh writer was Margaret Jones, from Rhosllannerchrugog near Wrexham, who left her home as a teenager to become a domestic servant with Frankel in Birmingham. When he followed his calling as a Christian missionary to France and then, in 1865, to Jerusalem, under the auspices of the London Society for Promoting Christianity among the Jews, she went with him and his family, and stayed there for four years, until a chronic hip injury forced her return to Britain. Some of the colourful letters in Welsh which she sent back to her family were published in the denominational press without her knowledge, and when she returned to Britain in 1869 and was facing expensive medical bills, they were collected by her friends for a fund-raising edition entitled *Llythyrau Cymraes o Wlad Canaan* ('Letters of a Welsh woman from the Land of Canaan'). In one letter, she describes a visit to the Temple Mount, and the Mosque of Omar:

> After that we were shown into the Mosque, which is a very wide, round building. The windows, which are about a yard and a half long by a yard wide, have been painted very beautifully, and their height, I guessed, was about 40 feet from the floor. The ceiling is of brass, and there are many railings in the building which have intricately carved out of wood. There are no benches or anything of that kind. I don't know how many doors are in it, only that I went in through one door and out through another, and that they were decorated with marble columns. There is a round open place by one of the doors, and columns around it holding up a brass roof. This is where it is said the angel appeared in order to halt the plague which God had sent upon Israel because David had conducted a census (see the last chapter of Samuel). But the most interesting thing in my eyes was the threshing floor which David purchased so that he could sacrifice to God for his sins. It is firm rock, and fills the centre of the Mosque.
>
> It could easily be a place of sacrifice, but I don't know how they could have threshed on it, because it's pretty uneven. They show an

> angel's footprint on it. When Mahomed went to heaven on the back of a white horse, and the threshing floor rose to follow him, an angel struck it on the rock with his foot to prevent it.
>
> There is a kind of door made of wire by the altar, and the Mohametans put pieces of thread through the wires if they wish to have children, or something else of importance; and indeed, every window is of wire and is full everywhere of little pieces of rag, or threads, which make it look very similar to a rag shop.
>
> But while that old Mahometan sheikh was telling us so much about his prophet, I was looking carefully at the place where I supposed my dear Saviour had sat among the doctors and had taught them in such a way that no man had ever spoken like that before, and I was saying the word 'Jesus' to myself. There was something so sweet about it next to the noise of the worshippers of the false prophet.[13]

Margaret Jones's example shows how even Welsh people of modest economic means were able to travel the world. She became well-known for her accounts of her travels. She later spent time in Morocco, and wrote about her experiences in her 1883 book, *Morocco a'r hyn a welais yno* ('Morocco and what I saw there'). In the National Library of Wales's collection of photographs is a full-length portrait of her in eastern dress, with an Islamic niqab, leaving only her eyes visible. Later, her appetite for adventure unabated, she emigrated to Australia, where she married a farmer. She died in 1902.[14] The Anglican mission to the Jewish people, of which E.B. Frankel and Margaret Jones had been a part, still exists, although the organisation, which celebrated its bicentenary in 2009, now operates under the more circumspect name 'The Church's Ministry among Jewish people'. Following the death of John Mills, however, the specific Welsh Calvinistic Methodist mission to the Jewish people was not sustained.

Nonetheless, another Welsh overseas missionary enterprise, which began, like the Jewish project, in the 1840s, was to be maintained for well over a century, and was to have lasting consequences. The mission to the Khasia Hills of north east India began in 1840, when the Welsh Calvinistic Methodists, the dominant denomination in Wales at the time, and now known as the Presbyterian Church of Wales, decided that they should no longer allow their missionary efforts to be conducted under the auspices of London-based agencies, but should run their own projects themselves. They decided to concentrate on the Khasia

Hills, which had recently been brought under British control, but were not yet evangelised. Within a year, the first missionary, Thomas Jones, had arrived in India, and, despite unpromising beginnings, the project grew and thrived. By 1866, there were 65 schools and 10 churches; by 1891, the entire Bible had been translated into the Khasi language; by the time of the Welsh religious revival of 1904, converts were counted in the tens of thousands; by 1928, there was a hospital and school of nursing, and by 1941, exactly a hundred years after the beginning of the mission, the local church was self-governing. The last Welsh missionary departed in 1969, leaving behind a people whose culture had been so transformed by the Welsh presence that their language is written with an alphabet based on that of Welsh, and their national anthem is sung to the tune of 'Hen Wlad fy Nhadau'. The history of the mission has been well documented in Nigel Jenkins's extensive 1995 study, *Gwalia in Khasia.*[15]

The Khasia area was not Muslim, but the Welsh missionaries would meet Muslims in neighbouring regions, and on the travels to and through India that were necessary to reach the Khasia hills. The next example of a portrayal of Islam comes from such a journey by one of the stalwarts of the Khasia work in the nineteenth century, John Roberts (1842-1908). Arriving in India in 1871, Roberts threw himself into the missionary enterprise, translating the Old Testament into Khasi, and revising the existing New Testament translation, and also contributing translations of *Pilgrim's Progress* and of no fewer than 73 Welsh hymns.[16] The following extract, quoting Roberts's own letters, comes from R.J. Williams's 1923 biography, *Y Parchedig John Roberts, D.D. Khasia.* It records meetings in Port Said and on the Suez canal:

> When one Mahommetan was in the middle of steering his boat ... the prayer hour came; he turned his face immediately towards Mecca; clapped the palms of his hands together, raised his thumbs to his forehead, or somewhere in the neighbourhood of the bridge of his nose, fell on his knees, and having set aside a patch of the boat and cleaned it, he put his forehead on it first, and then his nose. He did that several times as he murmured something in the way of a prayer. For a while he appeared as if he was taking no notice of anything around him; but, standing near him, was a youth who, one might suppose, did not respect his devotion in the slightest; rather the contrary, who played mischievous tricks around him. Eventually

> Mahomet Ali[17] caught him, and laughed out loud despite himself. However, having taken a little more possession of himself, he carried on as though nothing had happened. This Mahommetan came with us to show us Port Said; so I had the opportunity to look into his character a little; and if many Mahommetans are like him, then many Mahommetans are full of hypocrisy, and yet, there were in this brother some very praiseworthy things.

In Suez a Muslim Arab pilot came on board the ship to sail it from there to Aden. Williams quotes Roberts's comments:

> If I remember rightly he was on the ship for around eight days; but in all that time the spirit of prayer did not fall upon him so much as once, when he should have prayed five times a day. I asked him one day how he could spend so much time without praying, and his answer was, that his clothes were not clean enough, and that he had not had the necessary peace. But for the following days he would have to pray ten times a day until he had made the account up. He had no doubt in his mind that he would get to heaven when he died. He had one wife in Suez, for whom he had paid around £150; and as soon as he could he was going to get another for around the same sum, so that he could have one in Suez and one in Aden. Pity him, his ignorance is deep, and his hypocrisy is inexorable. It needs a very strong faith to believe that the day will come when every Mahometan will confess Christ as Saviour, and will abide in him for eternal life.[18]

Another example comes from the writing of one of the many women missionaries employed by the Welsh Calvinistic Methodists in India, Miss Elizabeth J. Jones. In May 1918 her denomination's journal, *Y Drysorfa*, published her account of her door-to-door evangelisation work below the Khasia Hills in the Sylhet plain, which was another focus of Welsh missionary activity. It is notable that Muslim practices and beliefs are portrayed with a utilitarian interest which extends only as far as is expedient for the purposes of evangelisation.

> As in most of the places on the Plain, there were Hindus and Mahometans living side by side – a family of Hindus here and a family of Mahometans a field away. It was to the Mahometans that I mostly happened to go. As a rule it is harder to make the Mahometans – especially the women – than the Hindus understand what is said to them, as they do not speak Bengali, but rather a mixture of Bengali, Hindustani and Arabic. The men understand, as they come and go and mix with the Hindus. In most of the houses,

> the women left their work and came to listen, the men sitting on one side of the yard, and the women and children on the other. I was amazed that they listened so well. When we went around like this, we would have a good audience at the beginning, who had come from curiosity and to hear the singing, but usually when we started to tell our message, they would go off one by one; but on this occasion most of them stayed until we had finished, and many asked questions at the end. Of course, it is the Doctrines of the Trinity and the Sonship of Jesus Christ that cause most of a stumbling block to the Mahometans, and they are very ready to draw us to argue with them about these subjects. At the beginning, in order to avoid vain assertion, we would try to stress the worth of Jesus Christ as Saviour and Advocate, rather than putting too much emphasis on His Person. The word about the Cross appeals to everyone, and the truth about the Atonement and the Second-Coming of our Lord has a great charm for the Mahometans. There is a great belief among them that 'the Prophet Jesus' as they call the Saviour, is to reappear without delay.[19]

Further literary testimony to the Welsh missionary enterprise in Sylhet comes from Elizabeth M. Lloyd's 1916 book, *Hanes Assam* ('The History of Assam'), which, in the course of an extensive description of Islam, heavily reliant on largely critical quotations from other commentators, has the following assessment of the author's:

> Purity and love are not considered as essential qualities of the Godhead, and the religion possesses no concept of the Atonement as we understand the word. According to Mahometanism, it is impossible for God to suffer; that would be a sign of weakness. It has no place for a deep feeling of hatred for sin. God is responsible for the bad as well as the good; as a result of this sin is not an offence against him. This religion is completely formalistic, devoid of spirituality.[20]

The evangelistic ministry in Sylhet did not meet with the same success as that in the Khasia hills, possibly due to the opposition from Islam which is frequently recorded in the missionaries' accounts. The full story of the enterprise can be found in the 1990 volume *Y Popty Poeth* ('The Hot Furnace') by Dafydd Gwilym Merfyn Jones (1916-98).[21] In 1981 he had published a brief personal diary of his own missionary work in Sylhet in 1943, in which he recalls being invited, on the occasion of the birthday of Muhammad, to address the main festival gathering: 'Not much to say about Mahomed;' he records: 'the prophet isn't one of my heroes! But I had the opportunity to remind the crowd of Mahomed's debt to Christianity.'[22] Jones served as a missionary in the region for 19 years until 1960, through a period of famine and sometimes murderous tension between Muslims and Hindus. He was fluent in four local languages,[23] and was often called upon to mediate in disputes.

It was not only in India and Palestine that Welsh Christians encountered Muslims, but also in Africa. The 1975 novel *Tu Hwnt i'r Mynydd Du* ('Beyond the Black Mountain'), by Urien Wiliam (1929-2006), tells the story of the Reverend David Williams (1856-81), a real-life missionary to Africa who followed the footsteps of David Livingstone but who died suddenly soon after beginning his career. The novel contains extracts from Williams's genuine correspondence, interspersed, for narrative purposes, with a larger number of imagined pieces, which are, nonetheless, very much in the spirit and style of the real-life letters. From the imagined letters comes the following condemnation of Islam for its failure to challenge the slave trade in Zanzibar:

> It is said one can buy a child here for a pound or two and sell him in Persia for twenty! Where is the voice of the Church and Civilisation to put an end to such a diabolical work? If anyone should doubt the need to bring the Gospel of Jesus Christ to Africa a single glance at the misery of these slaves would quieten any uncertainty. Oh! if only Wales and England and the whole world were burning to put an end to such an abominable trade! Most of the population are Moslems, and the spires of the minarets can be seen high above the dwelling huts; it is obvious this religion has nothing to say against slavery as the greatest part of that filthy commerce goes to the Arab lands, which are the strongholds of that chilly faith.[24]

Although, a few pages later, Williams is shown praising Arab traditions of hospitality, the picture of Islam in this imagined encounter is overwhelmingly dismissive, and as such accords with the indignation at perceived Muslim complicity in the slave trade which was a common attitude of British missionaries to Africa, as can be seen later in Chapter 10 when Henry Morton Stanley, another who followed in Livingstone's footsteps, gives his own pungent views on Islam.

One of the catchphrases of modern geopolitics is the concept of the ability to 'project power'. Looking at the literary output of the Welsh Christian church, it is striking the degree to which this small corner of Britain was able to send so many people so far and so often, and not by the necessities of emigration forced by poverty, but by choice. Wales may have been only a junior partner in the British Empire, but even so, compared with the colonised countries of that empire, many of its citizens were comparatively privileged and powerful, and desirous of, and capable of, projecting that power worldwide.

Certain socialist and nationalist streams in Welsh historiography have emphasised the comparative disadvantage of Wales relative to England in a wide range of areas, stressing how Wales was exploited economically by an essentially extractive capitalist system, oppressed linguistically by a hostile centralist state, and discriminated against by an Anglican establishment which held the rights of religious Nonconformists in scant regard. While all those perceptions undoubtedly have their basis in fact, the collective impact of the emotional stories, memories and cultural representations arising from those situations of injustice can sometimes create an impression of universal disenfranchisement which can obscure the fact that, during the same period in which those iniquities took place, Wales was actually, in world terms, a highly-developed, advanced and privileged society: literate, cultured, industrialised, and able to take advantages of the opportunities of empire. Enough Welsh people had sufficient disposable income to be able to afford to send missionaries abroad in large numbers, and individual Welsh Christians could afford to travel to the Middle East for their own spiritual edification and that of their co-religionists back home. The prominent Calvinistic Methodist, Sir Henry Lewis (1847-1923), lectured so often on his travels in the Holy Land that he was known as 'Thomas Palestina Lewis'[25] The sheer number of pilgrims' guides published for Welsh Christians is a testimony to the ready market for such material, and to the fact that at least some of the readers were assumed to be financially capable of making the trip. The content of the guides, meanwhile, shows that this indubitably colonised people also often knew just how to think and behave like colonists.

For example, in 1894 we find the prominent poet and Calvinistic Methodist minister Evan Rees (1850-1923) – the editor of *Y Drysorfa* at the time that Elizabeth J. Jones's article, mentioned above, was published – visiting the Holy Land, and publishing his experiences in *Gwlad yr Addewid* ('The Promised Land,'). Rees, known by his bardic name 'Dyfed', travelled extensively in Europe, Asia, South Africa and North America. He was Archdruid of Wales for the last 21 years of his life, and a National Eisteddfod adjudicator for the last 40.[26] In *Gwlad yr Addewid*, we find him using his critical faculties to interpret his experience of Islam. He describes the Arabs, 'one of the most remarkable nations under the sun', as proud but ignorant:

> While the world is in ferment, developing itself in knowledge, and perfecting itself in every branch of the arts, the Arab is stationary, and has set a kind of circle of prohibition around himself that no-one dares break through.
>
> . . .
>
> He has been described as a wild ass, and he's like enough to one not only in his wildness, but also in his inflexible stubbornness. His hand is against everyone, and everyone's hand is against him; and no matter how many attacks have been upon him, all the powers of the earth so far have failed to subdue him. He is of honourable lineage, but is fated to be a wanderer; and he feels that labour is a punishment to him. He looks on robbery as a duty, and begging is not shameful to him. In fact, begging and theft are the only two crafts he depends on, and he is unconscious of his own wretchedness because he is so ignorant of higher stations.
>
> . . .
>
> Although the land is fruitful, the most fruitless men dwell upon it, and the most leprous chieftain governs them. It is a pity to think that such darkness lies on the land, where the Light of the world once shone from within in his divine radiance.

Dyfed goes on to express amazement and indignation at the begging and poverty which he sees as shameless and endemic. He sees Islam as part of the problem:

> What is so dreadful is that there is nothing in the government of the country, nor in its religion, that can raise the people out of these depths.[27]

The Turkish rulers of Palestine come in for equally scathing criticism, although their perceived vices are different. In the next passage, Dyfed is in Jerusalem, contemplating the hill of Moriah, where the Temple Mount is situated.

> This is a hill on which it could be said literally that God had dwelt; but the king of Moriah today is the false prophet Mahomed. A Mahometan temple is on the ruins of the temple of the living God. Mahometan precincts, forbidden to the Levites, are around it, and the Castle of Antonia is a massive camp for Turkish soldiers. The present building stands undoubtedly on the site of the former temple, and the two courts, as they are, give a completely clear idea of the form and situation of the old ones that were erected according to the divine design. The place is regarded as more sacred and more sanctified than heaven itself, and it is death to anyone to tread upon the hill without permission. We had to consult with the Government before going in, and care was taken to send a Turkish soldier, fully armed, so keep us serious and to look after us. If he was an example of Turkish soldiery, then heaven forever and for eternity have mercy on such an apparition. He was no more than a suit of clothes, a pair of boots, a bent sword, and a red hat on top of the lot. He was too weak to cough without leaning heavily on his sword. Pity him! his spirit was clearly visible through his blue coat.
>
> In the portal of the temple we had to wear sanctified sandals, because the place is too sacred for the feet of the pagans; and unfortunately, I was given one of each pair, so, by the time I had reached the centre of the temple, I had lost one, and the hard sole of my shoe was defiling the place. In a moment it became a ruckus; and in the middle of a storm of screaming, I had to stand on one leg, frightened, in the middle of the temple, until a scrap of sanctity could be found to put under my horseshoe again. They are so jealous of the glory of the place that they would not care about stabbing a man to death for such a flagrant offence.[28]

Dyfed goes on to describe 'the present Mahometan temple', which he says is 'very splendid'. But he regrets the departure of the splendour of the old Jewish temple, and describes the present place of worship as that of 'the false prophet'. He says the stones of the old temple would weep to see 'false prophets repeating old legends of which a child of twelve in Wales would be ashamed. Such an extreme transformation on Moriah is enough to make a heart of marble break.' He says how this mountain is, for the Jews, a site of mourning for their lost glories, and, for the Christians, a place to contemplate the forgiving grace of God. But, as for the Muslims, he continues:

> To add to the Biblical connections of Moriah, and especially to the rock in the centre of the hill, the Mahometans have sown the most romantic legends. They say that from this cliff Mahomed ascended

> to heaven, and that the rock sprang up to follow him, only that some angel had put its hand on the rock to keep it down, and they show the handprints of the angel visible in the rock to this day. That's how they account for the cave underneath. They insist that the rock was stopped in its journey in the place where the angel touched it, leaving an empty space behind it. In the middle of this cave is an old closed-up pit, in which they say departed souls collect and from which they will be dragged out one day by their hair. Heaven help the bald ones, they'll be there for ever! It would give too much of tribute to folly to recite all the laughable legends that are given as gospel in the present temple.
>
> There is one other building on the hill, of a different design, and its form suggests that it was once a Christian church. A pity it ever fell into the hands of Antichrist. Among many interior decorations, there was once a host of intricate and artistic Christian symbols, worked into the walls all the way round, but they have all now been carefully chiselled away by the Mahometans. These cannot bear even the shape of a cross, nor any other Christian symbol, even if it had been worked in fine gold. No doubt the name of Jesus has been honoured and worshipped in this place; but it has been driven out centuries ago to make way for the most insane superstitions. It is an insult to the saints to show them Moses's prayer room on Moriah, when they have long learned that he was never in the land. I never felt more of a spirit of mischief than when we were shown the narrow gate to paradise. There are two old columns next to one another, and it would be very difficult to push between them. But everyone who is of the faith of Mahomed has to try to push through this gap. It appears that to succeed is a guarantee of salvation. There you see pilgrims pushing until they are out of breath, believing that paradise depends on the sum of clay that is upon them. As long as the man is no more than a spirit in a shirt he will succeed; but if he is possessed of a normal man's physique, it will look pretty grim for him, and he will take himself aside to grieve for the tragic misfortune of being fat. Blessed are the thin ones there, for to such alone is the kingdom of heaven. The Mahometans have heard that Christ at his second coming will take possession of the city, and that it is through the Beautiful Gate that he will enter. Therefore, they have blocked up that gate with stones, in order to make such a catastrophe impossible! O! Moriah! When shall thy glory return![29]

Elsewhere in the same volume, Dyfed has a poem 'Y Bedouin Arab', a long nine-stanza lyric depicting the desert nomads in largely negative terms as stubborn, hostile and deceitful:

> To wander, wander, is his doom,

to cheat, to cheat is all his mind;
without conscience is his bosom
and without labour all his kind;
his only heaven is deception.
such his life and such his way,
and for him to change direction
you may wait 'til judgement day.[30]

Later in the poem he says that the desert Arab has never awakened to learning: 'The superstitions of the wilderness / are a thick layer around him.' Although Dyfed praises Arab tenacity, endurance, courage and appearance, the piece is nonetheless an extended exercise in racial stereotyping, and while its prejudice is primarily racial rather than religious, as with the prose depiction of the Arab earlier, Islam is included within the poem's disapprobation. The same is true of Dyfed's poem, 'The Dragoman', depicting an Arab interpreter and guide in Egypt and published in the second volume of Dyfed's poetical works, *Gwaith Barddonol Dyfed*, in 1907.[31] It is given below in Alfred Perceval Graves's translation from *Welsh Poetry Old and New* (1912):

Of yellow face, heart black as burnt out brand,
Yet in his own esteem the brag o' man,
Dogging Time's footprints faint through desert sand,
While dogging ours, on stalks the dragoman.
About us like a phantom how he'll flit
Barefaced and barefoot under burning skies,
The Pharaohs' centuried crime and craft have lit
The fires of hell within his ugly eyes.

His memory is one jungle of tradition,
Wild tale on tale inextricably met;
He learned his land's most fatuous superstition
Before he knew its very alphabet.
Yet at his heart believes the world so blind,
'Tis fain submissive at his feet to sit,
And win all knowledge from his evil mind
Who could not read the simplest book e'er writ.

At cross road corners he is never missed,
His one pursuit to plague all passers by;
A cosmopolitan colloquialist,
In each and every tongue well skilled to lie.

On falsehood and deceit he so has thriven,
He counts himself as sacred in God's sight.
Is there enough of saving grace in Heaven
To wash the dragoman's black conscience white?[32]

Throughout the items collected in this study, it will be seen that it is aggressive begging and perceived petty deception by Muslims rather than any errors of doctrine that elicit the most vitriolic condemnation by the Welsh commentators. It seems that bad theology may be forgiven, but not bad manners. The memoirs of travellers to Egypt abound with accounts of indignation at the activities of beggars. The next extract is an example.

D. Rhagfyr Jones, of Treorchy in the Rhondda, a contemporary of Dyfed's and a fellow Nonconformist Christian minister, albeit of the Independent denomination, published his account of his visit to Egypt 1904 under the title *I'r Aifft acYn Ôl*, ('To Egypt and Back').[33] Egypt, which had been effectively a British protectorate since the last quarter of the nineteenth century, was a regular destination on the itinerary of Welsh travellers to the Middle East. Jones's book is written in idiomatic and colloquial style, with elements of dialect form. There is no doubt that the author could write with gusto and humour. But he could also write with sweeping arrogance, and his portrayals of Arabs particularly rank among the most pungent pieces of racial stereotyping found in Welsh literature. He gives an account of a journey with a Welsh friend and two Egyptian guides into the bazaar in Cairo and later to a mosque, which he refers to as 'one of the main churches of the Mahometans'. He portrays a visit to a Muslim 'church', where he finds thousands of men engaged in study of the *Qur'an* outside in the heat of midday. He is piqued by their refusal to move for his party, and he is later rebuked for joking loudly when passing through their study room. En route, recounting the mixture of races that are to be found in the bazaar, he comments that 'there is no difference between Jew and Greek', deliberately inverting the egalitarian message of the quotation from Saint Paul in order to suggest that both Jews and Greeks are equally deceitful.[34] And he describes a 'negro from the interior' in startlingly prejudicial terms: 'with more of the animal to them than anything else.'[35]

But it is the Muslims who come in for most criticism: 'It is not a sin for a Mahometan to cheat a man of a different religion in word and deed;' he says, and then adds; 'I'm not sure if it isn't counted a great virtue.' And in his description of the different races to be found on the street in Alexandria, he expends his descriptive abilities primarily on an Arab sheikh, and then, witheringly, on an Arab beggar:

> Here's the chief of some Arab tribe passing by, either in deep contemplation with his head on his chest, or in defiant spirit, with his nose in the air. As a rule the sheikh is a great lump of a man; tall, broad-shouldered, handsome, well-built, supple and strong; his skin black as pitch, his nose long and straight, his eyes small, dark and restless, as though seeking for enemies on every side, his lips thin, his nostrils narrow, his beard black and short, and his head long and narrow. He spits as he passes every European, and you can hear him mutter curses on your head as he goes past. If he and his tribe had their way, every dog of a Christian would be swept out of the region in no time. That's the real Arab type for you – strong, sly, cruel, superstitious.[36]
>
> . . .
>
> Ach! What's this thing bowing before me, and where did it come from? It looks like a pile of filthy laundry, or a pile of rags ready for burning. Here's an arm and a hand stretching out from under the rags towards me, and Oh! they're scarcely skin and bone at the best. A skeletal face stares at me from under an abominable head-dress, and two bright lamps burn in his eye sockets. I'm hardly afraid of him, and even less do I want him. I understand now that he's one of the country's beggars, in his groan and his gloom, and it was easier for Paul to shake off the viper from his arm than for me to get rid of this filth. In the east, the beggars are a characteristic class, and they're a plague and a pain to the visitor. They stick to you like a leech. To try to give some direction to his steps, I gave him a penny, but instead of going away, the old sinner still stretched out his hand, murmuring between his teeth and asking for more, like Oliver Twist. It was apparent he had made up his mind that I was an easy bird to pluck, and I was wary of his vulturish claws in case they went about the work for real. But I had swift proof that Providence cares for its children, one of the office men came out just as things were starting to wear a serious aspect – and as he saw how things stood, he drove the ugly and filthy beggar away with the quickest torrent of words I've ever heard. You wouldn't believe how quickly the creature gathered his things together and removed his unclean presence from the neighbourhood. Needless to say, he poured a flood of curses on

> my helper's head, and forgot to thank me for the penny he had received.[37]

That the animus here has a strong religious component can be seen by Jones's conclusion to his book. After praising British imperialism as a civilising influence, and taking his leave of Egyptian civilisation, he says:

> But what is civilisation without CHRISTIANITY? A whitewashed sepulchre, whose inside is full of filth and corruption – beautiful ornaments on a corpse – a cauldron painted, but death living within it. Without Christianity, no civilisation can save people, nation or country. Where now is Rome and its strength? Where now is Carthage, its rival in authority? Where is Greece, and its sculpture, its rhetoric and its philosophy? The most civilised countries on which the light of God ever shone, where are they now? Their civilisation did not save them, and their genius did not keep them alive. Thank God for civilisation, but thanks even more for CHRISTIANITY.[38]

While the Reverend D. Rhagfyr Jones was travelling in Egypt, yet another Welsh Nonconformist minister was touring the Holy Land The Reverend Thomas E. Roberts, of Aberystwyth published his travel guide, *Jerusalem: Y Ddinas Sanctaidd* ('Jerusalem the Holy City'),[39] in 1904. Unlike Jones's book, it does not rely on anecdote or the parade of personal opinion for its effect. Rather, it is a scholarly attempt to portray the history of Palestine with a view to instructing readers, primarily in Sunday schools. As the foreword puts it: 'It is a small country, and it would not be too much for every Welshman to be as well-versed in it as in the geography of his own country.' As will be seen in Chapter 6, dealing with the First World War, this ambition to create identification and familiarity with Palestine was to be greatly influential in creating British support for Zionism.

It is notable that the view of Palestine presented in books of this kind was selective. The vision is determinedly Judaeo-Christian, and the Muslim-majority Arab culture of the land is regarded largely as a mere background to the main drama in which the hope for the restoration of the Jewish people is bound up with the Christian narrative of Crucifixion and the hope for the Second Coming. With such cosmic events in prospect, the existing main religious culture of the country was, in the eyes of

Western Christian visitors, at best marginalised.

Roberts describes the essentials of the Islamic faith and practices in some detail, and without obvious distortion, and while his assessment of Muhammad's achievement is sceptical: '...the prophet made that religion a combination of every religion, true and false, that he knew about,' the description 'false prophet' has at least by now been put by Roberts in inverted commas. He goes on to describe Muslim society in Jerusalem:

> The city has been in the possession of the followers of the 'false prophet' for six centuries, and the results of this occupation are truly dreadful. Not only do they bring about no improvements and changes, but they insist on letting everything collapse and decay. The present Mahometans of the city number about seven to eight thousand, and of those there are no more than three hundred Turks. There are 700 soldiers there, and it is compulsory for every soldier in the land to be a Mahometan in full sympathy with the Turkish Power and the Mahometan Religion.[40]

While Muslim theology holds little attraction for Roberts, and while he notes that persecution of Christians is never far from the surface in the 'corrupt' Ottoman empire, he is much more conciliatory about the piety of individual Muslims:

> They are a very religious people... It is worth noting with what care and faithfulness they turn from any activity to obey the Muezzin's call to prayer. They do this wherever they are – in the house, in the shop, on the road and in the field. They do that no matter who is in their company or what work they may have in hand. Immediately, they wash and kneel on the Turkish carpet, if there is one to hand... I wouldn't dare say they do this other than with every sincerity, and watching them we should be filled with the desire to be much more faithful to our God and Saviour than we are.[41]

Roberts maintained an interest in the Holy Land for decades. Thirty years after *Jerusalem: Y Ddinas Sanctaidd*, he published *Palesteina Hen a Newydd* ('Palestine Old and New'),[42] a more extensive and more considered assessment of the state of the various religions in Palestine, written during the British Mandate period. Its portrayal of Islam is considerably more positive than in the author's previous volume. Special praise is accorded to Muslim Arab hospitality: '...giving lodging to a stranger on his journey is considered a matter of duty and honour. After such a one has been accepted into a house or a tent, and has eaten salt with the family, they and he will enter into such a covenant relationship – the traditional covenant of salt that Scripture talks about – that they would be ready out of loyalty to one another to lose their lives to defend one another.'[43]

Muslim faithfulness to the five pillars of Islam is commended too. Roberts enumerates the dangers facing pilgrims going to Mecca, and, noting that a third of them will not survive due to the hardships of the journey, he comments:

> It is wonderful to see the zeal of these people towards the dust of their leader in the earth of Mecca, compared with the indifference of we Christians to our living redeemer who left an empty grave behind him on the earth.[44]

Elsewhere he says he finds the flagellation and trances of the Muslim dervishes far from the kind of holiness commended in the New Testament,[45] but he approves strongly of Islamic ritual cleanliness and almsgiving, and the way in which Islam permeates the believer's daily life: 'One could fairly say this of the Mohammetans, that they do not confine their worship to the buildings, but rather that they are alive to the obligation to worship wherever they are when the time and the sign comes for them to do so.'[46]

A common pattern of pilgrim response to Muslim presence in Palestine is to be wary or disapproving of Islamic theology, and of Muslim control of the Temple Mount, while being considerably more positive about the devotion of individual Muslims. In such accounts, the Muslim collective is generally threatening, but the Muslim individual can often be reassuring. Elements of this can be seen in the work of Eluned Morgan (1870-1938) who visited Palestine in the early years of the century. Morgan was the daughter of Lewis Jones, founder of the Welsh colony in Patagonia, the man after whom the town of Trelew in Argentina is named. Born at sea en route to the colony, she was raised in Argentina, and spent many years living alternately in Wales and Patagonia before finally settling in Argentina. She was an adventurous and independent woman, a Christian of deep religious convictions, and a writer with a lively prose style. Best known for her evocative books about Welsh Patagonia, she also published an account of a visit to the Middle East, first in the magazine *Cymru* and then, in book form in 1913 under the title *Ar Dir a Môr* ('On Land and Sea').[47]

As with the previous accounts, the Christian visitor regrets seeing the Temple Mount under Muslim control:

> We spent one morning in the courts of the Temple, at Moriah Hill, which has a Mahometan mosque built on it, more's the pity. The old historic mountain looks pretty uncomfortable in the middle of such splendour and riches. All the same, as a structure, the Mosque of Omar, or, more correctly, the Dome of the Rock, is a miracle of intricacy and beauty: its walls shine with priceless gems, and the hundreds of lanterns which hang from its ceiling are of fine, polished gold, and it all looks like a child's dream of a Fairy palace; but, despite all that, it is a sight that saddens the thoughtful heart, and the mind cannot help but travel back to the time of the true Temple which was established by the wise and the good, and which was the chief beauty and pride of a chosen people, but which lost all its glory because the people lost their best ideals and chose the false instead of the true.[48]

Elsewhere, she describes the Arab inhabitants of the land as 'ignorant and superstitious'[49] as a result of the 'darkness which has overshadowed the land for so many years'. However, other Muslims whom Morgan meets on her travels are portrayed positively. In the next extract, she is sailing in to Joppa from Cairo:

> What if you could see the boatmen! Talk about the giants of Patagonia: they would only be feeble compared to the Arabs of Joppa. Rarely, I suspect, does one see humanity so gigantic and so powerful; and their noise and chatter corresponds to their size, and the look of them is so wild and lawless that it frightens fearful travellers; and seeing the boats being tossed like shells simply adds to the terror. But I was determined to get to Jerusalem, and this was the only way. So we ventured, perfectly silent, with our life in our hands. But fair play to the giant Arabs: they understood their work thoroughly, and watched every mountainous wave that came towards us, riding on its crest until we drew closer and closer to land; and they kept perfect time with their oars by singing together a psalm to *Allah*, and asking him to bring them safely to shore. Personally, I gloried in the splendour of the scene, and felt as much at home as a seagull on the breast of the deep.[50]

Coming to the work of more modern writers, we find the important Welsh-language poet David James Jones (1899-1969), known as 'Gwenallt', writing in his 1969 book *Y Coed* ('The Trees') about his experiences on a pilgrimage to Israel and Palestine in 1961. He shows deep empathy with the plight of dispossessed Arabs, as well as with the mindset of Jewish people seeking security from persecution. The following poem – by no means one of Gwenallt's better pieces – is about a visit to Jerusalem's Al Aqsa mosque:

Mosg Al-Agsa

Standing in front of the Mosque and listening to the muezzin from
the minaret,
Calling through the cup of his hands on the faithful
To leave their work and pray
(And he calls five times a day).
They say the meaning of his rhythmic call is:
'Great is God. I declare that there is no god but God.
I declare that Mohammed is the Apostle of God.
Come to prayer. Come to do good.
God is great. There is no god but God.'
Before going into the Mosque, shoes had to be removed,
And we did not fancy the dirty slippers at the door,
So I went inside in my stockinged feet along the Persian carpets
On the floor; carpets into which you sank.
The Arabic architecture was strange to me.
Above there was a costly ceiling given by King
Faroukh of Egypt; and beneath it there were windows
Letting clear light onto the central aisle,
An aisle between the marble pillars and the rose-coloured limestone,
And on the front of the aisle was an old intricate mosaic.
Apart from the old cedar pulpit at the front
There was no altar or image or Big Seat[51] or pews
So that the Mosque was light and bright and clear and open.
In the front end of the Mosque was a *mihrab* facing Mecca,
And in front of it worshippers knelt,
And bent until their foreheads were on the floor;
After the prayer they raised their hands to shoulder height
With their palms up to heaven,
And then drew their hands across their face
And across their chest so that the blessing of Allah
Can penetrate to every part of their body
The Mosque was too strange for me to worship and pray in.

But as an author I blessed the Arabs
For preserving the Greek classics in their language,
And transmitting them through their universities in Spain
To the Europe of the Middle Ages.[52]

Gwenallt's description of the place of worship and the devotions is faithful enough, but it is notable how his approval is granted according to Western criteria, with the Arabs commended due to their utility to the project of European enlightenment.[53]

Elsewhere in *Y Coed*, there are poems which touch on Islamic subjects. 'Dau Wareiddiad' ('Two Civilisations') depicts the mixture of modes of transport in the Old City, which include Arabs in expensive cars and others with mules and camels. The mention of the latter animal leads Gwenallt to reflect: 'According to the Moslem, his god, Allah, has twenty names, / But only the camel knows the twentieth. / And behold the old knowledgeable camel gazing from above scornfully / At the materialistic world of the West snarling by with horns blowing.'[54]

And in the poem 'Gabriel', given in full below, Gwenallt gives a rare depiction of a Muslim Arab convert to Christianity. The geography of this poem reflects the political boundaries prior to the Six Day War, when the West Bank was still Jordanian territory.

Not the Archangel, but our guide in Jordan,
Although, perhaps, he had been named after the Archangel
As he has an important place in the Qur'an.[55]
One afternoon he took us to the top of the Mount of Olives,
And showed us near the Church of the Ascension
The Israeli Jerusalem, and pointed at a row of houses,
And one of them was his former home,
A home he and his wife and children had been forced to
Flee, and leave everything to the enemy;
And he did not have a penny of compensation.

There must have been hatred in his heart towards the Jew,
And hatred towards Britain and America,
Like the hatred of the host of refugees we saw in Jericho,
In Bethany and next to our hotel in Old Jerusalem,
Refugees who live in tents, huts and caves,
And we had never seen such poverty:
Creatures refusing to do a scrap of work,
But living in bitter indignation on the ration card

> Of the United Nations: all they wanted was to return to their homes,
> And no-one loves home, family and tribe
> More than the Arab.
> Gabriel had to look for work to support his family
> In Bethlehem, as he could not afford to live in Jerusalem;
> And he thought he would like to be a tour guide in his own country,
> Tour-parties of British and Americans:
> So he went to it diligently to learn English,
> And to study the Bible carefully, and learn passages from it by heart;
> And it was the New Testament that turned him from Mohammed
> To the Lord Jesus Christ.
> There was no hatred in his heart when he referred to the Jews,
> And it would not have been wise to show his hatred of Britain and America:
> And perhaps this stocky, courteous Arab
> Had conquered his hatred through the power of the divine Refugee
> Who sweated affliction through his skin on the Mount of Olives.[56]

The poem seems straightforward enough. However, there are some subtleties to decode. The 'perhaps' is intriguing: Gwenallt is attributing to the convert a virtue, forgiveness, that he believes must be a result of his Christianity. However, Gabriel's hatred – again an attributed quality rather than a proven behaviour – is strongly associated with his Arab identity. If Gabriel hates, it must be as a Muslim-background Arab; if he forgives, it must be as a Christian. Even in a poem as sensitive to the plight of Palestinian Arabs as Gwenallt's, the privileging of Christian perspectives is active.

Another Welsh Christian visitor to Israel prior to the Six Day War was the Anglican clergyman Gareth Lloyd Jones, at the time a student of Hebrew and Judaism, and later head of the department of theology at Bangor University. His 1966 book *Yng Ngwlad yr Addewid* ('In the Promised Land') while naturally focusing on Jewish material, has the following observations, prompted by the muezzin's 'mournful' call to prayer.

> I wonder at the strength of Islam, the Arab religion. The word itself means 'submission'. And that is exactly what the Arab does before his god, namely to accept his will entirely without protest. If there is unemployment in his land, that is the will of Allah. What point, then, trying to reduce it? This is the religion of lands from Gibraltar to India and although those lands are often not united on burning issues, they are united in their worship of Allah. Some believe that

> Islam, and it alone, can in the long run unite the lands of the Middle East. If this is true, should not the nations of the world take note of it?[57]

Further explicitly political attitudes to the Israeli-Arab conflict will be explored in Chapter 9, but as the present chapter is concerned with the particular focus produced by pilgrimages and missionary work, we will move on to another pilgrim from the 1960s. William Emlyn Jones visited the sites of the churches of Asia Minor, and published his account, *Y Saith Ganhwyllbren Aur* ('The Seven Golden Candlesticks') in 1969.[58] Although Jones's quest is for traces of the churches mentioned in the Book of Revelation, he must face the reality that Christianity in the region has been supplanted by Islam. In the following passage, he visits the Selimye Mosque in the city of Edirne. He describes the building in detail and then says:

> It was lovely to sit in the quiet of the mosque, in the middle of such a riot of colours, and to listen to an old moslem brother[59] going through his prayers devotedly, at length and with plenty of fervour, if not of freshness.[60]

However, Jones finds the rest of the town disappointing and suggests: 'As a health official I came to the definite conclusion that only one thing could be done to this town, which is to leave the beautiful mosques and raze the rest of it to the ground and build a new town suitable for people to live in.' Later, he contemplates the culture of female modesty pertaining particularly in rural districts: 'Even though the traditional *yashmaks* have disappeared, the custom of hiding the face in the presence of men is still strong among the women. Not lightly does one forget the subordination of centuries in the *harem*.'

In Bergamo, Jones gets a sense of the degree to which Christianity has been replaced by Islam, although the impression he gets of Islam is that it is declining too, albeit for different reasons:

> When I asked what was the religious situation, I found out that there were eleven mosques here, but not a single Christian church, no-one bearing his name but everyone having denied their faith, and Antipas,[61] to all appearances, having been martyred in vain. Apparently the majority of people attend mosque on Friday, and the

> old people go there five times a day. I had heard this said before by people in Turkey, but I was given to understand as well that faithfulness to the mosque is quickly weakening. The boys testified that this was true, and they confessed as well that the young were not particularly faithful... In every mosque I had been in this time there was no need for a Muezzin to declare the prayer hour from the minaret, and there was a machine inside every mosque to broadcast a recording of the Muezzin's voice. Somehow I felt that this mechanisation robbed the soul from the act of calling the faithful to their spiritual duties.[62]

Asia Minor and its seven churches of the Book of Revelation were also the destination for another Welsh visitor, the minister and television presenter, Robin Williams[63] (1923-2003), whose *Herald Cymraeg* article on Muhammad Ali was mentioned in Chapter 3. Williams's 1986 book *Hoelion Wyth* ('The Eight-Inch Nails'), records his time spent in Turkey making a programme some three years earlier. Williams too gains the impression that adherence to Islam is in decline. Visiting Izmir, the Biblical Smyrna, and the location of one of the seven churches, he partakes of the holy atmosphere by reading from his Welsh Bible at the altar of St Polycarp's church. Then in company with his Turkish guide, Mehmet, the following morning, he has his first experience of Islam:

> It was an amazing experience too to be awoken early in the morning in the Hotel Karaca by the *muezzin* from the nearby minaret calling the faithful to the mosque to acknowledge Allah. I learned from Mehmet that the call happens five times every day, although he suggested that the response of many was by now pretty lame, adding that he himself was little better than 'a Mahommetan on paper'.[64]

A little later, Mehmet invites Williams to a ceremony to commemorate Kurban Bayrami, the Turkish name for the Eid al-Adha festival, in which a sheep will be sacrificed. The experience is the occasion for an extended and heartfelt meditation on justice, evil, sacrifice and faith which draws unselfconsciously on the traditions of all three Abrahamic religions. It begins when Williams asks Mehmet the reason behind the sacrifice:

> 'A very long time ago, the Got ... he ask Ivraim to sacrifice ... I think it was his daughter ... or maybe it was his son ... I am not sure –'

> 'Was it Isaac, the son of Ivraim / Abraham?' I ventured to ask.
>
> My question caused the eyes and jaws of Mehmet to open in surprise. Then an admiring smile spread across his yellow face, and he said, incredulously:
>
> 'You know? You *know* the story, yes?'
>
> I explained to him my background in Biblical education in Wales, suggesting at the same time that the influence of Judaism on Mohammetanism was quite strong.[65]

Williams attends the sacrifice: 'Were we not going to see the primitive drama of the first book of the Bible enacted before our eyes?' He describes the 'beautiful white sheep' which is the intended victim, listens to the slaughterers tell the sheep it is being offered to Allah, and wonders at the godlike power of life and death being exercised:

> As I stared inertly right into the eyes of those kind yellow eyes, the words of Isaiah became frighteningly meaningful: 'as a lamb that is led to the slaughter, and as a sheep before its shearers is dumb so he openeth not his mouth.'
>
> The left hand of the butcher was feeling gently below the sheep's chin, but then suddenly his knife split the throat wide open, and we saw the poor creature's blood flowing into the pit of the earth. And that is when I felt the terrible passion of that phrase, yet again from Isaiah: '...because he hath poured out his soul unto death.'
>
> I rose, shaken, from my crouched position, and walked over to Dinsher and Mehmet, and asked them how many sheep had been sacrificed that morning in Turkey. When Mehmet answered 'two million', I knew that my eyes were filling pools, and for a moment or two I could not speak a word. Because he had no language, the kind Dinsher [Dinsher Hazirol, the crew's Turkish colleague] held me, to strengthen me, I suppose.
>
> Remembering presently that I was a man visiting a foreign country, it was only fair for me to accept that this was their way of religion. And lest I should become in the slightest way self-righteous, I expressed to them my own inconsistency: that I did not, on the one hand, like to see an animal killed in cold blood, yet I was, on the other hand, fairly likely to eat mutton that very day.
>
> And it was somehow with raised eyebrows, headshaking, and half-smiles that the three of us acknowledged the weight of confusion that is in our own human nature.
>
> To this day, my mind insists on slipping back to Kemal's garden in Güzel Batshe. What on earth had that sheep done to anyone that it should deserve such an end? What god had willed that? Is it not

> the god, or the man – and not the animal – that is the beast all the time? Is it not the most innocent who have suffered in every age?[66]

A later essay 'Cusan Sanctaidd' ('A Holy Kiss') shows the intensity of Williams's experience of Turkey, as he recounts the way Dinsher Hazirol took leave of him at the airport at the end of the filming trip, unexpectedly kissing him on both cheeks and showing his affection '...with the strong embrace of the East and not with the limp, arm's-length handshake of the West'. He adds:

> What was painful, however, was the realisation that it wasn't so much a greeting that had taken place between Dinsher Hazirol and myself on the morning of our departure, as a farewell. And a farewell for ever. But for long as I live, I shall never forget that holy kiss on the airfield of Izmir.[67]

Robin Williams's writings on Turkey, which begin with cultural externals but which quickly progress to theological questions and to warm involvement, represent some of the most engaged pieces of writing by any Welsh Christian pilgrim to Muslim lands.

Theological reflections rather than the superficial questions of diet, costume or festivals, were also what drew the attention of the philosopher and theologian Hywel David Lewis (1910-92), when he met the Indian Muslim scholar Dr Syed Vahiduddin (1909-98) while visiting India for a theological conference. Both Lewis and Vahiduddin were prominent international figures. Lewis, born in Llandudno and educated in Bangor and Oxford, was Professor of History and Philosophy of Religion at King's College in the University of London. He became a Fellow of King's College in 1963. Vahiduddin was a philosopher and author of several influential books, as well as a well-known piece of Muslim devotional writing known as 'A Muslim's Prayer', a copy of which he gave to Lewis. In his 1971 book *Hen a Newydd* ('Old and New'), an account of his visit to India, Lewis gives Vahiduddin's prayer in full, as it had appeared in the *Islamic Review*. The following is the concluding paragraph:

> Blessed is he who has surrendered his all unto Thee and who has won his peace in Thy Pleasure. May my tears in constant remembrance of Thee sustain the heart and bring deliverance! Bless me

> with the fullness of life on earth and when the time comes make me return unto Thee united in the fellowship of Thy Loving ones, Lord! Grant me above all, I pray, the vision of Thy Countenance that Thou hast promised for those who are Thine.[68]

Lewis remarks: 'In these longings the Muslim and the Christian are not very far from one another, even though it is very difficult to find a place for the final uniqueness of Jesus Christ within the prospects of traditional Islam. The official belief is that the Koran includes all things which are essential for religion, and that it is the standard by which what has gone before is measured, It does not countenance any kind of incarnation.'[69]

The admiration of the Welsh theologian for his Muslim counterpart is evident. He mentions how he had been pleasantly surprised at Vahiduddin's liberalism, and by his desire that the *Qur'an* should be subjected to the same kind of higher criticism that had been operating in Biblical studies since the mid seventeenth century, and his wish that Islam would unbend accordingly. Lewis continues:

> However, it was not just about religion that Vahiduddin spoke with me, but about many other aspects of modern culture and education including our distaste for the lack of intellectual daring that kept the talented thinkers of today in the constrained ruts of their linguistic dogmatism. My friend's laughter was a delight to me, especially when he started laughing, in his chest as it were, at himself, something not unlike Gwili's[70] laughter years ago.[71]

Working in the second half of the twentieth century, Hywel D. Lewis was writing at time when religious observance in Wales had been in steady decline for over half a century ever since the tide of evangelical Protestantism had reached its high water mark in the religious revival of 1904. That decline was to continue, and to accelerate during the last decades of the century and into the third millennium. At the start of the century, Wales had been a centre of Christian fervour, sending missionaries around the globe. A hundred years later, it is the most secular nation of the United Kingdom, with regular monthly church attendance a mere 12 per cent of the population – around 360,000 people out of just under three million.[72] However, even in a society in which Christianity has experienced such a rapid reduction in influence and adherence, and where mission-oriented evangelicals now comprise only a small section of the total number of church members, some Welsh churches occasionally still have sufficient vigour to support missionary endeavours, even if, numerically, the activity is only a shadow of what had taken place in the past.

One example of an encounter with a Welsh missionary in a Muslim country is recorded by Stephen Griffith in his 1986 book, *Teithio'r Sahel*, ('Travelling the Sahel'), an account of a famine in Burkina Faso in west Africa, which he witnessed while working there as a teacher.

> The strongest religious sect in Burkina Faso is Mohammedanism, and mosques are to be seen the length and breadth of the country, but there are Catholic churches in Ouagadougou in addition. I had thought that the church opposite my lodging was Catholic, but the singing of the congregation did not confirm that. One evening I went across the road to listen to the service, and, to my surprise, it was English with a Welsh accent that fell upon my hearing from the chapel. After every English sentence there was a translation into the local language by one of the natives. At the end of the service I had a conversation with the preacher – Al Williams from the Rhondda. His wife was a black woman from Guyana. Al Williams explained that he had emigrated from Northern Ireland, under God's guidance, comparatively recently and he was gradually getting used to life in Ouagadougou. His wife was suffering from ill health. Pity them, neither of them knew a word of French, the official language of Burkina Faso, or of Mossi, the language of the majority of the population of Ouagadougou and the surrounding area. They were short of money because they had spent a great deal on expensive machines while they were in Ireland, in order to print programmes, hymns and the like, on behalf of the members of the church. I would like to return to Ouagadougou to see if the development of Evangelical Christianity is possible in a sea of Islam, and under the disadvantages experienced by Al Williams and his wife. Grant them grace.[73]

Griffith himself seems to show only limited interest in the majority religion of Burkina Faso. 'It is hard to avoid Muslims in Ouagadougou', he says a little later, before reporting an encounter which happened when he had visited the local airport just as an aeroplane landed for what appeared to be a grand civic welcome.

> I kept a hawk's eye on the aeroplane expecting to see at least a famous president appear at the top of the steps which had been set fussily alongside the door. But may the lord mayor and dignitaries of Ouagadougou forgive me for laughing so inconsiderately when the aeroplane door opened and around a hundred little men 'all in their gowns of white'[74] poured down the steps. Their sandals, nightgowns and arab head-dresses were shining white and the crowd reminded me of the Gorsedd of Bards crossing the National Eisteddfod field. But there was a difference. Each one of the aeroplane's passengers carried a shining copper kettle. Perhaps the travellers were returning from some international picnic?[75]

He says that after the 'uninteresting' welcoming ceremony, he managed to ask one of the travellers where he had been, and found out that they were pilgrims returning from Mecca, and that the kettles were to carry water for ritual ablutions, and for drinking, in the hot desert of Arabia.

Griffith's comments on Islam do not extend much beyond the externals of dress and custom. The comments of the missionary in the final extract in this chapter, Dr Rhiannon Lloyd, do engage with theological questions, although, as with some examples of earlier missionaries, the focus seems primarily on identifying areas in which Christianity excels over Islam.

Lloyd's 2004 book *Llwybr Gobaith* ('Path of Hope') tells of her work in Africa, particularly in Rwanda, where she carried out extraordinary reconciliation work in the wake of the 1994 genocide. Her work during the aftermath of that horrific episode forms the bulk of the book. However, it is the shorter time she spent in Liberia that provides the Welsh-Muslim contact that brings her work within the scope of this study. Lloyd had been asked by the government to use her Christian message to help rehabilitate young men and boys who had been brutalised by becoming killers in the service of a rebel army. She decides to preach to them about how God is a loving father:

> We'd been there for an hour now, looking at the different references. They were delighted. In the end, a young man put his hand up and said: 'I'm not a Christian. I'm a Muslim, but I have never seen a loving father like this in our faith. I don't want to be a Muslim. I want this loving father.'
>
> And down he goes on his knees in front of the group. Those who had become Christians were delighted, jumping up and down and

> running up to him, praying all the time for this boy. That said so much to me. Whatever our culture may be, whatever our experience may be, there is a need in our hearts to experience fatherly love. God has created us that way. And I learned something big, that having a revelation of the fatherly love of God is something that touches our hearts very deeply and attracts us to him.[76]

She adds that after she left Liberia she would get letters from some of the boys. They were affectionate and penitent, and said they could not understand what had come over them to make them killers. Lloyd comments that she thinks 'sorcery and black arts ... had opened the door for unclean spirits to get the chance to work through them.' She concludes by reporting that she lost touch with the boys when war broke out again in Liberia: 'I don't know how many of them are still alive, but God knows, and I know that I will see them in heaven even if I don't see them again on the earth.'

Lloyd's memoir is a very late example of the kind of evangelical Christian confidence which was once the normal inspiration for Welsh religious endeavour overseas. Although assurance such as Lloyd's is now remarkable for its rarity, her testimony nonetheless stands as a contemporary reminder of the strength of the religious ideals which have, over the centuries, taken Welsh people to foreign countries to share their own faith, and which have, as a result, brought them into contact with another.

Notes

1. G. Penar Griffith, *Hanes bywgraffiadol o genhadon Cymreig i wledydd paganaidd* (Cardiff, 1897).
2. Carl Bridge and Kent Fedorowich, (eds.), *The British World: Diaspora, Culture and Identity* (London, 2003) 57.
3. See the present author's *The Chosen People* (Bridgend, 2002) 55.
4. John Mills, *Palestina* (Llanidloes, 1858) 124.
5. *Ibid.* 89.
6. *Ibid.* 90.
7. *Ibid.* 94.
8. *Ibid.* 65.
9. *Ibid.* 341.
10. January 1857. For this information, and that in the next note, I am indebted to Geoff Ballinger.

11. Michael D. Jones, 'Y Cymry ac Ymfudaeth' ('The Welsh and Emigration') *Yr Amserau* (3 December, 1856)
12. The idea is not so outlandish if it is remembered that modern Israel and Palestine, often portrayed as a dichotomous Jewish-versus-Arab landscape, is actually a patchwork of communities, such as Druze, Bedu, Samaritan, and numerous Christian and Jewish groups. One relevant comparison might be the Circassian community, a Muslim group from the Caucasus removed to what is now Israel by the Ottoman Empire in the 1860s, the same decade that the Welsh project in Argentina began. The two Circassian villages in modern Israel maintain their own language and traditions. Other, larger communities, are located in Syria.
13. Margaret Jones, *Llythyrau Cymraes o Wlad Canaan* (Liverpool, 1869) 38-39.
14. Griffith Milwyn Griffiths, 'Jones, Margaret', *Welsh Biography Online*; http://yba.llgc.org.uk/en/s3-JONE-MAR-1902.html
15. Nigel Jenkins, *Gwalia in Khasia* (Llandysul, 1995).
16. Dorothy Elwyn Forrester, 'Roberts, John', *Welsh Biography Online* http://yba.llgc.org.uk/en/s-ROBE-JOH-1842.html
17. Probably an ironic reference to Muhammad Ali Pasha al-Mas'ud ibn Agha (1769-1849) known as Mehmet Ali Pasha, the Khedive of Egypt and Sudan, and a prominent international figure in the nineteenth century. In 1847, his portrait was painted by the Welsh artist Thomas Brigstocke (1809-81) of Carmarthen.
18. R.J. Williams, *Y Parchedig John Roberts, D.D. Khasia* (Caernarfon, 1923) 45.
19. Elizabeth J. Jones, *Y Drysorfa* 88 (May 1918),199.
20. Elizabeth M. Lloyd, *Hanes Assam* (Caernarfon, 1916) 109-110.
21. Dafydd Gwilym Merfyn Jones, *Y Popty Poeth a'i Gyffiniau* (Caernarfon, 1990). See also Gruffydd Aled Jones, 'Meddylier am India': Tair Taith y Genhadaeth Gymreig yn Sylhet 1887-1947', *Trafodion Anrhydeddus Gymdeithas y Cymmrodorion,* 4 (1997).
22. Dafydd Gwilym Merfyn Jones, *Blwyddyn y Newyn* (Caernarfon, 1981) 58.
23. D. Ben Rees, 'Obituary: The Rev D.G. Merfyn Jones': http://www.independent.co.uk/news/obituaries/obituary-the-rev-d-g-merfyn-jones-1143992.html
24. Urien Wiliam, *Tu Hwnt i'r Mynydd Du* (Swansea, 1976) 97.
25. Robert Thomas Jenkins, 'Lewis, Sir Henry', *Welsh Biography Online,* http://yba.llgc.org.uk/en/s-LEWI-HEN-1847.html
26. James Ednyfed Rhys, 'Rees, Evan', *Welsh Biography Online,* http://yba.llgc.org.uk/en/s-REES-EVA-1850.html
27. Evan Rees ('Dyfed'), *Gwlad yr Addewid,* 2nd edition, (Caernarfon, 1900) 24.
28. *Ibid.* 60.
29. *Ibid.* 64.
30. *Ibid.* 178.

31. Evan Rees ('Dyfed'), *Gwaith Barddonol Dyfed* (Cardiff, 1907) 206.
32. Alfred Perceval Graves (trans.) *Welsh Poetry Old and New* (London, 1912) 101.
33. D. Rhagfyr Jones, *I'r Aifft ac Yn Ôl* (Wrexham, 1904).
34. *Ibid.* 113.
35. *Ibid.* 61.
36. *Ibid.* 60.
37. *Ibid.* 61-62.
38. *Ibid.* 160.
39. Thomas E. Roberts, *Jerusalem: Y Ddinas Sanctaidd* (Caernarfon, 1904).
40. *Ibid.* 163.
41. *Ibid.* 164
42. Thomas E. Roberts, *Palesteina Hen a Newydd*, (London, 1933).
43. *Ibid.* 65.
44. *Ibid.* 66.
45. *Ibid.* 61.
46. *Ibid.* 74.
47. Eluned Morgan, *Ar Dir a Môr* (Abergavenny, 1913).
48. *Ibid.* 26.
49. *Ibid.* 70.
50. *Ibid.* 16.
51. Gwenallt is referring to the section of prominent special seating generally reserved for deacons in Nonconformist chapels.
52. David James Jones, ('Gwenallt'), Christine James (ed.), *Cerddi Gwenallt: Y Casgliad Cyflawn* (Llandysul, 2001) 332.
53. The entry on the Arabs in the 10-volume *Encyclopaedia Cambrensis: Y Gwyddoniadur Cymreig*, ('The Welsh Encyclopaedia'), published 1856-79 by Thomas Gee and edited by Rev. John Parry, says: 'The Arabs have fulfilled an important role for mankind, in the care with which they kept the intellectual treasures of the Greeks to this latter ages; and that they did so in the dark ages that followed the destructive incursions of the northmen into the most fruitful and civilised territories of Europe ... We do not have much to say about the customs of the Arabs of our day'
54. David James Jones ('Gwenallt'), *op. cit.* 335.
55. This is notable as an early usage of what is now the most widespread spelling of the Islamic scriptures in the Latin alphabet.
56. David James Jones ('Gwenallt'), *op. cit.* 339.
57. Gareth Lloyd Jones, *Yng Ngwlad yr Addewid* (Caernarfon, 1966) 71.
58. William Emlyn Jones, *Y Saith Ganhwyllbren Aur* (Llandybïe, 1969).
59. The term 'brawd', 'brother', is often used in Welsh to mean 'a fellow'. It carries connotations of respect.
60. William Emlyn Jones *op. cit.* 28.
61. A Christian martyred in Asia Minor in c.92.
62. William Emlyn Jones, *op. cit.* 45.
63. Williams was well-known as one of the members of 'Triawd y Coleg' ('The College Trio'), a popular group of male singers formed in the 1940s.

He later presented religious television programmes such as *Dechrau Canu, Dechrau Canmol.*

64. Robin Williams, *Hoelion Wyth* (Llandysul, 1986) 138.

65. *Ibid.* 147.

66. *Ibid.* 149.

67. Robin Williams, 'An Holy Kiss' in Meic Stephens (ed. and trans.) *Illuminations: an anthology of Welsh short prose,* (Cardiff, 1998), 214-216. First published in Robin Williams, *Tynnu Llwch,* (Llandysul, 1991). See also Meic Stephens, 'Robin Williams Sophisticated Welsh-language essayist' *The Independent,* 23 December 2003. http://www.independent.co.uk/news/obituaries/robin-williams-549141.html

68. Hywel David Lewis, *Hen a Newydd* (Caernarfon, 1971).

69. *Ibid.* 106

70. John Jenkins (1872-1936), known as 'Gwili', was a poet and theologian, and was Archdruid of Wales.

71. *Ibid.* 105.

72. Tearfund survey, *Churchgoing in the UK,* 2007.

73. Stephen Griffith, *Teithio'r Sahel* (Talybont, 1986) 21.

74. Griffith's quotation describes the appearance of the saints on the day of resurrection. It comes from an anonymous but well-known early nineteenth-century hymn entitled 'Bydd myrdd o ryfeddodau' ('There will be a myriad of wonders').

75. *Ibid.* 22.

76. Rhiannon Lloyd, *Llwybr Gobaith* (Caernarfon, 2004) 65.

'LION-HEART HATH COME AGAIN': WELSH-MUSLIM ENCOUNTERS IN THE GREAT WAR

Anyone who belongs to a minority community, or to a small nation, will be familiar with the message that small can not just be beautiful, but that it can be influential and significant beyond all proportion. Groups that feel marginalised can often compensate for apparent external insignificance by fostering affirmative narratives of uniqueness and importance. The Welsh are no exception, their advocates often attributing European or even global stature to achievements and characteristics of which Europe and the globe are often quite unaware. In all this understandable and largely harmless mythology of self-assertion – a 'world-first' here, a 'biggest-in-Europe' there – it is strange that one rarely hears the claim that the Welsh played a crucial role in changing the course of modern history and creating the world's most volatile political flashpoint. Strange, because, unlike many other assertions, this particular statement actually happens to be true. This chapter will show how Wales was pivotal in creating the State of Israel, with all the implications that event has had for world affairs and for the relationship of the West with Islam.

To understand how this came about, it is necessary to bear in mind two of the strands of thought and of historical process we have examined in previous chapters. Firstly, there is modern Zionism, which grew throughout the nineteenth century until, by the turn of the twentieth century, it was a political force sufficient to command the serious attention of the superpowers of the day. Secondly, there were influential strands of Protestant evangelical Christianity, which believed the Biblical promises that the Jewish people must return to their ancestral home and must convert to Christianity as necessary preconditions of the Second Coming of Jesus Christ. Although the objectives of Jewish Zionists and Christian Zionists could hardly have been more different on the question of conversion, or on the prospect of the return of Jesus

Christ, they were in close accord on the question of the physical return of the Jewish people to the land of Palestine. As Europe entered the convulsion of the First World War that was to leave the continent's empires shattered and its map redrawn, the promoters of the Zionist project found themselves with an opportunity that had not come the way of the Jewish people in the two thousand years since the Temple was destroyed and the followers of Judaism were scattered across the earth – the prospect of establishing their own state in the Promised Land.

A crucial figure in this climactic juncture of history is the one man who had it within his power to approve or refuse the ambitions of Zionism – David Lloyd George, the British Prime Minister, and the war leader of what was then the most powerful empire the earth had ever seen. He was a Welsh-speaking Welshman from Gwynedd, and had been raised a Baptist Christian in a land which was at that time markedly fervent in its evangelical Protestantism, a land in which, as he put it, knowledge of the history of the people of the Old Testament was at least as widespread as knowledge of Welsh history, and a land in which many people took the Biblical promises of the Jewish people's return to Palestine literally. It was a land where a sense of solidarity and identification with the Jewish people as fellow victims of oppression had combined with uncommon evangelical piety to produce a peculiarly potent type of Christian philo-semitism,[1] one which managed to thrive in the virtual absence of any real contact with the object of its admiration even as hostility to Islam had thrived in a similar vacuum.

Lloyd George may not have always adhered too closely to Christian ideals of fidelity in his private life, or those of probity in his public life, if one remembers some of his political activities such as his involvement in the 'insider dealing' share scandal of the Marconi Affair in 1912, or his cash-for-honours activities after the war. However, even if he was not always strict in observing its moral standards, his Christian upbringing and his early adulthood as a Baptist lay preacher had undoubtedly predisposed him to sympathy with the Jewish people whom he identified as a fellow small nation, oppressed, tenacious and imbued with a sense of destiny. As early as 1903, as a young MP, he had, at the request of a representative of the founder of Zionism, Theodor Herzl, used his position as a partner in a law firm to draw up a document for the first planned Jewish homeland in British domains, in Uganda. While that scheme was not advanced, it shows that when Lloyd George, as Prime Minister, fourteen years later, authorised the Balfour Declaration saying that the British Government would 'view with favour' the establishment of 'a national home for the Jewish people' in Palestine, he was not acting out of some passing wartime expedience, but out of a longer-term and more deeply-rooted conviction. The following passage is taken from a speech Lloyd George made to the Anglo-Jewish Historical Society in 1925, when he was looking back at the events of the previous decade, and on his decision to authorise the February 1917 declaration in the name of the then Foreign Secretary, Arthur Balfour. Tailoring his selection of the facts to his audience, and using a disarming rhetorical combination of candour and flattery, Lloyd George says of the decision that it:

> ...was undoubtedly inspired by natural sympathy, admiration, and also by the fact that, as you must remember, we had been trained even more in Hebrew history than in the history of our own country. I was brought up in a school where I was taught far more about the history of the Jews than about the history of my own land. I could tell you all the kings of Israel, but I doubt whether I could have named half a dozen of the kings of Wales. So that you must remember that was very largely the basis of our teaching. On five days a week in the day school, and on Sunday in our Sunday schools, we were thoroughly versed in the history of the Hebrews. We used to recite great passages from the prophets and the Psalms. We were thoroughly imbued with the history of your race in the days of its greatest glory, when it founded that great literature which will echo to the very last days of this old world, influencing, moulding, fashioning human character, inspiring and sustaining human motive, for not only Jews, but Gentiles as well. We absorbed it and made it part of the best in the Gentile character. So that, therefore, when the question was put to us, we were not like Napoleon, who had never been in a Sunday school and had probably read very little of that literature. We had all that in our minds, so that the appeal came to sympathetic and educated – and, on that question, intelligent – hearts. But I am not going to pretend there was not a certain element of interest in it, too. You call yourselves a small nation. I belong to a small nation, and I am proud of the fact. It is an ancient race, not as old as yours, and although I am very proud of it, I am not going to compare it with yours. One day it may become great; it

> will perhaps be chosen for great things. But all I know is that up to the present it is small races that have been chosen for great things. And there we were, confronted with your people in every country of the world, very powerful. You may say you have been oppressed and persecuted—that has been your power! You have been hammered into very fine steel, and that is why you can never be broken. Hammered for centuries into the finest steel of any race in the world! And therefore we wanted your help.

Lloyd George goes on to say how the scientist Dr Chaim Weizmann, the leading Zionist, had solved a pressing problem of munitions production for the allies, and that, as reward, refusing honours and offers of money, he had asked to put the Zionist case to the government who promptly agreed with his request.

Lloyd George's speech makes it all sound very straightforward. However, Weizmann, in his own autobiography *Trial and Error*, remembered the affair differently. His munitions work had certainly brought him into repeated personal contact with Lloyd George, and this had given him the opportunity to put the Zionist case. But there was no dramatic moment of exchange, of explosives for exodus. It was more a question of 'heartbreaks' and 'drudgery' and the gradual persuasion of a reluctant establishment of the merits of the project. As he remarked: 'history does not deal in Aladdin's lamps.'[2]

There were, of course, other motives behind the Balfour Declaration. As Lloyd George himself readily acknowledged, in later parts of the speech quoted above and elsewhere, there was also self-interest: the Allies believed an international Jewish lobby could help keep Russia in the war against the Central Powers, and could help bring in America on the Allied side too. Also, with a view to the post-war partition of the Turkish Empire, a Palestine populated mainly by Westernised Jewish settlers was seen as potentially a more pro-British client state in the Middle East, and one more likely to shield the prized protectorate of Egypt, than would a state composed mainly of Arabs.

However, if the crucial agency of Welsh Christian philosemitism in bringing about the Declaration should be doubted, it is only necessary to imagine whether the Declaration would have come about had a man of a different background been the British premier at the time, a man, for instance like Lord Curzon (1859-1925), the Leader of the House of Lords at the time of the

Declaration and later Foreign Secretary and Viceroy of India. He had been raised in the British Empire's ruling class, had served in India and had travelled extensively in Muslim lands, including Palestine itself. He was a strong opponent of Zionism, and in a paper to the War Cabinet in October 1917, as the government was considering promising Palestine to the Jewish people, said of the Arab inhabitants of that land: 'They and their forefathers have occupied the country for the best part of 1,500 years. They own the soil... They profess the Mohammedan faith. They will not be content either to be expropriated for Jewish immigrants, or to act merely as hewers of wood or drawers of water for the latter.'[3] He was overruled by Lloyd George. Had the roles been reversed, it is not difficult to imagine the Zionists and their supporters meeting a very dusty answer, and history having been very different as a result.

Most commentators readily agree that Christian Zionism played a major part in the policy of the British War Cabinet, many of whose members, either at the time of the declaration or later during its implementation, were either practising members of, or had their roots strongly in, Bible-believing evangelical churches. According to David Fromkin, in his study of the peace settlements that followed the war: 'Biblical prophecy was the first and most enduring of the many motives that led Britons to want to restore the Jews to Zion.'[4] Jill Hamilton, in her 2004 study of Lloyd George's role in the Declaration, *God, Guns and Israel*, says:

> In spite of the British tendency to glamourize Arab countries, Nonconformist ideas appeared to be a more persuasive force in shaping the attitudes of the politicians towards British sponsorship of Zionist aspirations. Generation after generation had heard the Bible read in church each Sunday, and many had a copy at home, which was studied daily. In many cases, the Bible was the only book, certainly the principal book. Its cadences, its music, its phraseology sank into men's minds. In remote villages it was the chapel, the church and the kirk that gave people their first music, their first literature and first ideals and philosophy, their first lessons in reading, their first moral code, their first sense of belonging.[5]

The historian of the Middle East, David Gilmour, described the Declaration as the result of 'those strange combinations of romanticism and strategic reasoning, zealotry and altruism, pro-Jewish sympathy and professed anti-semitism.'[6] The anti-semitism refers to one of the motives among at least some supporters of the plan, which was to remove unwanted Jews from Western countries.

The motives were, therefore, complex, but the centrality of the figure of Lloyd George, and the importance of his Welsh background, can hardly be overstressed. In the 1925 speech quoted above, Lloyd George went on to refer to Dr Weizmann having secured the 'conversion of the Gentiles running the war' to Zionism. He added: 'I am glad of it, both on the ground of sympathy and of interest, I was a very strong advocate of the conquest of Palestine.'

He certainly was. He belonged to what was called the Eastern Party, a school of thought which felt that as the war against Germany had reached stalemate on the Western Front, the best way to defeat the Central Powers was to break their weakest link, Turkey, in the east, and then attack their next-weakest, Austro-Hungary, in order to threaten Germany from the south and east. As will be seen, it is likely that Lloyd George's preoccupation with the eastern theatre of war may well also have owed much to his long-held dislike for the Turkish Empire and his desire to see it broken up and the nations under its control – particularly the Christian nations – set free. However, even as Prime Minister, Lloyd George faced steady opposition from many of his generals, who remembered the debacle of the 1915-16 Gallipoli expedition against Turkey, and were convinced that defeating the strongest adversary, Germany, was the priority. Lloyd George alluded to this in his speech to his Jewish audience:

> Some day I shall be able to tell the story of how near a thing that was, when we organised all our forces, took all our guns and munitions for the final attack with the idea of capturing Jerusalem, but the danger on the Western front very nearly forced us to take the troops away. If that had happened. I think Palestine would still have been in the hands of the Turk.

Two previous attempts had been made to enter Palestine from the British protectorate of Egypt. The First and Second Battles of Gaza in March and April 1917 ended with the Allied forces being repulsed with heavy and humiliating losses. It was only after

Lloyd George ordered substantial reinforcements and a new and trusted general, Edmund Allenby, that the Allies were finally successful, breaking through the enemy lines in November 1917, and just over a month later, on 11 December, capturing Jerusalem itself. Lloyd George, having first imposed a news embargo to ensure maximum drama, had the victory announced to the House of Commons, knowing what a boost the prestigious, symbolic victory would be for British morale. Knowing too the particular enthusiasm with which his home constituency in Wales would receive the news, he made sure that a Welsh contingent of troops led the victory parade into the holy city, and that they mounted the first Christian guard at the Church of the Holy Sepulchre since the Crusades. His home audience repaid the compliment, with Welsh journals recording the occasion with enthusiasm: 'Capture of Jerusalem. Another Triumph for Allenby. Enemy driven back by Welsh troops', was the *Western Mail* headline on 11 December. The triumphal moment is recorded in a painting 'Entry of the Welsh Troops into Jerusalem' by Frank Brangwyn, now kept at the National Museum of Wales in Cardiff.

So far, we have examined the influence of evangelical Christian philo-semitism on the British War Cabinet's decision to authorise a Jewish national home, and on the military campaign which made this possible, and have kept a particular focus on the Welsh element in that process. The material examined so far has largely been only indirectly about Muslims, in the sense that they were the main group whose land was being promised to the Zionists. However, there are three other aspects of the British involvement in Palestine in the First World War which have produced material revealing Welsh attitudes to Muslims: first, the specifically anti-Turkish attitude of Lloyd George; secondly, the policy of promoting Arab nationalism which was pursued in parallel with, and in contradiction to, Zionism; and thirdly the literature which was written about the campaign by other Welsh people and which casts a light on their attitudes towards Muslims. It is those aspects we will examine now, beginning with Lloyd George's attitudes towards Muslims.

It is clear that when considering Lloyd George's support for Zionism and for pursuing war in the East, his undoubted philo-semitism was only half the story. The other half is his marked dislike for the Turkish Empire, and for 'the Turk' as a symbol of oppression in general, and, oppression of Christian minorities in particular. Knowing that Muslims represented a quarter of the population of the British Empire, that they were a substantial minority in the prized but restive imperial possession of India, and that they were also a source of valuable manpower for the imperial armies, Lloyd George was always careful to stress that he was not condemning Islam or Muslims *per se*. But his caveats were just that: careful. His condemnations of that generic entity 'the Turk', on the other hand, were heartfelt, vivid and savage with the eloquence of true loathing. The following passage is taken from a speech he made at the City Temple in London in 1914 as Chancellor of the Exchequer on the occasion of Turkey's entrance into the war, and is typical of the attitude he expressed towards Turkey throughout the conflict, throughout the peace negotiations that followed, and in his memoirs afterwards. His antipathy could hardly have been expressed in stronger terms:

> But now we have been assailed by another national exponent of the higher culture – Turkey. I notice the same characteristics, even in the very way in which the war has been brought about. There is the same contempt for the elements, for the decencies, of international law. Harmless, defenceless towns are bombarded without any notice. We did our best to avoid the quarrel, but I cannot pretend that I am sorry this has happened. No one could have shown more patience in the face of insults and injuries that I could retail to you by the hour than Great Britain did, in face of the treatment which was accorded to us by this miserable, wretched, contemptible empire in the Bosphorus. It filled us with disdain and scorn that we should have to endure, even for a day, the insults of the Turk.
>
> But the quarrel has been taken out of our hands. We were in the hands of fate, and the hour has struck on the great clock of destiny for settling accounts with the Turk. I am not speaking of him as an enemy of Christendom. There is no more futile method of settling the conflicts of creed than a war. We are not fighting Mahomedanism, but the Turk. A very distinguished Mahomedan, who is very loyal to the British Empire, said to me the other day, 'After all, the British Empire is the greatest Mahomedan Empire in the world.' The Ottoman Empire is just a second-rate Mahomedan Empire, although it gives itself the airs of leadership of the whole Mahomedan world.
>
> Why, the Turk is the greatest enemy of his own faith, because he has discredited it by misgovernment. What has he in common with

> the cultured Mahomedan in India? In the loftier regions of thought, the Indian Mahomedan holds an honoured rank. The Arabs brought a civilisation of their own which has enriched Europe to this day. What have the Turks ever contributed either to culture, to art, or to any aspect of human progress that you can think of? They are a human cancer, a creeping agony in the flesh of the lands which they misgovern, rotting every fibre of life. They have ruled over most of the countries which are the cradle of civilisation; these lands were once the most fruitful and the most abundant of the world; they were the granaries of the East and of the West alike. In turn, they have been governed by Assyrians, Babylonians, Persians, Greeks, and Romans – all tyrants; but they left these countries prosperous and luxuriant.
>
> What about the Turk? He comes to these plenteous lands, and the tread of his blood-stained sandal scorches and withers life and fertility in whole territories. Every grain in thousands of square miles is shrivelled up. The sight of this Gorgon has turned bounteous plains and fields into stony deserts. The people he has subjected to his rule have for centuries been the victims of his indolence, incompetence, and lust, and now – now that the great day of reckoning has come upon the nations – I am glad that the Turk is to be called to a final account for his long record of infamy against humanity.[7]

On February 3, 1917, as Prime Minister, addressing constituents in his own Caernarfon constituency, he recalls how he imbibed his opinions of the Turkish character from the great Liberal statesman William Ewart Gladstone:

> The doctrine that the Turk is incapable of governing any other race justly, and even his own race well – that is another which I was taught. I remember very well as a boy having to walk some miles to the nearest railway station in order to buy Mr. Gladstone's famous speech on the expelling of the Turk, bag and baggage, from Europe for his misrule and his massacres.[8]

It is worth looking in detail at Gladstone's famous piece of political rhetoric, a piece so potent that the thirteen-year-old David Lloyd George went on a special journey to buy it. The pamphlet, *Bulgarian horrors and the question of the East*, had been published in 1876, when Gladstone, then in opposition to Benjamin Disraeli's government, was responding to reports of atrocities by Turkish authorities against Christian populations in the Balkans. The similarity of its sentiments and its rhetoric to Lloyd George's 1914 speech is striking:

> Let me endeavour very briefly to sketch, in the rudest outline, what the Turkish race was and what it is. It is not a question of Mahometanism simply, but Mahometanism compounded with the peculiar character of a race. They are not the mild Mahometans of India, nor the chivalrous Saladins of Syria, nor the cultured Moors of Spain. They were, upon the whole, from the black day when they first entered Europe, the one great anti-human specimen of humanity. Wherever they went a broad line of blood marked the track behind them, and, as far as their dominion reached, civilisation disappeared from view. They represented everywhere government by force, as opposed to government by law. For the guide of this life they had a relentless fatalism; for its reward hereafter, a sensual paradise.[9]
>
> . . .
>
> Let the Turks now carry away their abuses, in the only possible manner, namely, by carrying off themselves. Their Zaptiehs and their Mudirs, their Bimbashis and Yuzbashis, their Kaimakams and their Pashas, one and all, bag and baggage, shall, I hope, clear out from the province that they have desolated and profaned. This thorough riddance, this most blessed deliverance, is the only reparation we can make to those heaps and heaps of dead, the violated purity alike of matron and of maiden and of child; to the civilization which has been affronted and shamed; to the laws of God, or, if you like, of Allah; to the moral sense of mankind at large. There is not a criminal in an European jail, there is not a cannibal in the South Sea Islands, whose indignation would not rise and over-boil at the recital of that which has been done, which has too late been examined, but which remains unavenged, which has left behind all the foul and all the fierce passions which produced it and which may again spring up in another murderous harvest from the soil soaked and reeking with blood and in the air tainted with every imaginable deed of crime and shame. That such things should be done once is a damning disgrace to the portion of our race which did them; that the door should be left open to the ever so barely possible repetition would spread that shame over the world.[10]

The full text of Gladstone's long treatise on the iniquities of Turkish rule shows even more clearly the rage and helplessness he felt at the inability and unwillingness of Western governments to intervene and curb Turkish oppression. Forty years later, another Liberal statesman would finally get the chance to do what Gladstone could not. In a speech in Glasgow on 29 June,

1917, Lloyd George spoke of plans for the post-war fate of the nations which formed part of the Turkish empire:

> But they say, 'What is going to happen to those colonies? What is going to happen to Mesopotamia?' Well, if you like, take Mesopotamia. Mesopotamia is not Turkish, never has been Turkish; the Turk is as much an alien in Mesopotamia as the German, and every one knows how he ruled it. This was the Garden of Eden. What a land it is now! You have only to read that terrible report to see what a country the Turk has made of the Garden of Eden. This land, the cradle of civilisation, once the granary of civilisation, the shrine and the temple of civilisation, is a wilderness under the rule of the Turk. What will happen to Mesopotamia must be left to the Peace Congress when it meets, but there is one thing that will never happen to it – it will never be restored to the blasting tyranny of the Turk. At best he was the trustee of this far-famed land on behalf of civilisation. Ah! What a trustee! He has been false to his trust and the trusteeship must be given over to more competent and more equitable hands, chosen by the Congress which will settle the affairs of the world. That same observation applies to Armenia, a land soaked with the blood of innocents massacred by the people who were bound to protect them.[11]

Elsewhere, during the war, he spoke of 'The breaking up of the dark rule of the Turk, which for centuries has clouded the sunniest lands in the world',[12] and there was an echo of Crusading imagery in his statement to the Imperial War Cabinet on the military and naval position of the British Empire in March 1917:

> The Turk must never be allowed to misgovern these great lands in future. We owe it to these countries, for the gifts with which they have enriched mankind, that we should do something to restore their glory. There have been many expeditions from Christendom into that part of the world to wrest them from the grip of the destroyer. I believe this will be the last, because it is the one which is going to be successful, and completely successful. It is impossible that we should permit these lands longer to remain under Turkish government. Under Turkish rule they have been a constant source of irritation, and friction, and war. There has been no one cause which has been more fruitful of bloodshed in Europe than the misgovernment of the Turkish Empire and its results.[13]

There was a further echo in 1918 when Lloyd George published selections of his wartime speeches, including those mentioned above, under the title *The Great Crusade*, although it must be stressed that the title referred to the entire war, rather than the campaign against Turkey. However, while Lloyd George generally avoided using Crusader terminology to refer to the Turkish empire, there is no doubt he pursued his enmity with almost religious intensity. During the peace process in 1919, Lloyd George declared, 'We are undertaking a great civilising duty – a mission which Providence had assigned our race, which we are discharging to people living under the shadow of great tyranny, trembling with fear, appealing with uplifted hands for our protection. Turkish misgovernment ... shall come to an end now that Britain and the Allies have triumphed.'[14] Later, he recalled: 'There was not a British statesman of any party who did not have it in mind that if we succeeded in defeating this inhuman Empire, our essential condition of the peace we should impose was the redemption of the Armenian valleys for ever from the bloody misrule with which they had been stained by the infamies of the Turks.'[15] In the 1925 speech to the Anglo-Jewish Historical Society, quoted earlier, he showed that his opinion of the Turks as defeated adversaries was no higher than his opinion for them as defiant oppressors:

> ...it is idle to say that in the terms of peace you could have insisted on clearing Palestine. The Turk has not retired from any country from which he was not driven before the armistice. He has a way with him of signing documents. Say to him: 'Give up Palestine,' he simply says: 'Where shall I sign?' Say to him: 'You must give up Constantinople,' and his pen is ready. The Turk will sign any document you can present to him and he will never honour one of them. The Turk signed everything after the armistice, but he has never retired from a single yard of territory from which we had not driven him at the point of the bayonet.

However, as mentioned above, while Lloyd George undoubtedly felt a visceral distaste for the Turks as a governing power, and while he allowed that antipathy full rein in his speeches, he had to balance this antagonism with the need to placate Muslim opinion within the British Empire itself. Before he became Prime Minister in 1916 the British Government had issued clear promises to Muslims, via the Government of India in 1914, that the war was against Turkish power, not against 'the sacred seat' of the Muslim caliphate. In the Imperial Legislative Council in 1915 the British Government had promised that the holy places of Islam would remain 'inviolate' and would be defended by the Allies against all foreign invaders. These were promises that Lloyd George inherited when he came to power. He also made promises of his own, in a statement of war aims on 5 January, 1918, in which he said the aim of the Allies' fight was not:

> ...to deprive Turkey of its capital, or of the rich and renowned lands of Asia Minor and Thrace, which are predominantly Turkish in race... While we do not challenge the maintenance of the Turkish Empire in the homelands of the Turkish race with its capital at Constantinople, the passage between the Mediterranean and the Black Sea being internationalized and neutralized, Arabia, Armenia, Mesopotamia, Syria and Palestine are in our judgment entitled to a recognition of their separate national conditions. What the exact form of that recognition in each particular case should be need not here be discussed, beyond stating that it would be impossible to restore to their former sovereignty the territories to which I have already referred.[16]

This promise in particular caused problems during the peace process, as the Allies considered options for the future of Constantinople, including removing it from Turkish control, a proposal – not eventually realised – which some Muslims considered inconsistent with the pledge made during the war. Questioned in the House of Commons about the issue on 26 February 1920, and under pressure to abandon his promise, Lloyd George, in defending the pledge, was keen to balance his opposition to Turkish rule with expressions of respect for Islam and for Muslims. He said the 'carefully prepared' and perfectly deliberate' pledge of January 1918 was given '...after full consultation with all parties' to allay British workers' fears that the allied war aims were imperialistic and to allay Indian Muslim fears that Islamic holy places could pass to Christian control – fears which affected military recruitment in India. Once the pledge was made, Lloyd George said, Muslim recruitment increased:

> It is too often forgotten that we are the greatest Mahomedan power in the world. One-fourth of the population of the British Empire is Mahomedan. There have been no more loyal adherents to the throne, there has been no more effective loyal support to the Empire

in its hour of trial than came from the Mahomedans of India. We gave a solemn pledge, and they accepted it, and they are disturbed at the prospect of our not abiding by it. I can give you a statement made by the Viceroy. In May, 1919, we were considering this at the Peace Conference. He said: Moslem feeling is already deeply stirred. Educated opinion is probably prepared for extensive territorial losses but not for the loss of Constantinople, especially in view of the recent announcements made by the Prime Minister and Lord Robert Cecil. They depended on my Noble Friend's words just as much as they did on mine.

There were Mahomedan divisions that fought brilliantly throughout the whole of that Turkish campaign. Without their aid we should not have conquered Turkey at all. Were we to have broken faith with them in the hour of victory? That is what we were confronted with.

. . .

When the peace terms are published there is no friend of the Turks, should there be any left, who will not realise that he has been terribly punished for his follies, his blunders, his crimes and his iniquities. Stripped of more than half his Empire. His country under the allied guns. Deprived of his army, his navy, his prestige. The punishment will be terrible enough to satisfy the bitterest foe of the Turkish Empire, drastic enough for the sternest judge. My right hon. Friend suggested that there was a religious issue involved. That would be the most dangerous thing of all, and the most fatal. I am afraid that underneath the agitation there is not only the movement for the expulsion of the Turk, but there is something of the old feeling of Christendom against the crescent. If it is believed in the Mahomedan world that our terms are dictated by the purpose of lowering the flag of the Prophet before that of Christendom it will be fatal to our government in India. It is an unworthy purpose to achieve by force. It is unworthy of Britain, and it is unworthy of our faith. It never conquered by force. To attempt to conquer by force is the very negation of its fundamental principles.[17]

Despite Lloyd George's assurances, the prospect of the loss of Turkish control of Constantinople raised fears among some Muslims over the future of the pan-Islamic caliphate authority, traditionally based in that city. The issue became a *cause célèbre* for Muslim activists in India in particular, where, under the name of the Khilafat movement, it formed part of the growing independence campaign, and was supported by Mahatma Gandhi, who, though he was a Hindu, was keen to stress the mutual interests of Muslim and Hindu Indians. The Khilafat movement sent a delegation to Britain, which met with Lloyd

George on 19 March, 1920. *The Islamic Review*, of April that year reported the result of their embassy:

> The case of the delegation was very simple and clear. They approached the question of the future of the Turkish Empire not as a Turkish or an Arab question, but as a Muslim question, a question that vitally affected the clearest and some of the most essential injunctions of their faith. They took their stand on their religion and referred to texts in the Quran and the traditions of the Prophet in support of their threefold demand for the preservation of the temporal power of the Khalifa, adequate for the defence of the Faith, which involved the restoration of the *status quo ante bellum*, the Khalifa's wardenship of the Holy Places of Islam, and the Exclusive Muslim Control of the 'Island of Arabia' as delimited by Muslim scholars. But the reply of the Premier was simply disappointing. He made a passing reference to 'Mahomedans, sincere, earnest, zealous Mussulmans, who take a very different view of the temporal power (of the Khalifa) from the one which is taken by Mr. Muhammad Ali.'
>
> . . .
>
> The Premier took a tangential view of the question, and based his entire case on the application of the principle of self-determination which involves the dismemberment of Turkey. He repudiated the idea of treating Turkey severely because she was Mahomedan. He does 'not want any Mahomedan in India to imagine that we entered into this war against Turkey as a crusade against Islam.'[18]

In the event, Turkey's control of its former empire, including the Islamic holy places in Arabia, was ended. Constantinople remained Turkish, and the caliphate lingered, shorn of its temporal power, until it was eventually extinguished by the secular nationalist Turkish government in 1924.

Lloyd George's attitudes towards Muslims and Muslim lands were the product of a uniquely significant and intense context. They were expressed in respect of the fate of the Turkish Empire as part of a worldwide conflict, and at a time when the Welshman, as the political leader of the British Empire's war effort, was balancing the need to defeat two Christian empires and one Muslim empire, while retaining the support of powerful Indian Muslim allies, while recruiting Muslim Arab rebels to its cause, while placating its empire-hungry Christian ally, France, and while satisfying an influential evangelical Christian constituency at home, and a Zionist constuituency worldwide, all of whom had different and sometimes entirely conflicting visions for the fate of the Holy Land and the territories formerly ruled by Turkey. In such a situation, with the changing pressures and exigencies of war, it would be surprising if, during the four years of the conflict and the many years of the troubled peace that followed, there were not inconsistencies in the message or the policies pursued by the British Empire. Certainly, it is only too easy to see how some of the policies pursued were ultimately irreconcilable, and had probably been made in the knowledge that they were likely to be so; particularly the simultaneous and ultimately mutually exclusive promises of Jewish and Arab self-determination within the same geographical territory.

However, if expedience could trump principle in British policy as the empire sought victory in the east, it is notable that Lloyd George's position regarding Islam and Muslims within that conflict does remain largely consistent. Whether from a prudent desire to retain the confidence of Muslim allies, or a genuine aversion to advancing the interests of a religion by war, or a principled refusal to demonise the followers of another faith, or probably from a combination of all those motives, he was careful to avoid condemnation of the religion of Islam or its followers *per se*. At the same time, he was undoubtedly animated by a vitriolic, visceral antipathy towards the Turkish Empire, and towards 'the Turk' as a generic symbol of oppression, an antipathy in which his detestation of the mistreatment of specifically Christian minorities played a major part and which he sometimes expressed in terms which drew on the imagery of the Crusades. He had imbibed that animosity from the campaigning Welsh evangelical Christian and Liberal tradition of his youth, the same tradition as had given him his sympathy for the Jewish people, whose interests he was to advance so fatefully at the expense of the Muslim peoples of the Holy Land. Such were some of the currents of thought and feeling in this complex, charismatic, mercurial statesman from Gwynedd, a man who did more than any other individual to shape the geopolitical conditions under which the historic heartlands of Islam live to this day.

Lloyd George, though, was not the only man from Gwynedd to have had a major hand in shaping the Middle East during and after the First World War. In one of the strange coincidences of history, a man born at Tremadog, only a few miles from Lloyd George's boyhood home at Llanystumdwy, was prominent in promoting the Arab rebellion of 1916-18, against Turkish rule. This was Thomas Edward Lawrence (1888-1935), 'Lawrence of Arabia'.

Lawrence had become well-acquainted with the Middle East as an archaeologist before the war, and had learned Arabic; this made him very useful to the British forces as a liaison officer helping to guide the Arab revolt as a means of further weakening the Turkish Empire. The publicity his role attracted, and his own erudite account of the campaign in various versions of his memoir *Seven Pillars of Wisdom,* made him, as 'Lawrence of Arabia', an internationally recognised figure.

Lawrence was not of Welsh ancestry, and his residence in Tremadog was brief. His parents were Sir Thomas Robert Tighe Chapman, an Anglo-Irish landowner, and his Scottish partner, Sarah Lawrence, his former governess, for whom he had left his wife, and with whom he had left Ireland. They lived in Wales only for a matter of months after Thomas Edward's birth, at a house in Church Street called Gorphwysfa.[19] However, Lawrence took advantage of his Welsh birth in order to get a Meyricke exhibition to Jesus College, Oxford, a scholarship reserved for Welsh students, and after being accepted in 1911, he went on a cycling tour of Wales, presumably to acquire at least some knowledge of the country to justify his position. He concentrated on visiting castles, including Dinas Brân, Caernarfon, Harlech, Chepstow, Caerphilly and Raglan; this was an early manifestation of the interest in military architecture which took him to the Middle East to study Crusader castles and which led to his subsequent military and diplomatic career. Jeremy Wilson, Lawrence's official biographer, reports how the young Lawrence wrote to his family about his Welsh trip: 'After ten days in Wales, I ought to be able to sum up all the character, habits, peculiarities, virtues, vices and other points of the Welsh people. I am sorry I cannot do this yet. They seem to me rather inquisitive, more dirty, and exceedingly ugly. I am at last discovering where I got my large mouth from, it's a national peculiarity. At the same time they appear honest; I have had no extraordinary bills.'[20] The quotation shows how Lawrence regarded Wales very much from the position of an outsider, even as he claimed association as a native, in an early example of the contradictions and irony with which a great deal of his writing is marked.

In Lawrence's time, around half the student body at Jesus were Welsh, the college chapel services were held in Welsh twice a week, and the distinguished Celtic scholar Sir John Rhys was College Principal.[21] Among Lawrence's friends there was Arthur Glyn Prys-Jones (1888-1987), a pioneer of Anglo-Welsh poetry, and later a prolific author on Welsh subjects, who also wrote several memoirs of his friendship with his famous contemporary. Short of being in Wales itself, Lawrence could hardly have had greater exposure to Welsh society. In later life, troubled by his fame and oppressed by the memory of the very actions that had made him a household name, Lawrence craved anonymity and hid under repeated false identities, but his Welsh birth was one of the few items of his biography that he did not at one point or another choose to falsify. One must, of course, naturally be cautious about attributing this constancy to any irreducible patriotism; it is quite possible that he exempted this detail from falsification not because it meant to much to him, but because it meant so little. Nonetheless, those biographical facts are real enough to mean that however small the connection Lawrence may have claimed with Wales, Wales will always claim connection with Lawrence. That circumstance, and Lawrence's sheer historical status, would make it remiss not to at least give a summary of his writings about Muslims within the scope of this study, although in so doing, it must stressed that it is not suggested that his comments owe much to specifically Welsh attitudes on the subject.

Few authors in this study can have had closer experience than Lawrence of the life of Arab Muslims, or have come closer to the kind of desert experience in which Islam itself was born. He had worked in the Middle East for a long period and had learned Arabic before the rebellion in which he spent the best part of two years with the Arab irregular forces, sharing the hardships of the desert and the dangers of combat. His writings on the subject are notable in that, unlike those of most commentators, they show little interest in distinctions of theology, or in externals of practice; rather, they are deeply concerned with how the religion *feels*, how it is lived from the inside in the territory where it was born, and how the Muslim, particularly the Bedu, experiences God.

> The Beduin could not look for God within him: he was too sure that he was within God. He could not conceive anything which was or

> was not God, Who alone was great; yet there was a homeliness, an everyday-ness of this climatic Arab God, who was their eating and their fighting and their lusting, the commonest of their thoughts, their familiar resource and companion, in a way impossible to those whose God is so wistfully veiled from them by despair of their carnal unworthiness of Him and by the decorum of formal worship. Arabs felt no incongruity in bringing God into the weaknesses and appetites of their least creditable causes. He was the most familiar of their words; and indeed we lost much eloquence when making Him the shortest and ugliest of our monosyllables.
>
> This creed of the desert seemed inexpressible in words, and indeed in thought. It was easily felt as an influence, and those who went into the desert long enough to forget its open spaces and its emptiness were inevitably thrust upon God as the only refuge and rhythm of being.
>
> . . .
>
> The desert dweller could not take credit for his belief. He had never been either evangelist or proselyte. He arrived at this intense condensation of himself in God by shutting his eyes to the world, and to all the complex possibilities latent in him which only contact with wealth and temptations could bring forth. He attained a sure trust and a powerful trust, but of how narrow a field! His sterile experience robbed him of compassion and perverted his human kindness to the image of the waste in which he hid. Accordingly he hurt himself, not merely to be free, but to please himself. There followed a delight in pain, a cruelty which was more to him than goods. The desert Arab found no joy like the joy of voluntarily holding back. He found luxury in abnegation, renunciation, self restraint. He made nakedness of the mind as sensuous as nakedness of the body. He saved his own soul, perhaps, and without danger, but in a hard selfishness. His desert was made a spiritual ice-house, in which was preserved intact but unimproved for all ages a vision of the unity of God.[22]

While Lawrence's depiction of Islam is impressionistic rather than systematic, the intensity of his impressions is striking, such as when, describing 'the Wahabis, followers of a fanatical Moslem heresy', he goes on to speculate as to the rhythms of asceticism:

> It was a natural phenomenon, this periodic rise at intervals of little more than a century, of ascetic creeds in Central Arabia. Always the votaries found their neighbours' beliefs cluttered with inessential things, which became impious in the hot imagination of their preachers. Again and again they had arisen, had taken possession, soul and body, of the tribes, and had dashed themselves to pieces on

> the urban Semites, merchants and concupiscent men of the world. About their comfortable possessions the new creeds ebbed and flowed like the tides or the changing seasons, each movement with the seeds of early death in its excess of Tightness. Doubtless they must recur so long as the causes – sun, moon, wind, acting in the emptiness of open spaces, weigh without check on the unhurried and uncumbered minds of the desert-dwellers.[23]

It is perhaps, understandable that, living with the camel-riding nomadic desert tribes, pursuing their vision of freedom and fighting against the town-dwelling, train-riding, modernised Turks, Lawrence should identify authentic Islam primarily as a phenomenon of the wilderness: 'the monotheism of open spaces, the pass-through-infinity of pantheism and its everyday usefulness of an all-pervading, household God.' In common with most Britons of his time, he considered the Turkish empire irredeemably corrupt, bloodthirsty and effete, and the Arabs as representing a simpler, primitive but admirable ethic, one closer to the origins of Islam. Lawrence believed that, deprived of political power by the Turks, and with their language banned for official purposes, the Arabs had been thrown back on their religious heritage, finding in the *Qur'an* 'a standard by which to judge the banal achievements of the Turk'.

However, Lawrence was careful not to over-stress the role of religion in the motives of his Arab comrades:

> Of religious fanaticism there was little trace. The Sherif refused in round terms to give a religious twist to his rebellion. His fighting creed was nationality. The tribes knew that the Turks were Moslems, and thought that the Germans were probably true friends of Islam. They knew that the British were Christians, and that the British were their allies. In the circumstances, their religion would not have been of much help to them, and they had put it aside. 'Christian fights Christian, so why should not Mohammedans do the same? What we want is a Government which speaks our own language of Arabic and will let us live in peace. Also we hate those Turks.'[24]

The effect of Islam, as Lawrence experienced it, was characterised less by ideology and more by the practice of the austere virtues taught by the wilderness, such as passionate single-minded commitment, a quality which, with the symbolic capture of Damascus from the Turks, he claimed to have harnessed in the service of his dream of defeating his own country's enemies while advancing Arab freedom. While he worked with the Arabs as an 'undisguised' Christian (albeit an agnostic one, the evangelical Protestantism of his youth having faded in adulthood), and while he only once 'prayed in Arabia as a Moslem', and then only as part of an elaborate charade to fool the Turks, Lawrence nonetheless hinted that he was, in some way, aligned with the purposes of the Arabs' God in promoting their national interests:

> They were as unstable as water, and like water would perhaps finally prevail. Since the dawn of life, in successive waves they had been dashing themselves against the coasts of flesh. Each wave was broken, but, like the sea, wore away ever so little of the granite on which it failed, and some day, ages yet, might roll unchecked over the place where the material world had been, and God would move upon the face of those waters. One such wave (and not the least) I raised and rolled before the breath of an idea, till it reached its crest, and toppled over and fell at Damascus. The wash of that wave, thrown back by the resistance of vested things, will provide the matter of the following wave, when in fullness of time the sea shall be raised once more.[25]

Those 'vested things' were the harsh facts of *realpolitik* to which Lawrence was finally exposed after his forces had captured Damascus on 1 October, 1918, and when, in the negotiations that followed, it became apparent that conflicting wartime promises made by the Allies had left a range of different groups, including the British, the French, the Arabs and the Jews, competing for ultimately irreconcilable territorial and resource ambitions in the lands of the former Turkish Empire. Lawrence, torn between his country and the people with whom he had fought and struggled, found himself unable to deliver the freedom in whose name he had helped raise the tribes in revolt. Perhaps, in his idealised depictions of Arab Muslims as single-minded men of action from the desert whose purity of motive was always at odds with the corrupt and compromised town, can be seen some of his own frustrated idealism as the simplistic visions of freedom nurtured in the desert campaign gave way to the sordid realities of the conference chamber. Lawrence left the peace conferences disillusioned and disappointed. 'Time seemed to have proclaimed the impossibility of autonomous union for such a land,' he commented. He refused medals and honours from the British government, and retreated into a life of evasion, irony, ambiguity and introversion. However, although he was bitterly disenchanted, he nonetheless managed to produce, in his 1926 volume *Seven Pillars of Wisdom*, a memoir of monumental significance not only in its account of the historical events in which its author played a part, but also in its intensely-felt descriptions of the Muslim Arabs whose life and whose vision he had, for a time at least, come to share.

Conscious of the tensions of his position, Lawrence, like many of the British officers responsible for policy regarding predominantly Muslim lands, was careful to avoid using the potentially offensive language of the Crusades. Such inhibitions, however, did not affect many other commentators and participants, who, feeling less responsibility for the project of Allied diplomacy, reached for the convenient imagery made familiar and congenial by centuries of usage. One such was A.G. Prys-Jones, Lawrence's college friend, mentioned above, who had been unable to serve in the war due to ill health, and who, his biographer speculates, felt a frustrated patriotism as a result.[26] As the Allies captured Jerusalem, he wrote the following unashamed celebration of Crusading ideals, in a style reminiscent of the poet John Masefield, and portraying the Allied victory as a culmination of the ambition which had eluded even Richard the Lionheart:

Palestine 1192-1917

Gallant knights of Christendom riding out together
Down along the scorching plain, through the breathless noon;
Hauberk-mail of burnished steel, lance and plume a-feather,
And archers out of Cymric hills marching by the moon.

Brazen drums of Araby, strident bugles calling,
Calling from Damascus unto golden Babylon:
Saladin and Saphedin; and flaming Acre falling
And all the gates of Ascalon a-shimmer in the sun.

Towers of Jerusalem, marble-white and gleaming,
Pallid with the sorrow of the unredeeming dawn,
And silent in the tented sand – King Richard sick and dreaming,
Dreaming of your shadowed face – oh, weary and forlorn.

> Knights of Britain overseas, riding ever riding
> From Gaza unto Olivet, though centuries have flown:
> O Towers of Jerusalem – there is an end to biding,
> For Lion-heart hath come again to claim you for his own.[27]

The vast majority of British soldiers serving in the Middle East did not have the unusually close relationship with Muslims experienced by Lawrence and the small group of specialist liaison officers of whom he was a part. The bulk of the British military personnel lived in the closed exported communities of the Allied armies, for whom Arabs were not comrades but were simply the inhabitants of the land in which they happened to be fighting. In their diaries and letters home, unrestricted by the requirements of diplomacy, many Allied personnel routinely referred to their military enterprise in terms borrowed from the accounts of battles in the Old Testament, or from the Crusades. Curiosity regarding the religion of the local people, or that of their Turkish adversaries, was not common. Among commentators at home too, knowledge of the Islamic context of the campaign in the east was not salient.

There were, however, exceptions. One such was Sir Owen Morgan Edwards (1858-1920), the educationalist, MP, and pioneer advocate for Welsh in schools and in public life, whose career was summarised in Chapter 3. He was the editor of the influential and widely-read magazine, *Cymru* ('Wales'). In the September 1916 edition, one of his articles, 'Arabia', gave a view of the early stages of the Arab revolt, and showed an informed curiosity about the Muslim background:

> The war in Arabia has generated many causes for surprise. Amongst them is the revolt of the Arab against the Turk, and that at a time when the Turk supposed the invincible German was on the verge of setting him on his feet again, to rule and oppress and punish the infidel. Is not Turkey the most powerful Mohammedan power on earth? And is not Arabia the location of the faith's most sacred places – the grave of Mahomet in Medina and the 'House of God' in Mecca?
>
> I heard a friend of Lord Kitchener say that the minister of war was waiting for this to happen at any time. He knew the East, and he knew that the Arab too looked on the Turk as an oppressor.

Edwards goes on to describe the holy cities of Islam and

portrays Britain as a defender of Muslim interests:

> In fact, nearly all the pilgrims' paths, on land and sea, are under Britain's protection. As the majority of Mohammedans are under our banner, in India and Africa, we have been very careful always not to interfere with their religion; rather, we aid the journeys of their pilgrims.

His description of Islam itself avoids discussion of its theology, concentrating instead on the geographic setting of its birthplace, in a manner more romantic in its style and simpler in its understanding, but similar in its essential assumptions, to that of Lawrence:

> The Mohammedan faith is the child of the desert. The genius of the Arab gave it birth. The power of desert horsemen sent its flame across western Asia, north Africa and ancient Greece and Spain. And today more than two hundred million people look to Mecca as the most important place in the world.

Edwards praises the Islamic leaders for their enlightened policies, and contrasts these favourably with those of the Turks, for whom he displays the same condemnation as Lloyd George – both men had been part of the early nationalist movement Cymru Fydd ('Young Wales') – although Edwards's attitude to the Turks is more of a headmasterly disapproval than the lawyer's scathing forensic oratory deployed by Lloyd George:

> To these Arabs belong the love of learning and discoveries. From them came rulers like Harun al Raschid, the patron of science, and Al Mamun the knowledgeable. It was they who preserved the learning of ancient Greece for the new world, it was they who were the early teachers of science, mathematics and geometry. Then came the Turk from central Asia, one very different in language and in soul – coarser, rougher, crueller, more bestial. By around 1000 the Turks of Mahmud had conquered India; a hundred years later, the Seljuk Turks were despoiling from Armenia to the land of Canaan, a hundred years later the Osman Turks were beginning a campaign that would conquer Constantinople in 1453 and which would make them a scourge of the fairest lands on earth to this day.

Now, he says, 'come the Arabs to cast the yoke of the Turk from their necks.' He describes how the Islamic holy places are now free, and the Arabs independent 'but with the ready assistance of Britain.' Edwards gives a description of Mecca based on Sir Richard Burton's famous clandestine visit; he summarises some pilgrimage practices and discusses a photograph of the city sent by John Davies Bryan of Egypt (whose work on Islamic subjects will be discussed in Chapter 10 of this book). Edwards then concludes:

> To this extraordinary temple come millions of people from the four corners of the world. When they reach it they feast their eyes upon it. They spend the days of their pilgrimage within it, they sleep within it if they can, they feel every stone within it with hand and lip; the Black Stone has almost been kissed smooth. They faint from fervour, they see visions, they lose control of themselves in trances; some dance, some lie helpless. Wonderful is the hold that Mohammedanism has on the child of the desert and the many millions who have come to accept his faith.[28]

There is a similar flavour, and a similarly second-hand feel, to a series of two articles 'Dinasoedd Mahomet' ('Cities of Mahomet') by John Evans in *Y Traethodydd* in 1919, which in reporting the Arab recovery of the holy cities of Islam from the Turks, give a detailed account of the founding of Islam and of current pilgrim practices. Evans's primary source seems to have been the adventurer Arthur John Wavell's 1912 book *A Modern Pilgrim in Mecca* about an incognito visit to the holy city in 1908.[29] Evans's view of Muhammad is, however, negative: 'Very incompatible elements met in his character. He could sometimes be gentle and kind if he judged that to be to his advantage; he could also be deceitful, cruel and murderous. With a view to his prophetic claims, it is as hard to believe that he was always sincere as it is to believe that he was always deceitful and hypocritical.'[30]

Another exception to the general incuriosity about Islam's place in the conflict was Tom Nefyn Williams (1895-1958) who fought at Gaza with the Royal Welch Fusiliers. Later he was to become a minister of religion, and in 1928 was sensationally barred from ministerial work by the Presbyterian Church for holding unorthodox and radical religious views.[31] In 1917, however, that controversy was all ahead of him; he was simply a young man fighting for his life in a strange country. His enthralling 1949 autobiography, *Yr Ymchwil* ('The Search') shows how, as a young soldier, he displayed early signs of an inclusive religious world view. In the following passage, he and his company are preparing for the attack in the First Battle of Gaza, which was to end in an Allied defeat:

> To those of us familiar with the geography of the Bible and the colour of Ann Griffiths's hymns, and with the story of Dyfed's pilgrimage in the East,[32] and having exhausted ourselves tramping the harsh desert for the last ten weeks, the first sight of the hills of Canaan was a strange and enchanting thing. '*The blue hills of Judea*', that was the name we gave them; and they were so called because of a light blueness not unlike that of the cuckoo when he was a quarter of an acre away from us, or that of Carnedd Dafydd[33] before sunset at times in the summer. Soon we reached the lands of tall barley, and oranges, and the flat-roofed villages and pretty orchards. This was Jesus's homeland! One of the smallest countries on earth, and a land that could be counted a centre between east and west and north and south; and the moment the horses were set free, as though they had been possessed with the same joy as ourselves, they began to whinny and roll.
>
> It was not long, however, before the unpleasantness and the minor dangers of the journey from Egypt gave way to something harsher. After walking one day for miles from our hiding place under small brush-trees, hundreds of us Welsh were gathered into a scarred hollow below Gaza. It grew late. No-one's mouth was wetted with a ration of rum. Everyone realised that he was face-to-face with death, because we had been appointed for a surprise dawn attack on the web of Turkish and German defences. And great was the strain on emotion and thought, especially for those who had never before tasted the rush and tribulation of a great battle.
>
> In a moment, when it was around eleven o'clock at night, comes a tenor voice singing the first bars of the tune *Diadem*. 'Cyduned y nefolaidd gôr,' those were the words. In a stroke, exactly as though someone had pressed a rifle trigger, our confidence and our concern broke into the last lines of the verse. Like a rowing boat going from wave to wave, we slipped effortlessly from hymn to hymn: *Diadem*, then *Cwm Rhondda; Urbs Area*, then *Andalusia; Dwyfor*, then *Tôn y Botel; Gwylfa*, then *Crug-y-bar; Aberystwyth*, then *Rhos-y-medre.*
>
> A *cymanfa ganu* far, far from any place of worship, and on the threshold of the greatest danger! But why should I be surprised? Because it was in the night the shepherds heard the eulogy of the Spiritual World. It is in the night the night-scented stock releases its

perfume from the garden to the street. It was in the night that Samuel answered the Voice. It was in the night Jacob was given a glimpse of the angels' ladder. It was in the night our Lord and his friends sang their Psalm before crossing the Cedron. And it was in the night that Paul and Silas turned their prison into an opportunity to sing the praises of God. However, we did not have any hymn-sheets that night in March 1917, although we had been used to having them from the Sun Hall, Liverpool, and the Pavilion in Caernarfon, from Caersalem, Barmouth, and from Pen Llŷn; but we depended entirely on the hymnbook of the mind, the book that had been written quietly and gradually while we were children, rubbing along with our elders in the sacred places of Wales. The Holy Spirit's printing press, that's what services are for children.

Around midnight, when the dew was falling heavily and it was not too dark for us to see the frightening outline of the odd tree, we were ordered to leave the hollow, and to walk onwards to our grim task. As soon as we were in a relatively open place, there came a heart-rending cry. Not Welsh: not English either. Just as suddenly, an uncertain and strange silence descended again: the entire Turkish patrol had been killed. Had some of them prayed for the protection of Allah? Did some village or home flash into their memories, yes, faster than their cry? Had they been listening, perhaps, to our hymns about the cross and the love of Christ. The general opinion was that they must have heard us singing.

Moving ... hesitating; listening ... moving; waiting ... starting again; and that's how we were for hours, until we felt the spread of doubt that something had gone awry with our plan. At last daybreak came, but without us having attacked the high ground of Ali Muntar, nor lightened our path. Thick fog was everywhere, and sometimes we heard a nervous shot here and a nervous shot there, as though each side was uncertain of the other's intentions and movements. But sometime around eleven in the morning, blue sky appeared, and the table of empty ground we had to cross before Gaza could be won.

Talk about the old crusades, indeed! They were child's play.[34]

The tension between Tom Nefyn's religious beliefs and his military role is evident. After the war, he became a convinced pacifist. Other Welsh Christians, already pacifists during the war, had enlisted as medical staff. One such was Albert Evans Jones (1895-1970) known as 'Cynan', whose work was mentioned briefly in Chapter 4, and who was later to become one of the most prominent Welsh-language poets of the twentieth century, and Archdruid of Wales. In 1916, he joined the 'Welsh Students' Company', a unit of the Royal Army Medical Corps reserved largely for Welsh ministers and theological students.[35] Cynan served in Salonika in Greece and then in France and Macedonia. These campaigns brought encounters with local Muslims which prompted a poem which became widely anthologised. In Chapter 4, we saw how it was quoted by Captain Jac Alun. 'Salaam' is set in a romanticised desert location, and is an affectionate tribute to the Muslim custom of greeting people by wishing them peace. The following is a loose translation:

Salaam

I learned the greeting I love the best
When the sons of the east met the sons of the west.

Before they depart through the desert sands,
They bless one another with lifted hands.

Each on his camel before they tread
The track to the distance where dawn is red.

Their hand on their heart, they cry, 'Salaam,
'May the peace of God keep you safe from harm.'

Wherever you wander, though sun glows red,
May the Palmtree of Peace ever shade your head.

Wherever you stand in the parching drought,
May the Fountain of Peace ever cool your mouth.

Wherever you raise your tent each night,
May the Star of Peace give its restful light.

When you fold your tent at the break of day,
May the Breeze of Peace bear your ills away.

And when Allah brings us to our journey's end,
We will drink in the City of Peace, my friend!

* * *

I learned the greeting I love the best
When the sons of the east met the sons of the west.

And the wish they share is my wish too
– May the Peace of God ever be with you.

While that poem provides a highly positive portrayal, it must be noted that, in common with many of the literary responses of this period, it appears that the more some Western writers could safely confine Islam to the desert, the more they liked it. Generally, the further away from settled communities Islam is seen to be practised, and the further away it is placed in time and tradition, the greater the approval with which it seems to be viewed. There is a subtle, and very probably unconscious, pressure to exoticise and so to neutralise the religion as a contemporary phenomenon.

For one other Welsh soldier, the religion of his Turkish adversaries, and his Arab allies, was not a matter of polite interfaith curiosity or of anthropological interest; it was a matter of survival. Elias Henry Jones (1883-1942), later to become editor of the important magazine *Welsh Outlook* from 1927-33, and then registrar of Bangor University until his death,[36] was serving as an officer in the Indian Army when he was captured by the Turks early in the war. His extraordinary 1919 autobiography, *The Road to En-Dor*, tells of how he eventually escaped custody by conducting an elaborate and prolonged charade to convince his captors that he was a psychic medium, and so to be granted privileges which would allow him to escape. Jones was a capable amateur magician, and his campaign of deception saw him pretend to be mad, possessed and able to access supernatural knowledge. At one point, he managed to convince his captors that the strange language he uttered during his trances was evidence of his supernatural power. In reality it was his native Welsh. The title of his book is taken from Rudyard Kipling's poem of the same name which, referring to the Biblical story of King Saul visiting the Witch of En-dor to call up the spirit of the prophet Samuel, warns against the deceptions and dangers of spiritualism. Jones himself was not a believer in spiritualism, and his story is a fascinating account of how a modern secularised sensibility, familiar with the language of both Christianity and psychic phenomena, and also with aspects of Islam, could play on any and every belief and superstition of his captors in the service of one aim: freedom. In the following passage, having persuaded their captors they are insane, Jones and a colleague, the Australian officer C.W. Hill, are admitted to a mental hospital, and hear a fellow patient being mistreated:

> An idea prevails that the mentally deficient are handled with exceptional gentleness in Mussulmen countries. It is erroneous. No doubt they are believed to be 'smitten by Allah', but followers of the Prophet are no more patient than other mortals, and if a patient 'won't listen to reason', orderlies take it out of the poor devil.[37]

In another episode, he had convinced the Turkish commanders he could help them find treasure hidden by the local Armenian villagers they had murdered, or 'sent away,' as the Turks euphemistically described it to Jones. In this, Jones came closer to personal experience of the realities of the Turkish Empire's treatment of its Armenian subjects than many other domestic Welsh commentators, whose condemnation was based on second-hand accounts. Jones's closer perspective served only to confirm the picture of the unrepentant callousness with which the authorities and their servants regarded the fate of the Armenians:

> Behind the bald, cold-blooded statement lay a great tragedy, the tragedy of the Armenians of Yozgad. The butchery had taken place in a valley some dozen miles outside the town. Amongst our sentries were men who had slain men, women and children till their arms were too tired to strike. They boasted of it amongst themselves. And yet, in many ways, they were pleasant fellows enough.
>
> The mentality of the Turks is truly surprising. Supposing I had the supernatural power which the Interpreter and Commandant thought I possessed, was it likely that I, presumably a Christian and avowedly an enemy, would be ready to help them to the property of fellow Christians whom the Turks had most foully murdered? Yet they had put the proposal to me without a hint of shame. Englishmen are often upbraided with their inability to understand the Oriental. But sometimes it is the Oriental who fails to understand the Englishman.[38]

Jones conducted séances with the Turkish interpreter. In one instance, Jones was able to use his Welsh background, and the fact that Lloyd George really *did* know his father – he carried a picture of the two of them together – to add credibility to his claims of being a man of influence. In one séance, Jones makes his 'spook' answer the interpreter by saying: 'Either Jones or Hill can lead you to fame if you earn their joint friendship. By my help Jones's father raised Lloyd George to his present supreme position. He started more humbly than you.' The interpreter is captivated.

However, while Jones regarded men such as the greedy and self-important interpreter and the commander who had taken part in the atrocities against the Armenians with contempt, he also came across Muslims whose character he found much more congenial. One such was a fellow patient in the mental hospital, a man who was admitted there because of a physical condition rather than a mental one. His name was Suleiman Surri, and according to Jones he was:

> ...the son of a Kurdish chieftain and a very gallant soldier ... we owe him a debt of gratitude for many little acts of kindness, not least among which was his insistence that the other patients should treat our affliction with the same consideration as they showed to their brother officers. Suleiman Surri came from Diabekr. He had imbibed no western 'culture', but he was one of nature's gentlemen. Courteous, courageous, and full of a glowing patriotism, he was a man of whom any country might be proud to call their son, and if Turkey has many more like him there is yet hope for her.[40]

Jones's whole complex deception took around 18 months, and eventually did get him back home to Britain, albeit, in the end, only two weeks earlier than if he had waited for the Armistice. It is possible his extraordinary adventure will come to much wider attention in the future, as the novelist Neil Gaiman is adapting *The Road to En-Dor* for the cinema. It will be interesting to see what a twenty-first-century perspective makes of Jones's story.

One contemporary Welsh novelist who has revisited the Palestine campaign is Angharad Tomos (*b.*1958) whose 2004 novel, *Rhagom* ('Onward'), tells the story of two of her family members who served in Palestine in the two world wars, and is based on the genuine letters of the elder of the two, her great uncle William Henry Williams, who was killed at Gaza in 1917. Angharad Tomos is a committed pacifist and a tireless campaigner with Cymdeithas yr Iaith Gymraeg, the Welsh Language Society, for whose trademark non-violent protests she has served time in jail. In *Rhagom*, the perspective of a modern Welsh nationalist, opposed to war and sceptical of Western interests, is projected onto the participants in the First World War. In the following passage, two Welsh soldiers are preparing for the First Battle of Gaza:

'We're fighting an old, old, battle, you know,' said Mathrafal gravely.

'Are we?'

'Down in that town where we were yesterday – Kham Yuris, there was the ruin of an old tower.'

'Yes, I saw it. What was it?'

'One of the old castles from Crusader times. That's how old the battle is.'

'That's not so old for a lad raised in the shadow of C'narfon Castle,' Gwilym answered with a smile.

'Have you studied the maps of this area,' Mathrafal asked.

'Yes, a little,' answered Gwilym.

'Do you realise what is ahead of us – between us and Jerusalem.'

'I can't say I'm all that familiar with the towns.'

'They're very familiar names – Bethlehem, Hebron, Engedi.'

'Strange, eh?'

'Yes, and what are the names of the chapels in the town nearest to me? Jerusalem, Hebron and Engedi.'

'Outside C'narfon, we have villages – Bethel, Nasareth and Nebo. And there's an Engedi chapel in C'narfon too.'

'How many of these towns will be destroyed before we reach Jerusalem?'

'Depends how strong the Turkish resistance will be.'

'They have more of a right to the place than us, I reckon.'

'If you're willing to yield Jerusalem to pagans...'.

'Gwilym *bach*, they're no more pagans than us. They have their own god, and they take him as seriously as we do, even if they don't sing hymns.'

'But if you believe there is one true God . . . don't you think we are doing the right thing in liberating Jerusalem?'

'No I don't, but I'm not about to start discussing theology with you now. All I'll say is that this war has more to do with the Anglo Persian Oil Company than the Almighty.'

'Why are you fighting then, Math?'

'Because I've been forced to. I would be back home in Meifod if I had any choice in the matter.'

They were quiet for a long while afterwards. Gwilym felt that he had to believe that there was a purpose to their presence there. He wanted to believe that he was doing something right and honourable, that the whole battle had some dignity. There had often been fierce arguments among the crew of Cofis[42] but they had all volunteered to fight for some reason or another. The mindset of the conscripts was different, and he always forgot that.

It was depressing having no-one to talk to.

'Mathrafal?'

> 'Yes?'
> 'What are you thinking about?'
> 'About a poem I read today.'
> 'What was it a poem about?'
> 'About the war, by a young poet by the name of Wilfred Owen. Do you want to hear it? I learned it by heart.'
> There was something romantic about Mathrafal, because he was a poet probably. Gwilym felt envious of him being able to learn pieces of poetry by heart, that would be a comfort to him on occasions like this.
> 'I'm all ears. I'm not much of a one for poetry, but I like the sound of words. There's so much comfort to be had from them.'
> 'I don't know how much comfort you'll get from this one.'
>
> '*I am the enemy you killed, my friend.*
> *I knew you in this dark: for so you frowned*
> *Yesterday through me as you jabbed and killed.*
> *I parried; but my hands were loath and cold.*
> *Let us sleep now...*'[43]

In an afterword to the novel, Tomos says that she was struck when reading one of her great uncle's letters home which referred to 'The Holy Crusade against the Terrible Turks.' She comments: 'Did he say that ironically? Whether he did, or whether he was serious, I heard in it an echo of the '*War on Terrorism and the Axis of Evil*,' of the present day'.[44]

Given the political and historical equation that is the novel's starting point, it is perhaps not surprising that one of the novelist's characters, Mathrafal (who is named, significantly, for the old court of the independent princes of Powys) seems to have a sensibility owing more to the early twenty-first century than the early twentieth, not least in his ability to quote in 1917 from a Wilfred Owen poem not written until 1918, and not published until a year after that. It is also, perhaps, the novel's didactic intent and the need for explication that explains why the other soldier, Gwilym, seems to lack the Biblical, geographical and historical knowledge that was, in fact, widespread among the troops and the society from which they were drawn, as has been shown earlier. However, whatever may be the novel's anachronisms, in its recognition of the longer historical background of the Crusades, in its acknowledgement of the religious complexities of the Middle East, and of the part that energy resources can play in geopolitics, it is indicative of the reasons why Western involvement in Muslim countries during the First World War will continue to attract the attention of Welsh authors, even as their views of that fateful historical episode change with the passage of time.

Notes

1. For a fuller discussion of Welsh philo-semitism, and the smaller but important undercurrent of anti-semitism, see *The Chosen People* (Bridgend, 2002) by the present author. See also Jasmine Donahaye, '"By Whom Shall She Arise? For She Is Small": The Wales-Israel Tradition in the Edwardian period,' in Eitan Bar-Yosef and Nadia Valman (eds.) *'The Jew' in Late-Victorian and Edwardian Culture: Between the East End and East Africa* (London, 2009) 161.
2. Walter Laqueur, *A History of Zionism* (London, 1972) 187.
3. David Gilmour, 'The Unregarded Prophet: Lord Curzon and the Palestine Question', *Journal of Palestine Studies,* 25: 3 (Spring, 1996) 60-8.
4. David Fromkin, *A Peace to End All Peace*, (New York, 1989) 298, quoted by Jill Hamilton in *God, Guns and Israel,* (Stroud, 2004) 147.
5. Jill Hamilton *op. cit.* 147.
6. *Ibid.* 63.
7. Quoted in H.W.V. Temperley (ed.) *A History of the Peace Conference of Paris* 6 (Oxford 1969) 24.
8. David Lloyd George, *The Great Crusade Extracts from Speeches Delivered During The War*, (New York, 1918) 102.
9. William Ewart Gladstone, *Bulgarian horrors and the question of the East* (London, 1876) 9.
10. *Ibid.* 31
11. Quoted in Emily Greene, *Approaches to the Great Settlement* (New York, 1918) 143. See also David Lloyd George, *op. cit.*, 156.
12. David Lloyd George, *The Great Crusade op. cit.*, 144.
13. David Lloyd George, *War Memoirs of David Lloyd George* 3, (London, 1938).
14. Quoted in Humayun Ansari, *The Infidel Within: Muslims in Britain since 1800* (London, 2004) 90.
15. Margaret MacMillan, *Paris 1919: Six Months That Changed the World* (London, 2001) 378.
16. David Lloyd George, *British War Aims, Statement by the Right Honourable David Lloyd George* (New York, 1918) 4.
17. *Hansard*, HC Deb 26 February 1920, 125, 1949-2060.
18. *The Islamic Review*, April 1920, 140–41
19. Now called 'Lawrence House', it is a hostel for climbers and visitors. The room where Lawrence was born is now a bathroom.

20. Jeremy Wilson, *Lawrence of Arabia* (London, 1989) 41.
21. H.E. Salter and Mary D. Lobel, 'Jesus College', *A History of the County of Oxford: 3: The University of Oxford* (Oxford, 1954) 264-79.
22. T.E. Lawrence, *Seven Pillars of Wisdom* (private edition Oxford, 1922, public edition London 1926) References to 1940 edition (London) 40.
23. *Ibid.* 152.
24. *Ibid.* 103.
25. *Ibid.* 41.
26. Don Dale-Jones, *A.G. Prys-Jones* (Cardiff, 1992) 15.
27. A.G. Prys-Jones 'Palestine 1192-1917' *Poems of Wales* (Oxford, 1925) 5.
28. Owen Morgan Edwards, 'Arabia', *Cymru* (September 1916) 129-31.
29. John Evans, 'Dinasoedd Mahomet', *Y Traethodydd,* 74: 331 (1919) 116-22.
30. John Evans, *op. cit.* 74: 332 (1919) 148-58
31. He was reinstated in 1931.
32. See Chapter 5
33. A mountain in north Wales.
34. Tom Nefyn Williams, *Yr Ymchwil* (Denbigh, 1949) 38-40.
35. For an account of this company by one of its members see R.R. Williams, *Breuddwyd Cymro Mewn Dillad Benthyg* (Liverpool, 1964). It has a section (76-81) entitled 'Y Twrc', and based on the author's experiences in Turkey. However, it expresses no notable opinions on the subject.
36. Meic Stephens (ed.), *The New Companion to the Literature of Wales* (Cardiff, 1998) 375.
37. Elias Henry Jones, *The Road to En-Dor* (London, 1919) 275.
38. *Ibid.* 83-4.
40. *Ibid.* 276-77.
41. A nickname for natives of Caernarfon.
42. Angharad Tomos, *Rhagom* (Llanrwst, 2004) 213.
43. *Ibid.* 229.

'May we live in peace together': Welsh Experiences of Islam in the Inter-war and Mandate Period

The Allied capture of Jerusalem in 1917, the ending of 400 years of Muslim Turkish rule in the Holy Land, and the establishment of a 'Jewish National Home' in Palestine felt like a climactic moment of history for many observers. For the devout among the Jewish and Christian Zionists who backed the Allied campaign, it seemed, after many centuries of religious expectation, not only a culmination and a fulfilment of those desires, but also a momentous precursor to a new age of justice and peace. But history does not stop. Every climax has its anticlimax. After every dénouement, the cycle of action starts again. So when, after the peace conferences, Britain was granted a League of Nations mandate in 1922 to administer Palestine and Transjordan, and a mandate to administer Mesopotamia in 1920, it was only the beginning of a new chapter in the history of British relations with predominantly Muslim lands, and Welsh relations along with them. This chapter will examine the period between the First and Second World Wars. Much of the material relates to the Mandate experience, although some comes from other areas of contact.

The Mandate period marked the end of the Turkish empire, an empire long regarded with suspicion and distaste by Western commentators, religious and secular. The first extract in the present chapter provides the opportunity to examine the views of a Welsh author who, carrying the attitudes of a pre-war age, had the opportunity to observe the Turkish empire in its transition to a secular state. Rhys J. Davies (1877-1951), a Welsh-speaking former miner and trades unionist from Llanelli, was a prominent figure in the British Labour movement, and was M.P. for Westhoughton near Manchester from 1921 to 1951. For many years he was joint secretary of the British Group of the Parliamentary Union, which he chaired from 1945, and in this capacity he travelled widely, publishing an account of his journeys in Welsh in 1934 as *Seneddwr ar Dramp* ('A Parliamentarian on the Tramp'),[1] from which the following extracts relating to Muslims are taken. His comments provide insight into the longevity of the stereotypes in Western society of which we have seen evidence earlier.

> When I was a child, living in a little thatched cottage called Ysguborfach, in Llangennech, I would be terrified if anyone talked about the Turk. I cannot for the life of me think why. Perhaps my father had read to me once upon a time that a Welshman had been killed by a Turk on one of those ships that occasionally sailed into the little harbour of Llanelli. It is true that a terrible murder had indeed struck fear into our whole district at about that time. But that was a Welshman killing a Welshman. The idea that a Turk would dare to take a Welshman's life was beyond all understanding in Ysguborfach.
>
> However that may be, I decided in September 1934 to go and see the Turk in his own sty. Remember that my early idea of him was of a man with a sharp knife in his belt; and indeed, a similar picture was in my brain until I reached Istanbul ('Constantinople' before the most recent revolution.)
>
> Early influences are strange things. Until I met one, I could not for the life of me imagine a Turk as anything other than a false, bloody man, ready with his fist, flared of nostril, like a horse going to war! I should have known better, perhaps, having seen so many black and white people by now. But before I started for London, I was sure that the man who lived on the banks of the Bosphorus was a thief, and that I would have to have my wits about me if I was to get back to my own country alive and well and with a penny in my pocket.
>
> I had seen the yellow-skinned Arab, the Egyptian in his pitiful rags, the proud Italian, and the German with his arrogance and swagger. But what, I said to myself, would come of me mixing with the 'uncivilised' people of Turkey? Man is terribly conservative at best. Somehow or other, he sticks to his old ideas like a dog to a bone. He will never drop anything from his mind; he is like Thomas,[2] that time, wanting to see the mark of the nails every day. That was exactly my position in respect of the Turk. We will see presently if I will have to let my prejudice be consumed in the fire of truth like so many other ideas once we find how things are, and not how we supposed them to be.[3]

Davies went to Turkey on League of Nations business, travelling on the Orient Express. Finally, he reached Turkey:

> The sign of the Cross vanished when we left Bulgaria; it is the

> Crescent and Star from one end of Turkey to the other. Mohamed is the prophet of the Turk, as of the Arab and Egyptian. There is a place of worship almost on every street. Not a 'chapel' or 'church' either but a Mosque, if you please.
>
> . . .
>
> Remember, despite everything, that Istanbul is slowly but surely falling into ruin. The population has dropped by almost a half in the last ten years. And it is almost possible to say that the Turk as a man is losing ground – that he is deteriorating as a character. That is what is said to me by people who understand these things. A nation deteriorating. That's a strange idea, isn't it? Beware, little Wales, lest you follow the Turk! It is not an army or a navy or a Parliament either which determine civilisation; it is the morals and character which decide the fate of a nation.[4]

In his reflections on his visit to the League of Nations meeting, Davies expresses his socialist beliefs by saying he would like to put Trotsky, Stalin, Mussolini, Hitler and Pilsudski all in the same pot, and throw in William Randolph Hearst (the American newspaper magnate who had bought St Donat's Castle in the Vale of Glamorgan) for good measure.[5] He is equally scathing about the Sultan, in one of whose former palaces the League of Nations meeting was taking place, and who had been deposed in 1922 when the Turkish republic was established.

> He was the filthiest rogue imaginable. Imagine that old Sultan calling for a particular gift on his birthday. What was it, you ask? Well, well, a young girl not more than fourteen years old! I will let you guess the rest of the story. All Turkey rose like one man against the old fox, and he and his family were sent into oblivion.[6]

Davies cautiously approves the way that Turkey is being modernised, with women no longer veiled, and polygamy in decline. By the end of his journey, his earlier prejudices have been softened by experience, and he concludes with a valediction and a word of rhetorical advice:

> Well, farewell to you, Turk! You are a much better man than I imagined at the beginning. Remember, though, that new things are not always good.[7]

In his travelogue, Rhys J. Davies was comparing previous prejudice with present reality. Some other authors were in a position to provide a perspective on the Middle East which could compare the pre-war and post war situation. One such, in the case of Palestine, was Thomas E. Roberts, whom we encountered first in Chapter 5, as the author of the 1904 pilgrims' manual, *Jerusalem: Y Ddinas Sanctaidd* ('Jerusalem the Holy City'). He visited the region again nearly thirty years later, in 1933, for his updated guide: *Palesteina Hen a Newydd* ('Palestine Old and New'), in which he reflects on the changes he has seen:

> *Mohammetanism Today*. The departure of the Turks from the country, and their replacement by the British as governors of the country has not caused any change to the religion of the Mohammetans. They keep possession of their places of worship and all religious privileges as before. They feel much more satisfied under the government of the British than that of the Turk. Previously, it was against their will that they joined the Army of the Turk, and that they fought his battles. So they are glad of the change. They see that governmental authority is not something to keep them down and despoil them of all they possess; but rather that this is an authority which truly cares for them and helps them to get education, to get medicine, to experience sympathy and aid in their emergencies, as well as assistance to succeed as citizens of the state.
>
> It is said that the Mohammetans are not as hostile to people of other religions as they were, and that they do not now display that excessive zeal and dangerous religious hot-headedness that they used to show if anyone dared, besides they, the faithful, to tread close to the sacred places that have been in their possession for ages, and that there is not now a restriction on visiting the Mosque in Hebron, which has been so hopelessly closed.[8]

As mentioned before, Roberts's description of Muslim belief and practice is detailed, accurate and sympathetic. His assessment of Turkish rule, is, however, hostile. He says that it is Britain which was mainly responsible for setting 'the Turk' in power in Palestine in 1840, through allying with Turkey against the Egyptians, but that in the First World War, it was Britain which:

> ...had taken control of the country out of the hands of the Turk after four hundred and twelve years of oppressive government in union with the Mohammetan religion, and of keeping the inhabitants in the grip of superstition and chaos. A long while after the Age of the early Christians and the Age of the Crusaders, Christians are moving to reclaim their place in the land of Jesus.[9]

He is well aware, however, of the shortcomings of the Christians of the Holy Land, mentioning how their unseemly squabbling over custody of the Church of the Holy Sepulchre in Jerusalem and the Church of the Nativity in Bethlehem had resulted in Turkish Muslim soldiers having to keep the peace between the fractious Christian sects. He remarks: 'Should the contention continue now that the soldiers of Britain have taken the place of the Turkish ones, then the disgrace will continue too.' He goes on to commend the Muslim practice of praying not just in places of worship but wherever and whenever the appointed time of prayer may be.

While Roberts, as a visitor, saw a picture of increasing tolerance and decreasing fanaticism, the British Mandate forces were, in fact, struggling to control the ultimately irreconcilable forces of Jewish Zionists and Arab nationalists. One who sought reconciliation nonetheless, both in her life and her literary work, was Lily Tobias (1897-1984), a Welsh-speaking Jewish novelist from Ystalyfera in the Swansea Valley and an ardent Zionist. Her work is of enormous significance as a record of Zionism in Wales, and of the way it frequently found common cause with nascent Welsh nationalism. Her first book, *The Nationalists*, published in 1921, is a series of short stories about Zionism in Wales, and portrays evangelical Protestant philo-semitism from the Jewish perspective; its cover displayed a Welsh dragon within a Star of David. It is unashamedly propagandistic: all the author's interest seems to centre on people's attitudes towards Zionism, and all the stories' narratives, uncertainties and tensions are resolved by alignment with, and reference to, Zionism, an aim whose fulfilment in the case of many of her characters seems to extend no further than the simple goal of arriving in Palestine, or even, in many cases, simply coming to the existential decision to go there.

The idealism displayed in that work was tested by reality when Tobias and her husband Philip Valentine Tobias emigrated to Palestine in 1935. The decision made and the journey undertaken, they too then had to deal with the aftermath of a dream attained. They aligned themselves with movements that worked for understanding between Jews and Arabs.However, the tensions were beyond the remedy of good will, and Philip Valentine Tobias was killed in anti-Jewish violence in Haifa in July 1938. It was after this 'holocaust of terror broke over Haifa and overwhelmed my life'[10] that Lily Tobias completed work on *The Samaritan*, which she had been writing since 1936. It was published in 1939 and subtitled *An Anglo-Palestinian Novel.* In many ways a thinly-veiled autobiography, it tells the story of a Zionist woman's attempt to settle in that strife-torn country. The efforts of many of the characters of all faiths to behave with tolerance and mutual respect are commended by the novelist, as in this passage, where an Arab policeman, Saadi, visits a Jewish victim of an Arab riot.

> 'Honoured lady,' he began, as if resuming his errand, 'I came especially to tell you now – that you need have no fear. You shall be safe when you travel, at all times – you and your children – and the lady your companion.'
>
> 'I thank you, Saadi. But will you tell me this – am I and my family to be protected as English people? Shall we not be protected as Jews?'
>
> 'As Jews also, lady.'
>
> 'Ah, Saadi – it was not so in this bitter time we have passed through.'
>
> 'Had I known, lady, that you –'
>
> 'I am not thinking of myself alone. I say it was not so for my people, my brothers and sisters, in this old town where we have so many memories together – as in Hebron, and in Jerusalem itself.'
>
> The policeman made no reply. His eyes were still dark pools in an impassive face.
>
> 'Saadi – I thought you were my friend.'
>
> 'That is true, honoured lady.'
>
> 'And I thought you were the friend of my people.'
>
> 'That is true, also.'
>
> 'Then tell me – for my heart is very heavy, and I do not know how to bear such a heavy burden.' Involuntary tears broke again into her eyes and voice. 'I do not hold you personally responsible, Saadi, for the foul things that have been done by your brothers – but tell me why they have acted so.'
>
> Saadi hung his head. His words came slowly.
>
> 'Forgive us, lady. It is a great misery to many. They were deceived.'
>
> 'Who deceived them?'
>
> 'That I cannot tell. But messengers came to rouse the anger of my people against yours. Lies were told.'
>
> 'What lies?'
>
> 'That in Jerusalem the Jews were burning the great Mosque, and killing thousands of Arabs.'

> 'I see. And these lies your people believed so readily that they forgot all honour and friendship, and turned in great wickedness against the innocent.'
>
> 'Their fear and their anger led them astray. I am ashamed for them. You well know, honoured lady, that many will be punished. I wish you to know also that not all acted thus.'
>
> 'I know, Saadi, that you did your duty.'
>
> 'I do not speak of myself, honoured lady, nor of others who are officers of the law. But of men and women of my people, strangers to me and my family, who protected the lives of their Jewish friends at the peril of their own.'
>
> 'I rejoice to hear it.'
>
> Saadi leaned forward and spoke with a little more animation.
>
> 'It will please you, honoured lady, to know of the action of one of our women who had rooms in the town. She hid a number of Jewish children from the fury of those who sought them. When the children wept in fright, the woman sat on her doorstep and wailed in a loud voice, to drown the cries of the little ones.'
>
> 'That was well done.'
>
> 'There are many such, honoured lady. Mukhtars of villages and fellaheen gave shelter and comfort to their Jewish neighbours. In Gaza and in Artuf and in Tulkarem this happened. And at the quarry near Bethlehem our workers defended four Jews among them. Each was clothed in an abayah and taken to a village, where they lay concealed for two days, fed and guarded until they could be secretly convoyed to their homes in the City. This was done under fire and at risk of shedding Arab blood.'
>
> There was a soft clap of hands. Edith turned her head and saw Musa standing at the top of the stairs. Saadi did not stir, but his face showed awareness of the youth.
>
> 'That was a noble deed!' exclaimed Musa.
>
> 'It was an act of friendship,' said Saadi.
>
> The voices of David and Lexie now rose gaily from below. They were chattering to Marjorie. Edith left her chair, and Saadi, too, gathered himself up with dignity.
>
> 'I thank you again, Saadi,' said Edith, 'Father of Yusif, you have lightened my heart. May God bless you and your family and all your people. May we live in peace together.'[11]

The novel goes on to show how fragile is that hope of peace, as the honourable Arab policeman, a symbol of the acceptance the author would have liked the Jews to have received from the Arabs, is later murdered by young hotheads. Refused burial, his body is thrown on the village dungheap, from where the main protagonist's protégé, a young Samaritan called Musa, attempts to retrieve it so it can be interred decently. In the novel, the Samaritans symbolise the protagonist's hope for harmony between the opposing parties; they are seen as '...the remnant of Israel, that has never left the land – that has guarded the ancient ways of Jew and Arab with faith and fidelity – in the mountains of Samaria.'[12] However, this ideal, too, is shown to be painfully vulnerable, as Musa is stoned by Arab youths as he tries to rescue Saadi's body. The novel ends on a note of uncertainty as to the future prospects of coexistence for the people of Palestine.

> Jews and Arabs were standing together, brothers with heads bowed in a strange truce, the sons of Israel and the sons of Ishmael. The corpse of the murdered policeman lay in the dust at their feet. And between them, hostage or deliverer, was borne the body of the Samaritan.[13]

There is another revealing Welsh-Jewish literary testimony from this period. Judith Maro (*b.*1927) was born in Mandate Palestine. As an ardent young Zionist, she assisted the Jewish Haganah uprising against the British, yet fell in love with and married a Welsh soldier with the British forces, Jonah Jones, later to become a prominent sculptor and author. The couple moved to Wales, and brought up their family as Welsh speakers. As a declaration of solidarity with her adopted country, Maro published her memoirs of the tempestuous inter-war years in Welsh. In her 1972 book, *Atgofion Haganah* ('Haganah Memories'), she recalls how, as a child supporter of the Haganah in the 1930s, and one who could speak Arabic, she was sent in disguise to a mosque in Gaza to hear a speech by the Mufti of Jerusalem, whom she had encountered in an earlier chance meeting, and who it was believed was planning to incite violence against the Jewish settlers. The disguise arranged for her by her Haganah handlers, Moshe and Yam, was an elaborate one, and relied more on bravado than on unobtrusiveness: she was dressed as a blind boy, the son of a distinguished Muslim judge and friend of the settlers, and she was delivered to the mosque in a Rolls Royce borrowed especially for the purpose. Her face was darkened with thick lotion which was also used to give her eyes the appearance of blindness. She recounts what she found when she arrived at her destination:

In front of me, standing straight, and casting his eye over all the worshippers, was his Highness Haj-Emin el-Husseini, the Chief Mufti of Jerusalem. Our eyes met for a moment, Yes, that's who it was! My old 'friend' in the annex in Beshare the previous summer. And at that moment I was certain that he had recognised me.

When he began to speak, I listened eagerly to every word, and I paid attention to the tone, and the way he would raise his voice almost unconsciously. He recited some verses from the *Koran* – most of them relating to *Jihad* (Holy War) ... Moshe's knowledge of Arabic did not include the literary language or its devotional vocabulary, and Yam was somewhere at the back. (I doubted, in fact, if he was there at all...) I knew that it would be upon me that the responsibility would fall to make sense of what I heard, and in remembering everything, however unimportant it might appear. After the reading, the Mufti began in earnest:

'Brothers of faith and of blood! You, the servants of Allah and Mohammed his Messenger ... I greet you all!' A short pause, and then he raised his voice: 'Are you sheltering spies in your midst? Find them, unmask them!' The Judge sat a few rows behind me, but I knew he had not moved a muscle. Yes, I was fond of him. I missed a few words. '...Drive them out from here. We are Arabs in this Holy House, and Moslems all!' The screaming was now in the language of the marketplace, and the cultured, refined accent, and the precise intonation had completely disappeared. (As I listened to him, the inflammatory speeches of Hitler came to my mind; we would hear them from time to time on the radio).

'Prepare for the Great Day ... We are ready! You shall have a sign, seventeen days from now! The killing will start in Yaffo ... We will drive out the infidels, the conquerors of our country. We will throw the Zionists into the Great Sea.' And so on and so on, he continued to rave.

I thought of the peaceful Kibbutzim throughout the country, industriously taming the desert; of my friends in the school and the Youth movement; of my teachers, and the students in the nearby Technion. Peacefully we came to the Land, and we longed to live in peace. That was completely clear to even the youngest of us. So I listened to these terrible words flowing out of the gaping jaws in front of me, and I asked myself how it could be that this man should sow such seeds of hatred, seeds that would in the end grow into a crop of destruction for his own people. Because we all knew, even then, that we would never be moved, no matter what befell.

The Judge walked me back to the cottage outside the town, hand in hand as befitted a father and son. We walked slowly, without loitering, keeping apart from the noisy and riotous rabble, which was now, as a result of all the bragging and threatening they had

> heard, thirsty for blood. As we reached the outskirts of the town, I looked surreptitiously at his face. He looked stern and serious. His hatred of the Mufti must have been greater than his doubts about us, or he wouldn't have agreed to help us.[14]

A little later, she overhears Yam and the Judge bidding one another farewell:

> His last words have stayed with me to this day: 'It is a pity we cannot fight openly against him, beast that he is, and gather my people to your ranks against the common enemy ... But were I to do so, my friend, I would be a corpse before the day was out. No, I must fight in secret, as well as I can ...' Yam put his hand, heavy and weary, on the Judge's tired shoulders. I was watching the gesture in the driver's mirror. An inexpressible sadness came over me as I saw the tears gathering in the Judge's eyes. I believe that was when I ceased to be a child, except in name.[15]

Elsewhere, she recounts friendships with Arabs, particularly with a boy called Shareff, whom she befriends by teaching him Hebrew:

> Before long, we became great friends, and reaching such a situation was quite an achievement for one like Shareff: he was a Moslem – not used to speaking freely with girls. We spoke Hebrew when discussing literary and religious (!) matters, and talking about 'what the papers say'. Arabic was our language when we teased one another and messed about. We kept the English language for political matters – when the condition of the country was especially serious. We tried to avoid using English.[16]

In the highly politicised atmosphere of their period and place, the two young people shared a vision of a single socialist state of Palestine in which both Jews and Arabs would live harmoniously; they also shared an impatience with the British, whose position they regarded as untenable and dishonest. However, their dreams of a joint state for their two peoples were dashed with the violence which followed the United Nations decision to partition Palestine. Shareff, who by that time regarded partition as a reasonable compromise, was murdered by Arab extremists.[17]

A reflection of this relationship can be seen in Maro's Haganah-based 1974 novel *Y Porth Nid Â'n Angof*, published in English as *The Remembered Gate*, which has a highly-sympathetic

Arab Muslim, Khalil, as one of the main characters. Khalil is an illiterate slum-dwelling Arab street shoeshine boy, who becomes the friend of the young female Jewish protagonist. In one scene, a manipulative British intelligence officer, interrogating Khalil, tries to persuade him to inform on his Jewish Haganah friends:

> '...Khalil ... the Jews *are* clever – too clever for us – and *much* too clever for you. That's why we have to work together.' The hard eyes were penetrating into Khalil's soul. But hearing his own name was a balm to him. He thought hard.
>
> As a boy, in the old ruined Mosque in the *Suk* he had heard many an exciting sermon, and prayers full of hatred and vengeance came back to him now – as it were in a flash. He remembered the crazy screaming of the worshippers on those Friday mornings long ago. They sang in his ears. '*Itbach-Itbach al-Yahood*'. He was at the time too young to join his people's heroes in attacking Jewish villages and institutions, even though the general rage had excited his boyish imagination, and although he had joined in the chorus: 'Death to the infidel – *Alayhoom*!'
>
> Yes, but *that* was a different thing. The Arabs had not asked for Britain's help, as this officer was now asking for *his* help. In their riots before the War to challenge the conquerors who had betrayed them, they had not needed the help of the *Inglesi*; more than that, they had risen as one man to throw the detested *Yahood* into the sea! That had been truly glorious! Khalil remembered those heroes who had endangered their freedom by venturing down from their mountain hiding places to visit the mosques to recruit men and boys for Kaukaji's 'Liberation Army'. He remembered how colourful were their costumes, and how their swords had shone with gold and gems ... What a dream was that – for a ragged boy from the slums! Oh, that he could have been one of them.
>
> But he shook his head. No, things were not quite so glorious. Those Arab heroes had bled the poor to raise money for their cause, and had killed many good men for daring to speak out against them ... At the start, the Arabs feared no-one but their own warriors, although they took pride in their incredible victories over their enemy. But they had soon seen that the *Yahood* were not cowards, despite their reluctance to strike back; they had not fled the country or abandoned any scrap of land no matter how hard it had been attacked. More recently, a few of the *Yahood* had started shooting and killing. Now the Arabs, especially the poor ones, were really living in fear; in fear of the *Yahood*'s explosives; fear of the warriors' rifles; and fear of the *Inglesi* who were far from content with their lot...

> The officer released the Sergeant so he could be alone with Khalil. That was a relief to Khalil. He could breathe more freely without that threat at his side.
>
> 'You hate the Jews, don't you?' the officer asked, watching the doubts on the youth's face.
>
> Did he? When he heard hatred preached, his blood boiled. He was a good Arab and a faithful Moslem. But once he was outside the Mosque and needed customers, it was the *Yahood* that he sought. They were generous and would never treat him like dirt. Few of the Arabs wore shoes, and rarely would any of them need his services, with the exception of the landowners – and they were haughty; they would shut him up quickly enough if he tried to talk to them. As for the *Inglesi*, they were generous, but somehow they made him feel as though he belonged to some lower class of human being. Khalil hated their fake courtesy, even though he would take their money thankfully, and bow to them deeply enough; the poor had no choice but to kiss the hand – or foot – that fed them.
>
> 'No, I don't hate the Jews,' he answered.[18]

While it is clear that Maro has an unswerving commitment to the narrative of the Zionists as peaceful settlers forced into defensive violence by the irrational hatred of Muslim extremists, her extended and sympathetic portraits of Arab Muslim friends, like the similar portraits in the work of Lily Tobias, stand as a testimony to the hope that existed, prior to Partition, of the possibility of a harmonious relationship between Jews and Arabs in Palestine. It was a hope that has so far proved unrealisable, as Maro's work, like that of Lily Tobias, shows: in both women's books the moderate Arabs of whom the authors approve tend to become victims of extremists themselves.

The degree to which the Holy Land has been a cauldron of contending loyalties can be seen by the fact that in Mandate Palestine, a Welsh Zionist like Lily Tobias could find herself in tension with the British regime being upheld by soldiers from her own home country. In Chapter 9, which deals with Second World War experiences, we will look at the work of one of those soldiers, Elwyn Evans (1912-2004), a soldier with the British forces in Palestine, who wrote two impressive sequences of poetry about his experiences. However, Evans was not the only major Welsh-language poet to have spent a period in the British Mandate territories of the Middle East. John Tudor Jones (1904-85), known as John Eilian, and, like Elwyn Evans, a graduate of Jesus

College in Oxford, worked in the region as the editor of the *Macedonian Times* and the *Iraq Times*. A mercurial, pugnacious character, Jones spent only a brief time in the Middle East, which was one of many short-lived appointments in his career. However, the experience produced a sequence of poems 'Wrth Afonydd Babilon' ('By the Rivers of Babylon'), which was published in the magazine, *Y Llenor*, in 1930, and which gave some vivid depictions of Islamic life in Baghdad. Although John Eilian was only eight years Elwyn Evans's senior, the superficial and romantic artistic sensibilities of these poems, written as they were in the 1930s, seem to belong to an earlier age, and are closer to the style of thought and expression of the late nineteenth century. This is the first of the five poems:

In Baghdad

Thou holy Arab cleric
Atop thy temple fair
Calling to thy brothers
Through the silky evening air,
What balm have you to offer
The traveller today? –
The strong call from the minaret
'Awake! And come to pray!'

'The all-forgiving Allah
Is mankind's only friend;
Awake! And make obeisance,
Communion without end;
The spirit that possesses
Creation's farthest place
Shall give like dew of morning
The blessings of his grace.'

I offer, gentle Arab,
My hand and heart to thee,
Your evening call will always
Be sacred unto me;
My people too are noble
Although of poor estate,
And they too know the secrets
That God keeps from the great.[19]

The remaining four poems, all in a similarly florid lyrical style, portray a jasmine-scented world of Arabian Nights romance, full of seductive black-eyed maidens, and tented encampments beneath the desert stars. Apart from one rather incongruous poem about the dubious pleasures of cocaine, this is an idealised and exoticised view of the Arab world; the religion and God of Islam are treated as little more than local colour, as the following extract from 'Arab wrth ei Gamel' ('An Arab to his Camel') shows:

> O, forward now, Zabia
> And bring Basra to hand
> We twenty miles must travel
> Through unforgiving sand.
> Until we fall, exhausted
> By heat and dust oppressed,
> And seek Allah, the Highest,
> In prayer before we rest.[20]

Unlike the Muslims of Elwyn Evans's Mesopotamia and Palestine, these people are portrayed less as being of intrinsic value within their own context, and seem to serve more of an extrinsic decorative function for a Western sensibility. The politics of recent years has thrust Iraq into the headlines, but the work of Elwyn Evans and John Eilian is a reminder that British, and Welsh, involvement in the country is not just the product of world affairs of the early twenty-first century, but has its roots much further back in time.

Yet another Welsh writer who visited Iraq during this period was Tom Madoc Jones, known by his bardic name 'Madoc o Fôn' ('Madoc of Anglesey'), who later, as an RAF chaplain, came to prominence as the organiser of the Cairo Eisteddfod of 1943, whose history will be examined in the next chapter. Jones's interest in the region predated the war. He made a visit to Palestine, Syria and Iraq in 1931, and recorded his impressions in his 1953 travelogue *O'r Aifft i Baghdad* ('From Egypt to Baghdad').[21]

> The first view of Damascus was an enchanting one: there she was like a grey pearl in a green circle of orchards; the minarets of mosques rising from among its thousand terraces, and sometimes a piece of ruined wall as a reminder of times gone by. Somewhere in its midst I imagined the Street called Straight that the apostle Paul

escaped from in a basket over the wall; here too is the grave of Saladin, the Mahometan ruler who gave such a drubbing to the crusaders in the year 1187 and who ended the Christian Kingdom of Jerusalem and indeed completely flattened the crusaders. Despite that, there were superb elements in Saladin's character, not least his kindness to the poor. Even though he had amassed great wealth in his campaigns, he died poor after sharing it all; and we are reminded by H.V. Morton that a friend of Saladin had recorded that they had to borrow the money to buy the necessities of burial, even the small amount of straw to mix into the clay to bake the bricks of his tomb. Above the chapel of his sepulchre is an Arabic inscription written centuries ago:

'O God, receive this soul, and open to him the gates of heaven, the last victory for which he has been waiting.'

Much sharp mockery is to be found between the covers of world history; perhaps none is harsher for the Christian than to be forced to admit that one of the greatest enemies of their religion had shown that he was, in essence, a better 'Christian' than the majority of his opponents.[22]

In Iraq, Jones finds himself in a country emerging into a modern form of nationhood, with urban dwellers imitating the modern West: 'and to a degree sacrificing much of the charm and naturalness of the true life of the country.'

I noticed this in the country's religious practices. The great majority of the people are Mahometans, and it is a common sight every day to see the people on their knees in the fields or in the streets offering prayer at particular times of the day. Was there not once something of the kind in Wales when prayer meetings were held in the cabins of the quarries of the North and in the black bowels of the South?

We took a train journey from Baghdad to Basra more than once during my stay in the country, but I shall not forget the first time I went. The journey was very tedious – the weather hot, clouds of dust coming into the carriage and mixing with the food I was trying to swallow. The same bare plain stretching either side of the iron road. But exactly half way to Basra the train stopped in a station, exactly on the special hour of prayer according to the religion of the Mahometans. As soon as the train stopped, scores of people got out and unrolled little carpets, and the travellers all knelt on them and practised their devotions and prayers as naturally as the Welsh or the English might have gone to look for tea or something stronger in the railway stations of Britain. After the devotion, everybody got back on the train, and on it went with its journey.[23]

The final extract from T. Madoc Jones's memoir is included not specifically because it says something about Muslims, but because it indicates the seamless identification between British imperialism and Welsh-speaking culture that was possible, and common, even as late as the 1930s, but which would seem unimaginable in the work of most post-war Welsh-language writers, who identified increasingly with a nationalist position which opposed Britishness and the Crown. In this passage, Jones's travels have taken him to Tehran in modern Iran.

> During my visit I called at the official residence of the ambassador of Great Britain to pay my tribute to him and to let him know I was in the city. Doing this is a requirement for Britons; and were it not, I know of nothing more fitting in a foreign country. The ambassador is the stay and the 'father' of every Briton away from home, who can turn to him for succour and counsel in any need he might feel. It is a little part of the mother country within the boundaries of the court, and it is inviolate. Gathered within these walls are all the power and authority of the empire, and the most humble of the citizens of Britain can claim shelter and protection beneath the roof-tree of the representative of the Crown.[24]

As with so many of the items collected here, the encounters with Islam recorded by Welsh authors in this chapter are by-products of travel undertaken for other purposes, whether politics, military service or religious emigration. For the teacher and translator Cyril Pritchard Cule (1902-2002)[25] the circumstances which took him into the Middle East and to contact with Islam were those of simple necessity. Cule had left the University of Wales, Cardiff, in 1925 during the Depression and could not find work. Several months and fifty job applications later, he was teaching in a Quaker school in the mountains of Lebanon, then ruled by France under the League of Nations Mandate arrangements. Cule recorded his impressions in his first book, a 1941 memoir, *Cymro ar Grwydr* ('A Wandering Welshman'), which begins with a meditation about the spiritual value of the desert:

> It was in the desert that the Lord's call came to Moses. It was in the desert that Jesus Christ defeated the tempter. Mohamed was a man of the desert. So was Buddha. It was in the desert that Elijah heard the 'still small voice.' Why? because all other voices had been stilled. It is the tropical forests, where life is dangerous and complex, which

> are the home of polytheism. It is the desert which is the home of healthy monotheism.[26]

If that passage represents a common response of a Westerner musing on an alien landscape, Cule's second chapter, entitled 'Iaith Mohamed' ('The Language of Mohamed'), is more original. Uniquely, as far as this study has been able to establish, it provides a comparative Arabic-Welsh linguistic analysis of the Muslim call to prayer:

> Syria, Palestine, Arabia and all the lands of north Africa – those are the lands of the desert, and those are the lands of the Arabic language, the holy language of the Prophet of Mecca – the language of Paradise according to his teaching. Whatever may be the case about the life to come, this is one of the main languages of this world. It is spoken by some 40,000,000 people.
>
> To describe the charm of Arabic, the best I can say is this: that it is a language no-one would ever think of calling 'thin'.[27] It is the language of thunder – a language full of the majestic music of Old Testament poetry. Here is a sentence of it – the most famous sentence ever spoken in it, the Mohametans' call to prayer:
>
> Al-la akbar. La ila li Al-la wa
> God (is) great. (There is) No god but God and
> Mohammed rasul Al-la
> Mohamed (is) God's Prophet.
>
> Notice the extraordinary conciseness here. There is no word that corresponds to the English 'of', and so 'God prophet' is said the same way as in Welsh, through juxtaposing these two words. The verb 'to be' has no present form either. It is dispensable. It will be seen too that the Arabs understand the art of brevity, and delete every unnecessary word, saying many things in few words.
>
> They have a definite article, but they do without the indefinite article, just like the Welsh. 'Al' is the article (the 'the') and so it can be seen that the meaning of 'Al-la' is 'The God', namely the only true God. That last word is uttered very reverently by them, with the last syllable drawn out.
>
> I have heard that word in many common phrases, courtesy greetings and so on. An Arab will never express the hope that you have had a good time. He must hope that *God had willed* that you had had a good time, and you must answer 'Thanks be to God, I had a good time.
>
> I remember a six-year-old boy in the school where I was teaching,

> on being told the good news that one of the teachers had left – one of whom the children were not very fond. 'Nashkor Al-la,' 'Thanks be to God,' the little lad said, looking to heaven with a very sermonical look on his face.
>
> You can tell a man's religion by noticing his manner of greeting – and his way of cursing! The Mahometan greeting is 'Salaam aleikum,' which is 'Peace be upon you,' but if you say that to a Mohametan, he cannot answer you in the same way, when you are an 'unbeliever'. He can say nothing better than 'Peace be upon the faithful!' You can be sure that he wishes that you will at some time be converted and have the privilege of being one of the Prophet's faithful. 'A privilege, a privilege, to have fellowship with the saints!'[28]
>
> 'Mesheen', or followers of the Messiah, is what Christians are called in Arabic. That is the literary name, but in common parlance the Mohametans have a nasty name for us, namely 'Nasrini' – Nazarenes. It is a terrible insult to a Mohametan to call him a 'Nasrini,' and it is not uncommon to hear a man cursing his horse, his camel or his ass by calling it 'Ibn-en-Nasrini', which is 'Son of a Christian!' 'A curse on he who prays for you!' a taxi driver once said to the driver of another motor on our road, and I thought that was one of the most comprehensive curses I had ever heard.[29]

Cule was teaching in Lebanon at a time of change, with European colonial cultural influences and the mechanism of the industrial age disrupting traditional ways. The English missionary enterprise to which he was himself attached he regarded as a benign one, which improved the lot of the local people and contented itself with everyone retaining their own traditions and their own religion – whether Christian, Muslim, Jewish or Druze – as long as all was permeated with 'the spirit of Jesus Christ'. Although he was himself employed as a teacher of English to mainly Christian Arabs, Cule views with distaste what he saw as the more inhumane manner of the promulgation of the French language to Arab schoolchildren, and the readiness of some parents on their part to abandon their native language. He compares it to the similar pressures exerted in Wales in earlier years to discourage Welsh. Cule, a socialist, was moved to political reflection, suggesting the land would be better off independent than under European control, and dismissing as 'opportunism' the imperialistic rationale that believed that European mastery was necessary to ensure peace between the region's warring religious sects.[30]

In manners, Cule far preferred the natural courtesy and unstinting generosity of Arab hospitality to the ways of the *bourgeoisie* – 'the moneyed class who have nothing to commend them but their wealth'.[31] As for the introduction of capitalism, he says he has mixed feelings in seeing it supplant the 'splendid traditions' of feudalism. As an example, he recounts how some local people welcomed the arrival of European-style banks, which they saw as a way of safely depositing money; but he adds that some of 'the old Muslim faithful' had refused to receive interest payments, as Muhammad had branded usury a sin. He reflects: 'More's the pity, the unclean money of the usurer is the essence of the unchristian and un-mohametan system that is born when Feudalism perishes, and we have to accept this diabolical system, as the clock cannot be turned back.'[32]

The wide spectrum of Welsh experience of the Middle East during this period is clearly illustrated if it be considered that while Cyril Cule was teaching out of economic necessity in a mission school for poor children in the mountains of Lebanon, a distinguished fellow-countrymen was also engaged in scholarly work in the Middle East, albeit at the other end of the economic and educational spectrum. Sir Idris Bell (1879-1967) was a renowned international scholar and a world expert on ancient papyri. He was English-born, but his mother was Welsh, and he identified with her country, learning Welsh and becoming an influential translator from Welsh to English. His translations were standard works for a generation and made a huge contribution to Welsh scholarship. However, his international reputation was based on his work on ancient manuscripts at the British Museum, where he spent his entire working life. He was a world authority on his subject, and was awarded a host of honours, including being elected President of the British Academy,

Part of his role for the museum was to expand its collection of papyri, and it was in this capacity that he made several journeys to Egypt in the 1920s on behalf of a syndicate which was trying to acquire important manuscripts for Western scholars. He gave an account of his experiences in the prose memoir 'Hela'r Papyrus' ('Hunting the Papyrus'), which was published serially in *Y Llenor* in 1929 and 1930. Bell was not specifically a scholar of the Islamic period in Egypt: his speciality was Roman Egypt, and the preceding Greco-Egyptian culture. However, 'Hela'r

Papyrus' nonetheless contains some descriptions of contemporary Egypt and its Islamic culture, although, like John Eilian, Bell reaches for the ready imagery of oriental romance:

> But it is in the native district that one finds the real Cairo. The moment he goes there a man finds himself in the world of the Thousand and One Nights, and apart from the odd motor car and British soldier, it would be easy to imagine that we are living here in the age of Haroun al Rashid. It is a dense labyrinth of small narrow lanes, with the occasional wider street crossing them here and there. On every side there is an endless row of shops, especially in the Bazaar district, and the tall native houses with their unglazed windows open to wind and sun. Yonder rises a mosque from the corner of the houses, with its walls decorated with intricate tracery in masonry and plaster; from the minaret, its tower, swim the notes of the muezzin calling the people to prayer – 'No-one is great but God; I bear witness that there are no gods but God, and Mohammed is his prophet. Come to prayer; come to safety. Only God is great; there is no god but God.'[33]

As Bell's specifically scholarly interests in Egyptian history did not extend into the Arab Conquest, it might be suggested that he finds the modern country, for all its romance, rather less evocative than the polytheistic ancient world. In one episode, he visits a newly-discovered temple at Faiyum to the crocodile god Sobek, known locally as Petesouchos and Pnepheros:

> By today, the crocodile has vanished from the land, his temples are roofless and deserted, and from the dozen minarets the muezzin testifies that there are no gods but God.[34]

In the vicinity of Luxor, however, Bell finds that it is the mosques which seem neglected, while it is the domestic architecture which excites his imagination with its sense of a continuity with the pre-Islamic past:

> In the biggest villages, above the other roofs, rise the towers and minarets of the mosques, most of them in a ruined state; it is strange that a people as religious as the Muslims should hold their places of worship so cheaply. Although it looks old, it is the mosque in fact which is the only building in the villages which looks recent; in terms of their external appearance, the houses could have survived from the time of the Greeks and Romans.[35]

In 1946, Bell published a further two-volume account of his travels in the 1920s, under the title *Trwy Diroedd y Dwyrain* ('Through the Lands of the East').[36] He devotes an entire chapter of the second volume, 'Cyffes Abdw Mwhammad' ('The confession of Abdu Muhammad'), to a portrait of his eponymous Arab guide. The passage begins with Abu helping Bell haggle, successfully, for some papyri. Later, they have lunch, and Bell commits a *faux pas* by offering to share his sandwiches with Abdu, who, after inquiring as to the kind of meat, politely returns them. 'They had ham in them,' says Bell. 'And like every good Muslim, he could not touch them. I cursed myself for being such a graceless and thoughtless fool.' Later still, harmony restored, Abdu approaches his employer:

> Shortly afterwards, after completing the ablutions required by his religion, Abdu crossed over to me and, squatting on his heels before a pillar at my side, he began to talk – on general subjects to begin with, but he soon delivered himself of a kind of confession:
>
> 'You would notice, sir,' he said, 'that at Hamed Hamid's there was much talk before he would take your price?' I said I had noticed that. 'Well, sir, to make him take it I tell him a little story – I am very sorry, sir; I ask you to forgive me – I ask Allah to forgive me, but it is often necessary in the way of business to tell little stories. I do not like it, sir – you know, we Muslims believe – I hope you do not mind me talking to you of our beliefs?' 'Not at all,' I said. 'Well, sir, we believe that when we die and the soul goes out of the body, three kings – we are forbidden to say gods; there is but one God, that is Allah? – three kings, sir, will come to us, and they will say to us: "What is your faith?"; and we shall reply: "Your faith is my faith and your God is my God!" And they will say – you know, sir, we shall be very thirsty, terribly terribly thirsty – and they will say to us: "If you will deny your faith we will give you water to drink", but we shall reply: "No, your faith is my faith and your God is my God!" and then they will let us go through into Paradise. But at the end of the world, at the day of judgment, we shall be examined of all our deeds, and everything will be known: the hand will testify against us, "I did this," and the tongue will say, "I said so and so." I wish to do the will of Allah, sir; I am a good father to my children, I do not betray my friend, I do not steal, or do injustice; but in the way of business it is necessary to tell little stories – you cannot do the tourist business without little stories. I hate it, sir; I wish to go to Mecca, to make the *hajj*, sir, and then to return and go away from the world and be a holy man, be alone with Allah. I do not like the world, sir; it is not a good place;

> everybody is evil, men betray their friends, they hear a secret and tell it to others, they are all anxious only for gain. Look at me sir – I am only thirty-eight, sir, but I am sick of the world: I am fed up, sir, fed up,' and he repeated the colloquial expression with heartfelt feeling.
>
> And that, after some pruning and abridgement of its repetition and loquacity, was the substance of Abdu Muhammad's confession. I understand that the Egyptian does tend to talk about and around without every getting to any point at all, and I have no doubt that Abdu was back at his old business with travellers the next day, telling his 'little stories' to them as before and trying to get what he can out of the pocket of the innocent; but if we men wish to avoid being condemned ourselves, then we have to be judged, not alone, not even first, according to our deeds, not by the small confessions and deceits that are pushed upon us by the hustle and turmoil of life, but rather we should be judged also by our hopes and those shy desires which are never practically expressed; somehow I feel that I had for a moment been able to see into an Egyptian's soul. And so true, so true and so completely typical was Abdu's confession. We start our journey with such high hopes and such generous and honest wishes, but then we are pressed by the sullied activities of the world around us – and as we deal with business, we begin to tell 'little stories'.[37]

Another prominent Welsh scholar made a visit to a land with Islamic heritage during the inter-war years. Iorwerth Cyfeiliog Peate (1901-82) was from humble roots in Montgomeryshire, but became a successful academic and museum curator, who was instrumental in setting up the Welsh Folk Museum (now the National History Museum), at St Fagan's near Cardiff, and who became the new institution's first curator, just after the Second World War. In 1928, while he was still working in the archaeology department of the National Museum of Wales, he took an extended trip to Spain, recounting his experiences in an article in *Y Llenor*, in which he goes into detail about the Islamic past in the southern part of the Iberian peninsula. He describes the 'sublime' Mosque at Cordoba, 'the main monument to the religion of the Moor in Spain', and adds: 'Cordoba is a kind of Spanish St David's and the beauty of the body of the old tradition pushes its elbows through the whitewashed dress of the twentieth century.'[38] A little later, he finds himself in another place where the Islamic architectural tradition is preserved, Granada's Alhambra:

> But behold, where is the Arab palace? All that can be seen at first glance is the ostentatious building erected by Charles V with the help

of Moorish money and at the expense of destroying much of their finest work. But I turn through a little gate, pay a peseta, and paradise opens before me:

> *palais que les génies*
> *Ond doré comme un réve et rempli d'harmonies,*

as Victor Hugo said. I came shortly to the *Patio de la Alberca*, the Court of Myrtles, the *alberca*, or the narrow lake of green water, with goldfish in the middle, and a hedge of myrtle either side of it. It is hard to forget that glimpse of the greatest beauty of Spain.

The decorations of the Alhambra are full of that rich intricacy that one imagines is to be seen in fairyland. Every inch of the walls are covered with arabesques of incredible splendour, with inscriptions declaring the greatness of Allah and the deeds of Moslem kings.[39]

He goes on to describe the building in greater detail, and to suggest that every child in Wales should read *The Alhambra* by Washington Irving, the American author who had studied extensively in Spanish history, who was his country's minister in Spain, and who wrote a biography of Muhammad. Peate concludes his description of his visit to the Alhambra in terms which are close to a spiritual epiphany:

> The memory of the glimpse I had of the masterpiece of the Moors comes back to me from time to time like the gentle spring breeze. This place is something more than 'the old inn of the world where we stay a little while': the church in the city below seemed ridiculous in comparison, and I could not stand to stay long there after descending from the beauty. But the city was as fair as before: the transformation was within me, and the Alhambra was to blame.[40]

There were other Welsh visitors to Spain during the period between the First and Second World Wars. However, these were drawn not by heritage or culture, but by politics: they were the 174 Welshmen who volunteered to fight with the International Brigades, the multi-national forces which were formed to support the Spanish socialist government when nationalist and fascist forces rebelled against it in 1936. The appeal to foreign socialists to join the fight against fascism found a strong response in Wales, where there were hundreds of thousands of miners steeped in socialism. Of those who joined the International Brigades in their ultimately unsuccessful fight to prevent a fascist victory, a total of 33 lost their lives. The literary account of contact with Islam brought about by this episode in Welsh history is an unexpected one. It is not, as with Peate, a transcendent experience of the architectural glories of the long-vanished Moorish culture in Spain, but something more earthy, and much more dangerous: a fight to the death against 'Moors' themselves.

General Francisco Franco, leader of the nationalist rebels, had launched his campaign to conquer Spain from a base in the Spanish colonial territories in Morocco in North Africa, using Spanish regular forces, augmented by an estimated 80,000 Moroccan Muslim recruits, known at the time, by both sides, by the now-archaic term 'Moors'. Although many of these Moroccan soldiers had fought against the Spanish colonists, they had joined Franco's forces through a combination of coercion and financial incentive. Franco's personal bodyguard was made up of Moroccan Muslims, and the 'Moors' in his forces were among the most feared of his fighters.

Critics of Franco's claim to be fighting for Christianity were quick to point out the inconsistency of his army relying on Muslim troops. However, it is notable that even left-wing critics of the Spanish fascists found it possible to employ prejudicial stereotypes of Muslims in pursuit of their main objective of discrediting fascism. This can be seen in the anonymous column 'Dyddiadur Cymro' ('A Welshman's Diary'), in the magazine *Heddiw* ('Today') published between 1936 and 1942, which gave a platform of support for the Spanish Republic. The article is partly a rebuke to an influential minority in the Welsh nationalist movement, represented particularly by the founder of the Welsh nationalist party, Saunders Lewis (1893-1985), who, partly out of neo-Catholic conservativism, were willing to support Franco.

> I pity those people who still believe that the battle in Spain is between atheism and Christianity. If I believed that, if I believed that people like De Llano[41] (a man who is sick in mind) and Franco were the true defenders of Christianity, then I would be prepared to say that the sooner they were swept from the face of the earth the better. We are not so blinkered as to claim that the other side are blameless, but one thing must be remembered, that they are the product of a reaction against a particular kind of religion, a healthy enough reaction we believe, a religion of capitalism, a religion of the vested interests. And the motive of the rebellion was to defend land and

> property, not to defend religion. In essence, the weakness of the Puritans who 'won' America, and the Catholics who 'preserved' Spain over so many centuries was the same. Look at who are the allies of the rebels. Mussolini, the defender of the Moslem faith, Hitler the persecutor of orthodox Protestants and Catholics in Germany, and pagan Moors, who are willing to murder for pay. No, faced with Spain, Christianity has little to say, little except to repent in sackcloth and ashes.[42]

While the point about the illogicality of the fascist position might be pertinent, the use of the casually prejudicial term 'pagan Moors' indicates that considerations of interfaith sensibility counted for little compared with the aim of political point-scoring among warring parties within Christian nations. Islam is once again subordinated to a Western agenda.

The same can be seen in another left-wing journal of the same period, *Tir Newydd*, ('New Ground'). The author of the following passage is one of Saunders Lewis's opponents, the Reverend Gwilym Davies (1879-1955), a Baptist minister and peace activist, who was at the time the Honorary President of the council of the League of Nations in Wales. Davies was a tireless promoter of international understanding, a man who had attended every General Assembly of the League of Nations in Geneva between 1923 and 1938, and a man whose draft plans for educational co-operation were used as the basis for the constitution of UNESCO. In Wales, Davies is perhaps best remembered for his initiative in setting up, in 1922, the annual goodwill message from the youth of Wales to the world, a tradition which, under the auspices of Urdd Gobaith Cymru, the Welsh-language youth movement, continues to this day.[43] The quote below comes from the leading article of a special edition of *Tir Newydd* in 1938, devoted to the ideal of freedom:

> Hitlerian Germany does not just aim to conquer in the political world: it aims to conquer in the intellectual world as well.
>
> Hitlerian Germany should always be considered as the Islam of the twentieth century, looking at democracy as an unclean thing and on a democrat as an infidel.
>
> To hundreds of thousands of Germans today, Hitler is a god, and there is no God but he.[44]

While the condemnation of Hitlerism, or the identification of it being a movement with a religious character, is inarguable, it is notable how a man of liberal religious views such as Davies could, in pursuance of his argument, use Islam as though it were an unquestionably pejorative term. Together with the previous quote from *Heddiw*, it is reminiscent of the way in which, in earlier periods, Islam was used as a shorthand insult in inter-Christian religious disputes. In some respects, the use of the term in this manner is similar to the way that the word 'Nazi' is now used as a brief – and often lazy – means of discrediting opposing viewpoints by association.

A portrayal of the actual contact between Welsh volunteers and the Moroccan soldiers is given in the 1992 novel, *Crystal Spirit*, by Welsh author Roger Granelli (*b.* 1950) which follows the fortunes of a young man called David Hicks, who joins the International Brigades under the influence of his communist uncle, Billy. As part of his research, Granelli interviewed the last Welsh survivors of the International Brigades, including his former high school teacher, Morian Morgan. In the following passage, Granelli shows the Welsh Brigaders encountering their Moroccan opponents in a battle near Madrid in February 1937, presumably the battle of Jarama, when International Brigades, including many Welsh volunteers, formed part of the Republican forces fighting the Nationalists, of whom Franco's Army of Africa was a major component:

> A sea of Moors washed towards them. Billy galvanised the Maxim back into action, and he was right, it was good at killing. It cut a swathe through the Moors, a cruel scythe that took many, yet they came on blindly, crying hatred and pain at their adversaries. David fired one shot that he knew hit its mark. He saw a man fall to the ground, he landed on his back and stayed there, like an overturned turtle. That man was dead, he was sure of it. There was a clammy emptiness in his gut, an intoxication of shock and power. Billy clapped him on the back. 'Well done, young 'un, you've opened your account.'
>
> In this way, David's taking of a life was lauded. Later he learned that the Moors carried little Christian hearts over their own, to protect them from the bullets of the ungodly. They made perfect targets.[45]

As with so many examples of Welsh-Muslim encounters, many of the episodes recorded in this chapter have stemmed directly or indirectly from one kind of conflict or another. In the next chapter, we will examine the legacy of contact brought about by the twentieth century's greatest conflict, the Second World War. But before doing so, it is worth reflecting that the prominence of the two world wars as agents of Welsh-Muslim contact should not be allowed to create the impression that they were isolated periods of encounter. As this chapter has shown, extensive contact had continued, and not merely for political or military reasons, throughout the intervening years, and reflections on the Islamic world were published regularly throughout that period for the Welsh reading public by some of the country's most prominent authors. There have been times when the conversation between Wales and Islam has been more audible than others, but there has never been silence.

Notes

1. Rhys J. Davies, *Seneddwr ar Dramp* (Liverpool, 1934).
2. 'Doubting' Thomas, the disciple of Jesus of Nazareth who required convincing of Jesus's resurrection.
3. Rhys J. Davies, *op. cit.* 113.
4. *Ibid.* 118.
5. *Ibid.* 119.
6. *Ibid.* 121.
7. *Ibid.* 122.
8. Thomas E. Roberts, *Palesteina Hen a Newydd* (London, 1933) 93.
9. *Ibid.* 73
10. Lily Tobias, *The Samaritan* (London, 1939) Author's Note.
11. *Ibid.* 27-9.
12. *Ibid.* 314.
13. *Ibid.* 320.
14. Judith Maro, *Atgofion Haganah* (Liverpool, 1972) 99-101.
15. *Ibid.* 102.
16. *Ibid.* 189.
17. *Ibid.* 190.
18. Judith Maro, *The Remembered Gate* (Liverpool, 1974) 34.
19. John Eilian, 'Ym Maghdad' *Y Llenor,* 9:3 (October 1930) 133.
20. *Ibid.* 136.
21. Tom Madoc Jones, *O'r Aifft i Baghdad* (Liverpool, 1953).
22. *Ibid.* 29.
23. *Ibid.* 41.
24. *Ibid.* 68.

25. D. Ben Rees, 'Cyril Cule' *The Guardian*, 23 April 2002, http://www.guardian.co.uk/news/2002/apr/23/guardianobituaries2
26. Cyril Pritchard Cule, *Cymro ar Grwydr* (Llandysul, 1941) 10.
27. In Welsh, the English language is sometimes referred to as 'yr iaith fain', 'the thin language.'
28. Cule quotes the opening line of an eighteenth-century Welsh hymn.
29. Cyril Pritchard Cule, *op. cit.* 10-12.
30. *Ibid.* 16.
31. *Ibid.* 20.
32. *Ibid.* 21.
33. Idris Bell, 'Hela'r Papyrus', *Y Llenor*, 9: 1, (Spring 1930) 27.
34. Idris Bell, 'Hela'r Papyrus', *Y Llenor*, 9: 3, (October 1930) 169.
35. Idris Bell, 'Hela'r Papyrus', *Y Llenor*, 9: 2, (Summer 1930) 91.
36. Idris Bell, *Trwy Diroedd y Dwyrain,* II (London, 1946).
37. *Ibid.* 37-38.
38. Iorwerth Cyfeiliog Peate, 'Tua Granada', *Y Llenor,* 8: 4 (Winter, 1929) 203.
39. *Ibid.* 205.
40. *Ibid.* 207.
41. Gonzalo Queipo de Llano y Sierra, (1875–1951), Nationalist general.
42. Anon. 'Dyddiadur Cymro', *Heddiw*, 3: 6, (January 1938) 225.
43. Meic Stephens (ed.), *The New Companion to the Literature of Wales* (Cardiff, 1998) 159.
44. Gwilym Davies, 'Rhyddid a Chymru', *Tir Newydd*, 14, (November 1938) 5.
45. Roger Granelli, *Crystal Spirit* (Bridgend, 1992) 165. Republished 2005.

'THE EFFENDI AND THE EISTEDDFOD': WELSH AND MUSLIMS IN THE SECOND WORLD WAR

As Britain went to war for the second time in generation, hundreds of thousands of British men and women found themselves in Muslim lands. Many thousands of these service personnel were Welsh, as around 300,000 people from Wales served with the British forces during the conflict. This meant another extensive round of Welsh encounters with the Islamic world. A short Welsh-language poem by a serving soldier will serve to illustrate the geography of the territory covered by this chapter. Written by W.D. Williams in April 1941 and published in 1942, the poem is called 'Yr Hogiau' ('The Lads'), and is given in full below minus its first and final stanzas, which mentioned no place names:

> Robin is in Arabia, – and Dewi
>   On the gold sands of Libya,
> Non and Sem on Iceland's tundra,
> And Dan in Macedonia.
>
> Old Bob is in Nairobi, – Huw and Rhys
>   Are in Egypt, effendi,
> Sam El with the Somali,
> And Now Rhyd Sarn in the Red Sea.
>
> Sionyn's in Abyssinia – Deio'r Bont,
>   Poor beggar, in India,
> Ned y Rhiw in Somerset far,
> And Stan in Palestina.
>
> Sianco Puw in Singapore city – and Huw Fôn
>   A submarine mate, you see;
> No one knows where Trebor may be
> Nor Dei'r Maes, except 'at sea.'[1]

The poem is written in the *cynghanedd* metre, as a sequence of four-line *englynion*, each with a complex system of end and internal rhyme, syllabic count and consonantal symmetry. *Cynghanedd* is virtually impossible to translate into English while retaining its metrical features, so I have here replicated the line structure and given an approximation of each stanza's single end-rhyme. The choice of personal names and place names is the same as in the original, and with its juxtaposition of words with similar consonantal structures, such as 'Robin ... Arabia' and 'Sam El ... Somali', it gives an idea of some of the effect of the strict metres.

The poem, even allowing for what is lost in translation, is, of course, of very slender literary merit, but it and the other pieces in the volume *Cerddi'r Hogiau* ('The Lads' Poems') of which it is the title poem, must have proved popular with contemporary audiences, as the collection was already in its third edition in 1943. It is chiefly of interest for this study because it conveniently shows just how many of the lands of Islam had become the temporary homes of Welsh service personnel. Of the thirteen place names mentioned, five are places whose majority population is Muslim, and four have substantial Muslim minorities. Although the choice of place names of Islamic significance is entirely incidental to the purpose of the author, who was merely trying to show how far his community had been scattered, the use of it serves to illustrate the extent to which the war brought people from Wales into contact with Islam.

Nowhere was the relationship more extensive than in Egypt, the traditional centre of British power in the Middle East, and the base for Allied operations in the Mediterranean, the Balkans and the Arab world. During the Second World War more than 140,000 British service personnel were stationed in Egypt, with thousands of Welsh people among them. In Cairo and Alexandria they found themselves in cities which, although alien in many respects, had institutions and facilities tailored to Western sensibilities, and it was these which enabled one of the most extraordinary expressions of Welsh culture in a Muslim country: the Cairo Eisteddfod of 1943.

For those unfamiliar with the eisteddfodic tradition, some brief context may be necessary. An eisteddfod is a cultural festival dating back to at least 1176, and characterised by song and poetry competitions. Its modern incarnation dates to the late eighteenth and early nineteenth century, when it was revived and revised as a vehicle of renascent Welsh cultural identity, and with the addition of neo-druidic ceremony. The centrepiece of the National Eisteddfod is when the winning bard is enthroned by the Gorsedd, or assembly of bards, each of whom has an adopted bardic sobriquet, and each of whom wears druidic robes. Eisteddfodau are held, with more or less ceremony, in communities of all kinds in Wales, from schools, to chapels, villages, and counties, right up to the annual National Eisteddfod, a week-long festival which can attract over a hundred thousand visitors.

The Cairo Eisteddfod of 1943 took place in Sharia Soliman Pasha in a requisitioned former cinema, which, under the patronage of Lady Dorothea Russell Pasha, the English wife of the Cairo chief of police, had become the centre of a programme of cultural activity for British exiles under the title 'Music for All'. The event, which attracted an audience of around two hundred people, drawn from the Welsh expatriate civilian and military community in the city, was organised under the auspices of the Cairo Welsh Society by the Reverend T. Madoc Jones, whose work we examined earlier, in Chapter 7. The role of Archdruid was taken by Richard Aethwy Jones, while the Right Reverend Llewellyn Gwyn, Bishop of Egypt and Sudan, was the Day President. As the majority of the participants were in military uniform, there was an added poignancy, not to say irony, in the enactment of the traditional ceremonial Eisteddfod litany in which the Archdruid solemnly asks the assembled audience 'A Oes Heddwch?' ('Is there Peace?') to be answered 'Heddwch!' ('Peace!').[2]

The Eisteddfod, which was repeated in 1944, was an addition to the Welsh exiles' existing cultural programme of concerts, Sunday religious services and *cymanfa ganu* hymn-singing festivals, and it proved the catalyst for adding another enterprise to Welsh activity in Egypt – a monthly newspaper. The man behind the idea was a young RAF officer, T. Elwyn Griffiths (*b.*1918) and he called the newspaper he founded *Seren y Dwyrain* ('Star of the East'). It was circulated every month to Welsh societies in Cairo, Alexandria, Jerusalem, Haifa and Casfarit in the canal zone until the end of the war. After the end of hostilities, it provided the model for the formation of *Undeb Cymru a'r Byd* ('The Union of Wales and the World'), in 1948, an organisation for the Welsh diaspora, and for its journal *Yr Enfys* ('The Rainbow'), of which Griffiths became the editor.

In 1955 a memoir of the Cairo Eisteddfod and of the Welsh newspaper was published under Griffiths's editorship, under the same title as the periodical, and including examples of the kinds of contributions which servicemen had made to the journal. Two examples from the collection show different aspects of the relationship between the British and their Egyptian hosts. In one essay, 'Yr Effendi a'r Eisteddfod' ('The Effendi and the Eisteddfod'), published under the pseudonym of 'Anarawd', a Welsh soldier proudly takes an Egyptian friend to one of the eisteddfodau. It is given in full below:

> In the evening of the last Saturday Night in September, I strode down Soliman Pasha Street in Cairo. Suddenly, someone called my name, and as I turned, who was there but my friend Hassan Awad Effendi.
>
> 'What's the hurry?' he asked.
>
> 'Didn't you hear,' 'I answered, 'that the Welsh in the forces in the Middle East are holding their first eisteddfod tonight in the Music for All hall?'
>
> 'Eisteddfod! What is an eisteddfod?'
>
> 'Well indeed, Effendi, this isn't the time or place to explain what an eisteddfod is, even if I had time to do that. I'll tell you what! Come with me now to this eisteddfod, and you will see for yourself what a Welsh eisteddfod is.' He agreed politely with my suggestion and off we went.
>
> At the threshold of the hall, we stood surprised because the place was full to overflowing – I'm sure there were over six hundred there – and every one was listening intently to the address of the venerable president, the Bishop of Egypt. He told of his recollections of his youth – an eisteddfod in Swansea, playing rugby in Merthyr – the miners, holidays in north Wales, and every touch would spark a response from someone in the audience. To end with, he stressed that religion was the foundation of all true culture.
>
> 'Is an eisteddfod just a meeting to listen to speeches.' asked the Effendi. 'It would have been easy enough for you to have explained that to me without bringing me here with you,' he added.
>
> 'Wait a minute,' I said, 'that's the leader, Padre Baker, announcing that the bass solo competition is about to start.'
>
> Five singers came to the stage and the enthusiasm rose to a pitch as we listened to them – a man from New Zealand, an Englishman from Bradford singing about the road to Mandalay, a Welshman praising Devon, and a lad from Bala warming the hearts of the crowd with his call to 'Brave Ones of Wales'. When the singing ended, I explained to my friend the difficult task that faced Sergeant Harry Gabb and his assistants, Aneurin Griffiths and Walter

Hopkins, as they tried to assess these basses.

But the singers were forgotten for a while when the Reverend Madoc Jones came forward to adjudicate on the literature. In select Welsh, he divided the wheat from the chaff with light touches that raised the eisteddfodic cheer in the hearts of the audience.

'What prize will the candidates have for their efforts?' Hassan asked.

'Nothing,' I said, 'but the praise and the pleasure that comes from trying to do something to promote the culture of Wales. It's true that eisteddfodau in Wales, speaking generally, give financial rewards, but it is just as true that the prize is small compared with the effort that is made to win it.'

By now, the congregational singing had started, and with real feeling, under the direction of Flying Officer Elwyn Griffiths and the able accompaniment of Gwyn Bryant. The Effendi listened intently to the crowd singing 'Cwm Rhondda', 'Llef' and 'Aberystwyth', with passionate conviction.

Then we had a feast listening to the melodic tenors, and it was good to see a Welsh sailor on the stage, and to hear that over twenty competitors had appeared in the tenor and bass preliminary competitions during the afternoon. And now, behold the crowd silent and waiting expectantly for the chairing of the bard, and here comes the procession of the Gorsedd bards, ascending to the stage. These must be some of the strangest bards ever! 'Poeta nascitur non fit', says the Latin proverb; but not so these. They had been made bards at the vote of the committee and their names showed that they belonged to the tradition of the Cockle Poets.[3] Here they are – Aethwy of Egypt, the archdruid with his voice resounding to the far corners of the hall; the Chief Bard of Misra singing the songs of Gwalia on the banks of the Nile; Melody of Suez, who tried to justify being called from the world of music to the circle of bards by mentioning the virtues of such unpoetic things as bully beef; mischievous Tudor of Helio; Bard Mena who had never spent a night in that not unfamiliar hotel; Martin Tybie of Casfarit; Gwilym Aden carried the sword with great devotion; Eos Marlais and Siôn Tawe performed a great feat by walking the length of the hall carrying the victorious poet, and that without the trace of a smile despite the mockery of some of their friends in the crowd; Trumpet of Memphis sounded the ceremonial horn, with such passion that it might almost have raised some of the Pharaohs of Memphis from their Pyramids; and finally Ioan Penmon, who sang 'Cartref' ['Home'] until all our hearts melted. At the centre of the whole ceremony was Gwyndaf, for once able to sit still with a contented smile on his face, because was it not he, of all the men who had dwelt in Egypt in her thirty centuries of history, who had been invested as its chaired bard?

> 'I suppose,' says the Effendi, 'That Welshmen wear these djelabirs at home when they're not in the army. Am I right?'
>
> This stroke was almost enough to knock me off my chair, but I had enough strength to mumble, 'Shh! Here's "Hen Wlad fy Nhadau." Let's stand! If I have time, sometime, I'll try to explain to you about druids, and the Gorsedd and Iolo Morgannwg and so on. But for tonight, I shall sing the national anthem with more passion and pride than ever.'
>
> 'You have every right to do so'. said Hassan Awad, and after the singing, 'Good night, I have had the privilege tonight of seeing the Welsh at their best.'[4]

But of course, the Welsh were not always at their best. In the above scene, the Egyptian and the Welshmen seem to have a frank and friendly relationship. But not all Welshmen were as egalitarian. Another essay from the same volume, 'Bygs' ('Bugs'), published under the pseudonym 'Hyd', shows a different aspect of Welsh and Egyptian interaction. The author complains that films and the popular press portray the East as a land of romance and enchantment. However, he finds the reality less alluring:

> But in reality, what about the bugs? You, correspondents and editors of the daily papers of America and Britain, what about the bugs? You would be better off refusing to pay for articles about Egypt and the Middle East unless they mention something about the bugs.

Seeking relief from his irritation, he goes to speak to Achmed, the dhobi, or laundryman.

> 'Saieda, Achmed,' I said to him.
>
> 'Saieda, effendi' he replied.
>
> 'Well, Achmed,' I said, 'these bugs are making "mungaria" of me day and night, and I have come to you to find out what is the best thing to keep them away.'
>
> 'They will keep away baadin,' he answered.
>
> 'What do you mean, Achmed,' I asked. 'Are you trying to tell me that my blood isn't wog-like enough yet to save me from being bitten by the bugs?'
>
> 'Aiwa' he answered. 'Your blood is too English and sweet, and until your blood becomes something like ours, you will be bitten.'
>
> 'Well, I said. 'I will have to wait for months for such a salvation.'
>
> 'Aiwa', he answered.
>
> 'Mush quayes,' I said quietly to myself in my throat as I started back to my tent, knowing that another uncomfortable night lay

> ahead of me – waking and scratching, and lighting matches under the blankets to search for those diabolical little creatures called bugs.[5]

The author adds a short Arabic-Welsh glossary explaining that 'Saieda' is good day; 'mungaria' is food; 'baadin' is 'in due course'; 'aiwa' is yes, and 'mush quayes' is bad. However, despite the effort he had made to acquire some Arabic words, his use of the casually derogatory racial epithet 'wog' is enough to give a reader more than an insect-bite of discomfort today, and shows that not all Welshmen were as enlightened as the author of 'The Effendi and the Eisteddfod' might have liked. As an antidote to the Welsh myth of peculiar benevolence, however, it is valuable as a record of how some Welsh servicemen really did think and speak.

A further brief example can be found in the special twentieth-anniversary edition of *Seren y Dwyrain* published in 1963. Among several retrospective pieces, it included an article, 'Ebeneser', by an author identified only as 'Cyfaill' ('Friend') which quotes an anonymous poem 'Y Muezzin' ('The Muezzin') sent to him by a fellow soldier:

> Hoarse crier of the dawning
> From the pulpit of the minaret,
> His flock to prayer is calling,
> And I to my cigarette.
>
> I turn over in my bed again
> When I hear his croaking cry,
> I close my eyes, in grateful thanks
> That one of Christ's am I.[6]

Another record of the indifference of some servicemen to Islam can be found in the 1960 novel *Ym Mhoethder y Tywod* ('In the Heat of the Sand'), set in Egypt during the war, and written from personal experience by William Hydwedd Boyer (1912-70),[7] a son of the manse from Pontardawe, who served as a cartographer with the Royal Engineers in Egypt between 1940 and 1945.[8] It gives what feels like a realistic portrayal of the behaviour of young men far from home in circumstances which make considerations of culture, morality and religion seem secondary to the daily challenge of survival and of the search for pleasure or distraction in the face of violence and death. On a visit to the city in search of hashish, Boyer's characters encounter beggars, child-prostitutes, and a confusing jumble of poverty and piety:

> Les turned left into a dark alley. Huw almost tripped over a beggar who was lying on the ground by the entrance.
>
> He was shouting 'Salaam Alaykum,' and something about 'Allah.'
>
> The pair went up the alley for a short while and then turned right. A number of women glided past them, like monks in their eastern dress. All they could hear was the rustle of their clothes. From one of the dwelling houses on the left the voice of a believer praying arose melodically, like a breath of fresh air among the overpowering smell of Egypt. He had a note of the old Welsh hwyl [fervour] in his voice.
>
> 'Listen to that old bastard going at it,' was all Les said, but as for Huw Prydderch, he felt that his heart was almost warming and his soul being exalted and his troubled mind comforted.
>
> 'God is in every place, present everywhere.'[9]
>
> The melodic prayer was a symbol of the unity of the nations in the Great Creator, and yet ... and yet, the nations were at one another's throats, and he, Huw Prydderch, was taking part in the violence.[10]

The rougher character, Les, epitomises the unthinking superiority and distaste which the author attributes to the British imperial mentality generally, while the more sensitive Huw, who is animated by Welsh national consciousness and by religious sensibilities, experiences pangs of conscience over his place in another people's country, and over his participation in war itself:

> Two Egyptian nightgowns went past them quietly. They went past without greeting them.
>
> 'These wog devils don't want us in their country Huw.'
>
> 'No they don't. Any more than you'd want to see them swaggering through Caernarfon square.'[11]

The crisis of conscience experienced by the character Huw reaches a climax when, on a mission to Syria, he goes absent without leave, and visits the holy sites in Jerusalem associated with his boyhood faith. There, a spiritual epiphany leads him to confess an earlier crime, although this does not bring about the resolution he desires, and he is cast back into the fray, from which only physical disablement seems to offer a release.

Hydwedd Boyer, as a minister's son, found his faith challenged by the experience of war, although it is noteworthy that he found his religious sensibility offended more by the coarse materialism of fellow Britons than by the values of devout local Muslims, whose piety he finds congenial and familiar. This was a not uncommon reaction. Exiled servicemen of a religious persuasion could find that being in the company of the foreign worshippers of an omnipresent God brought them closer to home than the company of irreligious men from their own country.

This can be seen in the work of another Welsh-language author of the same period, Glynne Gerallt Davies (1916-68) from Ro-Wen in the Conwy valley, a minister, poet and scholar. In 1945, he published a volume, *Y Dwyrain a Cherddi Eraill 1942-1945* ('The East and Other Poems 1942-1945), which dealt with war experience in the Middle East. His lyrical elegy, 'Y Balmwydden' ('The Palm Tree'), from that volume, is a sensitive evocation of fellow-feeling with devout Muslims.

The last tanks now are rumbling
  Their way to El-Kab-ir,
And from their smoking nostrils
  Their fumes the skies besmear,
But to disturb this peaceful land
  They shall no more appear.

And you, the handsome soldier,
  From foreign parish far,
You slumber in Askarit
  Where no fierce engines are,
You sleep beneath my branches,
  And go no more to war.

You shall not see the pilgrims
  In robes of varied hue,
Depart across the desert
  A grave religious crew,
To call Mahomed's blessing,
  Their broken lands unto.

You shall not see the lovebirds
  In gauche and shy embrace
As, wing to wing, they hover
  And dance through endless space,
Nor hear among my palm-fronds
  The nightingales sing grace.

No more to hear the Arab
 Give sober, thrilling cry
Among the rocks of Amon
 With prayer to wake the sky,
No more to hear his chanting
 In praise to God on high.

Your countrymen shall never
 Behold your grave again,
Nor halt the hungry woodworm
 From feasting on your name,
The flimsy cross of boxwood,
 Above your shattered frame.[12]

The piece is inevitably reminiscent of Thomas Hardy's famous Boer War poem 'Drummer Hodge or The Dead Drummer', particularly in the way it combines an almost callous acknowledgement of physical dissolution with the impersonal sympathy of the natural world. The Welsh poem is, though, more religious, with a seemingly genuine respect for Islam, and also with the apparent suggestion by the author that the Western presence in Muslim lands is transient, as symbolised by the native fauna rapidly consuming the shallowly-planted cross.

On the theme of theological reflection occasioned by contact with Islam, the 1963 edition of *Seren y Dwyrain* mentioned above contained a notable essay 'Yr Hyn a Erys' ('That Which Remains') by Gruffydd Glyn Evans (1915-97), a wartime R.A.F. officer in Egypt and Cyprus, and later a further education official in Montgomeryshire. In his article he reflects on the memories of his war service which have most endured. In concluding with what he says was his strongest memory, he seems to find himself drawn to the unitarian Islamic vision of God:

> It is quickly growing dark. The forms and the shadows of the hills and hollows and plains between me and the horizon quickly vanish. Between the two lights, it cannot be seen that they are all sand. Due to the distance in every direction, the line of the horizon is straightened. Above: the firmament, without a cloud to cut across the blue-black, purple-black, black-black expanse. Smooth silk, hard silk, riddled by the sharp stars. I stand outside the tent conscious of the immensity, the distance and the silence. There are no houses, no streams, not a shade of the congenial companionable creations of man and nature anywhere. Nothing but the cheerless emptiness.

> Bleak and comfortless thoughts are forced upon me – about beginnings and endings, about an immeasurable universe, about the insignificance of man. I feel the weight of some impersonal cruelty pressing upon me. In the sand under the stars, an interest and belief in pantheism, trinity and humanism is irrelevant. There is nothing but Allah, the strong, the one, and the only one. I seek refuge in my tent. I long at times to have that experience again. It would do me the world of good.[13]

Another serviceman moved to speculation by his experience in Egypt was Llewelyn Williams, of Rhosllannerchrugog near Wrexham, who also served in North Africa, Egypt, India and the Far East. His 1964 memoir, *Rheng o Dri* ('A Rank of Three') tells of the experiences he and two fellow Welsh speakers had during their war service. The following passage describes Islam in Cairo:

> I wonder if the zeal of the Mohamedan has something to do with the fact that his religion was born in the furnace of the desert, or if the zeal arises from the sincere nature of Mohamed himself? Certainly, there is fire in this religion, a fire you would expect to course out from the souls of wild men, familiar with the harshness of the desert. It is an intolerant religion, based on the uniform belief that there is no God but Allah and that Mohamed is his prophet ... It's thought-provoking to speculate what might have been the course of civilisation had Christianity and Mohamedanism set themselves to search for the strengths, rather than the weaknesses, in one another's credos!'[14]

Another son of the manse who found his faith and morals challenged by wartime conditions was Elwyn Evans (1912-2004), the son of the popular minister, poet and Archdruid, Wil Ifan (1882-1968). Elwyn Evans served for four years in Libya, Syria, Iraq, Egypt, Jordan and Palestine. His 1975 collection of poetry, *Amser a Lle* ('Time and Place'),[15] contains an impressive sequence of poems, 'O'r Dwyrain' ('From the East') written in 1948 and showing understanding of, and sympathy for, Islamic subjects. The sequence was submitted for the Crown of the National Eisteddfod at Bridgend that year, where it came second.[16]

> Beneath me is the Near East
> Spread out like an Isfahan carpet:
> Arched towns and lazy heaps of sand
> And river and fields and pyramids and sea

Flowering together in one perfect and intricate
Pattern like the pattern on the wall of the mosque
Woven from the letters of the holiest verse
in the Holy Koran.[17]

He is aware of how tenuous and ephemeral is the British claim to empire, and remarks that the Bedouin had seen many a conqueror come and go.

And now it's our turn,
Fragile conquerors,
Passing them in a lorry to govern the world.[18]

However, despite his knowledge that British dominion must be short-lived, he shares the attitude almost universal among British troops serving in Muslim lands during the Mandate and Second World War period, that regarded current Muslim societies as decayed vestiges of former glory. Referring to Baghdad, he asks:

Was it from this enfeebled city
That the Caliph's Viziers once rode out
To demand tribute from Spain to Samarkand?
And the thin voice of the muezzin
At the top of the minaret
Called the faithful to prayer and to war
When Islam and the world were young.
Today the heavy boots of foreign soldiers
Trample on their kings.[19]

In Chapter 9, which is dedicated to responses to resurgent Islam in the post-Second World War period, we will look at some later poems by Evans, dating from the time when he made a return visit to Israel and found himself having to work out his reaction to the intensified Arab-Israeli conflict. As those compositions belong to the changed circumstances of the post-war era, they will be considered in that context, and we will remain for the present with the period of the war.

Not all the Welsh people in the Middle East during the Second World War were involved with the armed forces. In Egypt particularly, there was a substantial extant expatriate British civilian community, with the inevitable proportion of Welsh people among them. One of these was the scholar David Gwyn Williams (1904-90), originally from Port Talbot, who was educated at Aberystwyth University and at Jesus College, Oxford, and who began a career as an academic in the Middle East in 1935, working as a lecturer in Alexandria, Benghazi, Cairo and Istanbul. In September 1942, Williams became head of the English department at the newly-established Farouk I University in Alexandria. There, he became part of a group of expatriate British academics and writers, including Lawrence Durrell, and he engaged in spirited poetic exchanges with them.[20] Some more of his work will be examined in Chapter 10, but in the context of this chapter, it is worth examining one of his books which deals specifically with the Second World War.

Williams's 1984 novel, *Y Cloc Tywod* ('The Sand Clock'), has a somewhat bizarre premise: two Welsh-speaking Second-World-War servicemen, an airman and a sailor, go missing in the Libyan desert, where they join a tribe of Senussi nomads. One of the men identifies so strongly with the tribe that he becomes fluent in Arabic and is adopted as the tribe's blacksmith and craftsman.

> He was more and more accepted as a member of the section of the tribe with whom he was living, although he would never be a full, equal member. He was now El Hadad; he had his own tent and a right to his share of any fortune which came the way of the tribe, whether it was the result of barter or a lucky shot at a gazelle. No-one tried to turn him into a Muslim; he was considered a kind of fool, innocent if not holy, like the thousands who were tolerated in the Islamic world from one end to another. And the concern that the men of the tribe had about any contact that might take place between Hadad and the women disappeared almost entirely, as he did not show any interest in them. Some of the men who had young women muttered that he should be castrated, but that was too dangerous for one of his age, and they could not afford to lose him. The elders of the tribe laughed at the suggestion.[21]

Later, an extended visit to the Senussi oasis from a travelling Tuareg group allows El Hadad to indulge in sexual activity with a succession of the visiting tribe's young women, whose morals seem more lax than those of the Senussi. The author describes these encounters with specific reference to the *Arabian Nights*. *Y Cloc Tywod* is a curious work. As well as the story of the two servicemen, it also weaves in the narrative of four women who leave the louche environment of post-war Alexandria to seek the temple of an ancient Greek goddess. The overlapping tales seem to have the common theme that the austerity of the desert, and the rigours of Islam – conceived of here as essentially a desert religion – are contrasted with modern Western values, largely to the detriment of the latter. As such, as with so much material examined in this study, the Islamic elements in the setting form part of a backdrop of exoticism whose primary aim is to allow the questioning of certain qualities within the Western experience.

There is exoticism, although with no particular didactic intent, in the account by Geraint Dyfnallt Owen (1908-93) of his visit to the Casbah, the traditional citadel region of the city of Algiers, while he was serving there as a British intelligence officer in 1944. Owen, yet another minister's son and yet another alumnus of Jesus College, Oxford, spent his post-war career as a BBC producer, while maintaining a rigorous and highly productive regime of historical scholarship.[22] In 1985, only eight years before his death, he published his war memoirs as *Aeth Deugain Mlynedd Heibio: Dyddiadur Rhyfel* ('Forty Years Have Passed: A War Diary'), which included a record of his experiences in Algeria, then a French colony, where he spent some time en route to the Balkans, a region in whose culture and languages he later became a specialist. His visit to the Casbah was unauthorised – the district was forbidden to soldiers except those on official business – but it was undertaken in the company of a group of sixty British and Americans, perhaps in the assumption that there was safety in numbers.

> Visited the Catholic church, St Philippe, which had been built on the ruins of the Mahometan temple which had been transferred by the Arabs to the French. In it is the grave of Geromino [sic], an Arab who had converted to Christianity in the sixteenth century and had been martyred. The pulpit is the same one as had been used before in the temple, although a cross has been put on it instead of the symbol of the new moon. Many of the decorations of the church belong to the old temple. On we go to the Temple of the Fisheries, the only religious building that it is allowed for Christians to set foot in. It was built in the sixteenth century by a Christian architect who built it in the form of a cross – the only one of its kind. From there to the Citadel in the Casbah; an incomparable view of the bay and the Atlas mountains; guns stolen by pirates from the Spaniards stand

> frowning at the sea. There are two purposes to this citadel – to pacify the city should unrest occur there, and to defend the port from the mountain tribes. By the fountain is the place where prisoners or criminals were beheaded in the old days. Beheading is anathema to the Mahometans, as no-one can enter Paradise without a head. The custom, apparently, is for the families of the executed to stitch his head to his shoulders before the funeral. Opposite the house of the Janissaries' wives, or the *harem*, is the old Pasha's palace. Here the French consul was struck by the Pasha in 1839, a clout that led to war between the two countries, and to French supremacy. Outside the palace is the Pasha's court of justice, and the gate and the chains where criminals were kept until the Pasha decided their punishment by dropping a coin from the window of his counsel chamber above the gate. From there to a house which is characteristic of the old town – the house of Barbarossa, the famous pirate, according to the story. Here can be seen every kind of information about the Turk's customs, e.g. the circumcision ceremony, where a boy was sent from the *harem* at the age of seven and music was played to drown his screams, even though he was only expected to let out one scream during the harsh treatment. And the women's custom of shaving themselves every Friday and of going to the cemetery that day. As far as that is concerned, no man has the right to climb to the roof of his house, for fear that he should catch a glimpse of the wives of his neighbours. The women wear veils over their faces, as the Prophet has enjoined them to be modest. This is the custom of every woman, apart from the Tourags [sic] and of unmarried women.[23]

Owen's reflections are external, verging perhaps on the superficial. The appropriation of an historic mosque by the French colonial authorities is described in almost euphemistic terms – 'transferred by the Arabs to the French' – with no apparent sense of the tensions that 'transfer' involved, tensions which resulted in the building being turned back into a mosque only 17 years later, in 1962, when Algeria gained independence after a bloody guerilla war. Owen himself refers to Muslim places of worship only as 'temples', never uses the word 'mosque', and, nearly a century after Turkish rule of Algeria had been ended by the French in 1830, seems to use the term 'Turk' to denote Muslims in general. Owen's detailed and authoritative post-war scholarship shows that he was far from being an incurious man, but it should be remembered that his illicit visit to the Casbah, in the necessary company of sixty soldiers, many no doubt in boisterous mood, was probably unconducive to acquiring anything other than a rough impression of his surroundings. His war diary is perhaps best understood as indicative of the kind of sketchy acquaintance with a subject which was all many soldiers, even cultured ones like Owen, could manage in the pressured and often highly transient world of their war service.

The transitory nature of so many service personnel's experience is well illustrated by the next item, which comes from the letters of Alun Lewis (1915-44), a poet and writer of short stories, and the greatest Welsh author of the Second World War. Lewis was born in Cwmaman near Aberdare in the Cynon valley of south Wales, and he overcame his early pacifism to enlist in the Army, earning a commission as an officer and being sent to India, and then to Burma. Already recognised as an author of great achievement and even greater promise, he nonetheless struggled with depression, with ambivalence about the war, and with the tension caused by an extra-marital love affair with Freda Ackroyd, a married woman he met while recuperating at her home in southern India. He carried on a passionate correspondence with her as well as with his wife, Gweno Ellis, whom he had married in 1941. On 5 March, 1944, he was found with a head wound inflicted by his own pistol and died a few hours later. A subsequent army inquiry ruled the death was accidental, although many commentators believe Lewis killed himself, a theory strengthened by the evidence of his intense and troubled letters. The extract below comes from his correspondence with his wife, and was written on 9 August, 1943. It serves to illustrate just how hasty and snatched were so many of the experiences of men caught up in what Lewis, in a letter to Gweno, the month before his death, called the 'massive hurry-scurry of regimental mankind.'[24] Here, he is passing through what is now Pakistan:

> To continue my ragged existence, I'm sitting in the shade of a tree casting its limes upon me – today it's Lahore yesterday it was Delhi, the day before, it was in the train all day and before that Bombay. Tomorrow I hope to arrive in Karachi. I shall have travelled for eight consecutive days! Delhi was wet and sticky and it was only distaste of the station that pushed me forth into the town. I didn't 'enjoy' the splendours, partly because the guides and beggars worry and pester you all the time, but thinking it over, there was a considerable nobility there. The great fort and palace of the Moghuls was a cool spaced construction of beautiful proportions, square marble buildings

> among neat lawns, red paths and cypresses. And the mosque – three marble domes, four red towers, nothing else except the great exalted square of worship and the fountains in the middle – struck my mind as harmoniously as music.[25]

Generally even more fleeting than the contact with Islamic culture experienced by many soldiers was that experienced by sailors, who often saw little more of a country than its quaysides. One such traveller whose war service brought him to a Muslim land was the poet Thomas Henry (Harry) Jones (1921-65), from Breconshire, who was at university in Aberystwyth when war interrupted his studies. Jones volunteered for the navy and served as a signals telegraphist aboard a minesweeper, in which capacity his travels took him to Benghazi in Libya. Again, exoticism is to be found in his use of Islamic versions of stories of the Jewish patriarchs in his short poem 'Djinn-master Solomon', which refers to the Qur'anic account in which King Solomon is enabled to bind djinns to his service and in which these mysterious non-human spirits form part of the hierarchy of his court.

> Djinn-master Solomon
> Had never such delight
> From all his wives
> As I from one
> Dark princess of my mind.[26]

It is worth reflecting a little on what general patterns emerge in terms of the wartime Welsh sojourners' responses to the Islamic world. It would seem fair to say that any perceived weakness or corruption calls forth a mixture of contempt and distaste, mixed with condescension. Respect is more readily accorded to the safely vanished glories of the past, and is almost always given to the uncompromising devotion of contemporary Muslim believers. Rather like the attitude of Giraldus Cambrensis visiting the Welsh in service of an imperial master, the Welsh in service of the British Empire seem most likely to approve tenacity rather than servility in the natives they encounter, but prefer the distant chivalry of the past to the challenge of the present.

Although fewer than twenty years had passed between the end of the First World War and the beginning of the Second, the decline in the importance of religious belief is noticeable in the written responses of Welsh soldiers, reflecting as they did the changes that had happened in Western society as a whole during that period. In the First World War, it was common for service personnel of all ranks to express religious views ranging from simple unquestioning personal piety through to the kind of committed evangelical conviction which could attribute messianic and prophetic significance to their role in the conflict. A generation later, the disillusionment caused by the horror and waste of the first war and the economic depressions and political uncertainties of the inter-war years had done their work and religious certainties were much less in evidence; Welsh observers recording their responses to Islam were at least as likely to draw comparisons with the *Arabian Nights* as they were with the Bible. One example of continued Biblical reference can be found in the work of D.J. Morgan (1884-1949), a long-time columnist with the *Welsh Gazette.* A minister's son from Llanddewi Brefi in Ceredigion, he was already sixty at the time of writing this second-hand commentary about wartime experiences in north Africa, and it can perhaps be taken as representative of an earlier frame of reference that was already sounding antiquated compared with the more cynical and disenchanted voices that were characteristic of the literature of the period. In this extract from a collection of his articles for the *Welsh Gazette*, published posthumously in 1953, Morgan is recounting the experiences of a younger friend, Gwyn Morgan, on active service.

> Apart from the land which is cultivated by the French, the ox and wooden plough are to be seen scratching the surface there in North Africa, and as Morgan says, the odd mule as 'lead horse'. You may see an old man watching the flock or a woman drawing water from the well, and old faces here and there like pictures from the Old Testament, according to Morgan's description again: 'They have learned the craft of being able to stand and stare, as the poet W.H. Davies says.' Imagine the 'Muezzin', the man who calls the faithful to prayer in the Mosque, receiving 'chewing gum' from a soldier at the temple gate and smiling as though Allah had vouchsafed it to him. Morgan had a shock, as he puts it, 'It was as though I had heard about a prophet drinking ginger pop.' Gwyn is a boy from Llandre. His father should compose a verse to the 'Muezzin'.[27]

Also writing in the post-war era was Glyn Ifans (*b.*1920), from Penrhiw-coch in Carmarthenshire, who later became head teacher of Tregaron Secondary School. He won the first prize for a short prose work at the National Eisteddfod at Rhyl in 1953 with his essay 'Tua'r Dwyrain' ('Eastwards'). Ifans served in Far East in the air force in the Second World War, travelling there via Egypt and Suez, and he recorded his thoughts in a diary, *Coron ar Fotwm* ('A Crown on a Button'), published in 1960, in which, in some passages, he expresses his distaste at what he sees as English arrogance towards Welsh people and towards natives of the colonies alike.[28] His essay 'Tua'r Dwyrain' is a meditation on the romance of the 'East' as perceived by Western sensibilities. He points out that there are many different kinds of Eastern societies, and says:

> But for me it is the East of the desert that attracts me. The east of Sahara and Sinai; the East of the lonely places from Beersheba to Babylon; the East my father's uncle tramped through in the wake of Roberts of Kandahar. The East that gave a resting place to my cousin and the East I cursed a hundred times for its dust. The East of the Khamsin whose first breath would send me to tighten the tent ties, to bury the meat tin and straighten the centre pole.[29]

Returned to the compromises and uncertainties of post-war Britain, Ifans clearly hankers after the clarity and simplicity of life in the East, particularly as expressed by Islam.

> ...you will recall that it is Islam, and not the West that manifests completeness and continuance. What has the West to offer from Morocco to Alexandria? Roads, ports, factories, hospitals, hotels, scabby cars and airports. But these are entirely improper; detached in their relationship to the land, and the history and civilisation of the land. Look at the villages of the *felaheen* – an organic extension of the landscape – with only a mound here and there, entirely in keeping with their background.[30]

It is interesting to note that as Ifans was extolling the virtues of the simple peasantry of the East, living close to the earth and untouched by the evils of mechanisation and materialism, the great Welsh priest-poet R.S. Thomas (1913-2000) was saying exactly the same kinds of things about what he called the 'peasantry' of the Welsh hills, whose pre-industrial life was being transformed by mechanisation. Both men were responding to the challenge of modernity which was changing Western society irrevocably, and sweeping away the last traces of older patterns of rural life. Faced with such irrevocable change, Thomas resolutely looked West, seeking parishes ever more remote, untouched and Welsh; Evans, for his part, looked East:

> I look from Alamein across the wadi to Benghazi or from Karachi to the edges of the Sind. On a canvas like this the labourer on his ass travelling towards the sunset dwindles to the size of an ant in the face of heaven. The people are part of the landscape. They borrow the simple muteness of the sand. Not so the Westerner. He is busy hiding from heaven with his cement and his concrete and his steel, either in impudence or in fear. On the edges of the desert, my inexpressible East, the cement shibboleths are pathetically inadequate. They are an attempt to hide from the achievements of the twentieth century. But in the native part of the city on the edges of the long desert in the blue of the morning, I hear the muezzin calling to prayer, calling across the patched roofs of the faithful. To those who are familiar with it, it is no more than a mournful cry, a scream. But, to the traveller, sometimes, its early pang echoing from minaret to minaret, the call, of all sounds the saddest, comes as though from the centre of the soul. I heard this call in Massawa. I hope to hear it again between the pagoda and the temples. It calls upon man to separate himself from the enchantments of his sweet dreams. It calls life to be fearless in its service once more.[31]

After the war, Ifans's continued interest in Islam can be seen in his 1975 volume *Gwynt yr Ynysoedd Bach* ('Wind of the Small Islands'), an account of an educational voyage to the Mediterranean with a thousand Welsh children on the *S.S. Uganda*, in July 1970. It is perhaps his background as a reluctant agent of empire that, as the voyage approaches Muslim North Africa, leads him to recount with unusual attention and sympathy the information imparted to his young charges about Islam. Approaching Tangier, he reflects on the Arab Muslim conquest of the region 'with a sword in one hand and the Koran in the other,' and on 'the religion of the Arab' in general:

> He learns the Koran entirely by memory. The women and children fear the camera and connect this with the tradition of the Evil Eye. They want to go to heaven whole but they believe part of them is lost when the picture is taken. I am ready to believe there is something in

> this. (Certainly the television set has long unsouled those who would like to be important men.)[32]

He recounts listening to an onboard educational film about 'The World of Islam' in which he sees parallels between the lives of his own young Welsh charges and those of the young Muslims, who are portrayed having to leave their home communities to seek education. He remarks: 'In the film, a great deal of space is given to the Koran. The religion of the Arab, like the religion of the Jew, has kept its national character.'[33]

The Second World War was in many senses a transitional point in the Welsh relationship with the Muslim world. Part of the change was in Britain and the West itself. In the religious sphere, the spiritual assumptions and certainties that had dominated discourse in previous ages were being increasingly marginalised by growing disillusion and secularisation. As for the romantic viewpoint which perceived the world of Islam in terms of exotic sensuality, the loss of Empire which swiftly followed the war dealt a fatal blow to the sense of national and cultural superiority which was essential to the objectification inherent in orientalism. And the revelation of the full horror of the European Holocaust which emerged at the end of the war would provide a permanent check on subsequent assumptions of European religious and cultural superiority. At this point, the religious and orientalist approaches, while largely moribund, had not yet been replaced by any dominant alternative mode of perception. In the following chapter, we will see how, in the period following the Second World War, a developing Welsh political consciousness would come to be a newly significant mode of processing encounters with Islam.

However, the other main catalyst for the change in the Welsh relationship with the Muslim world was not a factor operating within Western society or within Wales as part of that society: it was the political, economic and religious resurgence of the Islamic world itself. Post-war, the European empires were themselves in decay, exhausted by their own battles with one another, and were gradually being forced to yield independence to the countries they had colonised, and it was the turn of Islam to assert itself. Many Muslim countries were part of the process of decolonisation, and the Islamic world, growing in spiritual, material and intellectual confidence, was rising to face the West with new challenges.

Notes

1. W.D. Williams, *Cerddi'r Hogiau*, third edition, (Llandybïe, 1943) 3.
2. The event was recorded by the BBC, and extracts can be played on the Wales on Air/Cymru ar yr Awyr website: http://www.bbc.co.uk/wales/walesonair/database/egypt.shtml
3. John Evans (1827-88) was an unschooled cockle-picker from Menai Bridge, Anglesey, whose unintentionally comic verses made him a kind of Welsh William McGonagall. He shared with his Scots contemporary the same ambition and self-belief, and the same absence of talent and self-knowledge. Ironically feted by wags as the 'Princely Arch-Cockle-Poet of Wales', he became a byword for unintentionally bad poets.
4. T. Elwyn Griffiths, (ed.) *Seren y Dwyrain* (Bala, 1955) 59-61.
5. *Ibid.* 65.
6. *Ibid.* 34.
7. The unusual first name makes it likely he is also the 'Hyd' who wrote 'Bygs'.
8. An extended study of Boyer's work can be found in Gerwyn Wiliams, *Tir Newydd* (Cardiff, 2005) 208-14, a thorough and authoritative examination of the Welsh-language literature about the Second World War.
9. The first line of a nineteenth-century Welsh hymn by David Jones (1805-68), seemingly used here to indicate the presence of God in the Muslim's devotions.
10. William Hydwedd Boyer, *Ym Mhoethder y Tywod* (Liverpool, 1960) 38.
11. *Ibid.* 40.
12. Glyn Gerallt Davies, *Y Dwyrain a Cherddi Eraill 1942-1945* (Liverpool, 1945) 11.
13. *Op. cit.* 20-2.
14. Llewelyn Williams, *Rheng o Dri* (Llandybïe, 1964) 44.
15. Elwyn Evans, *Amser a Lle* (Llandysul, 1975).
16. For an extended critical study of the sequence, see Gerwyn Wiliams, 'Mab yr Archdderwydd yn Hyrwyddo Achos Islâm – y pennawd na fu!', in *Barddas*, 273 (June/July/August 2003) 30, and Gerwyn Williams, *Tir Newydd* (Caerdydd, 2005)101-111.
17. Elwyn Evans, *op. cit.* 27.
18. *Ibid.* 32.
19. *Ibid.* 32
20. A selection of Williams's contributions to these exchanges was published as *Flyting in Egypt* (Port Talbot, 1991). For Williams's own account of his experiences as one of the expatriate authors, see David Gwyn Williams, 'Durrell in Egypt' *Twentieth Century Literature* 33: 3, Lawrence Durrell

Issue, Part I (Autumn, 1987) 299.
21. David Gwyn Williams, *Y Cloc Tywod* (Talybont, 1984) 52.
22. Elwyn Evans, 'Obituary: Geraint Dyfnallt Owen' *The Independent*, 22 February 1993 http://www.independent.co.uk/news/people/obituary-geraint-dyfnallt-owen-1474551.html
23. Geraint Dyfnallt Owen, *Aeth Deugain Mlynedd Heibio: Dyddiadur Rhyfel* (Caernarfon, 1985) 16-18.
24. Alun Lewis in Gweno Lewis (ed.), *Letters to my Wife* (Bridgend, 1989) Letter of 23 February 1944.
25. Alun Lewis, *op. cit.* 388.
26. T.H. Jones, 'Djinn-master Solomon', in Don Dale-Jones and P. Bernard Jones (eds.), *The Complete Poems of T.H. Jones* (Cardiff, 2008) 44.
27. D.J. Morgan, 'Gair o Ogledd Affrica', *Detholiad o Ysgrifau* (Aberystwyth, 1953) 23.
28. See Gerwyn Wiliams, *op. cit.* 217.
29. Glyn Ifans, 'Tua'r Dwyrain', *Cyfansoddiadau a Beirniadaethau Eisteddfod Genedlaethol Cymru, Rhyl, 1953* (Liverpool, 1953) 26.
30. *Ibid.* 27.
31. *Ibid.* 28.
32. Glyn Ifans, *Gwynt yr Ynysoedd Bach* (Llandysul, 1975) 68.
33. *Ibid.* 70.

'THE NEWS SHOWS ME MORE THAN I WANT TO SEE': WELSH RESPONSES TO ISLAMIC RESURGENCE.

At the end of the Second World War the British Empire had reached its zenith. It was the largest empire in history. It controlled a quarter of the world's land surface and a population of 700 million people, and it had just emerged victorious from the worst conflict in the history of humanity. At the darkest point of that struggle, its political leader had inspired its people by referring, in a flight of rhetoric, to the possibility of the British Empire and Commonwealth lasting 'for a thousand years'.[1]

It scarcely lasted a generation more. This climactic moment between supreme achievement and swift decline is described perfectly in the masterly history of the British Empire, the *Pax Britannica* trilogy, by Jan Morris, writing at the time as James Morris:

> The end of it was not surprising. Once the almost orgiastic splendour of its climax had been achieved, once the zest went out of it, it became rather a sad phenomenon. Its beauty had lain in its certainty and momentum, its arrogance perhaps. In its declining years it lost the dignity of command, and became rather an exhibition of ineffectual good intentions. Its memory was terrific; it had done much good in its time; it had behaved with courtesy as with brutality, rapaciously and generously, rightly and in error; good and bad had been allied in this, one of the most truly astonishing of human enterprises. Now its contribution was over, the world had moved on, and it died.[2]

When it died, the assumptions inherent in it died too: the superiority of the white race, of Christianity, of European culture. European nations had, for the second time in a generation, laid waste to their own continent, and in the Holocaust of the Jewish people had committed an unprecedented atrocity that would scar their collective conscience ever afterward. It was not only the British Empire that had reached a point of exhaustion;

so had the confidence of the wider Western culture of which it was a part. The success of independence movements in one European colony after another in the post-war period simply turned into external fact what was already internally evident – that the age of European supremacy was over.

There had been around 100 million Muslims in the nations of the British Empire. Now, one by one, and starting with the most populous possession, India, in 1947, the nations of the Empire broke free. At the same time, the Islamic civilisation itself was gaining in confidence, bolstered by political independence, and fuelled in many cases by new oil wealth. In innumerable ways it began to reassert itself on the world stage. The crisis of Western imperial confidence coincided with, and was related to, the rise of an assertive Islam.

For centuries, Britons, the Welsh among them, had been accustomed to regard the Islamic world by means of a repertoire of more or less detractive responses: Muslims and their culture and religion were frequently portrayed as indolent, ignorant, backward, fanatical, greedy, and cruel. And when Britons did find something to praise in the world of Islam, they often did so according to a Western agenda: the safely-departed glories of long-vanished Caliphates; the reassuringly private, uninfectious piety of individual believers; the sensually exotic romance of the *Arabian Nights*. Rarely had Muslims and their culture and religion been taken seriously on their own terms.

Now, those conditions were changing. This chapter will look at how Welsh writers have responded to resurgent Islam, paying particular attention to conflicts of the post-war period: the events of post-Mandate Israel and Palestine; the Suez Crisis; the process of decolonisation; the Islamic revolution in Iran; the Rushdie Affair; the Gulf Wars, and of course 9/11 and its aftermath. Prior to this era, the British might sometimes have fought Muslims, as with Mahdists in nineteenth-century Sudan or Turks in the Middle East in the First World War. They might have hated Muslims, whether they were importunate beggars on the streets of Cairo or oppressive Turkish overlords in the Balkans. And they might occasionally even have respected Muslims. But they had not generally feared Muslims, not since the Crusades. Now, however, those who held the faith of the Prophet were being treated with a new seriousness. In the passages that follow, which largely follow the chronological order of the events to which they respond, we will see assumptions reassessed, allegiances renegotiated, criticism withheld and praise redirected.

Nowhere is the interface between Western heritage and the Islamic world seen more starkly than in Israel and Palestine, and in Jerusalem in particular: the city sacred to the three Abrahamic monotheisms, but so politically and religiously divided that it is a flashpoint for the world's tensions. So it is fitting that this chapter's first passage should come from the work of a writer who engaged deeply with the conflicting loyalties and aspirations of the Holy Land. We first looked at the work of Elwyn Evans in Chapter 7, quoting his poems on the subject of Islamic encounters and reflections based on his time as a British soldier in Mesopotamia and Israel during the British Mandate period, a political dispensation which ended in 1948 with the creation of the State of Israel.

Looking back, in the 1970s, on his Middle East experience, Evans, by then a BBC producer, composed a thoughtful and nuanced sequence of poems with specific reference to Palestine, called 'Jerusalem Divided', and examining both Arab and Jewish standpoints. The first poem, given here in full, is written from the viewpoint of an elderly Arab who remembers being dispossessed in the wake of the establishment of the State of Israel.

> The door of heaven is closed, but between it and the threshold
> There's still a flickering line of scanty gold,
> Across the rushy western slopes, a yellow stain is rolled.
>
> We rode across the slopes one time, and stayed
> Among my father's servants while they strayed,
> To lead as all his bleating wealth an endless pilgrimage made.
>
> A lad upon the hills I heard the voice
> Of birdsong rising to the azure skies:
> For such an hour I'd forego Paradise.
>
> I journeyed to Mecca so I might implore
> That before I die I'd tread my land once more
> But Allah did not answer: closed is heaven's door.

The second poem, also given in full, is written from the perspective of a more radicalised younger Arab.

I never saw the city more given to night
But its intestines are a riot of bright
Appliqué lightning which drags until first light.

The dun-coloured face grows harsher still and greyer
As it watches the alien race below the wire
There's a hatred there that's purer than gunfire.

My beggar's candle stammers a lying fate:
Thin are the arms that guard my son's estate:
And, mixed with mother's milk, he sucks in hate.

The wind grows cold that flees the naked hill.
The old men in their flimsy tents grow chill
And their shivering shanty children that a cough could kill.

But in the dawn of vengeance we shall see
The Arab peoples like one man agree
And rise and drive their enemies to the sea.[3]

In a later sequence, 'Taith yn Ôl' ('Return Journey'), the speaker recounts how, decades after the war, he travelled back to Israel to visit a former wartime lover and a young Jewish family friend from Cardiff who had emigrated for religious reasons. While the emphasis of that visit is firmly on Jewish matters, Evans's sympathy with the Arab position in the face of defeat and displacement is evident:

Israel at last.
'You'll notice great changes', said the taxi man,
It was a true word.
Under the shadow of Carmel, a shattered mosque beside the sea
And the door hanging on one hinge. No more
Comes the sacred shriek from the minaret
To the faithful in the slender overcrowded houses
Before daybreak: 'Prayer is better than sleep.'
Where are the godly old men? And the straight-backed, pretty girls
Swaying delicately in their black cloaks.
Where are the graceful youths
Happy-exhausted? Here in their place
Have come the busy immigrants from Bucharest and Vienna,
Hasty walkers. Their homes are beginning
To disfigure all my Mountain. I see them
Like chalk heaps along the fields of Wales,

On the second ridge defacing the gentle spot
I knew,
When Europe was on fire, made glorious by spring.[4]

The work of Elwyn Evans, coming as it does from an extended, dangerous and passionate involvement with the Muslim world, and matured with the wisdom of hindsight, provides one of the most artistically satisfying Welsh portrayals of Islamic subjects. His sympathetic depiction of Arab disenfranchisement is one of the first signs that the underdogism which had, for more than a century, fuelled the sympathy which Welsh people had felt for the Jewish people and which had led to almost unquestioning Welsh support for Zionism, was transferring to the people whom the successful Zionist project had displaced.

While Israel was, and remains, the primary focus of tensions in the Middle East, by no means has it been the only one. In Egypt, Arab nationalism had gathered strength throughout the twentieth century, and by the immediate post-war period was strong enough to challenge Western power directly in what had long been the centre of British influence in the region, and where, in the Suez Canal Zone, Britain still maintained a huge military presence of some 80,000 personnel. In 1954, the Egyptian nationalist leader Gamal Abdel Nasser negotiated British withdrawal from the zone and then, in 1956, forcibly nationalised the canal, taking it out of the control of its British and French shareholders. The action made him a hero of Arab nationalism in Egypt and beyond, but provoked a British, French and Israeli military invasion. Although the invasion was a military success, it was a political disaster for Britain, as the United States forced it and its allies to withdraw, a debacle which ended Britain's ability to take unilateral military action in the Middle East.

The following extract from a 2010 novel by Stevie Davies (*b.*1946) is set in the period leading up to the Suez Crisis. Davies is one of the most important novelists of modern Wales and was the winner of the 2002 Wales Arts Council Book of the Year Award. The daughter of an RAF family from Wales, Davies travelled widely as a child before settling in Swansea. She spent part of her youth in Egypt, and her novel *Into Suez*, which is set in that country, shows the tension between Britain's colonial influence and growing Egyptian nationalism, which has, in this case, a strong Islamic component. In the following extract, Davies's female protagonist, visiting the market, experiences first-hand some of the political tensions of the region:

> 'Death to the British!' the youth shouted. Burly military policemen bore down on him.
>
> 'Evacuation with Blood!' He roared this slogan in English straight into Ailsa's face. For a shocked moment, she thought of menstrual blood. His mouth seemed to come at her; she smelt garlic breath; saw milk-white teeth, the pink inside of an open mouth. The whole face seemed to rear at her, a colt stampeded (for he was young, in his teens). She saw the whites of his eyes. And then he was taken. One towering military policeman at either side lifted the lad sheer off his feet. At once he went limp in their hands, still close to Ailsa on the surging pavement, where a new pandemonium had ensued, one he took no part in. She saw that his eyes were beautiful. Dark brown pools of sudden serenity, with long, curling lashes. His lips moved silently, as if praying, and this quiet at the eye of the storm seemed to go on for an age, which in reality could only have been the seconds it took for Ailsa to step back.
>
> When the policeman's fist slammed into the young man's stomach, he bent double and cried, *Allahu Akbar*! God is great.
>
> Scattering in all directions, passers-by cried, *Allahu Akbar*!
>
> Ailsa's hands flew to her own stomach, in sympathy. She'd never seen, never imagined such violence. When one is struck, we all are. No man is an island, entire of itself. She whimpered out a cry like a cat's mew.
>
> 'Are you hurt, Madam?' Another khaki man held her gently by the top of one arm. The boy gushed blood from nose and mouth. They were searching him, shoving their hands between his legs, lifting his gallabayya. The boy's blood spattered Ailsa's blouse. Two front teeth hung from his lips on strings of bloody mucus. They'd beat him to a pulp in jail, she knew.
>
> We'd beat him rather.
>
> Both her hands reached out to the young man, as to a child. But he shrank back. In a way he'd not done from the military policemen. To be touched by a woman. A foreign female without modesty, an infidel. Pollution. Taint. Infection. Defiling his perfect martyr's moment and blocking the path to heaven. The knowledge flashed through Ailsa in a second that there was no sign she as a woman could offer that she abhorred these injustices, this occupation. For to them she was of no more worth than an army's *impedimenta*. Chattel. Breeding stock.
>
> Brakes squealing, more jeeps arrived, and an army truck. Rifles sprang up everywhere. The young man was lugged away and tossed

> into a truck, from which another boy in white was gazing out, eyes wide with terror. She glimpsed her boy for a fraction of a moment, before they slammed the doors.
>
> 'Did the bastard molest you?' asked the tender policeman.
>
> 'Not at all.'
>
> 'Thank goodness.'
>
> 'He's just a child. He wasn't armed, was he? What was he supposed to have done?'
>
> The word terrorism was spoken. But anti-British slogans constituted the extent of the schoolboy's trespass apparently. That was our justice and democracy, Ailsa saw. A bitter taste flooded her mouth. We are thugs. We take our thuggery all round the world, calling it civilisation. But it hurt her to think this. She did not want to think it. We were the civilisers, the educators. Recoiling, Ailsa said she was perfectly all right now; she would walk back alone. When she was ready. Not before. Thanks very much. The policeman wouldn't take no for an answer. Should they alert her husband? *What, to come and round me up too?* Certainly not. She would go about her business.[5]

The passage also highlights contrasting attitudes towards women, with the protagonist, Ailsa, uncomfortable both with the British and Islamic versions of patriarchy, although not necessarily to the same degree. Shortly after the incident in the street, she finds herself in a 'native' Egyptian cafe, where Arabic love songs sung by a woman are playing on the radio:

> Heartbroken, abandoned, the voice asserted the sensual desire forbidden by Moslem culture between man and woman. Which all the men in the cafe heard with unembarrassed ecstasy.
>
> Within half a century, Ailsa thought, I don't suppose there'll be any more veils or head scarves in Egypt. Or in the world. Women will be full citizens, they'll enjoy equal rights just as we do, she inwardly informed the inhabitants of the cafe. They'll walk free and proud as I do, a citizen, the peer of any man. You can't stop us.[6]

Egypt was also the background for the reflections on Islam published by J. Gwyn Griffiths (1911-2004), a Rhondda-born Egyptologist, author and prominent Welsh nationalist. He and his wife, Kate Bosse-Griffiths (1910-98), a Jewish Holocaust refugee, spent nearly a year in Cairo, where J. Gwyn Griffiths was a visiting professor, in 1965-6, as tensions between Egypt and Israel were increasing in the period leading up to the Six Day War of 1967. J. Gwyn Griffiths had been to Egypt before, as an archaeological assistant in Sesebi in Lower Nubia with the Egypt Exploration Society between 1936 and 1939. A highly accomplished scholar, learned in English, Welsh, German, Greek and Latin, he pursued with his complementary academic, political, religious and literary interests for the rest of his long life. His numerous publications included poetry, and the first extract below comes from the posthumous 2007 collection *Hog dy Fwyell* ('Sharpen your Axe') edited by his son, Heini Gruffudd. The first poem, 'Fflam Casineb' ('Flame of Hatred'), is a confrontation with Arab hatred of Israel, and is given in full below:

It was a new bookshop
and the welcome to the official opening was luxurious:
the books arranged attractively
Arabic ones, English and German and French
the latest magazine section
perfumed the air
and the virgins who were serving,
smiled answers in many languages
sherry for the Europeans –
fadal, have another!

We wandered over
to the Dictionary section
and saw a shining row of English ones.
Opened one somewhere in the middle
and noticed something strange –
one word had been crossed out
with blue ink.
What word, I wonder?
After looking more closely it became clear:
Israel.
I look again at a dozen or so dictionaries
to find that poor Israel
has been deleted in the same way
in every one.

And that is the truth about the Arab's aim:
to destroy Israel
to annihilate it, to lay it waste
as a nation and as a state.

In Egypt there is all the courtesy
and all the civility in the world;

> Yet there blazes freely all the same
> The eternal flame of hate.[7]

In implying anti-semitism among Muslims, this poem is rare among the work of Welsh writers. It is worth noting, though, the poem's own apparent stereotyping, with the generalisation represented by its reference to 'the Arab'. Further extracts from the work of J. Gwyn Griffiths and Kate Bosse-Griffiths, will be examined in Chapters 10 and 11.

Although the Arab nationalism which had ended Britain's unilateral power in the Arab world with the Suez Crisis, had strong Islamic elements, as did the opposition of Arab states to Israel, the Islamic Revolution of Iran in 1979, while still composed of religious and political components, had the emphasis firmly on the religious. As such, it presented the West, and the world, with a new and unexpected challenge.

The Islamic Revolution, in which an alliance of religious and political forces swept away the extravagant and oppressive pro-Western monarchy of the Shah of Iran in favour of an Islamic theocracy, did much more than transform the governance of that ancient nation. In a way similar to the French or Russian Revolutions, the consequences of this upheaval were global rather than merely national, as they set in motion forces far beyond the borders of the land where the revolution took place, and as the proponents of the revolution actively tried to export the ideology. The historian Vali Nasr, author of *The Shia Revival*, described it by saying that the revolution 'made Islamic fundamentalism a political force that would change Muslim politics from Morocco to Malaysia'.[8] In a Cold War world accustomed for decades to a binary, oppositional model of capitalist West versus Communist East, there was, very suddenly, a powerful new force to be reckoned with, a force whose influence across the Muslim world was inspiring a challenge to the Western economic and cultural hegemony which had taken the place of the cruder previous political dominance of the colonial era.

The earliest Welsh artistic response collected here comes itself from rather an unexpected source: the novelist Richard Llewellyn (1906-83). It is unexpected because Llewellyn made his name as a novelist a full forty-three years earlier, in 1939, with his worldwide bestseller *How Green Was My Valley*, the most famous Welsh novel ever. If one recalls how archaic the Oscar-winning 1941 John Ford film version of the book looks today, it is hard to imagine the author of the original novel tackling the modern complexities of the Ayatollah Khomeini's project to transform the Islamic world in the 1980s.

It becomes more understandable if one remembers that Llewellyn was only 33 when he wrote his bestseller, that he carried on writing for the rest of his life, and that he had spent his latter years in Eilat in Israel, becoming well acquainted with at least some aspects of the Middle East. His 1982 novel, *I Stood on a Quiet Shore*, written the year before he died, is set in Arabia and Iran, and depicts the Islamic Revolution from various standpoints. It tells the story of Jonathan Tewkes, a long-term expatriate British oil executive in the Gulf, who finds himself caught up in the events. The novel opens with a Western oil executive bemoaning the effects of the upheaval, and the destruction of his company's plant by its Iranian employees, who are, he says, 'not even a generation away from the desert':

> Chaos. Unless they bring in the Russians or the Chinese. It'll be a very long time before there's the production we had. But they won't. That damned Ayatollah and the lunatics with him want another way to live. Islamic law. Sharia. Do them any good? Of course not. A mediaeval bollix![9]

Llewellyn shows understanding of the revulsion the revolutionaries felt at the greed and callousness of the Shah's regime – 'The poor were of no consequence and were not to be worried about'[10] – but more often he allows his characters to express violent antipathy to 'the Black Dog, as many called that little old fraz, Khomeini',[11] and to condemn the excesses of the 'puritan' revolutionaries generally: 'An utter nuisance. These idiots want to bring in Islamic law. But it's long out of date. It's infantile. In countries selling millions of barrels of oil? Monstrous.'[12]

His descriptions of his characters and their society can contain elements of an orientalism which seems to belong to an earlier age, and can involve some apparently alarming generalisations:

> Never fool with Arabian women. Beautiful as they may be, they can be poison because their men are adamantine and so is their law, and

> the Arabs are a fierce people. They have no room for compassion, and mercy is unknown.[13]

When compared with Llewellyn's other work, including *How Green Was My Valley* and its sequels, it can be noted these passages are not noticeably more ethnically essentialist than his portrayals of his Welsh or English characters, or of the peoples to whom they belong. Llewellyn was given to essentialism in dealing with the ethnic or cultural properties of his material generally, and was not making a special case of doing so with his Islamic subject-matter. Nonetheless, the particular cultural assumptions implicit in his treatment of the Islamic subjects are worthy of note. In the case of *I Stood on a Quiet Shore*, it is clear that qualities of uprightness and rectitude, and the corresponding defects of intransigence and mercilessness, are attributed to his Islamic characters, as in this description of the Arab emir's son:

> They were of a different breed, upright in all their dealings and honourable in all their ways. They were devoted to a particular way of being, a daily religion, and any slightest departure became a crime, without any excuse.
>
> That is true.[14]

As well as the political events which provide the context for the novel, Llewellyn, as an author whose works generally contain a large romantic element, gives considerable attention to the position of women in Islamic countries. In the following passage M'aroukh, an emir's glamorous daughter, who has experienced Western freedom, chafes at the restrictions of her society:

> '...I still don't think you understand the Arab way. Or the Arabs. Or my father. Or me. We can play with other ideas. We can pretend. But we can't cheat ourselves. We have nothing to do. We must obey!'
>
> 'Why?'
>
> She shrugged and it bounced her breasts, tight, small.
>
> The Koran,' she said. 'Women are slaves. How many years until we fight free? It will depend on the mass of women in all the Arab countries. How *are* we to get together? There are millions of us. We can't. The men stop us. We are slaves. We must do as we are told. I *hate* it!'
>
> 'Same sort of battle's going on everywhere,' I said, for something to say.
>
> 'I went to a couple of meetings at Oxford. Marvellous enthusiasm.

> I saw what's being done in America. *I'd* like to make my own decisions. Perhaps my granddaughter will make hers, but I'll never have the smallest chance. Have you seen our women around here? If I suggested any of my ideas, I'd be stoned to death!'
>
> 'No!'
>
> 'Oh yes. There's no moral fervour so vocal or poisonous as Islam's. It's a real chance for everyone to play the holier-than-thou. We are lunatics ... I had almost five years away in England and America. I loved the freedom. I no longer had to ask advice, permission. I consulted my *self*. Then I came back here to the tenth century. Everything except the chains. Make a mistake and they throw stones until you are dead. You didn't know that?'[17]

I Stood on a Quiet Shore was Llewellyn's final novel, and, thanks to the author's extraordinarily long writing career, it provides a rare interface between the earlier pre-Second World War attitudes – the author had spent six inter-war years as a soldier of the British Empire in India and the Far East – and the transformed world after the Islamic revolution.

The shock caused by the Islamic Revolution can hardly be overestimated: a nation which seemed set on a course of Westernisation suddenly repudiated the project wholesale and embraced a seemingly atavistic vision of society; in a world of growing secularism, a modernising industrial society adopted a theocratic form of government.

In 2006, the theologian, Professor D. Densil Morgan, writing in *Y Traethodydd*, reflected on the Islamic Revolution: 'To us in the West it was simply incredible! An "enlightened' Anglicised regime, one with which we could easily co-exist, overthrown by a system entirely alien to our way of thinking but entirely acceptable to uncounted millions of ordinary people in the lands of the east.' The subsequent Rushdie Affair, then, he says, shook the 'secular orthodoxy' to its core: 'It was funny to see non-religious people, people whose imagination could not cope with any truth beyond their one-dimensional idea of truth, entirely clueless in the face of thousands of people who could not help but show extreme sensitivity to what they understood as blasphemy, a shameless attack on their *religion*.' These events, Morgan says, have put religion back in the centre of public debate.[16]

Among many Western observers, whose societies had seen great recent advances in the status of women, it was the effect of the Islamic Revolution on women which excited most surprise, concern and fascination, perhaps because its effects were so iconically visible – the women clad head-to-toe in black chadors, and the segregated schoolrooms and public places – and perhaps because it seemed such an obvious rejection of Western ideals of equality and democracy.

One of the Welsh authors who have written most extensively about this subject is the important English-language poet, Sheenagh Pugh (*b.*1950). In Pugh's impressive 1990 sequence, 'M.S.A.', a fictional male narrator, watching reports about the Iran-Iraq War on television in 1987, reflects on that conflict and on the lives of the Iranian students with whom he had studied in Germany in the 1970s, prior to the revolution, including one – whose initials are M.S.A. – with whom he was briefly in love.[17] Pugh's poem, substantial extracts of which are given below, has a particular focus on the sexual repressiveness of the Iranian regime. Its narrator's indignation at what it perceives as the Islamic Republic's cynical exploitation of youthful piety and idealism is undisguised:

> The news shows me more than I want to see.
> I hold the *Guardian* between the screen
> and my eyes; peer around at the Persian boy
> coughing poison gas over his uniform.
> I know with my eyes shut what he looks like:
> dark smudged eyes, long lashes, skin
> like ivory. That's how they look
> in my memory, the ones who must be
> sixteen years older now.
>
> The camera slews round; shows women
> shapeless in black cloth, and I go back
> to the paper. One hidden face
> is like another, and any one could be yours.
>
> She was twenty-three
> in Berlin: there was a busload
> down on a student trip
> from the north. (The Shah sent them
> West, to study science
> and be out of the way.)
> There were a dozen, all
> dark-haired, pale, willowy,

but she was *die Perserin*,
the only woman.

She stood out anyway
from the others; she laughed
a lot. The boys didn't laugh;
they were intense and pure
and a little ludicrously
serious, and very young.

Any of these young eager soldiers
tumbling like puppies towards death,
eyes shining, brain in neutral, could be them.

They're forty now, if they're alive,
but when that boy crouches miserably,
doglike, vomiting war, it's as if
none of them had grown a day older.

That was a hot summer:
we found a lake
in the *Zoo-park*, and talked,
while she held her long fingers
in the water. They bowed down
under the turquoises: blue
roughcut masses; her dad
traded in them, she said.

She was going back
to him, when she'd qualified
as a textile chemist. The West
was fine, free and easy; the boys'
fiery purity passed her by,
but he had a walled garden
full of old roses, a house
full of old books, and whenever
she spoke of him, she smiled.

There are a kind of thieves that come by day
with dogmas, policies and manifestos
and steal your country when you aren't looking.
Before you know it, you've no pride
any more; immoralities are uttered
in your name; your consent inferred
to actions that disgust you

. . .

The news shows me more than I want to see.
Whenever I watch some woman
behind a chador, scurrying for cover,
veiling her voice, I hope it isn't you.
Those boys ... they believed
so much, it hurt. Their hate
kindled when they spoke of SAVAK,[18]
the pliers, the shocks. It did sound
pretty bad, I said; she eyed
them from a distance:
'Yes, but they'd do it too.'

There's a night club, called
the Cheetah; probably refers
to the price of beer. The Persian
boys drank coke, sickly-sweet,
innocent, just like them.
They looked askance at her dancing:
she laughed gently,
said things were changing.

They changed all right, I've seen them. I've read
about the squads of the pure-minded, keeping
the streets clean of unveiled women. I hear
they beat them on the soles of the feet.
Those boys were soft, frail; they'd surely flinch
from the sight of pain. Perhaps they close their eyes.

What happened in your country, when one
murdering old con-man replaced another?
How many girls hid their glinting hair,
their clear voices: how many sweet-faced boys
got a taste for torture? It's bad enough
he wastes their bodies in his wars:
firm flesh, straight bones, bright eyes, spilt
for a wizened bag of rheum. It's worse
that he made use of innocence; bought
ardour and hope at market in amounts
expedient to his needs. But the worst
would be if he insinuated craft
and hardness into their wide eyes,
made them like him.[19]

It is perhaps no accident that the newspaper which the narrator hides behind in the opening lines of the poem is the *Guardian*, the widely-recognised symbol of British liberal thought, a newspaper whose readers are regarded as progressive, left-leaning, anti-racist and anti-colonialist. It establishes the speaker's political credentials, guards against suspicions of conservatism, and makes clear the basis for the narrator's opposition to the regime in Iran is that of a concerned supporter of liberty.

This was not the only occasion that Pugh has dealt with the gender politics of the Islamic Republic. Her poem 'The Tormented Censor' from her 1999 collection *Stonelight*, continues the theme of querying the private complexes underlying the outward manifestations of sexual oppression. The poem is given in full here:

He sees what is not given to others,
the foreign magazines before they are made
fit for the faithful. He makes them fit.

All day long, he sifts indecent women.
Runner's World; his glinting scissors meet
and part; amputate bare legs and arms.

All through *Hello*! his soft felt-tip is busy
stroking a chador of thick black ink
over celebrity cleavages.

Even in *Woman's Weekly*, some minx
moistens her lips with the tip of a pink tongue:
he rips it out. The whole page.

They all get shredded, the silky limbs,
the taut breasts, flesh cut to ribbons.
He is devout, and keeps none back,

but after work, walking home, if a woman
should pass, decently veiled, all in black,
his gut clenches; he tries not to look,

as the little devils in his mind whisper
what they know; melt cloth; draw curves
on her dark shapelessness.[20]

The place of women in the face of increasing Islamic fundamentalism worldwide is also the subject of the next item, by Rhiain M. Phillips, based on her contributions to the Radio Cymru women's programme, *Merched yn Bennaf* ('Mainly Women'), in 1984 and 1985 about her experiences travelling the world with her husband, Professor Glyn O. Phillips, a prominent scientist. In 1986, Phillips collected her talks for publication in a volume entitled *Cefndir* ('Background'). In the following extract, she comments on Islam in Malaysia when resurgent fundamentalism was beginning to trouble the Suharto regime:

> For centuries it was a religion with a gentle nature, but, since the early '70s when a host of students travelled abroad, merciless and puritanical elements came to prominence. As a reaction against Western customs, many women voluntarily went behind the veil, saying they felt safer and more independent that way. I had a hint more than once in these countries that Western women were looked down on because of their appearance and their behaviour. One of the research workers in the University there was guiding me around Kuala Lumpur once, and various barbed comments came to the surface. One I remember was his observation that western women always had so many blemishes on their skin! There was surprise among a social group once too when I asked for juice to drink. 'But white women all drink alcohol,' was the response.[21]

The Islamic Revolution and the Iran-Iraq War were not the only conflicts in the Muslim world to attract the attention of Welsh writers. In 1979, the year of the revolution in Iran, the Soviet Union embarked on its ill-fated military occupation of Afghanistan, seeking to secure the future of a pro-communist government there, and initiating a conflict which was to continue for a decade until the Soviets withdrew in 1989. As with so many Cold War conflicts, the Soviet invasion of Afghanistan was a proxy for other competing ideologies elsewhere in the world, including Islamism, communism, capitalism and nationalism. Towards the end of this chapter, it will be shown how a Welsh novelist views the later American-led invasion of Afghanistan in 2001 through the lens of Welsh nationalism. For now, though, it is appropriate to note that during the Soviet occupation, at least one Welsh writer of a nationalist persuasion was moved to comment on the resistance of the Afghan fighters to foreign domination.

The work comes from the copious writings of the Calvinist Christian evangelical poet Bobi Jones (*b.*1929), a former Professor of Welsh at Aberystwyth. His poem, 'Affganistân Acw 1988' ('Afghanistan Yonder 1988'), seems to approve the tenacity of the religiously-inspired Muslim resistance movement against the communist invasion, a resistance which by this time was looking increasingly successful:

> despite the essential investment of traitors
> and everything except absence dead
> from their prayer they draw their battle...

The text is characteristically abstruse, with no capitalisation or punctuation, but it seems to express admiration for the fighters' faith, their determination to defend their country, and their use of primitive resources in their battle.

> in a uniform universe which celebrates ill fortune
> they throw to the million their proverb mules
> until pacified again is their invisible nation
> of a caliph-song against cost a eulogy rises
> until pacified again is their invisible nation
> saying no will mean we do
> passionate are these who make a land from scraps
> saying no will mean we do
> to allah against an alien sacrifice
> wanton bullets will make sharpened hearts
> for allah in the teeth of an alien sacrifice
> and the lovely mules defeat the million.[22]

While an author as uncompromisingly conservative in his Christianity as Bobi Jones cannot, in this poem, be expected to be approving the detail of Muslim belief or the implied aspiration for a caliphate, the poem appears to extend approbation to the way Muslims put God before materialism and before atheism, as represented by communism. It is reasonable, given Bobi Jones's unvarying support for Wales and other small nations to have their distinct identity recognised, to suppose he is approving the Afghan resistance movement as an example of an anti-imperial intransigence which, in general terms, he shares.

In the wake of the Rushdie affair, when novelist Salman Rushdie faced death threats from Islamic extremists for publising a novel, *The Satanic Verses*, which they held to be blasphemous, we find David G. Bowen co-ordinating the written responses of Bradford Muslims in the 1993 collection *The Satanic Verses: Bradford Responds*, and the Reverend Gethin Rhys, reviewing the book in the magazine *Cristion*, comparing the position of the Muslims as a minority with that of the Welsh.[23] A similar intellectual alliance between nationalism in the Muslim world and that in Wales is explored in the curious 1989 novel, *Any Old Iron*, by the distinguished English author Anthony Burgess (1917-93), best known for his 1962 futuristic dystopian novel *A Clockwork Orange*. In *Any Old Iron* Burgess recounts the supposed rediscovery of King Arthur's sword Caledfwlch, or as he spells it, 'Caledvwlch', the legendary Excalibur, which becomes a focus for renewed Welsh national aspirations. In the scene which follows, Caledvwlch is exhibited at a London Welsh venue. Among the dignitaries is one unexpected figure in Arab robes and dark glasses:

> 'The Celtic cause is a common cause,' the fat man said. 'We have a struggle in common with the overweening English. We appreciate Irish help as we appreciate the help of those of our sundered brethren in America North and South. The freeing of the small enslaved nations is the theme of our age.'
>
> 'What's that bloody nignog doing up there?' a Welsh voice called.
>
> 'Please, let us have none of this racial abuse. It is very much in order that the justness of our cause has carried even as far as the Middle East. I invite Mr Ibrahim ibn Mohamed Saud to speak a few words to you.'
>
> Ibrahim ibn Mohamed Saud kept on his dark glasses as he addressed the microphones. He said little in a very refined English, but that little was coloured by no romantic nonsense.
>
> 'The curse of colonialism is less the curse of oppression', he said, 'than the curse of waste. Welsh coal has fired British trains and British ships, but Wales is more than its coal deposits. The exploitation of new minerals, in which the mountains of Wales are rich, is more appropriate to the nuclear age that is upon us than the scraping at coal seams that are approaching exhaustion. If I may allow folk mythology to intrude for a moment, we of the Arab nations have always regarded the Welsh people as that lost tribe of the Ishmaelites or Kahtanites which migrated north and settled in a land which the word of the Prophet could not reach. This may be unhistorical fantasy, but such fantasies are not to be despised. Certainly, the struggle of the Palestinian Arabs finds a parallel in the struggle of the

> Welsh. The scimitar and the sword are forged from the same metal. Long live a free and prosperous Wales.'[24]

The passage is notable as a portrayal of the way Welsh nationalistic support for the perceived victims of injustice was shifting from the Jews to the Arabs. While the setting may be fanciful, the process it illustrates is a real one.

Other major events which have prompted significant literary response by Welsh writers in the post-Second World War period are the Iraq wars, the attacks of 11 September 2001, and the war in Afghanistan. These will be examined in a little more detail presently, but first, it is worth collecting some other materials from the same period, which, although they all deal with perceived conflicts in and with the Islamic world, and although they all illustrate underlying attitudes, cannot readily be grouped with other material.

Firstly an extract from the work of the Welsh-language poet, Eluned Phillips (1914-2009), who won the crown of the National Eisteddfod twice, in 1967 and 1983. Her only volume, *Cerddi Glyn y Mêl* ('Glyn y Mêl Poems'), published in 1985, features a long series of poems about Saudi Arabia, where a cousin of the author's worked in the oil industry. The sequence portrays Islam as admirably simple, but productive of fatalism. The sequence's exact intentions towards Islam are conflicting and unclear, although it would be fair to say that, at the very least, it is an unromanticised portrait of the religion, and although it is based in the new oil-rich economic realities of the Arabian peninsula, its attitudes seem to be a combination of the exoticism and suspicion of an earlier age, perhaps not surprising if it is remembered that the author was indeed the product of an earlier age, having been born in 1914:

> The blessing of Allah
> is upon the capitalism of the long narrow table in the OPEC room.
> Tomorrow again
> the man who sold camel dung to the poor
> will shoot across the world
> in the womb of the Great Concorde.
>
> The vomit of the black wealth bubbles
> from the entrails of the earth.

> Everything has changed
> except the cry of the Koran in the soul,
> and the thrill of the flesh in the harem.[25]

In the sequence, the material wealth brought by oil is shown to be corrosive of the values of those who seek to exploit it. Abdullah, the Arab protagonist who has gone from uncouth goat-herd to international oil magnate, is portrayed as materialistic and shallow. In the poem 'Gwario' ('Spending'), he squanders his money in casinos, and the poet comments: 'Perhaps Allah / does not work nights in London.'[26] But if the exiled Welsh oil engineer, Wil Ffynnongarreg, is shown to have been severed from his home environment and to be diminished as a result, the underlying values of the Welshman's home community – hard work, fair play and faith – as shown in the letters he receives from home, are unquestioned. While Abdullah is equally deracinated, the fundamental values of the Arab's society are regarded with scepticism. Here, Abdullah is portrayed at Friday prayers, which are themselves depicted somewhat irreverently: 'Rows of head-dresses bowing to the floor / a transient crop of backsides ascending from the earth':

> Here
> is Abdullah of the Pickaxe and the Faith
> straggling leisurely from the arms of Mohamed
> from his beseeching in the dust:
> 'In the name of the warhorses who strike fire with their hooves
> and who tread down enemies with the lightning-clouds of their charge,
> O! Giver of water, let the overflowing of my joy
> arise from the pitcher in the secret of the sands.'
> Fate continues to torture him
> 'What will be ... will be,'
> despite the pillars of his faith:
> Faith ... Prayer ... Alms-giving ... Fasting ... and Idleness.[27]

Oil is never far from the politics of the Middle East, and it was at the root of one of the major conflicts of the post-Second World War era, the First Gulf War. This conflict began in August 1990 when the Iraqi dictator Saddam Hussein invaded and annexed neighbouring oil-rich Kuwait, triggering a response from a military coalition led by the United States which expelled Iraqi forces by February of the following year.

First-hand literary accounts by Welsh participants in this war, as in the Second Gulf War which finally overturned Saddam Hussein's regime, and in Afghanistan, have not yet been forthcoming. Unlike the First and Second World Wars, where large conscript armies had included many writers, the more recent conflicts have involved small professional armies. Although many Welsh service personnel have taken part in these conflicts over the years, the closest we have to a first-hand account of the Iraq wars by a Welsh writer is by Robert Minhinnick (*b.*1952) the former long-time editor of *Poetry Wales* magazine, and one of the foremost English-language authors of his generation in Wales. His 2002 volume, *After the Hurricane* contains several poems based on his travels as an artist and film-maker in war-torn Iraq. The poem 'Voices from The Museum of the Mother of All Wars', extracts of which are given below, has several Islamic references:

The Museum

Soldiers who spoke
A terrible language
Broke into the mosque.
look, here are the words they wrote
In the blood of the boy who serves the priest.
Our translator weeps.

The Guard

A woman brings me bread and dates.
I give her toilet paper.
So we stand under the green star and listen
To the night's first sirens,
To the muezzin through his microphone.
Then slowly, faint as reeds in the Tigris,
Starts our own murmuring.[28]

Minhinnick won the Best Individual Poem category of the prestigious Forward Prize in 1999 for his sequence 'Twenty-five Laments for Iraq', which was based on a visit to the scenes of the conflict in 1998 when, as a committed environmentalist, he was working on a film about the use of depleted uranium weapons. Below are some extracts:

The muezzin voices break the night
Telling us of what we are composed:
Coffee grits; a transparency of sugar;
The ghost of the cardamom in the cup's mosque.

★

Before hunger
  Thirst.
Before prayer
  Thirst.
Before money
  Thirst.
Before Thirst
  Water.

★

Since the first Caliph
There has been the suq –
These lemons, this fish:
And hunched over the stone
The women in their black –
Four dusty aubergines.

★

Over the searchlights
And machine-gun nests on Rashid Street
The bats explode like tracer fire.

★

Yellow as dates these lizards
Bask on the basilica.
Our cameraman removes his shoes,
Squats down to pray.

★

In the hotel carpark
One hundred and fifty brides and grooms
Await the photographer.
All night I lie awake
Listening to their cries.

*

Moths, I say.
No. Look again, she suggests.
Fused to the ceiling are the black hands;
Of the children of Amiriya.[29]

Amiriya is a district of Baghdad, where, on 13 February, 1991, around 400 people were killed when a bunker they were using as a public air-raid shelter was destroyed by American 'smart' bombs. In the chapter 'The Thief of Baghdad' in his 2005 travel book *To Babel and Back*, which won the Wales Book of the Year Award, Minhinnick gives a prose account of his visit to the bunker. He says he noticed black shapes clinging to the roof of the building, and thought initially they were bats until it was explained to him they were the hands of the victims which had fused to the roof as they clawed to escape the fire, and which had remained there when the rest of the bodies were removed.[30]

To Babel and Back, contributes further powerful depictions of Baghdad during the Second Gulf War, including one passage reflecting on the continuing legacy of hatred of the Iran-Iraq war, where Mohammed, an official at the Ministry of Information, tells him how the Iranians had used children in human wave attacks:

> But there were no weapons to give them. Instead, the children were issued with keys that they carried on chains around their necks. With these they advanced on the Iraqi positions. It didn't matter if they were killed. The mullahs told them they were the keys to Heaven. If they died for their country they would find salvation.
>
> So, shrugs Mohammed, they were shot in the battle Then of course, they went straight to Heaven.
>
> And Mohammed sits at the table with his coffee unsipped and tears of laughter streaming down his face.[31]

The means by which Robert Minhinnick visited Iraq, television journalism, had become an increasingly important method of contact for Welsh people with the Muslim world in the last few decades of the twentieth century. One of the major catalysts for the growth of overseas television reporting by Welsh media was the establishment in November 1982 of Sianel Pedwar Cymru, known as S4C, the Welsh-language television channel, the realisation of a long-held ambition of supporters of the language to secure a full and dedicated television service for Welsh-speakers, as a means of safeguarding their culture. Although Welsh-language television programmes had existed for many years before the establishment of S4C on the schedules of the BBC and commercial channels for Wales, the consolidation of this programming on a single channel, augmented by new money for large amounts of extra programming, led to a quick expansion in the quantity of Welsh-language television provision in all kinds of genres, including foreign correspondence and travel programming. This meant a new generation of articulate Welsh cultural practitioners found themselves encountering overseas societies, including those in the Muslim world, and interpreting them for their domestic audiences.

Such was the expansion of this field of cultural enterprise that by 1993, the journalist Dylan Iorwerth could find enough written material to edit a collection of Welsh-language foreign reportage, *Deuddeng Mlynedd o Ohebu Tramor* ('Twelve Years of Foreign Corresponding'). The collection contains first-hand testimony from TV journalist Tweli Griffiths, about his meeting in the mid 1980s with Colonel Muammar al-Gaddafi, the leader of Libya who had seized power in 1969. Griffiths's description of his conception of the role of a Welsh journalist is indicative of the newly assertive attitude of many of those who were culturally active through the medium of Welsh in the wake of the radicalising campaigns of the 1960s onwards, and displays that numerically small but influential group's conscious divergence from British, and to some degree from Western norms.

> Ever since the policewoman, Yvonne Fletcher, had been shot outside the country's embassy in London in 1985, I felt that a deeper analysis than that which was seen on the news was needed. What was Gaddafi's Green Book and was there any value in the philosophy it offered – a middle way between capitalism and communism? What about the Moslem religion, then? In Cuba and Libya, doors were opened to us that journalists from England had not bothered knocking on. Of course, we were dealing with countries that were politically sensitive and we had not got our own government with its ideological and worldwide financial interests and investments to create a 'line' for us to follow. As a result, the various guards sensed that we were more open and less prejudiced. That's one explanation

> why I found myself sitting in the tent of Colonel Gaddafi, at the feet of the man himself...[32]

Although it must be noted that Griffiths's assumption that English journalists toe a government line while nationally-minded Welsh speakers are peculiarly objective, open and unprejudiced might itself be considered to be ideological baggage of a particular kind, he is not reverential about Gaddafi. He tells a story of how the Colonel had once invited five Western magazine journalists to his home to see how normal was his family life, only to yield to temptation and to invite three of them to bed. He goes on:

> It's said too that Gaddafi is a homosexual, that he likes wearing women's clothes, and has long spells of depression. Although many of these tales are probably the fruit of the CIA's imagination, his behaviour is strange enough ... for example the time he decided to change the names of the months. 'There is a good reason for the changes,' one of the government's officials told me. 'But neither I nor anyone else can tell you what it is.'[33]

Later, Griffiths recounts a visit to an elite school where children are indoctrinated in Gaddafi's philosophy, which includes 'pan-Arab unity in face of the Jewish enemy', and fierce incitement to export the revolution worldwide: 'We must have a revolution to win freedom for the Arab world,' he quotes the sloganising children: 'America should burn in hell.' Griffiths ends his account by saying that the Libyan leader had sought to be a pan-Arab leader in the mould of Gamal Abdel Nasser of Egypt, but that Gaddafi's leadership had been 'disastrous from the start'.[34]

Another collection of travel writing, *Y Teithiwr Talog* ('The Cheerful Traveller'), from 1998 and edited by Gwyn Erfyl, contains an article by Betsan Powys, later to become a presenter of the BBC current affairs programme, *Panorama*, and then BBC Wales's political editor. In it, she tells of her experience reporting on the situation of Bosnian Muslims in the Balkan conflict of the 1990s, where that ethnic and religious group were the victims of many of the genocidal 'ethnic cleansing' operations carried out by rival communities, events which have contributed to tension between Muslims and non-Muslims worldwide. Powys's fixer,

Vera describes the troubled politics of the region for her Welsh visitor, who is making a return trip as a BBC journalist six years after having reported on the height of the conflict for the commercial television station H.T.V.:

> 'This is how I see it. The English are the Serbs, the Scots are the Croats, and you, the Welsh, are the oppressed Moslems! Welcome!' And off she goes to the car, a Croat with a Serbian name, who loves the Moslems, and who tells us that the Land Rover she had hired used to belong to Welsh Water and that I should therefore feel at home.[35]

Powys's attempts to persuade the official of the Serbian Information Ministry not to record her country of origin as 'Engleska', met with no success. Neither did her attempts to explain that as 'a Welshwoman, who knew what it was like to feel under siege' she understood the Serbian desire to 'protect the language, traditions and separateness of the Serbs', although not to the point of tearing the country apart along its fault lines. She was 'too young to understand', she was told.[36]

She tells of staying in the house of a middle-aged Croat man who poured a cup of tea for her each morning with the hands he had used the previous night to fire mortar rounds at Muslims. Later, she and Vera drive through the outskirts of Sarajevo:

> Driving through completely deserted villages, and asking who used to live there. Sometimes, Vera remembers. Moslems lived here, farmers – but it's mainly Croats in this area now. Passing a mosque burnt to ashes. Sometimes she is not so sure, can't remember which faction turned on which. These are signs of fire here, not bullets. No-one wasted bullets on ordinary people when fire was sufficient to destroy them.[37]

They are listening to a Welsh-language rock band on the Land Rover's sound system, and Powys tries to interest Vera in the latest manifestation of language politics in Wales: the criticism received by the band when some of its members set up another mainly-English-language group. Vera laughs that she can hardly understand what is happening on her own doorstep, let alone anywhere further away.

In the divided Croat and Muslim district of Mostar, one of the most iconic locations of the Balkans conflict, Powys passes a

Muslim cemetery, noting that many of the pictures on the graves are of young people, and then visits a youth centre where some reconciliation work is underway under the leadership of a broad-minded Croat administrator called Miro. Here the comparison between Wales and the Muslims is brought out again. Had the theory been advanced by a Welsh person, it would surely seem an impertinence to compare the lot of a minority linguistic community in Britain with that of a religious minority in the Balkans which has been subjected to thousands of genocidal murders. But the fact that such a correlation is willingly used by Powys's Balkan interlocutor shows that the desire to interpret a minority experience is a compelling one, even if it results in disproportionate comparisons:

> Vera explains the theory that we Welsh are the Moslems of Britain. Miro is delighted. As it happens, he has just heard a joke that is appropriate for Moslems – and Welsh people. A little boy hears his religious education teacher claiming that God is omnipresent. 'Is God in my house, Sir?' 'Yes, lad.' 'Is God in my bedroom, Sir?' 'Yes.' 'Is he in Sasha's kitchen?' 'Yes.' 'And even in Mujo's cellar?' 'Yes, there too.' I can see the punchline coming from a long way off. 'Now I know you're telling lies, Sir. Mujo hasn't got a cellar!'
>
> I have heard it before but – Vera to the rescue again – I haven't heard the Bosnian version of it at all. Sasha is a Croatian name, and Mujo is a Moslem name. But the little boy isn't doubting that God is looking after Mujo because he's a Moslem, but because he just hasn't got a cellar. 'Do you understand? You're supposed to think it's a joke about Moslems – and then you realise it's just an innocent joke. Just a joke.'
>
> Suddenly it starts to pour with rain. It's been threatening to do so all morning, and now the noise is deafening. Off goes Miro to close doors and windows, the director and comedian turned caretaker. I begin to understand his joke, and his sermon too. There used to be so much significance to being a Croat or Moslem, Miro is working hard to persuade everyone around him that they have the right now not to give a damn – if that's what makes it easier for them to carry on living in Mostar, together. The jokes – 'just a joke' – is part of the sermon.[38]

Crossing to a Muslim district a little later, she comes across a Muslim youth:

> He wasn't intending to go to the mosque, he said. But since the war

> he cannot help but come over when he hears the sound of that mournful call to prayer coming through the loudspeaker. He had slackened his grip on the Moslem culture completely until the war but when that culture became, overnight, something worth dying or killing for, he had been forced to embrace it in a hurry.
>
> Kamel is his name, the trendy DJ of Radio X, the station for young people in Mostar. He's delighted with the promise that there'll be a pack of CDs in the post when I get home. Welsh will scarcely be popular here, but he's promised to play the odd song. It's American stuff that goes down well, in his experience, the cool DJ sitting on a wall outside the mosque, an embodiment of the tension that still tears Mostar apart.[39]

Powys's account is a conscientious and detailed examination of the complexities and tensions of the Balkans, and is one which acknowledges the difficulty in finding objectivity in the face of confusing circumstances and contending narratives, as Powys says at the end of the article: 'Witnessing, without guessing, without interfering – that's what's difficult.'[40]

Meanwhile, in Wales itself, the violence against Bosnian Muslims elicited a rare contribution to the Welsh-language press by one of the small number of Welsh-speaking Muslims. In her article, 'Y Ffordd i Feca' ('The Road to Mecca'), in the magazine *Cristion* in 1993, Norah A. Malik remarked:

> At the start, they came for the Jews; now it is the Muslims of Bosnia who are suffering merciless oppression and cruelty. It is incredible, to say the least, in a world which takes pride in its technological maturity and its civilised standards, that man could pour out so much indignity on his fellow-man and without thinking twice about it, and without the rest of us thinking too much about it either.[41]

Malik goes on to examine the anti-Islamic tradition in the West, dating back to the Crusades and colonialism before concluding with a simple summary of what her faith involves: a monotheism which respects both Christianity and Judaism, and which provides 'an eternal law which encompasses life in its entirety'.[42]

> No way of life offers purity of body, spirit, economy and society better than Islam ... clear statements and meditations from the Almighty, who made the heavens and earth. May we heed His eternal word and live at peace.[43]

Another Welsh Muslim, Siân Messamah, expressed similar sentiments, also in an article for *Cristion*, in 1998. She expresses gratitude for the religious grounding given to her by her upbringing in the Presbyterian Church of Wales, and although she is now a convert to Islam, she sees much in common with Christianity and Judaism, both in theology and morality.[44]

Peace between Christians and Muslims, however, seemed in short supply in the last years of the century. Before examining the two specific conflicts of the Iraq wars, and 9/11 and its aftermath, it is worth noting, in passing, a few other treatments of conflicts involving the Muslim world in the literature of the period under consideration.

The 1997 novel, *Dim Ond Un* ('Only One'), by the scientist, essayist, novelist and religious sceptic, Eirwen Gwynn (1916-2007), is set in a near future where a nuclear-armed and prosperous Arab-led Muslim League threatens an enfeebled and decadent Europe. One Welsh character reflects:

> Religion had no influence in Europe these days. But the Muslims clung stubbornly to their faith in all its extreme fundamentalism. They despised the westerners for what they saw as their moral decadence, and were pretty haughty in their behaviour towards them as they saw their economic prosperity in the world increasing every day, and their confidence had been greatly increased by the recent alliance between a number of Muslim countries. The Muslim bloc had become a threat to world peace.[45]

A little later, the main character, Meleri, is reflecting on Islam and its adherents following a recent visit with a delegation to the Middle East:

> She could not for the life of her cope with the Muslims – as much as anything because of their attitude to women. Although they were not obviously discourteous to the women in the delegation, to Meleri their patronising attitude suggested contempt. They were a chauvinistic people, and to Meleri, that was one of the greatest sins. And not just that. She supposed they did not have the same concern for the condition of their fellow men or for securing world peace as the representatives of the European Union. She doubted whether using a nuclear weapon would cause one of them to lose a night's sleep.[46]

It is possible that Eirwen Gwynn's experience as a feminist, and as the only woman in her Honours science class at inter-war Bangor University, where she encountered sexism, sensitised her to the gender issues associated with Islam, and informed the indignation and unease with which her character Meleri speaks.[47]

Anxieties about not offending Islam are examined in Sheenagh Pugh's poem, 'The Embarkation of the Pigs', published in 1997, which depicts the porcine characters of children's books going into exile because they are no longer politically correct, implicitly because of sensitivities about Islamic taboos.[48]

The Embarkation of the Pigs

On hearing that British publishers no longer welcome pig characters in children's books.

Piglet can take a hint. He walks off
page four, leaving a small white space
among the swirling snowflakes. Pooh wanders on,
his paw grasping at air, toward the place

where the Hundred Acre merges into Nutwood,
and Rupert stares at a Podgy-shaped gap.
Meanwhile, houses of brick, sticks and straw
open their doors, and out the Three step,

suitcases in their trotters. At every turn,
some other joins the band: on some page
a word fades. They follow Pigling Bland
down to the pea-green boat at the tide's edge,

that will take them to the eternal wood
where the Piggywig stands; where the round moon
will countenance their portly, tolerant curves.
This is where outlaws dance. Shine on; shine on.[49]

Other perceived threats from Islamic sources had a more realistic setting. In Geraint Vaughan Jones's 2000 thriller, *Omega*, Kurdish militants inspired by Islam are the main villains faced by the novel's protagonists. In the following passage, a Kurdish militant, Reza Kemal, recruited to commit terrorist acts against Jewish people in London, 'through the hand of Allah', is pondering the arguments of an English contact who has proposed an alternative non-violent approach, and is now considering how to a persuade the prominent militant, Zahedi, of the merits of a political, as opposed to a violent, solution:

> As the Englishman had said, it was time for Zahedi to realise that Russia was no longer the great political power in Europe. And the rest of what he had said had been true too, that the West had been more of a friend to Islam than the communist bloc had ever been. Was not Russia's bloody record in Afghanistan and in the Balkan countries, and more recently in Chechnya, proof of that? And was it not the lands of the west that had opened their doors and their hearts over the years to refugees from the lands of Islam? And the more he thought about it now, the more he agreed with the Englishman that the greatest enemy of the Kurd was the Arab himself. Who had trampled on his people over the centuries? Who had persecuted them and denied them a recognised land as a home? The West? No, but rather false individuals who had claimed hypocritically that they were followers of Allah; men whose aim was to glorify themselves rather than to promote the welfare of their people.
>
> Was not Ataturk a Muslim? Was not Saddam Hussein a Muslim? Was not Ruhollah Khomeni a Muslim? But how much brotherly love had they ever shown the Kurds within their boundaries? How much goodwill was ever shown by Shi-ites to Sunnis? And every Kurd worth his salt was Sunni! 'No,' said the leader-in-waiting of the PKK to himself, 'with the power and influence of Western Europe and America to support us in our battle, then the Englishman's plan is the one which offers us the best hope for the future. But how can Zahedi be persuaded of that?[50]

While the prospect of a terror attack in Britain or the United States may have been the stuff of a fictional thriller as late as 2000, the events of 11 September of the following year, the Afghanistan and Iraq wars which followed, and their legacy of terrorism and suspicion, made the threat a real and ever-present one.

Certainly, one of the most significant and substantial responses to 9/11 by a Welsh author is by Merryl Wyn Davies, an anthropologist and political writer of international standing, and one of the British commentators who has done most in recent years to interpret the West to Islam and *vice versa*. A native of Merthyr Tydfil in the south Wales Valleys, she worked as a journalist and as a BBC producer before spending 10 years working in television in Malaysia. A convert to Islam, she became the media officer for the Muslim Council of Britain before her appointment as Director of the Muslim Institute. The author of a number of volumes, her work on Islam has come to prominence primarily through a series of high-profile books co-written with the prolific London-based Muslim scholar, critic and journalist, Ziauddin Sardar, including *American Dream, Global Nightmare* (2004), *The No-Nonsense Guide to Islam* (2003), and the controversial 2002 bestseller, *Why Do People Hate America?*

Merryl Wyn Davies's work is different to the bulk of material collected here. The vast majority of other passages compiled in this book are comments *en passant* about Islam and Muslims by non-specialist writers. As the intention of this study is to trace cultural attitudes through the centuries, those comments are of interest primarily because of the attitudes they reveal, not because of the quality or originality of the observations in themselves. By contrast, Davies's work is the product of deep and extensive specialist engagement with Islam. As such, while committed and forthright, it is of unusual depth and detail. And as the product of a Muslim perspective, it is uniquely valuable. Davies's work is wide-ranging, seeking to debunk myths about Islam, to counter stereotypes and preconceptions, and, perhaps most significantly, to meet the anxious and sometimes hostile questions of non-Muslim commentators and observers about Islam with challenging questions of her own. In *Why Do People Hate America?* for example, the American television series about presidential politics, *The West Wing*, is examined and is accused of having a 'trademark recipe for all problems – pluralism,' an ideal against which all other competing value-systems – with Islam implicitly among them – are seen as intolerant, rigid and totalitarian. The book is not content to allow the programme, and the cultural assumptions it represents, to draw such a conclusion, and consequently highlights the tradition of pluralism in Islam.[51]

Davies's work with Ziauddin Sardar represents one of the most influential contributions to the intense debate about Islam and the West in the wake of the attacks of September 2001. Given Davies's importance as a contemporary Welsh interpreter of Islam, it is worth looking in detail at one of her own works of single authorship, an article entitled 'Wilful Imaginings', in *The New Internationalist* in May 2002. It begins with Davies's personal testimony as a Welsh convert to Islam. As such, this could be considered as belonging with the material about Islam in Wales collected in Chapter 11. However, it is given in the present chapter because its subject matter deals largely with post-9/11 conflict. The article is quoted at some length as its analysis of orientalism can illuminate this entire book, whose scope as a collection of primary materials does not otherwise allow for extensive surveys of the critical and theoretical literature about the relationship between Islam and the West:

> 'How does a nice, sensible Welsh girl like you end up joining a religion of militant fundamentalists who suppress women?' Interviewers have endlessly asked me this question. The question is predicated on the proposition that nice and sensible people do not become Muslims, and by implication therefore that no Muslim is either nice or sensible. The lack of niceness or reason is proved by the second assertion: Muslims in totality, and presumably by their nature, are militant. Militancy is synonymous with the dread word fundamentalist that clearly needs no definition. The logical consequence of militant fundamentalism is the self-evident observation that all Muslims suppress women. In the perception of the interviewer these terms belong together: because Islam offers no alternative, become a Muslim and that is what you get.
>
> Of course, interviewers often play devil's advocate asking aggressive questions to stimulate robust rebuttal. In which case, they must be aware of the possibility of an alternative view. So why does it never occur to them that devilishly reductive stereotypes actually impede and often preclude sensible discussion of the alternative view? Neither the conventional questions nor the rote answers they are designed to elicit describe or help anyone understand who I am, the world I inhabit, how I know and understand Islam, and the condition of being a Muslim.

Davies says Muslim identity has been problematised for Western observers from its inception due to Orientalism, a mixture of polemic and propaganda which justified the Christian case to reclaim the Holy Land:

> The basic representation of Muslims that emerged was of militant, barbaric fanatics, corrupt, effete sensualists, people who lived contrary to the natural law – a concept defined by canon laws and philosophy of Christianity. Even when Muslims were portrayed in popular medieval literature as equivalents of knightly Western counterparts, they were completely Other because they were beyond the pale of Christianity, addicted to wrong religion which they persisted in passionately believing. The failings of Muslims stemmed

> from their beliefs. What medieval Europe made of Islam and Muslims has been described by British historian Norman Daniels as 'knowledgeable ignorance', defining a thing as something it could not possibly be, when the means to know it differently were available.

Such attitudes were revived, she says, with the rise of the Ottoman Empire impeding European access to the riches of the Far East, and then again in the European colonial period, when Orientalism provided a rationale for 'ruling and managing the subject people.' Orientalism informed an entire method of approaching and analysing other communities, but, says Davies, it did so on false grounds:

> ...Orientalism is not simply prejudice, it is also knowledge. The real problem with Orientalism and the authority it gives to Western experts on Islam and Muslim affairs is not that it is knowledge, but that it is knowledge that does not appreciate it is wrong. The authority of Orientalism is that it makes Muslims incomprehensible yet predictable.

She adds that due to this attitude 'Islam and the West have been engaged in a clash of civilizations since Prophet Muhammad began preaching his Message.'

> There is a sense in which Osama bin Laden is utterly predictable, since he embodies so many of the essential details of the time-honoured image of what the West expects from a Muslim iconoclast in ideas, rhetoric and action.

Orientalism has led to prejudice among both the educated and non-educated in the West, so that it 'finds its outlets in plasterboard movie villains as well as strategic political thinking', and leads to racism and discrimination even among 'well-meaning and well-intentioned nice, sensible people.' However, Davies says, in recent years Orientalism has become an even greater problem:

> It has become the scapegoat, the shield and sword of Muslims themselves. Among Muslims the existence of Orientalism has become the justification for every sense of grievance, a source of encouragement for nostalgic romanticism about the perfections of Muslim civilization in history and hence a recruiting agent for a wide variety of Islamic movements. It has generated a sense of exclu-

> sivity, of being apart and different within Muslim communities and societies that has no precedent either in Islam as religion or Muslim history.

She says the fact of Orientalism, 'or its latest buzz word Islamophobia', has forced some Muslims into a defensive posture where they feel obliged to condone or at best ignore even the indefensible within their own community out of a sense of embattled solidarity. For Davies, this is unworthy of Islam's ethical framework, and has caused: 'modern Muslims to become reactive, addicted to a culture of complaint and blame that serves only to increase the powerlessness, impotence and frustration of being a Muslim.' Rather than critical engagement, Muslim identity becomes 'a projection of perfections that makes arriving at a contemporary interpretation of how to enact and live by Muslim beliefs and ideas almost impossible.' She concludes:

> So, what we have is not a clash of civilizations but mutual complicity in proliferating mutual incomprehension. On both sides, wilful, determined, distorted imaginings and knowledgeable ignorance propels, fuels and then justifies aggression, oppression, dispossession and dehumanization of anyone who is not 'us'. The consequences are real, appalling human suffering whether in Palestine or Israel, Baghdad or New York or on the streets of Britain.
>
> With two complicit systems of self-justification and self-fulfilling incomprehension reinforcing the divide, is there any way forward? There is. In the root of antipathy, where difference and distance were manufactured, we can recover the building blocks of a new sense of interrelationship, compatibility and mutual enlightened interests. Orientalism makes Muslim civilization the dark alter ego of European civilization. Muslim Occidentalism makes the West the dark, despoiling nemesis of its contemporary existence. Both leave out an essential detail. There would be no Europe as we know it without Islam, without the constant interconnection with Muslim civilization. And there is no Muslim existence today or in the future that can be conceived without interconnection with the West.
>
> We have to go back to history and see how much Europe gained from the knowledge and ideas in science, technology, philosophy, literature and culture of Muslim civilization. There are thousands of words in English – such as algebra, zenith, alcohol – that are route maps of the positive contribution Muslims made to European ways of life. Indeed, Europe acquired its crowning glory, liberal humanism, from Islam. Islam taught Europe the very idea of reason as well

> as how to reason. Muslim thinkers like ibn Rushd, ibn Sina and al-Haytham, who had their names Latinized, became integral parts of the rise of knowledge and technical progress in European life. This contribution occurred and was possible because both Islam and the West had a common context and legacy from the Greco-Roman world and both, as monotheistic worldviews, had to revise and critically evaluate the ideas of Greek thought. Christianity and Islam share the common legacy of the Abrahamic tradition. There are values, precepts and ideals, as distinct from specific doctrines, that are common to both or markedly similar. There is a retelling of history and ideas to be undertaken.
>
> The West has the task of learning to think differently about where it came from. The Muslim world must rethink where it is. It needs to learn how it values: its moral and ethical impulses are not a separate order but integral part of the common concerns of contemporary human dilemmas. Muslims want sustainable improvement, human betterment, are concerned about where science is going, how to save the Earth, how to attain a just, equitable and inclusive social and political order. To these common concerns they bring a particular way of seeing problems, and no simplistic definitive answers.
>
> The trouble with hopeful alternative strategies is they begin with a change of mindset. They can operate only if we are prepared to unlearn, become self-critical and conscious of the false constraints we have taken for normality and authoritative knowledge, that deform our potential, divert us from the most constructive use of our insight and abilities. In short we have to admit to errors and remedy what we have got wrong. To do that we have to be able to explain ourselves, make our debates not predictable but comprehensible to each other.[52]

Davies's is an important contribution to the debate about Islam and the West in the post-9/11 world, distinctive in its combined Welsh and Muslim perspective, and significant in its depth and erudition.

Of course, many other Welsh writers have engaged with the events of 9/11 and its aftermath, and even if their work cannot, like Merryl Wyn Davies's, be the product of years of involvement in the field, it can nonetheless illustrate important attitudes in Welsh society. Among Welsh literary responses to the events of 9/11 were the powerful 2006 e-mail epistolary novel *Eleven* by David Llewellyn, which will be examined in Chapter 11, which is devoted to portrayals of Muslim people residing in Wales itself, and a 2002 poem by Gwyn Thomas (*b.*1936), later to be appointed the second National Poet of Wales in 2005. Thomas's poem is entitled 'Y Mae'r Tyrau Mawr yn Torri' ('The Great Towers are Breaking'), and while it does not address Islam specifically, it leaves no doubt that the author regards the attacks as manifestations of evil:

> To the New World,
> An old grief arrived,
> An old, old evil,
> An old, old hatred –
> Signs of the mark
> That we received, we men,
> Red upon our being
> From the dark pit of our past.
> That red mark is here,
> It is in the midst of our present.[53]

The events of 9/11 precipitated two major American-led Western military actions, which have had far-reaching ramifications for Western relations with Islam, and which have also produced literary responses from Welsh authors. The first was the invasion of Afghanistan in October 2001, aimed at toppling the fundamentalist Taliban regime and thereby denying a safe haven to the extremist al-Qaeda group, which had used the country as a base while organising the attacks on the United States. The second was the invasion of Iraq, the Second Gulf War, in May 2003, aimed at removing the Ba'athist regime of Saddam Hussein because of his claimed support for terrorism and his alleged possession of weapons of mass destruction.

From the Second Iraq War, comes another poem by Gwyn Thomas. Published in his 2005 volume, *Apocalups Yfory* ('Apocalypse Tomorrow'), the poem 'Muhammed Said Al-Sahhaf, Diweddar weinidog gwybodaethau Irác' ('Muhammed Said Al-Sahhaf, Former Iraqi Information Minister'), pokes fun at the indefatigably, and unrealistically, upbeat spokesman for Saddam's doomed regime, who had continued to give impossibly optimistic interpretations of the progress of the war to foreign journalists, even as Iraqi forces melted away before the invaders.

> 'I have been given knowledge
> Beyond the discernments
> Of human and earthly beings

> 'For his sake, his Majesty,
> Gentle Saddam, I have been given,
> Strength to transform our calamity
> And all darkness
> into un – truly – defeatable light.'[54]

The poem satirises not only the absurdity of Al-Sahhaf's version of events, but, more seriously, the reality of the regime he was serving, by suggesting that his denial of the obvious truth, and long years of similar denials by others, had concealed the oppressiveness of Saddam Hussein's rule.

The same conflict provides the background to the novel *Un Diwrnod yn yr Eisteddfod* ('One Day in the Eisteddfod') by the innovative post-modernist Welsh-language novelist, Robin Llywelyn (*b.*1958) the director of the italianate village of Portmeirion in Gwynedd, which was designed by his grandfather, the architect Sir Clough Williams-Ellis. *Un Diwrnod yn yr Eisteddfod* won the 2004 National Eisteddfod's Daniel Owen Memorial Prize for novels. It tells the story of a Welsh-speaking British soldier, Wil Chips, who has returned from two troubling tours of duty in Iraq, and who is spending a day in the Eisteddfod with old friends. The incongruity of the soldier visiting a festival many of whose adherents espouse pacifism and who are at the very least sceptical of the values of Britishness, is a source of some of the tensions in the novel's narrative, allowing for an interrogation both of Britishness and of certain constructs of Welshness, as the following extract shows. Wil Chips is recounting a confrontation with Gwyn, who is opposed to the war:

> 'So you've finished your vandalism in Iraq,' he asked then. 'What was it, Wil Chips, couldn't take the strain?'
>
> 'I don't want to discuss it,' I said, curtly, feeling something starting to gnaw my stomach again.
>
> 'Why didn't you stop the looters and the arsonists?' said Gwyn. 'The history of our whole civilisation is in the balance.'
>
> 'What are you rambling about, now?' I said. 'Stop who doing what?'
>
> 'Only destroying the National Library and all its archives', said Gwyn, starting to get agitated. 'The Royal Archive of Iraq and the history of the Ottomans, and the most important collection of Arabic manuscripts in the world. There were pictures of parchment and manuscripts rolling through the gutters, letters from the court

> of Sharif Hussein of Mecca to the Ottomans in Baghdad, letters of recommendation to the courts of Arabia, reports of attacks on pilgrims in the desert. Genghis Khan's grandson burned the city in the Middle Ages, and the river Tigris was black with the ink of its books. And now here's the same thing happening again.' He looked at me out of the corner of his eye. 'Why? That's the question.'
>
> 'No idea,' I said. 'You're the one who gets excited about old books. You're the one who thinks a library's more important than the life of the librarian.'
>
> Gwyn looked at me a second time, and then turned to flick a spider off his shoulder. 'The Arabs had a saying that their books were written in Cairo, bound in Beirut and read in Baghdad,' he said.
>
> 'Good job they read them before they got burned, then,' I said.[55]

As its title suggests, *Un Diwrnod yn yr Eisteddfod* is a story whose primary material is the society of Wales itself, as focused in the intense atmosphere of the annual national celebration of Welsh-language culture. The Iraq war, and its Muslim context, serve the purpose of exoticising the soldier, thereby making him an outsider and a more effective foil for the idiosyncrasies of the Welsh people he encounters. As so often, the Muslim background is subordinated to a domestic Welsh agenda.

While 9/11 and the wars in Iraq and Afghanistan might locate conflict with the Muslim world at a distance, other events brought the tensions closer to home. On 7, July, 2005, four British Muslim extremists detonated suicide bombs on the London transport system, killing themselves and 52 passengers. While not explicitly a response to those attacks, a poem published in *Barddas* magazine in early 2006 by the Welsh-language strict-metre poet, Gwynfor ab Ifor, addresses the issue of suicide bombing. Entitled 'Addolwr' ('Worshipper'), the poem is a series of *englynion*. It is given in full below in a metrical version reproducing some elements of the original form; the accompanying endnote gives a more literal translation:

> My God, I shan't abandon, – to His just
>   Anger, I shall bow down;
> Loyal, live the religion
> His eyes' fist is upon.
>
> To the clear sky, if rain fall – Him be praised,
>   And praise Him through rainsquall

To hold me against downfall,
The book in my hand, through all.

I fight my wolves to the end – with my rod
  My sheep I shall defend;
Naming the book will commend
My soul's polluted riverbend.

For us there still remains one – His city
  And through us the waves come
Of the faith we sailed upon;
For Allah's sake, I'm a bomb.[56]

Further tensions came in September 2005, when a Danish newspaper published satirical cartoons of the Prophet Muhammad, challenging a widely-held Muslim taboo on depicting the Prophet's image and sparking a worldwide storm of protest as many Muslims denounced what they saw as a deliberate insult. The controversy intensified as some other Western media outlets republished the cartoons, citing defence of free speech as their reason for defying Muslim anger. Mainstream UK media outlets did not join that counter-protest, but two Welsh journals did get caught up in the row. *Gair Rhydd* ('Free Word'), Cardiff University's mainly English-language student newspaper, reprinted the cartoons. The college authorities reacted by recalling the 8,000-copy print run and having it pulped. The editor was suspended and later published an apology. A month later, *Y Llan* ('The Church'), the Anglican Church in Wales's Welsh-language journal, reproduced a later cartoon from the French newspaper *France Soir* in the context of an article stressing the relationship between Christianity and Islam. The cartoon depicted Muhammad sitting on a cloud in company with other religious figures and being told: 'Don't worry, we've all been caricatured here.' Again, the print-run, of some 400 copies, was recalled and pulped, this time by the Church in Wales, acting on the authority of the Archbishop of Wales.

Support for *Y Llan* came from three prominent intellectuals in the nationalist community in Wales: Dyfrig Jones, Siôn Jobbins and Simon Brooks. Jobbins, the former Plaid Cymru mayor of Aberystwyth, writing in the Welsh heritage magazine, *Cambria*, was indignant that other politicians and public figures had not defended the paper's right to free speech. His article, 'Llanistan', is one of the most outspoken on the subject of the perceived clash of values between Islam and the West, as experienced in Wales. Describing the reaction to the editor's publication of the 'intelligent, ecumenical article', he says:

> What do you do if you see someone being mugged on the street? Well, if you're the Welsh Establishment you just walk on by, and even go back and give the poor man another good kicking just to make sure he's down.

Jobbins says the article was 'an intelligent critique and a balanced argument on interfaith commonality. It was an outstretched hand of fellowship, believer to believer in a secular world.' But for the 'crime' of publishing an image of Muhammad, the editor 'was given a bell to hang around his neck, clanking and tolling his political uncleanness for all to hear.' He said the editor's treatment would probably have been better had he been an apologist for Palestinian suicide bombers of Tel Aviv's cafés.'

Jobbins is scathing about the supposition that a publication circulating among 'that most threatening and dangerous of constituencies, the bara brith-munching, tea-sipping Welsh clergy and its parishioners' could have sparked anger across the Muslim world, and is incredulous at the thoroughness of the Church in Wales's suppression of the edition.

> Along with thousands of others I haven't been allowed to make my own judgement on the article but I assumed that at least a copy would be at hand at the National Library of Wales. However, so diligent (or paranoid) was the Church in destroying any last copy of the edition, that even the one sent to the National Library, our citadel of conscience, was asked to be returned. So there we have it, a reader at the Library can order and see a copy of *The Protocols of the Elders of Zion* or even *Fiesta's Reader's Wives Special* (two publications I have never ordered, I hasten to add) but not *Y Llan*. Was the March 2006 edition of *Y Llan* such a threat to civil society and morality that even the copy sent to the National Library had to be withdrawn? That edition has now been airbrushed from history. Even the historians of the future won't be able to read it.

He challenges the view that an article of offensive intent could not be distinguished from a well-meaning one, and the supposition that the depiction of the Prophet is entirely forbidden in Islam.

> There are good moral and practical reasons to show sensitivity towards the Muslim community in Wales, as a minority can always be susceptible to scapegoatism. There is also a need to educate the public of the majority culture about the subtleties of the minority. But withdrawing every copy of *Y Llan* demonstrated the cringe factor at its worst.
>
> Do we really think that some evil men are hunched in the slums of Gaza or the coffee houses of Cairo or even the mosques of Cardiff cursing and plotting against the editor of *Y Llan* because of this offending cartoon as they struggle to master the voiceless alveolar lateral fricative of its title? And if so, should not we, the media, the Church, the state and the police in a free democracy, be defending the editor of *Y Llan* for his right to free speech rather than slapping him down like an errant dog? Is Western liberal democracy so shallow that it cowers to bigots and murderers and those who threaten murder? Or are the majority of decent Muslims as represented by the Muslim Council of Wales too afraid or disrespectful of Western liberal democracy to accept its traditions too?
>
> The depiction of Mohammed isn't against Islamic law nor even every Islamic practice or tradition, and there was certainly no malice in the piece (from what I've read or heard in interviews) nor was there any intention to offend. In fact it was the opposite. So, why was it that virtually the whole of Welsh civil society crossed to the other side?

He said the Welsh press, with the exception of *Barn*, withheld its support, and that of the 104 elected, fully-paid Welsh representatives in Westminster and the National Assembly, not one stood up for the editor or made an attempt to balance the affair.

> 'Is it not inconceivable that not even 1% of the Welsh population thought, 'hey, come on, boys, lets put this in perspective'? If so, not one elected representative was willing to give that constituency a voice. *Shame on them.*[57] [author's emphasis]

Jobbins's article referred to the monthly current-affairs journal *Barn* ('Opinion'), which had published three articles in which the commentator Dyfrig Jones and the editor, Dr Simon Brooks, one of the foremost intellectuals of Welsh-language culture, condemned the way the *Llan* affair had been handled.

Dyfrig Jones's article 'Cenhadon Casineb' ('Missionaries of Hatred') is 'illustrated' with 12 empty spaces, each containing only a verbal description of the contents of the Danish cartoons, and the word 'censored'. In the article itself, Jones compares the cartoon furore with the Rushdie affair: 'The cowardly attack on Rushdie's right to be express himself had been defended to the hilt by every section of civilised European society.' By contrast, he says, the publication of the cartoons had not attracted such support, with politicians trying to please all sides by saying the editor had a right to publish the cartoons, but should not have done so. Jones concludes:

> The pity of the situation is that the violence of Muslim extremists has succeeded in restricting our freedom to express our opinion, or at least on the freedom of the press... It is the threats of Muslim extremists which are at the root of this self-censorship. Unlike the row over *The Satanic Verses*, violence, this time, has succeeded in winning the day.[58]

In his adjacent editorial, 'Wyneb Mohamed' (The Face of Muhammad'), in the same issue of the magazine, Simon Brooks says he has copies of the Danish cartoons on his desk, which he had bought in a copy of the German newspaper *Die Welt* in Caernarfon. He supports the decision to publish the cartoons in the first place, and to republish them in other European newspapers, and condemns the self-censorship of the British press, blaming the 'Trojan Horse' of political correctness, 'one of the great diseases of our age', for liberals' abandonment of liberal values. He quotes a statement by the Federation of Muslim Students of Wales, criticising *Gair Rhydd* for publishing the cartoons: 'The insensitive actions of a few individuals should not, and will not, stop the atmosphere of respect and tolerance that exists at the university.' Brooks comments: 'This is a devious, two-faced use of the inclusive rhetoric of a multicultural society. Notice how "insensitive" is used to mean "unacceptable", "respect" to mean "Censorship" and "tolerance" to mean "shutting up". A University of all places refusing to allow freedom of opinion!' He continues:

> Is there something wrong with Islam, then, and do we have a right to criticise it? The events of the past weeks have shown clearly that Islam does not appear to realise that secularism in public life is one of the cornerstones of European life. This does not mean that there

> should be any opposition to Islam in private life. The right to faith, the right to worship, the right to places of worship: these are some of the most fundamental human rights. And the right too to express peaceful opinion about blasphemy, and to protest against it if desired.
>
> But as far as law and order are concerned, this is a secular society, and we have every right to keep it that way. Here it appears that the Western World and Islam exist on two different planets.

Brooks blames the lack, in the Islamic world, of a process comparable to the European Enlightenment. He condemns as 'foolish' the way some critics of the cartoons equated religion and race, and describes as 'shameful' the protests on the streets of London where extremists called for the execution of journalists and cartoonists.

> My decision as the Editor of *Barn*, then was a simple enough one. I wanted to publish them. Not in order to celebrate blasphemy, but in order to resist the Islamic extremists who choose to support their religious world-view with threats of violence and murder.
>
> And yet, you will not see any of these cartoons in *Barn*. Why so? Simply enough: cowardice. I had better be honest about this rather than insulting everyone's intelligence. The length and breadth of Britain editors are filled with fear. And I am no exception.
>
> Of course, failing to publish these cartoons declares that violence and terrorism are victorious over the values of a civilised society. It means that the rule of Law is no longer strong enough in Britain to guarantee the freedom of the press. This is a tragedy for us all. But publishing these cartoons would be too dangerous. For the first time in Britain for three hundred years and more, the punishment for criticising a religion is the death penalty. Shame on these Islamic extremists who have brought this about, and shame too on everyone who makes excuses for them.[59]

In the following edition of the magazine, an article with an opposing view appeared from the Plaid Cymru politician, Gwenllian Lansdown, a councillor for the Riverside district of Cardiff, where around one in seven of the population is Muslim.[60] In the article, entitled 'Y Gwir yn Erbyn y Byd?' ('The Truth Against the World?'),[61] Lansdown expresses no opinion as to whether the Muslim protests were justified or proportionate, and focusses instead on the limits of free speech in the West, claiming that the idea that freedom of speech is an absolute unconditional right has been 'thrust on us by neo-conservative Anglo-American ideology.' She points out that freedom of speech is limited, for instance, by libel laws, by 'tradition and courtesy', and should be exercised responsibly. The publishing of the Muhammad cartoons was therefore, she says, 'irresponsible'. She adds that any example of casual prejudice should be taken seriously:

> In that respect, it could be argued that the rationale for protecting the rights and interests of Welsh speakers compares with the right of Moslems in Wales not to have their sense of self-respect destroyed by comparisons which claim they are terrorists.

The article concludes by saying the 'most frightening' thing about the cartoons affair was that the editor of the Danish newspaper had not published caricatures of Christ 'because that would cause too much disturbance and ill-feeling in the country'.

> So why treat the followers of Islam differently? Why attack a group of people who are, compared with the majority, powerless? Of course, it is necessary to have an open and comprehensive debate about multiculturalism but let no-one create bogeymen about some 'clash of civilisations' or the failure of pluralism in Western society. After all, that is not a new phenomenon and none of us would have to look back very far in our own histories to see that cultural, linguistic or religious pluralism is the foundation of who we are too. That means that we have a special duty to think carefully about the implications of our actions on other people in society and not just to claim the sanctity of some great truths that do not necessarily exist.[62]

Gwenllian Lansdown's article appeared next to another, briefer, editorial by Simon Brooks, in which he defends *Y Llan*'s republication of the 'completely innocuous' cartoon from *France Soir*, and in which he criticises the Archbishop of Wales's response and that of the Assembly Equality minister, who had welcomed the editor's resignation. He says the editor's home and workplace were now under police guard:

> The editor of a Welsh-language magazine living in fear of attack. And the reaction of the Welsh establishment? 'Apologising' for his 'offences' which are not contrary to any law, and knifing him in the back. I cannot be the only one in Wales who believes that this has all been extremely shabby.[63]

The articles in *Cambria* and *Barn* in the spring of 2006 provide one of the few, and certainly one of the most intense, discussions of conflict related to Islamic exttremism in Wales in recent years.

As for literary engagements with the subject of extremism, there is a passing mention in the work of Dannie Abse (*b.*1923), the doyen of English-language Welsh poets. In 2007, he recorded his unease at the views of the radical Islamic cleric, Abu Hamza, jailed in February 2006 for inciting murder and racial hatred. Writing in *The Presence*, his poignant memoir of his grief at the death of his wife Joan in a road accident two years earlier, Abse says he had seen reports of the Abu Hamza court case on television, and remarking on the preacher's charismatic quality, he says: 'Abu Hamza is obviously half-insane and would inoculate his followers with his madness.'[64] However, Abse's comment was only a passing reference in a wider discussion about the power of oratory generally. In 2008, another Welsh poet, Patrick Jones (*b.*1965) sought to locate one of his volumes in the area of free speech and religion, including Islam.

The poetry collection, *darkness is where the stars are*, attacked various forms of religion, including aspects of Christianity and Islam, from an atheist perspective. Jones, an English-language poet, of strongly radical political views, precipitated a controversy in advance of publication by sending some of the poems to Christian and Muslim organisations and to the far-right group Combat 18, requesting 'feedback'.[65] When the pressure group Christian Voice, named in the book, duly threatened to protest at his book launch, claiming the publication was obscene and blasphemous – one poem contains the repeated line 'just like mary magdelene / i fucked jesus'[66] – the event was cancelled by the host bookshop and had to be relocated. No protests by Muslim representatives were recorded in press coverage of the issue, however, the Prophet Muhammad was not actually mentioned by name in the book, which confined its criticism of Islam to bombings, jihads and burkhas, alongside examples of extremism from other faiths, as the following extracts from the poem 'hymn', show:

> cover my face
> with burkha so unnatural

i'm so ugly in your eyes
or is it my vision is so clitoral

. . .

go to bed with jihad so young
fasten my vulva with catholic tongue
decapitate me while i kneel
as all my sisters bow like culled seals

just like mary magdalene
i fucked jesus
just like mary magdalene
i am in each of us[67]

The poem 'moment of light', given in full below, sets out the author's carefully comprehensive manifesto against all supernatural belief, Islam included:

the world turns
people stand still
stare from suburban windows
looking for a sign

the trees wait
eyeing the chainsaws
splinters and papyrus
guide our todays
as shopping malls and stainedglass windows
bring us to our knees

as subservience is all we feel

religion the new race
followers are easy to replace
so belong or be gone
as blindfolded women with stapledshut eyes
are paraded through villages
to lie beneath stones
and the love of men labelled evil
and rucksacks scream the word of god
place the veil, the hood, the orange boiler suit
to mark your ground and plead for enemies and infidels
and poppies flower in spilledblood sommed silence
as taleban lords harvest opium crops

to numb the masses
like bloodless crucifixion upon wooden crosses
and bush declares god is on our side
and blair expects significant ... losses

so.

today
i have become a born again

atheist
bow to a river bank not the parting of the sea
sing to a star not an invisible man in the sky
and

i pray for prayers to be abandoned
mosques deserted, synagogues closed, churches morphed into poundshops
and the congregations will commune with one another
talk with one another laugh with one another

could this be how the shelling stops?

on a tiny piece of earth with no ownership manual
no ritual no prayerline 0800 number no tube of holy water
that guarantees eternal life
no jihad no them no us

then they shall all be fucking saved
from a lifetime of waiting
because
the verb is more important than the noun
hey
oh, mighty father?

The final treatment of the post 9-11 world by a Welsh creative author, is Llion Iwan's 2008 novel, *Yr Anweledig* ('The Invisible Ones'), which tells the story of the war in Afghanistan from the twin perspectives and tangled fates of 'Jon' – real name 'Mohammed' – an assimilated Muslim U.S. Air Force pilot fighting a war he finds increasingly unjustified, and Hani, a simple Pakistani village boy exploited by unscrupulous jihadist demagogues and turned into a suicide bomber.

The novel's attention is focused with an intensely sympathetic interest on the perspective of Muslim villagers in the mountains on the Afghan-Pakistan border. These scenes are rich in detail of village life in central Asia, informed by the author's earlier travel in similar regions. The American forces and the jihadists are portrayed as intruders who disturb the peaceful mountain idyll for their own ideological ends.

Neither intruder is depicted positively: the brand of Islam followed by the jihadists is shown to be harsher and more intolerant than that which the villagers had habitually practised, and the jihadists' exploitation of Hani's naiveté and grief is shown to be cynical and ruthless. Nonetheless, the novel's disapproval of the jihadists is not as heartfelt as that reserved for the Americans, who – with the exception of the conscience-stricken Muslim protagonist – are given an almost cartoonishly villainous portrayal. In one passage, an American serviceman says: 'The only good Arab is a dead Arab; the women bear children, and the children grow up to be men.'[68] In the following passage, an American captain is advocating the indiscriminate bombing of mountain villages:

> 'Wrong? They're all enemies, so how can we be wrong? Only the fools in the press claim such nonsense.' But he remembered what had happened to the last officer who had ordered the bombing of a village. 'But just in case, best to call for a seed-planting raid. Just in case...'
>
> He was referring to a new, secret policy, where it could be arranged for special forces soldiers to land in helicopters at the site of any bombing, to plant arms and to take pictures in order to prove that it had been the real enemy who had been hit that time. And if anyone innocent in the area had been killed, then it was their fault for giving shelter to the enemy. That's what the nameless colonel, in his expensive suit, had said in the meeting in their headquarters in the desert.
>
> The junior officer made the two calls over the radio despite his fears that another massacre of innocent people was about to happen. An order was an order. In minutes warplanes were heading for the wedding to vomit their lethal cargo. In another camp, soldiers in black clothes were stepping into their helicopter carrying bags of weapons and video cameras before leaving for their raid. Everyone was sure they would be back in time to watch the latest George Clooney film in the camp's cinema.[69]

As well as giving more rounded and sympathetic portrayals of its Muslim characters than its American ones, the novel also emphasises the suffering of the victims of American violence far more heavily than that of the victims of the jihadists. The death of Hani's mother, in an incendiary attack by American jets, is depicted in gruesome detail over several pages, while the victims of the later jihadist suicide bombing are dismissed in a single line – 'the bodies of dozens of men, women and children who were standing nearby were torn apart'.[70]

The novel ends on a note of conciliation, with 'Jon', returned to the United States, after the trauma of his war service, embracing his true identity – and his real name – as a Muslim American, and finding unexpected acceptance. However, while American tolerance is shown as commendable, though rare, the overall impression given by the novel is of an almost idealised poor and virtuous mountain community resisting the depredations of a technologically superior but morally inferior and more materialistic empire. It is a perspective that would be recognisable to a Welsh nationalist schooled in the influential narrative of history as a series of episodes of heroic resistance to unwarranted incursion, which has been promulgated over the last sixty years or so among a substantial constituency of politicised Welsh speakers. But it is a long way from that watershed moment of the end of the Second World War, where we began this chapter, when British people, the Welsh among them, still largely shared a world view formed by a past in which they were not the victims of empire, but its masters.

Notes

1. Sir Winston Churchill, speech to the House of Commons, 18 June, 1940: 'Let us therefore brace ourselves to our duties, and so bear ourselves that, if the British Empire and its Commonwealth last for a thousand years, men will still say, "This was their finest hour."'

2. James Morris, *Farewell The Trumpets: An Imperial Retreat* (Harmondsworth, 1978) 556.

3. Elwyn Evans, *Amser a Lle* (Llandysul, 1975) 84. See also: Gerwyn Williams, *Tir Newydd.* (Caerdydd, 2005)101-111.

4. Elwyn Evans, *ibid.* 74.

5. Stevie Davies, 'Into Suez', extract published in advance in *New Welsh*

Review (Winter 2009), 53.
6. *Ibid.* 58.
7. J. Gwyn Griffiths in Heini Gruffudd (ed.) *Hog dy Fwyell* (Talybont, 2007) 207. The poem is also printed in Bethan Mair and R. Arwel Jones (eds.), *Cerddi'r Byd* (Llandysul, 2005) 66.
8. Vali Nasr, *The Shia Revival: How Conflicts within Islam Will Shape the Future* (New York, 2006) 121.
9. Richard Llewellyn, *I Stood on a Quiet Shore* (London, 1982) 1.
10. *Ibid.* 152.
11. *Ibid.*
12. *Ibid.* 9.
13. *Ibid.* 11.
14. *Ibid.* 5.
15. *Ibid.* 56.
16. D. Densil Morgan, 'Crefydd ar ôl 9/11', *Y Traethodydd,* 161: 679 (October, 2006) 246-252.
17. Sheenagh Pugh website, FAQs http://sheenagh.webs.com/faqsonspecificpoems.htm Pugh notes that the initials were used to protect the safety of the woman concerned.
18. The Shah's secret police.
19. Sheenagh Pugh, 'M.S.A.', *Selected Poems* (Bridgend, 1990) 11-18.
20. Sheenagh Pugh, 'The Tormented Censor', *Stonelight* (Bridgend, 1999) 47.
21. Rhian M. Phillips, *Cefndir* (Denbigh, 1986) 65.
22. Bobi Jones, *Casgliad o Gerddi* (Aberystwyth, 1989) 309.
23. Gethin Rhys, 'Ymateb i Rushdie', *Cristion* (January/February, 1993) 4.
24. Anthony Burgess, *Any Old Iron* (London, 1989) 306.
25. Eluned Phillips, *Cerddi Glyn y Mêl* (Llandysul, 1985) 35.
26. *Ibid.* 38.
27. *Ibid.* 30.
28. Robert Minhinnick *After the Hurricane* (Manchester, 2002) 78.
29. *Ibid* 7-11.
30. Robert Minhinnick, *To Babel and Back* (Bridgend, 2005) 20.
31. *Ibid.* 14.
32. Tweli Griffiths, 'Yn y Drych Aneglur' in Dylan Iorwerth (ed.) *Deuddeng Mlynedd o Ohebu Tramor* (Cardiff, 1993) 18.
33. *Ibid.* 19.
34. *Ibid.*
35. Betsan Powys, 'Bosnia' in Gwyn Erfyl (ed.) *Y Teithiwr Talog* (Llanrwst, 1998) 12.
36. *Ibid.* 13.
37. *Ibid.* 14.
38. *Ibid.* 17.
39. *Ibid.* 17.
40. *Ibid.* 20.
41. Norah A. Malik, 'Y Ffordd i Feca', *Cristion* (July / August, 1993) 13.

42. *Ibid.* 14.
43. *Ibid.* 14.
44. Siân Messamah, 'Yn enw Duw; y mwyaf grasol, y mwyaf trugarog', *Cristion* (January-February, 1998) 17.
45. Eirwen Gwynn, *Dim Ond Un* (Llandysul, 1997) 161.
46. *Ibid.* 162.
47. Meic Stephens, 'Obituary: Eirwen Gwynn, Welsh nationalist and writer,' *The Independent*, 30 January, 2007: http://www.independent.co.uk/news/obituaries/eirwen-gwynn-434251.html
48. Correspondence with the author.
49. Sheenagh Pugh, *Id's Hospit* (Bridgend, 1997) 48.
50. Geraint Vaughan Jones, *Omega* (Llanrwst, 2000) 183.
51. Merryl Wyn Davies, Ziauddin Sardar, *Why Do People Hate America?* (London, 2002) 30.
52. Merryl Wyn Davies, 'Wilful Imaginings', *New Internationalist,* 345 (May 2002), http://www.newint.org/features/2002/05/01/wilful-imaginings/
53. Gwyn Thomas, 'Y Mae'r Tyrau Mawr yn Torri', *Barddas,* 303 (April/May/June, 2009) 23.
54. Gwyn Thomas, *Apocalups Yfory* (Swansea, 2005) 78.
55. Robin Llywelyn, *Un Diwrnod yn yr Eisteddfod* (Llandysul, 2004) 15.
56. Gwynfor ab Ifor, 'Addolwr', *Barddas,* 286 (February/March, 2006) 47. A more literal translation might run as follows: 'From my God, I shall not depart – to his righteous / Anger I bow down; / I shall obediently live in the faith / With the fist of his eyes upon me. // To the clear sky, if the rain comes – praise him, / Praise him through the beating rain; / To sustain through all competing melodies / I name the book in my hand. // I shall fight my wolves; – with a rod / I shall shepherd my sheep; / Naming the book whitens the mud / In the rivers of my soul. // There is one city of us – remaining / To Him, but there runs through us / In waves the faith given to us; / For Allah's sake, I am a bomb.'
57. Siôn Jobbins, 'Llanistan', *Cambria* (August/September, 2006) 28.
58. Dyfrig Jones, 'Cenhadon Casineb', *Barn,* 518 (March, 2006) 4-6.
59. Simon Brooks, 'Wyneb Mohamed', *Barn,* 518 (March, 2006) 7.
60. The 2001 Census shows 1,751 people in the Riverside ward identified as Muslims, a total of 14% of the ward's population.
61. A reference to one of the major ceremonial statements of the National Eisteddfod of Wales.
62. Gwenllian Lansdown, 'Y Gwir yn Erbyn y Byd?', *Barn,* 519 (April, 2006) 4-5.
63. Simon Brooks, *Barn,* 519 (April, 2006) 7.
64. Dannie Abse, *The Presence* (London, 2007) 94.
65. 'Poet "stirred up" storm over book.' BBC News Online, 15 November, 2008: http://news.bbc.co.uk/1/hi/wales/7730396.stm
66. Patrick Jones, *darkness is where the stars are* (Blaenau Ffestiniog, 2008) 34.
67. *Ibid.* 34.

68. Llion Iwan, *Yr Anweledig* (Llandysul, 2008) 85.
69. *Ibid.* 143.
70. *Ibid.* 177.

'Strange is the magic of the East': Welsh Travellers in Islamic Lands

Travellers' tales of their meetings with Muslims and their impressions of Islam have formed a major part of the preceding chapters. There, as a way of emphasising the main engines of Welsh-Muslim contact throughout history, the travellers' accounts were grouped into some broad themes in order to examine particular significant historical periods, such as military campaigns, or particular mechanisms of contact, such as missionary work or seafaring.

The present chapter is intended to capture the many travellers' accounts which fall outside those categories. As such, it is something of a miscellany, but is, I hope, useful because the large number and the variety of the commentators involved, and their distance from an explicit religious or military context, means that they can act as a kind of control group for the entire study, allowing us to assess to what degree the attitudes expressed in the other themed chapters were representative of Welsh views generally. It also serves to illustrate how many and varied have been the means by which Welsh people and followers of Islam have met over the centuries.

The earliest extract is not a first-hand account, but a report of a traveller's tale, and of an apocryphal one at that. But it illustrates the view of Muslim countries common on the streets of Wales two hundred years ago. Published in several pamphlet editions in the last decade of the eighteenth century, it comes from the work of Edward Pugh ap Fyllin, a Welsh-language balladeer from Oswestry in Shropshire, at that time a Welsh-speaking area. It shows that travelling to lands ruled by the 'Turk' – 'lands without religion ... Morocco, the land of the fez' – was viewed as an inherently dangerous enterprise for Christians. The poem is entitled 'The story of the son of a gentleman from Lancashire who went travelling,' and its own introduction provides a summary of its contents, and, incidentally, an indication of its quality:

> He was taken to prison, on account of his religion, in the country of the Turks, and the king's daughter fancied him, stole the keys and set him free making a condition that if she could come over to England within seven years, he would not marry in the meantime, but the son married another, and on the bidding feast the night before the wedding the king's daughter came according to her word, and the son was very surprised, he refused his betrothed and married the daughter of the king of the Turk.[1]

If ap Fyllin's poem cannot be taken as a high point of inter-cultural understanding, it can at least provide a marker as to attitudes prevailing in Welsh popular culture at the time, and as such can be compared with the 1762 *anterliwt* (or folk drama), *Hanes y Capten Ffactor* ('The History of Captain Factor'), examined in Chapter 4, which had equally simplistic, albeit more extensive, portrayals of Muslims. Siwan M. Rosser, in her 2005 study *Y Ferch ym Myd y Faled* ('The Woman in the World of the Ballad') has shown that numerous Welsh versions of this ballad were in circulation, themselves adaptations of an English ballad known as 'Young Bateman', part of a genre of similar stories popular throughout Europe, and known as the story of 'the Saracen Princess'.[2]

Once genuine first-hand accounts are available, they become more informed, and, over the years, gradually less prejudiced, although the next example is by no means free from that defect; in fact, it is probably the most challengingly unreserved in this chapter. It comes from the memoirs of the great African explorer, Henry Morton Stanley (1841-1904). Stanley's real name was John Rowlands, and he was born into poverty in Denbighshire, north Wales, where, as an illegitimate child of a teenaged mother and alcoholic father, he suffered poverty, including a spell in St Asaph workhouse. At the age of 18, he emigrated to the United States where, after serving with both sides in the Civil War, he became a successful journalist and adventurer, most famously discovering the missing Scottish explorer and missionary David Livingstone in Uganda in 1871. During the early part of his career as an explorer Stanley had himself briefly been taken prisoner in Turkish lands, when, in 1866, he embarked on an expedition to Syria; he and his party were captured by outlaws, and, until an intermediary secured their release, were badly ill-treated – at least according to Stanley's account.

That caveat is necessary, because while there is no doubt that many of his exploits were spectacular, this copious memoirist was also given to exaggeration. Fortunately, our present study is an examination of attitudes rather than an assessment of factual accuracy. In the following passages from Stanley's 1878 book *Through the Dark Continent*, he tells of his meeting in 1875 with Mtesa, ruler of Uganda, and reveals an attitude to Islam which somehow manages to combine deep respect and callous dismissiveness. He is pleased to find Mtesa 'nearly half-civilized':

> All this is the result of a poor Muslim's labour; his name is Muley ben Salim. He it was who first began teaching here the doctrines of Islam. False and contemptible as these doctrines are, they are preferable to the ruthless instincts of a savage despot, whom Speke and Grant[3] left wallowing in the blood of women, and I honour the memory of Muley ben Salim – Muslim and slave-trader though he be – the poor priest who has wrought this happy change. With a strong desire to improve still more the character of Mtesa, I shall begin building on the foundation stones laid by Muley ben Salim. I shall destroy his belief in Islam, and teach the doctrines of Jesus of Nazareth.[4]

Stanley reports how he threw himself into his missionary work in a series of ten interviews:

> I showed the difference in character between Him whom white men love and adore, and Mahommed, whom the Arabs revere; how Jesus endeavoured to teach mankind that we should love all men, excepting none, while Mahommed taught his followers that the slaying of the pagan and the unbelievers was an act that merited Paradise. I left it to Mtesa and his chiefs to decide which was the worthier character. I also sketched in brief the history of religious belief from Adam to Mahommed. I had also begun to translate to him the Ten Commandments. The enthusiasm with which I launched into this work of teaching was soon communicated to Mtesa and some of his principal chiefs, who became so absorbingly interested in the story as I gave it to them that little of other business was done.[5]

Stanley wrote to his newspapers, the *Daily Telegraph* and the *New York Herald*, appealing for a Christian mission to be sent to Mtesa.

> I have, indeed, undermined Islamism so much here that Mtesa has

> determined henceforth, until he is better informed, to observe the Christian Sabbath as well as the Muslim Sabbath. He has further caused the Ten Commandments of Moses to be written on a board for his daily perusal, as well as the Lord's Prayer and the golden commandment of our Saviour, 'Thou shalt love thy neighbour as thyself.' This is great progress for the few days that I have remained with him, and, though I am no missionary, I shall begin to think that I might become one if such success is feasible. But, oh I that some pious, practical missionary would come here! What a field and harvest ripe for the sickle of civilization![6]

Stanley's chequered reputation meant that his appeal to religious sentiment was met with some scepticism. However, the professional missionaries who did later follow up Stanley's lead seem to have been less successful than the amateur: the bitterly competitive Christian sectarianism they introduced to Uganda so disappointed Mtesa that he told them to return to Europe and come back when they had agreed which type of Christianity was the true one.[7]

While the accounts of many travellers are, by their nature, records of transient encounters, one particular Welsh overseas enterprise resulted in extended contact, and, as a result, a deeper engagement with the Muslim world. It has already been shown how Egypt was the centre of British interests in the Middle East. Britain had extensive commercial interest there, not least the Suez Canal itself. Egypt was a crucial crossroads for an Empire for whom contact with India was of huge importance. Accordingly, Cairo became a major centre of British commerce, and, as so often, prominent among the British community were the Welsh.

The most extensive Welsh connection in Egypt was brought about by the Davies Bryan brothers, who founded Cairo's major department store. The full story of the brothers' enterprise can be found in Siân Wyn Jones's 2004 study, *O Gamddwr i Gairo – Hanes y Brodyr Davies Bryan (1851-1935)* ('From Camddwr to Cairo – The Story of the Davies Bryan Brothers').[8] The business was founded by John Davies Bryan, (*d.*1888) a shopkeeper from Llanarmon-yn-Iâl in Denbighshire, who emigrated to Egypt in 1886 partly for health reasons, and partly due to the encouragement of his cousin, Samuel Evans, who was already a prominent public official in Egypt, and whose writings we examined in

Chapter 3. John Davies Bryan founded a succession of shops, eschewed the local habit of haggling in favour of a fixed-price policy, and prospered. His brother, Robert Bryan (1858-1920), a well-known minor poet, said in an introduction to his late brother's writings published in 1908 that the pricing policy was an act of principle: 'I heard him say that he had decided to live, so that his life would be a sermon to the Musselmen about Christianity.'[9]

Whatever its motives, the policy worked. The firm was reputed to be so widely trusted that Arabs would deposit large sums of gold there, without written security, rather than put them in the bank.[10] The business grew to the extent that John Davies Bryan could send for two of his brothers, Edward and Joseph, to join him in Egypt. Although John Davies Bryan died from typhoid at the age of 33 in 1888, the business continued to grow under the family's ownership. Eventually, it had branches not only in Cairo but in Alexandria, Port Said and Khartoum. By 1910 the brothers could afford to build their own department store, St David's Buildings, at one time the biggest modern building in Africa; purpose-built to their own design, it sported the triple-line symbol of the Gorsedd of Bards and the carved motto beloved to eisteddfod-goers: 'Y Gwir yn Erbyn y Byd' ('The Truth Against the World').

The eisteddfodic motif was apposite, for these were not just sharp men of business; they were also cultured lovers of literature. A collection of John Davies Bryan's writings, *O'r Aifft* ('From Egypt'), consisting of his letters to the periodical *Y Genedl Gymreig* ('The Welsh Nation'), was published posthumously in 1908. One of the articles, recounting a sea voyage, gives a portrayal of Muslim fellow passengers who boarded at Algiers:

> Despite their sonorous names, these were poor and dirty creatures – they had very few clothes, and they appeared pitiable enough. The main occupation of most of them was smoking – women and men, but two or three were very devout. They would spread their mats and turn their faces to Mecca many times a day in view of everyone. A pity that such devoted worshippers could not come to know the 'God that should be worshipped'.[11]

John Davies Bryan also wrote an authoritative series of

articles on Islam for O.M. Edwards's popular magazine, *Cymru*, in 1912 and 1913. It was noted in Chapter 6 that many Welsh people of the period were steeped in Biblical stories and were predisposed to support Zionist claims to the Holy Land on the basis of their shared belief in Old Testament prophecy. That is certainly true, but it is nonetheless worth pointing out that, by this stage of history, the Welsh reading public was by no means ignorant of Islam; those same Welsh people, at least if they were readers of *Cymru*, had been exposed to detailed and thorough accounts of Muslim history, belief and practice, thanks to the work of the Bryan family. Of course, in the same way that Arabism such as that of Lawrence of Arabia was a sideshow in British cultural life when compared to the power of Christian philo-semitism, so was knowledge of Islam in Wales much less widespread, and less resonant, than was knowledge of Judaism. The work of authors such as the Bryan brothers shows that it was, however, not entirely absent.

The articles by John Davies Bryan, entitled 'Islam a'i Phroffwyd' ('Islam and its Prophet'), explain the historical and religious background of Islam, and the life of Muhammad himself, in considerable detail. They are largely factual accounts drawn from the *Qur'an* and from common and undisputed biographical and historical sources. But the following extracts contain some personal opinion, and give some insight into what John Davies Bryan actually thought of Muhammed himself. In the second of the articles, about the early life of the Prophet, Bryan gives a sympathetic account of Muhammed's religious revelations:

> His whole nature was inspired. He fled to the caves of the hills, and to the magnificent loneliness of the mountains in order to be closer to God. There, with his face in the dust, and with pain in his heart, he cried out in the words of the Fatiha, which were set out later as the first words of the Koran.[12]

In the third article, when Muhammad's reforming campaign is underway, there are some more critical comments. Bryan notes that Muhammad's knowledge of Christianity has come from 'some very corrupt sources'[13] and that the Prophet's rejection of Christianity was due to the unedifying behaviour of Christians themselves: 'It is obvious that the greatest barrier to the spread of

Christianity, then as now, was the character it had been given by those who professed it.'[14] Had Muhammad been literate, says Bryan, he would have been able to understand Biblical texts better: 'He would have avoided also one or two of the atrocious errors that are to be found in the Koran.'[15] Referring to Muhammad's series of spiritual revelations, which caused him much disturbance of mind, Bryan remarks that his desire for these evidences of God's communication with him was 'unhealthy'.[16] However, Bryan's conclusion to his account of Muhammad's early career ends on a very positive note, owing much to Thomas Carlyle's famous essay on Muhammad in his 1841 book, *On Heroes, Hero-Worship and the Heroic in History*. He praises Muhammad's achievement and says he was 'entirely sincere in his belief, there is the ring of sincerity in his teaching, and his courage was heroic'.[17]

By April 1913, Bryan's series had moved on to a later stage in the prophet's career, the year 623, when, at a low ebb in Muhammad's fortunes, his followers took part in caravan raids, whose moral legitimacy is still a matter of controversy today. Referring specifically to the seventh raid, at Nakhla, undertaken during a sacred month contrary to the customary truce and resulting in the death of the caravan leader, Bryan is in no doubt this action was unjustified: 'It was through betrayal that blood was first shed for Islam, and the action was given the authority of "divine revelation" to justify it.'[18] Depicting the battle of Badr, a year later, Bryan, whose article is entitled 'Buddugoliaeth Gyntaf Islam' ('Islam's First Victory'), tells how the Muslims defeated their Meccan opponents. However, Bryan's treatment of Muhammad is somewhat sceptical, as he depicts him leaving the battlefield at the first bloodshed, and fainting 'either from excessive worry or from fear'.[19] After the battle, with the Muslims victorious, Bryan says Muhammad spared most of his captive enemies, although he also reproached the corpses of his dead opponents. Bryan comments:

> In his behaviour now, in the hours of his first victory, we can see the double nature of the prophet very clearly. At one time behaving tenderly towards the defeated in a manner far in advance of the custom of the age; and at another time casting his vengeance upon a fallen enemy with barbaric cruelty. From heartfelt and passionate prayer, we see him moving on to discussing worldly matters with his

> grumbling followers about the division of the spoils; and then, with the prescience of a wise statesman, conversing with the prisoners he hopes to attract to his party.[20]

It is with this impression of ambiguity that John Davies Bryan closes his account of the early years of the prophet's life. However, if his portrait of Muhammad is not entirely complimentary, it is detailed and engaged and contains many positive elements. It should be noted too that Bryan is careful to compare the prophet's activities implicitly with those of the British Empire, then at the height of its power, and to imply therefore, that any failings of which Mohammad may have been guilty are more than matched by those of the empire to which readers of *Cymru* belonged:

> By now the prophet had become what some European authors would call a talented chief highwayman. Had Mohamed dwelt in these latter times, and had he carried out his actions on a wider scale, no doubt he would be called the founder of an Empire.[21]

While John Davies Bryan was providing heavyweight articles on Islamic history for *Cymru*, his younger brother, Robert Bryan, was contributing a series of articles entitled 'Adlais o'r Dwyrain' ('An Echo from the East') in which he provided versified Welsh translations of Egyptian proverbs, some with a distinct Islamic flavour, such as the following one, which refers to Muhammad as 'El Amin', 'The Faithful':

> 'I cannot battle for Islam,
> Too sultry has the weather been,'
> 'Hell will be a hotter clime.'
> Answered fiercely El Amin.[22]

Robert Bryan was an able lyric poet and composer, best known now for writing the words to the lullaby 'Suo Gân' a long-time favourite with folk singers and choirs, and brought to international prominence in 1987 when it was used as a musical motif in the Steven Spielberg film, *Empire of the Sun*. While not a permanent resident of Egypt like his brothers, he spent the winters there from 1903, and he wrote a considerable amount on Egyptian and Islamic themes. One of his poems, published in 1921, after his death in Cairo the previous year, is a rarity – not for its quality, which is at best indifferent – but for its subject matter. It is given in full below:

El Jihad

'Why must the sword be raised on high?'
said El Amin, of fearsome eye,
        To Islam's faithful men one day
        'For men to choose if they should pray
and live for God, or else should die.

'In Eden once did God impart
His holy law to human heart.
        Man disobeyed, and angels cast
        Him from the garden at the last,
The fruit had held death's fatal dart.

'His ways did all the world offend
So All Forgiving God did send
        Noah to teach the righteous way,
        But stubborn were the sons of clay
And flood did their defiance end.

'Then Lot was sent to clear the stain
Of sin from cities of the plain,
        To cleanse the evil men and vile
        Who holy angels would defile
And God destroyed with fiery rain.

'God spoke on Sinai's mighty height
In smoke and thunder, fire and light,
        And Moses came from Yahweh's face
        To where all Israel did abase
Themselves, transgressing in his sight.

'God pitied this poor world of ill
And quiet grew his voice, and still
        And Jesus came with God's own love,
        And grace to earth from heaven above –
To bear a cross to Calvary's hill.

'Take up the sword of God alone
Against the pagan gods of stone,
        Against the faithless Jews reviled,
        And those who worship Mary's child.
No god but God; not three, but one.

'These evil men destroy accord,'
Said El Amin, the fiery lord.
    'But by the heavens, they must submit
    To God alone or die for it.
Men of Islam, unsheath your sword.'

Out flamed a host of shining steel,
A third of all the earth did feel,
    Through family of El Amin
    The sword-blades pitiless and keen,
The lust for blood of lips of steel.

***

The sword will cut the hand that draws,
Islam knows this for all its wars;
    It never shall return to sheath
    Nor rest, until the world beneath
The crescent moon obeys its laws
And every hill declares its cause.[23]

A second, shorter poem, 'Bacshîsh' ('Backsheesh'), shows Bryan's distaste for the begging which he encountered in Egypt, a custom which for many Welsh authors, was a bigger source of ill-feeling towards Arabs and Muslims than any theological difference.

The endless call, 'Backsheesh, backsheesh,'
    On every hand disturbs all peace,
    In mosques and graveyards, fields and towns
'Backsheesh, backsheesh,' all quiet drowns, -
Is this the romance of the east?[24]

Edward Bryan died in 1929, and the last of the four brothers, Joseph Bryan, who was chairman of the Alexandria British Association and of the chamber of commerce, died in 1935 at the age of 71, leaving a fortune to the National Library of Wales and the university at Aberystwyth, where a hall of residence was named after the family. The business remained in Welsh hands, however, through the firm's accountant, Fred Purslow of Coedpoeth near Wrexham, who had joined the company in 1929 and who continued to run it until 1956 when it was nationalised by Nasser's government. Divided now between other businesses, the building still stands, and although no longer a home-from-home for Welsh expatriates, it still attracts curious visitors from Wales who try to make out the gradually-fading Welsh symbols and lettering on its carved facade.[25]

The Davies Bryan family, and Robert in particular, were friends of Thomas Gwynn Jones (1871-1949), one of the major Welsh-language poets of the twentieth century, a winner of the National Eisteddfod Chair in 1902 for his strict-metre Arthurian ode, 'Ymadawiad Arthur' ('The Passing of Arthur'), and later Professor of Welsh Literature at Aberystwyth. In 1905, troubled by incipient tuberculosis, he made an extended journey to the drier climate of the Mediterranean, taking in Egypt and a visit to the Davies Bryan family on the way. He returned in April 1906, the shadow of the disease having lifted. His 1912 book, *Y Môr Canoldir a'r Aifft* ('The Mediterranean and Egypt'),[26] an account of his experiences, contains numerous colourful passages about Islam. The following passage tells of his visit to Tunis. Having visited the French-controlled European quarter, and having reported his delight at its variety, order and liveliness, he then ventures into the Arab quarter on the last night of Ramadan in company with his friend Llywarch and an Italian guide.[27]

> Almost everyone has a cheerful look, and they don't take the slightest notice of us – much less, indeed than the people of Caernarfon or Liverpool would take if two Arabs in their national dress were to wander the streets of those towns staring at the religious Association day, or the Horse Race.[28]
>
> . . .
>
> What is this endless crowd doing? Here's one creature alongside us who is going at it with all his power to make some dreadful din. I thought to myself that he was ill and groaning in pain, but Llywarch told me that he was singing. I would never have thought it.
>
> Now again I see something on the floor in the gutter almost at my feet. It looks like a pile of dirty clothes. I almost stepped on it, but I hear the great word 'Allah', and the Italian tells me that the heap of clothes is a woman, and that she is praying.
>
> Yonder are tall, handsome men, walking gracefully past, but there are masks on the faces of all the women. Yet their stately gait leads me to believe that there is beauty behind many a mask, and there is many a shining eye sparkling above the veil.[29]
>
> . . .

> Suddenly, I hear a voice. If I had not known well where I was, I would have thought I was back in Wales and listening to some old brother praying in the spirit. His intonation, whoever he is, is identical. I ask the Italian to tell me what is going on.
>
> 'There they are,' he says, pointing his finger at a building some distance away.
>
> There, I see about half a dozen mature men sitting like tailors on benches, and rocking from side to side while reciting something, or rather half-singing, half-reciting something.
>
> 'They are reciting prayers and extracts of the Koran,' says the guide.
>
> This street gets darker and lonelier all the time, but now we take another turn and come to a more open and lighter place. There are two men arguing with one another and fighting in their drink. Yes, they are Italians. I never saw a Mohametan drunk. They don't take strong drink. They leave that to us Christians, and I fear that we are abler at that than at just about anything, more's the pity.[30]

In a private letter home, collected in David Jenkins's 1973 biography of Jones, we find the poet putting a less positive gloss on this kind of experience: 'The Arabs are a cussedly thieving and cheating people, for all their godliness. In the evening here, they pray or chant parts of the Koran until they nearly deafen you. I heard one of them last night singing just like some old Welshman at prayer, the same tune exactly. But all their prayer does not teach the devils to be honest or truthful.'[31]

Returning to Jones's book, we find him, the following day, visiting the city again. He has criticism for Jewish storekeepers he encounters, finding them pushy and insincere 'like a dog fawning after being whipped', but has warmer words for the Muslims, commending one old chieftain, 'a Mohametan of the most precise order', who abhorred electric trams as a sign of godless modernity.[32]

Jones's journey takes him on to Egypt, where he reflects on the religious history of that country and of the East in general. He observes some 'Egyptian girls sitting by the side of the road, with their faces wrapped in their scarves so that you could only see their eyes.' He says they show no curiosity about present distractions and seem to be 'looking far, far back into the ancient past, and daydreaming about the greatness that once was; or looking forwards through the ages, dreaming of some glory that shall come.'

> Whatever it may be, the West and its skill and its glamour and its little cares, which lives among them, does not make them so much turn and cast their eyes upon it. That's the serene quietude of the East, and its leisure and its rest, and its strange secret. Is it sleeping? Perhaps. Once it was very wakeful, and you might almost think that if it sleeps, then it is only the sleep of such as has seen, as once did Solomon the Wise, that 'vanity of vanities, all is vanity' is, after all, the best description of the life of man.
>
> Strange is the magic of the East, and beside it you feel that the world is very old and tired and that there is nothing new under the sun.
>
> The dream of the East is upon you too, and the magnificent climate means that you need not bestir yourself.
>
> And there comes the Muezzin's cry from the minaret of the mosque calling the faithful to evening prayer.
>
> Without doubt, nothing could be better. The East is the home of religion.[33]

Jones then recounts a visit to the 'splendid and very spacious' Al-Azhar mosque, built in 970, and the home of an Islamic university ever since. He and his companion are offered slippers to allow them to enter the holy place, a requirement he regards with some rancour: 'the polluted feet of the infidel dare not tread upon its floor.' Once inside, Jones gives a lengthy description of the mosque with its scholars, comparing the scene to a Welsh Sunday School. He is drawn to one good-looking youth at prayer, and considers sketching him until his companion advises him not to 'for fear I should disturb the students' hot-headedness.' Jones continues:

> I agree, feeling that Llywarch is right, What would a congregation of Welsh people have said if a Mahometan came among them and started to draw a picture of someone in the middle of their prayer?[34]

He marvels at the quiet and dedication of the thousands of students, and while he doubts if the study is productive by Western standards, it makes him long for a time when the pace of life in Wales was more leisurely, and Welsh scholars had the time and commitment to produce religious manuscripts as beautiful as the copies of the *Qur'an* in the Arabic Museum in Cairo.

> The education that is given in the Mohametan university is not, perhaps, of any use for scarcely anything in the life of the world

> today, as we live it, but the lads who learn a bit of English and 'English history' in the English schools in Cairo are not after all half as gentlemanly as the students of the El Assar mosque. If Egyptian education grew from its own historic roots, and kept its natural leisure and quietness, it would teach self-respect and trust, and the Egyptian would not for much longer be like a servant in his own country.
>
> As we turned our back on the place, the sun shone brightly on the alabaster pillars and on the classes that were scattered across the floor, busy studying the one book that is everything to them, but outside, perhaps there are some men, some who are scorned so often in Britain, who are slowly developing a plan that will turn the gaze of the Egyptian on the thousands of years of glorious history that are behind them. I met some of those leaders, and they told me of their dreams, and about what they are doing to turn their dreams into facts.[35]

Jones goes on to say how he once found himself in a mixed company of Arabs and Europeans in a club for the advancement of Egyptian interests, where, through an interpreter, an elderly Arab explained his hopes for a revival in Egypt's national fortunes, with the children being taught their own language, and Egyptians being trained to become teachers of their own people. Significantly, Jones's response does not align his own views about Muslims with those of his fellow-Britons, the English, but rather with the Muslim people as fellow underdogs struggling against alien British rule.

> Listening to the old Arab speaking his mind, I could not help but remember the schools I attended in Wales, where they tried to teach everything to us apart from the history of my own land and people. And remembering such things, I could not but sympathise with the Arab who demanded that the children of his own country should know something about the magnificent history of ancient Egypt rather than be forced to learn the history of minor English kings during some brief period of a thousand years. It is easy enough for we Britons to chafe about other nations showing towards us a bit of the independence and the self-respect that we count such an achievement.[36]

The first serious modern attempt to press for greater Welsh political independence, the Cymru Fydd ('Young Wales') movement, which had been founded in 1886 and which had counted David Lloyd George as one of its early leaders, had come to an end in 1896, some 15 years before T. Gwynn Jones was writing. Jones and Lloyd George were friends and had shared the nationalist ideals of the movement. The drive for greater independence resumed in 1925 with the founding of the Welsh nationalist party, but only really moved from the fringe to the centre of Welsh politics in the last third of the twentieth century, attaining the majority of its goals with the establishment of The National Assembly for Wales in 1999 after a referendum vote in 1997. Jones's comments nearly a century earlier, equating the issues of Wales with those of another colonised country, are among the earliest expressions in this study of what could be called political nationalism.

As he was in Egypt for an extended period, Jones managed to form friendships with some Arabs, or at least, as he put it: 'as much as it is possible for East and West to be friends'.[37] One of these friends, called Abdul, was 'a convinced Muslim', whom he recounts courteously debating religion with a Christian and eventually agreeing to disagree:

> 'That is what your priest tells you,' he said, 'and my priest tells me otherwise. So we are both somewhat the same.'
>
> And that was it. Abdul went straight off to check on the mules.[38]

Later, Jones and Abdul share a journey into the desert, where Abdul abstains from the wine which Jones offers him. 'Water is better,' he tells him.[39]

Jones ends his book with an extended reflection on the use of imagery of the desert, and of Egypt, drawn mainly from Biblical accounts, in Welsh religious poetry and hymnody. Most see the desert as a place of threat, deprivation and danger; only few see it as a place of spiritual promise and opportunity, of pilgrimage and rest. In the concluding section, given below, Jones's aesthetic vision transcends differences of language, religion and geography as he finds parallels between the religious experience inspired by the desert and that represented in the ecstatic hymnody of the Welsh Methodist mystic from Montgomeryshire, Ann Griffiths, (1776-1805), who was mentioned in Chapter 3:

> I myself saw pilgrims, only they were Mohametan ones, sitting under the palms, and chanting their prayers and praises to Allah, the God

apart from whom there is none. Ann Gruffydd sang even more excellently, and it was her verse that made me think of the hymns about the desert. She felt that 'worthy grapevines' flourished there.

'Worthy grapevines grace the desert land.'

On a lovely morning in the month of November, I was in the desert, at least five miles from the nearest town, and with no living soul in sight. To the west, the river Nile was flowing slow and white-grey, and on its broad breast boats with white sails in the great distance like seagulls on the Menai. Beyond it the Pyramids rose up towards heaven, the eternal dreams of a people who believed the soul was immortal. To the north was Cairo, and the two intricate minarets of the mosque of Mohamed Ali like two needles lost in the blur of the sky, and the dome between them as if it were floating in space. To the east stretched the desert, and to the south, the same aspect, until the distance was nothing but a rolling sea. I sat myself down to dream about the life which was once on the banks of the Nile and now is no more. And to the south-east, something drew my attention. The Bedouin had kindled a fire in the far distant desert. Through 'the thin clear air and splendid quiet heat,' as Elis Wyn[40] put it, I saw two blue-white columns rising straight upwards like two pillars, and climbing higher, higher, slowly, slowly, up, up, until they were lost in the eternal blue of the firmament. I stood up, out of respect to the girl from Montgomeryshire, the poetess who saw in her imagination so clearly and so perfectly the things her eyes had never looked upon:

'Oh, to rise from out the desert
   Like the columns of smoke above
Unwavering to the throne of Him
   In Whose face is only love!'

And as I was thinking of Ann Gruffydd, the columns of smoke rose upwards unwavering to the bright blue sky, that was so silent and so deep, so motionless, that it disturbed the columns not at all, and upon whose serene face there was no crease or frown.[41]

David Jenkins's biography of T. Gwynn Jones notes that on his Egyptian visit, Jones spent time with a Dr Beddoe, a young doctor of medicine from south Wales whose novel, *The Honour of Henri de Valois*, Jones had read before leaving Wales. Beddoe's maternal grandfather was Thomas Lewis (1759-1842), a black-smith of Talyllychau in Carmarthenshire, who was famous as a hymn-writer. Beddoe, however, Jones reported, was, like himself, 'not too orthodox in his faith'.[42]

That may well be true. What is certain is that David M. Beddoe, whose work seems almost entirely forgotten now – and needlessly so, given its quality – was an able historical novelist whose extensive knowledge of Egyptian life and of Islam allowed him to provide some of the most thorough, informed and sympathetic portrayals of Muslims in Welsh literature. He wrote two novels. The first, in 1905, was *The Honour of Henri de Valois*, which was set in Egypt and Syria between 1828 and 1834, during the time of the ambitious statesman Mehmet Ali Pasha's rise to power as an Egyptian-based challenger to Ottoman Turkey. The second novel, *The Lost Mameluke*, published in 1913, was set in Egypt in the late eighteenth century, when French and British forces were contending for influence during the last decades of power of the Mameluke dynasty. In both cases, the main characters are Europeans, but Islam and secondary Muslim characters are depicted with intelligence and insight.

The Honour of Henri de Valois tells the story of a motley group of European mercenaries and veterans of the Napoleonic wars – formerly enemies now united in the service of the Turkish state. One is Irish, one French, one Italian, one English, and one, whose background is a mystery to the others, is actually a Welsh aristocrat, Geoffrey de Braose, exiled after being unjustly accused of murder, and living under an assumed name, with only his Celtic harp to remind him of his homeland. Almost all are Christian; none are devout. One, Vassili the Greek, is 'a Musselman, a creed he found it advantageous to profess with an ostentation which shamed many a true believer.'[43] Under Ottoman rule, non-Muslims were barred from the upper echelons of power, and some who sought to rise higher would convert to Islam in order to further their ambitions. The pressure to convert, and the dilemma over whether or not to do so, is a recurring theme in both novels. While the cast of European mercenaries, adventurers and rootless fortune-hunters are hardly pious Christians, they are nonetheless reluctant to convert. Some are deterred by the rigours of the religion. For others, it is the internal barriers of prejudice, cultural loyalty and identity which make conversion, at best, a suspect undertaking. One of the mercenaries refers to another convert, a Frenchman: 'Tush! a lot Soleiman cares for reekahs or mosques, save as a stepping stone to his ambitions.'[44] Vassili, the villain of the piece, is depicted as a sinister renegade, whose conversion to Islam has been an excuse for cruelty and sensual indulgence, as the following passage, describing Vassili's house, shows:

> And a fortress it is, a paradise if you will, but a cage nevertheless within whose walls the Mussulman owner encloses his womenfolk. Here they would come when their master had paid the price to the slave-dealer, and here they would live and die too, stepping not beyond the walls save when perhaps as a special favour their despotic lord would have them driven through the city in a closed carriage with their yashmaks on. The Bastille in the days before the Empire was not more jealously guarded than some of these houses.
>
> Heaven only knows the unspeakable crimes, the bloody deeds which have taken place in some of these secluded buildings.[45]

Vassili has used his power to abduct and imprison a European woman, who, in the long tradition of stories in which Christian women are snatched from captivity in cruel harems, is, in due course, rescued.

The historical setting of the novel, and much of its external action, relates to Mehmet Ali's war with the Turks, and the Europeans' role in it. The complex internal tensions of this war between powerful Islamic factions are rendered by the novelist with confidence and understanding. In one scene, Mehmet Ali attempts to secure the support of the Grand Mufti, Egypt's highest religious official, for his challenge to the Sultan, the nominal head of the faith. Mehmet Ali argues that he himself has done more for Islam than has the Sultan. In handling this scene, as many others, Beddoe shows considerable understanding of the tensions within the Islamic community.[46]

However the emotional centre of the novel is the redemption of the good name of one of the mercenaries' former comrades, the eponymous Henri de Valois, whom they believe to have betrayed them and who has died in disgrace. In fact, it transpires that Henri had been framed by the villainous Vassili, a fact only revealed when Geoffrey de Braose, for the platonic love of Henri's daughter, entrusted to the mercenaries' care, decides to redeem Henri's honour at the expense of his own by allowing Mehmet Ali to believe that it was he, not Henri, who was the traitor. A last-minute revelation spares him this ultimate sacrifice; he is freed, Vassili is exposed and punished, and honour is restored.

Conversion to Islam was a mark of a renegade in Beddoe's first novel, but it plays a much more central role as a plot device in his second novel, *The Lost Mameluke*. Set in the last years of the eighteenth century, the novel tells the story of a young English trader and former army engineer, Stephen Hales, who, with his wife Margaret, is living an aimless and disconsolate existence in Egypt following the death of the couple's young son, who was swept away in the Nile. Stephen is given a second chance at life when he rescues a prominent Mameluke from assailants and is rewarded with a position as an official engineer. He grasps the opportunity, converts to Islam, takes a Muslim bride and abandons his wife. He discusses his decision with a cynical Frenchman, Maxime, who has taken a similar path:

> 'Ay, 'tis a good religion for men, *mon ami*, saving the water and the fast of the Ramadan, though even that one can get over by a convenient ailment for which the hakeem will give one dispensation; no, I repeat it, no religion can be wholly bad which allows one to get rid of a nagging wife by simply saying, 'I divorce thee by the triple divorce;' he was no fool was the Prophet.'[47]

However, another Frenchman, Jules Lefebre, a friend of the abandoned Margaret Hales, has a different perspective, as he comes to bring her the news of Stephen's remarriage. He speaks bitterly of 'logic à la Moslem', and calls Muslims 'imbeciles' for practising what he believes is an indolent fatalism, which ascribes all events to the will of God. Margaret Hales reproaches him:

> 'I have never heard you speak so bitterly of the Moslem religion before.'
>
> 'Never had I such good reason,' murmured the other to himself, but aloud he added, ' 'Tis no fit religion for one brought up with Western ideas, it degrades, poisons the mind, and is foreign to our ideas of honour and rectitude.'
>
> 'How now, what ails you?' exclaimed Margaret; for Jules, staunch Catholic as he was, had always been tolerant to the religion of the race amongst whom he lived, ever ready to praise its rigid tenets of fasting and alms-giving.[48]

Jules is reluctantly forced to tell her of her husband's remarriage, and the scene ends with him 'murmuring maledictions on Stephen Hales, his apostasy, and on the Mohammedan religion which permitted such things to be.[49]

As Napoleon's forces begin to threaten Egypt, disturbing the delicate *modus vivendi* of the longer-established European residents, the tensions between moderation and extremism in Islam are portrayed through the different influences operating on Abdullah, the disciple of the tolerant and saintly Sheik Fadl. Abdullah is being drawn, despite his teacher's misgivings, increasingly towards hot-headed fundamentalism. In the next passage, Abdullah takes a day off work to visit Cairo's most influential place of worship, 'the seven-gated mosque of el Azhar':

> Four thousand students were there, gathered from all those quarters of the globe where Allah and Mohammed, his prophet, rule over the hearts of men. Grey-bearded age squatted alongside lisping childhood and was not ashamed, for in the sight of Allah were not all equal?
>
> Hither they had come, lean Algerians, grave-faced men from Turkestan and the Persian bazaars, wild-eyed fanatics from the holy cities, and ebony-skinned Nubians from the Soudan, to hear the word expounded in this, the most famous university of el Islam.[50]

Here, in 'the nursery of Moslem fanaticism and intrigue' Abdullah is privy to a planned insurrection against the French occupiers in Egypt. The narrator comments:

> In common with all Moslems, Abdullah had an overpowering contempt for all other religions; it is a sentiment inculcated into them from the cradle, but his natural antipathy had been increased by the pride of serving the Sheik Fadl; not that there was anything intolerant in the teaching of that simple, tolerant old sheik himself, but Abdullah had mixed with others at that hotbed of fanaticism, the el Azhar, and had imbibed intolerance and hatred to the full.[51]

At the same time, Abdullah continues to visit his gentle old teacher, the model of the kind of quiescent Islam that European powers would find convenient. Abdullah tells him he longs for 'the banner of el Islam triumphant' and for the 'cursed Nosrani' to be 'hurled out of the country':

> The old sheik looked up in surprise. 'That we can leave to Allah, my

> son, in his own time he will doubtless bring it about.'
>
> 'Ay, and that time is not far distant,' murmured the lad; but the sheik continued, 'Behold, I have had it in my mind to speak with thee, my son, and take it not amiss, but I have seen with regret that thou dost frequent the orations of the Sheik el Tantawi, who will surely do much harm in inciting the people, and thou art ever too much outspoken and rash. Beware, my son, lest such lead thee into trouble, for, as thou knowest, any mischance to thee would grieve my soul more than aught I know, more even than the loss of my manuscript,' and the old sheik smiled pleasantly. 'And remember, these Franks, though Nosrani, have not behaved as ill as the mamelukes themselves would have done had they been in their place, and many Moslem conquerors too have done in the past, as even the learned Macrizy and Abu Aza tell us.'
>
> 'Nevertheless, I would prefer a kick from a Moslem to a blessing from a Nosrani,' replied the lad warmly.
>
> 'Yet are they all children of the most High; however, it is late, and thou must be weary; may no evil spirit disturb thy dreams.'
>
> The almost sullen face of the lad softened and going up to the old man he took his hand reverently in his and kissed it.[52]

While Abdullah's mixture of piety and national pride is authentically shown, it is clear from the way that Beddoe depicts the moderates more sympathetically than the extremists, that, for all his understanding of the Muslim perspective, he does rather wish that the Muslims could feel a little more positive about being conquered by Europeans. For example, two other Muslim characters are given their own commentary on the French occupiers, a commentary which, while it contains some well-aimed criticism of Christians, seems to ascribe to the defeated Egyptians a magnanimity which can only be the product of a conqueror's wishful thinking:

> 'I like these Franks,' put in the other, 'there is something about them which attracts me. It is a bold enterprise this, to seize on a country so far from their own, to conquer it, and then to treat the people as they treat us; behold, they know that I bore arms against them yet here I walk the streets free and unmolested, and when I was sick, did not the French hakeem attend to me as though I was a brother, and of the many who knew of me not one breathed a word, though there was a price on my head.'
>
> 'They are a strange people,' put in the other musingly, and could I be born again with the choice of my destiny, then would I of a truth be a Frank.'

> 'What, not a mameluke, Radouan Effendi?'
>
> 'Not even a mameluke,' smiled the other;' the days of mamelukes have passed, they died two hundred years ago, not as you think at Embabeh; that was but the axe laid to the rotten root.'
>
> 'But to be a Nosrani, one whose religion sits so lightly upon them?'
>
> 'It is a fine religion nevertheless, that taught by the prophet, Eesa; have I not read it, and though these Franks keep it not, it is not the religion that is at fault; the doctrine is too high for these sons of dogs.
>
> 'It preaches peace, yet they make war; it forbids them to steal, yet they seize on the country of another; it orders them to commit no murder, yet the bones on the plains of Embabeh bear witness against them; it forbids them to take the wife of another, yet thou dost know as well as I the lives that they have lived here in Cairo, and behold,' he broke off, indicating a now ragged proclamation that flapped in the wind from the wall of a house near by, 'it says thou shalt not deny the Lord thy God, yet does not the Frankish general say hereon,' and he pointed with scornful finger, 'that he is of a truth a Moslem? Liar!
>
> 'No, no, there must be better Nosrani than these, Osman, else their religion would have died long ago, and remember that it is seven hundred years older than the time when el Nebbi brought the light.'[53]

The novel concludes with the arrival of the British, who defeat and expel the French. Stephen, still separated from his wife, finds a form of redemption by breaking his vow to his Muslim paymasters and aiding the British invading force, in the course of which action he is killed.

Abdullah, meanwhile, is revealed to be Stephen and Margaret's son, rescued, unknown to them, from the Nile, and raised a Muslim. Appraised of his true origins, he nonetheless vehemently rejects the prospect of ever seeing his now-widowed mother, due to his contempt for Christianity. Heartbroken, Margaret resorts to donning the Muslim veil and waiting, incognito, outside the mosque for an occasional glimpse of her estranged son from afar. Eventually, unable to bear the separation any longer, she takes a momentous decision, setting in motion the events of the moving final scene of the book. Having previously accepted poverty and loneliness rather than endorse her husband's apostasy, she now proposes conversion herself, not for material advancement, but for love. She confesses her intention to an appalled Jules Lefebre, who exclaims: 'But thy soul, madame, thy immortal soul?' She replies: ''Tis my child I want.' Against Lefebre's advice, she visits Sheik Fadl to ask him to accept her conversion. The following passage represents the novel's final scene:

> The old sheik was at home, and though much surprised at the visit, received her with his customary kindly and grave courtesy.
>
> 'Thou art in trouble, my daughter?'
>
> 'Even so, O sheik, and to thee have I come for help.'
>
> 'Allah alone is omnipotent,' he murmured, 'but tell me, ya sitt, perchance I, his servant, can help thee.
>
> 'Ah, 'tis of the lad Abdullah that thou wouldst speak,' and his face looked troubled. 'Patience, ya sitt, patience, I have seen signs, Allah will in his time make all things straight.'
>
> 'No, no,' she burst out, 'preach not to me that doctrine, it is finished.'
>
> 'Tell me all then, O sitt, what it is that thou dost desire.'
>
> Squatting cross-legged on the divan the old sheik listened, whilst seated on an ottoman at his feet Margaret poured out her soul to him, and no penitent confessing to a priest of Rome ever had a more fitting confessor than Margaret Hales in this old sheik of the Mohammedan faith.
>
> The outer door opened, but neither heard it, nor the stealthy footsteps of a boy, who, coming in, stopped at the sound of her voice, and creeping up to the entrance, listened with flushed and intent face.
>
> The low murmur of her voice came distinctly to his ears, mingled with an occasional sob, and the soft encouraging voice of the Sheik Fadl.
>
> 'Wallahi,' it came in surprise, 'and thou wouldst turn Moslem then?'
>
> 'I would, I would, if I could but get my son by it.'
>
> 'But is it not commanded in thy religion not to forswear thy God, and is not Eesa a God?'
>
> 'Yes, yes, but I want my child.'
>
> 'And dost thou not think that thou wilt lose thy soul thereby, O sitt?'
>
> 'Perhaps, perhaps, but I want my son.'
>
> 'Wallahi, but thy love is great,' and the old sheik's voice sounded full of wonder. 'But I have seen things, O sitt, which tell me that perchance this sacrifice will not after all be demanded of thee. Remain here, O sitt, I will pray to Allah, who knowest all things, to give me light in the darkness, and holding his rosary in his hand he went off to his own room.
>
> Margaret, overwrought, fell on her knees before the divan and

> sobbed bitterly, it all seemed so hopeless.
>
> Slowly a slim reddish-headed figure moved across from the entrance, his large grey eyes alight with a strange enthusiasm, and soon a brown, sunburnt arm moved protectingly over her shoulder, some one was kneeling beside her, and into her ears there breathed a boyish voice, glad and broken by emotion, uttering words that she had scarcely hoped to hear, 'Ya ommi, ya ommi – My mother, O my mother.'
>
> When the old sheik returned he saw two sobbing figures kneeling together with arms around one another's necks, and softly he let fall the curtain, as ticking off his beads he murmured, 'Thanks be to Allah, the merciful, the compassionate, extolled be the perfection of the most High.'[54]

Although *The Lost Mameluke*'s rendition of the political situation in eighteenth-century Egypt reflects some of the paternalistic and colonialistic attitudes of its age, it nonetheless gives an unusually detailed and informed picture of the lives and beliefs of its Muslim characters, who are as rounded as the Christians and who consequently represent some of the most early, if not the earliest, credible Muslim characters in Welsh fiction. Its treatment of the human dilemmas of its characters of both faiths is assured and truthful, and in its affirmation of the shared values of compassion and love rather than the differences of dogma and theology it prefigures some of the more liberal strands of inter-cultural relations emerging nearly a century later.

Egypt continued to be an important centre of British power until at least the Second World War. The privileged and influential position of the British in Egypt meant that the country provided not only a crucial military base but also a wide range of commercial and employment opportunities, as we saw with the story of the Davies Bryan family. Another Welsh writer who took advantage of this situation was the scholar David Gwyn Williams (1904-90), whom we encountered in Chapter 8, and who spent many years lecturing at universities in Islamic countries. His first contact with the Islamic world had actually come when he was only 23, when, in 1927, in company with another Welsh friend, he went to the city of Tanta, north of Cairo, to work as a teacher. There, he found lodgings with three other single young Welshmen, in an example of the kind of economic chain-migration now more familiar as a means by which some people come from Muslim countries to the West. He described his impressions of the city and its Islamic heritage in his 1981 memoir *ABC of (D)GW*, where he recalls visiting the Said el Badawy mosque and seeing an ascetic Muslim holy man carried in procession in 'a strange, barbaric event':

> Dervishes led the way, whirling slowly along the main street, and the captured Crusader armour was brought out from the mosque and carried in the procession, usually one man or boy one piece, rusty swords, battered shields and chain mail. For us it was best seen from a balcony, to avoid the happy, smelly crowd, many of whom forced their way forward to kiss the hem of the Khalifa's robe, or at least to touch it.[55]

Gwyn Williams also recorded some impressions from his period in Turkey, and in Kurdistan, where he muses on the missed possibility, at the end of the First World War, of creating a viable independent Kurdish state, and where he wonders whether Henry Tudor might not, in like manner, have been able to create a Celtic federation instead of reaching for the crown of England.[56] In his only volume of Welsh-language poetry, the pamphlet *Y Ddefod Goll* ('The Lost Rite'), from 1980, Williams has a poem entitled 'Arap Baba o Harput yn Anatolia' ('Arap Baba from Harput in Anatolia') about the eponymous Muslim holy man whose mummified body is kept on public display in Harput. Williams says he would prefer the body had been allowed to return to the elements naturally. He concludes:

> Let him go, people of Harput.
> Perhaps something escaped
> through the hole drilled in his skull
>
> but the body I am sure longs
> for salvation from the cold
> purgatory here on the top of Harput rock.[57]

Another major Welsh writer who spent an extended period in the Muslim world was Richard Hughes (1900-76), best-known as the author of the 1929 novel *A High Wind in Jamaica*. English-born, of Welsh parents, Hughes identified strongly with Wales, living there for many years and involving himself closely in the Welsh literary scene and public life. In 1927, he realised a boyhood ambition by travelling to the Atlas mountains of Morocco, where, as his biographer Richard Poole, who knew him during the last years of his life, says: 'he found the splendour of the Atlas no betrayal of his child-imaginings, and a living source of mystery.'[58] In his introduction to the collection of Hughes's writings about Morocco, *In the Lap of Atlas*, compiled posthumously from the author's papers, and published in 1979, Poole says that Hughes and a painter friend, Jim Wyllie, made their way to Marrakesh and travelled in the interior of the country with a guide furnished by T'hami el Glaoui, Pasha of Marrakesh, Hereditary Lord of the Atlas, and a descendant of the Prophet Muhammad. Hughes then made a return visit in 1929, again travelling extensively, but also living in a house he bought the Casbah, the citadel quarter, of Old Tangier. Poole says:

> ...the arrival of a Christian proved extremely unpopular. 'When I came to move in,' wrote Hughes, 'the neighbours commented that to have a Nazarene living in the street would send down the real-estate value of the whole district.' The hereditary saint who lived next door, a magnificent and important personage whose Prophetic ancestry rendered him infallible, was thoroughly ashamed of his wall-to-wall proximity to an infidel. But eventually Hughes's neighbours became reconciled to his presence: for not only did he strictly observe the Moslem code of good manners – never staring at anyone, never glancing through an open street door, and above all refraining from mounting to his roof at sunset (the time when Moslem women go up to theirs to take the air) – but he showed himself ready to help them in their dealings with authority.[59]

The stories collected as *In the Lap of Atlas* are a combination of first-hand experience mixed with second-hand travellers' tales and oral tradition. As Poole says: 'Hughes did not feel that a faithful representation of the actual circumstances in which he first encountered a tale necessarily served the best interests of his art.'[60] One of the major sources of Hughes's information was the *Times* correspondent in Morocco from 1887 until 1933, Walter Burton Harris, who appears in fictionalised form in the stories[61] and who is represented by the figure of the uncle in the first extract below, taken from the story 'A Woman to Talk to'. The story's first-person narrator is depicted as a callow schoolboy, perhaps in order to allow Hughes to express the kind of intense admiration which might be forgivable in a youth but which might be questionable in an adult. In reality, Hughes was in his late twenties when he first visited Morocco. In the following extract, the young narrator is present when his uncle is visited by the magnificent and enigmatic chieftain, Kaid Omar el Medouli, Prince of the Anti-Atlas and Pasha of Taroudant. Not knowing he is breaching rules of courtesy, the boy asks Medouli how his left hand came to be badly scarred. The chieftain mildly replies that it was a cooking accident. Shortly afterwards, the boy and the visitor are briefly left alone together:

> On a table lay a beautifully illuminated old Koran, that my uncle had somehow contrived to buy.
>
> Omar el Medouli, without speaking to me, picked it up, kissed it reverently, put it in his sleeve, and walked out of the house: and further I knew he meant me to see what he did.[62]

The uncle then returns and reproaches the boy for asking about Medouli's scar, explaining that in reality it had been incurred in an act of desperate heroism, but that the chieftain's modesty forbade him from talking about his exploits. The boy, chastened, then tells of how Medouli had taken the holy book. The uncle responds:

> 'What a fool I was to leave it about!' he said. 'But Omar was right. It would have been an impious act for him to leave it in the hands of an Unbeliever.' He paused, and made a wry face. 'It cost me a hundred and fifty pounds,' he added.
>
> Then, as we parted: 'I wish I had a God I could serve as Omar serves his.'[63]

Later that week, the boy goes hunting with Medouli on a fine mare lent to him by the chieftain for the occasion. Medouli himself rides a beautiful dappled Arab stallion. The following day, the boy is surprised to find the mare still in his own stable. He tells his uncle, who grins:

> 'I have sent word,' he said, 'that she awaits the return of my Koran.'
>
> By midday came Medouli's answer – no Koran, but a slave, leading that lovely dapple stallion, with a message: 'Since the mare is to live the rest of her life far from her native pastures, I have sent this

> old friend of hers to keep her company.'
>
> His own favourite mount – and what that means to an Arab, we all know! The gesture was superb: he would do anything, it meant, except the blasphemy of surrendering The Holy Book. Uncle Robert was beaten – as he seldom was, in a contest of will. He sent back the stallion, of course; but he kept the mare, whose money worth was much the same as that of the manuscript.
>
> All this while they were meeting every day: but neither mentioned the subject.[64]

The comment made by Hughes's fictionalised uncle – 'I wish I had a God I could serve as Omar serves his' – expresses the kind of piety-envy common in many of the passages collected here, when travellers from the Christian world encounter devout Muslims. It is possible to take such responses at face value as sincere expressions of admiration for a faith which the speaker simply happens not to share. However, in a wider context, a different interpretation is possible: perhaps depictions of pious Muslims are being used by increasingly secularised Westerners as vehicles to express suppressed religious aspiration, while simultaneously, due to the apparently irreducible otherness of Islamic culture, absolving the aspirant of the demanding necessity of actually practising a religion. It is worth speculating as to whether the same class of people who readily express admiration for Muslim piety would have expressed similar sentiments so freely about the piety of Christian clergy, monks, nuns, or even that of devout lay people. Is it possible that Muslims, being safely exotic, and with their religion seemingly an ethnic birthright to which a Westerner could not hope to fully aspire, are an object onto which disillusioned Westerners, unable or reluctant to face the requirements of religious commitment readily available within their own culture, can safely project their frustrated longing for transcendence without ever being challenged to emulation?

Certainly, Hughes found the religious gulf almost unbridgeable, and it is on the dangerous interface of irreconcilable differences that he finds excitement and stimulation. Later in the same story, Hughes touches on the enmity towards Christians he himself had found, as he mentions the ill fortune of a group of explorers taken captive by the 'fanatical native of those localities' who would not allow 'the filthy Christian to defile his pure Moslem air'.[65] Hughes's Morocco is an *Arabian Nights* world of harems and magicians, of slaves and chieftains, of injustice, honour, heroism and cruelty; a world in the final years of its immemorial traditional life, as the French imperialists wait to supplant the native dynasties, of which Medouli's is the most powerful, with their own ways.

Towards the end of 'A Woman to Talk to', the disconsolate Medouli searches his immense harem for the eponymous woman. He searches in vain. The passage in which this happens contains some of the most trenchant observations this study has found relating to the Islamic female veil:

> The veiling of women in the East – that strange sense of modesty which will make an Arab woman lift the hem of her skirt to cover her lips at the approach of a stranger – seems always to excite the most pleasurable surmise in the Occidental breast: but few seem to have paused to consider what effect the veil must have on the face it covers. Fish that live for generations in caverns to which no light can penetrate lose their eyes: and faces which are never (or very seldom) exposed to public gaze, seem in the same way to lose all mobility: they become, indeed, as inexpressive as any other part of the body that is habitually covered. That is the greatest shock which comes to those who have had occasion to see respectable or prized Eastern women unveiled – greater, even, than the often elephantine girth of their ankles: the doll-like woodenness of those faces which have never learnt to smile or frown, to darken or lighten, in harmony with open conversation. It is not only that these faces have nothing to express, they could express nothing if they had.[66]

Hughes knows this is a society in transition, and he shrewdly identifies the potential future importance of a resurgent Islamic society, rich with mineral wealth, which would manage to combine its inner faith with the outward advantages of modernity. Medouli himself is shown making a treaty with the French to keep his own territory inviolate, even as he sends his own sons to French universities and invests in French banks in order to acquire wealth and knowledge to modernise his own lands, and to exploit their mineral wealth – 'opened up by Moslems who had learnt the skill of the Nazarene'. By so doing, he plans to keep those lands out of European control, and to 'set the flame of his lamp of Islam burning brightly once more in the modern world'.[67]

> He played up to them of course; it suited his purposes for them to *think* they had him on a line, since it was the only terms on which they would trust him. But he knew, he alone knew, that he was free as air. For there was a bedrock of asceticism in that great voluptuary which no one – except, perhaps, my uncle – suspected. It was the last trump card that he held. A great lover of magnificence, a lover of wealth, of power, of beauty, yet, had the French ever pushed him to the last resort, ever demanded of him something he was determined not to give, he was prepared, in his spirit he was fully prepared, to walk out on them; to leave everything in their hands that they thought he most valued: and, an ageing man, start life again as my uncle had first found him, with no other property than a gun, a ragged jelaba, and his belief in God.[68]

Many and varied were the motives that took Welsh travellers to the lands of Islam: the Davies Bryan family had travelled for trade, T. Gwynn Jones for his health, and Richard Hughes for adventure. The next author in this study, Rhys J. Davies (1877-1951), travelled for reasons of state. Davies, whose background was given in Chapter 7, which dealt with the inter-war period, where some of his writings about Turkey were examined, visited Cairo in his capacity as a British politician, and recorded his impressions in a 1934 memoir, from which the following extracts are taken.

> They rise early, early, and before sunrise they have to pay tribute to the Great Prophet, Mohamed.
>
> They respect our Saviour; but Jesus is no more than a great man like Moses in their opinion.
>
> In Egypt, one woman for the Christian, but as many as he can maintain for the Moslem. The Moslem's wife is never seen even in her own house. The man is the master of everything. And the strangest thing of all is that the woman is content with her position![69]

In Cairo, Davies engages in what, as the twentieth century progresses, can be seen to be an increasingly common activity of nationally-minded Welsh-speaking travellers: namely to proselytise on behalf of their country of origin; the desire to stress its difference from England growing as national self-confidence increases and British imperial prestige wanes. For his part, Davies asks the 'learned old Pasha' who has been guiding him around Cairo's antiquities if, in either the Coptic, Arab or Ancient Egyptian museums, there were any books in Welsh. The question, which had been asked, surely, more in hope than expectation, elicits a negative response. Davies, undaunted, promises to send them a Welsh Bible. A little later, after a dinner party, he asks if the group knew anything of Wales. Before long, he is singing them Welsh hymns. 'Fair play to Joseph Parry,' he comments, mentioning the famous composer of hymn tunes, 'Had it not been for him, the people of the far reaches of Egypt would not have learned any of our songs.'[70] This is an early example of the way that for many Welsh-speaking travellers, devotion to their culture and its values gradually replaces religious faith as the trading goods of cultural exchange.

A similar tendency can be seen in the work of Tom Madoc Jones, whose career was noted in Chapter 7, where his travels in inter-war Iraq, Syria and Iran were examined, and again in Chapter 8, touching on his work in Egypt during the Second World War. Jones continued his involvement in the Middle East after the war. After retiring as an airforce chaplain in 1959, he became an organiser for Christian Aid, and travelled extensively bringing relief to refugees, particularly in the Middle East. In his 1969 memoir *Ar Gerdded* ('Travelling') he tells how he visited camps in the hills of Lebanon occupied by refugees from the Arab-Israeli conflict in Palestine, 'both Christians and religionists of Islam'. In one school, the head teacher insists on the children displaying their linguistic attainments by serenading the visitor with 'God Save the King'. Jones remarks: 'After thanking them for singing so well, I told them that there was another language in Great Britain, and I proved that by trying to sing "Hen Wlad fy Nhadau"!'[71]

Later in the journey, he visits a district near the Dead Sea, in Jordan, in search of a tribe called the Asasmi, who were known to be suffering extreme hardship.[72] He accepts the tea that they offer as a sign of hospitality, and then is able to tell them the good news that the first of a series of regular convoys of food aid is on its way to them from Amman, and due to arrive in two days' time.

> Hearing this, the chief of the tribe got to his feet and stretching his arms towards heaven said 'Great is Allah!' We said something similar from the standpoint of professing Christians, and we believed that we both, Arab and Briton, worshipped God in truth in that remote corner beside the Dead Sea.
>
> Before leaving, a word of blessing was given to the chief and his

> people. His response to us was the most emotional we had ever heard under those kinds of circumstances – he in his poverty, we in our sufficiency. He said: 'I wish you and your people in your own country the blessing and protection of Allah, and the fullness of good things to man and animal within your gates.' This was a man in the extremity of hardship, short of everything except selfless graciousness, and a simple faith in the God he worshipped.[73]

In Chapter 7, we saw how Tom Madoc Jones, in a visit to Damascus in the inter-war period, was moved to reflect on the virtues of the nemesis of the Crusaders, Salah ad-Din. The comments of another Welsh visitor who trod the same paths in the 1960s are strikingly similar. William Emlyn Jones was the author of a number of travel books in Welsh, including, in 1963, *Tua'r Dwyrain* ('Towards the East'), which includes an account of his visit to Syria. Jones remarks on the beauty of the city's mosques. At the Umayyad Mosque, he comments on the conduct of the worshippers: 'There was a peaceful atmosphere to this place and somehow we could not but feel that there was some mystical element to the religion of Islam that could not be fully appreciated by we westerners.'[74] Next to the mosque, he comes across the tomb of Saladin.

> Saladin was the great enemy of Christianity and Richard Coeur-de-Lion and others. And yet, perhaps he possessed more true Christian virtues than almost all of the barbaric knights he fought against. Around the tomb and outside the entrance there were a host of old men in loose white clothing, guarding the spot, and as we went past on our way out one of them got up, despite his frailty, and brought a stone dish full of water to us from a spring which arose nearby. Everyone drank from the same dish, unfortunately, but the water was beautifully cold and very acceptable. In seeing the kindness of the old man, I thought that we had seen the true meaning of the word which speaks of cold water to a thirsting soul.[75]

The 1960s, too, was the period when J. Gwyn Griffiths (1911-2004), whose work was introduced in the previous chapter, and his wife, Kate Bosse-Griffiths (1910-98), were living, and writing, in Egypt. German-born Bosse-Griffiths, an Egyptologist, of partly Jewish ancestry, came to Britain to escape the Nazi persecution, which was to claim the life of her mother. At Oxford, where she found work as an academic, she met her future husband. They moved to Wales, where Bosse-Griffiths learned Welsh, and the couple became highly active in Welsh-language literary circles as central figures in *Cylch Cadwgan*, a circle of Welsh-speaking nationalist, Christian and pacifist authors. They spent most of their subsequent life in Swansea, where she curated the Egyptian collection at the city's museum, and he was Professor of Classics and Egyptology. Both left a literary legacy of their year in Egypt, a legacy informed by deep scholarship and by an instinctive curiosity about, and sympathy with, other cultures and religions.

In the foreword to Bosse-Griffiths's 1970 memoir *Galwad yr Aifft* ('The Call of Egypt'), the author begins by saying it is the Muslim practice to thank God rather than man while accepting any favour or gift, so she bids *al-hamdu l'Illah* to those who have helped her complete the work. Although she acknowledges that her primary interests and those of her husband are in ancient Egypt, she felt the volatile situation in the Middle East made it worthwhile her recording her impressions of a period when Egypt seemed to be at a historical crossroads, with the choice of pan-Africanism, leadership of 'dark-skinned nations', or 'leadership of the Arab Islamic nations'.[76]

In Luxor, Bosse-Griffiths notes a remarkable example of religious continuity, with the ancient Egyptian custom of the ritual sailing of sacred boats on the Nile in honour of the gods Amon, Mut and Khonsu being reflected in the contemporary ritual to commemorate the thirteenth-century Islamic saint Yusef Abu'l Haggag, where boats are also used as part of the ceremonies. Bosse-Griffiths recounts the content of the ceremony in detail, including the ritual slaughter of a bull on the mosque steps, and the recitation of the entire *Qur'an*. She believes the contemporary Islamic religious observances, combined with those from an earlier Coptic Christian period, link with Ancient Egypt to mean that the celebration of a similar festival in the same place goes back more than four thousand years.

> This experience happens in Egypt again and again, that the sanctity of a place remains, and that only the name changes (and I think that it would be good for many a Christian to realise that the Muslims and Pagans do not have a 'different God' ... God is the same ... if

> there is a God ... it is only the spectacles of the believer that vary).
>
> There is one amusing aspect to this Saint. His mosque is so respected by the faithful that it makes it impossible for archaeologists to get hold of this part of the temple of Amon in Luxor. And thank goodness for that, I say; why should they get their rapacious revelatory way every time?[77]

Bosse-Griffiths devotes an entire chapter of the book, 'Ar lwybrau Islam' ('On the paths of Islam'), to explaining contemporary Muslim faith and practice. Much of the chapter is factual, although it does contain some sections where the author's views are expressed. For instance, after explaining the significance of Ramadan, she says that having breakfasted before dawn, in the Muslim fashion, she was later taken aback to see a man in a Greek cafe eating breakfast publicly during the period of the fast:

> We looked at him with some surprise, feeling that he was challenging the faithful. It is strange how quickly one is ready to accept the moral attitude of one's environment – we having eaten our breakfast as always in the house. At the same time, we felt admiration as we realised that there were in the capital no shortage of men who took their religion sufficiently seriously to keep a fast in the month of Ramadan: not eating during the day and not drinking or smoking either, with the aim of sanctifying their thoughts.[78]

She confesses herself mystified by what she sees as extreme fasting followed by overeating during the same day, and believes she has identified a fundamental difference in Christian and Jewish fasting and that practised by Muslims: the former abstaining in order to purify the mind to be reconciled with God; the latter doing so in order to better enjoy God's gifts. 'There is nothing unreasonable to them in the fact that they go to extremes both in the day and in the night.'[79]

In company with an Egyptian Muslim friend, Mohsen, she explores some Islamic practices and festivals in extensive detail. On one occasion, she encounters 'a sticking point' as her friend insists that the son Abraham had planned to sacrifice was Ishmael, not Isaac. They have to agree to disagree.[80] On another occasion, she and her husband find themselves invited to a *zikr* prayer ceremony at the Saida Zeinab mosque, in which whirling dervishes will be taking part. As it is a major public event, she and her companions find themselves in the middle of an immense throng. At one point, to make room for trams to pass, police baton-charge the crowd, some of whose members had begun to use the street for emulative displays of ecstatic dancing. Arriving at the mosque, which was dedicated to a female Islamic saint, the Prophet Muhammad's granddaughter, Zeinab, Bosse-Griffiths finds herself nonplussed:

> ...when we got to the entrance the Mosque guardian refused to give me permission, as a woman, to go any further. Men only!
>
> I wondered rather at the unexpected situation of refusing permission for a woman to go into a mosque which is *sacred to the memory of a woman.*
>
> But there were plenty of poor women sitting hunched on the floor outside the Mosque, and hoping for bread and alms.[81]

At the end of the event, she reflects:

> That night revealed a new aspect of Egypt to us – one unfamiliar to we sun worshippers and Museum-attenders; the faithful of Islam worshipping a female saint, folk mystics seeking God through *ecstasis*, and crowds running in panic before the police.[82]

At the *zikr*, Bosse-Griffiths had shown her surprise at gender roles in Islamic culture. A further sub-chapter, on marriage, gives her further opportunity to explore the subject. She views with affectionate amusement the attitudes of Mohsen's 17-year-old son, who is in love with a 'girlfriend' who lives across the street from him, and whom he has never met. Despite his inexperience, however, she finds he has firm plans for married life, as he intends to marry four women: one for beauty, one for money, one to work for him and one for fun. 'He was joking, of course,' she says: 'But he was not claiming anything that was impossible according to Islamic morality.'[83] She notes polygamy is now largely confined to the countryside, but that many city men nonetheless contrived to have many wives due to the ease with which Islamic law permitted divorce.

'And how do women look on the situation?' she asks. She explains how common is arranged marriage, and that Mohsen's niece's engagement was arranged for her even though she was an educated woman studying at commercial college. When the apparently amicable arrangement is then dissolved due to the niece's desire to continue with her studies, Bosse-Griffiths remarks: 'So, despite all the arrangements, a woman has a certain amount of choice.'[84]

> One thing that astonished me about Egyptian women was the fact that they did not take much part in public religious life, despite the fact that religion takes such a prominent part in Egyptian life, and although the mosques are often full of men praying.[85]

Having examined festivals, religious practices, and gender roles with all the thoroughness of a professional academic, Bosse-Griffiths finally moves on to Islamic architecture, whose avoidance of narrative and depiction she finds unappealing and 'uncomfortable'.[86] Finally, however, she found her aesthetic sense satisfied in Cairo's ninth-century mosque of Ibn Tulun, whose 'dignified simplicity' she praises.[87]

> Outside, there are crowds of people, filth and decay, disturbance and poverty. But as soon as one comes in through the entrance and takes off the street shoes, there is quietness and cleanliness and space to breathe and peace for the troubled soul. And yet, this is not the quiet of the cemetery. In the shadow of the open hall young boys can be seen hunched over, learning the Qur'an, and men kneeling and praying. Under the blue firmament, surrounded by white pillars, I had a feeling of height and breadth like the endless space of the desert.[88]

For his part, J. Gwyn Griffiths recorded his impressions in a number of poems which, informed by his scholarship and by his extended contact with Islamic culture, are among the most insightful of Welsh-language responses to Islam in the twentieth century. While Griffiths could be uncompromising in challenging perceived prejudice, as was seen in his poem in the previous chapter about Arab hatred for Israel, it should not be thought that his views on Islam focus on negative aspects. Many of his poems show intimate and respectful knowledge of the religion. The poem 'Y Mis Sanctaidd' ('The Holy Month'), excerpted below, gives an insight into the Muslim month of fasting, and compares Islamic practice favourably with that of many Christians:

> No right to swallow saliva, complete abstention
> from sunrise to its setting

is the way of things in Ramadan.
No smoking, no glass of mint tea,
let alone a bowl of beans or eggs.
For this is the month that the olden Prophet
was given the pure revelation of the holy Scripture,
the Koran itself,
and inscribed it on palm leaves.

. . .

How guilty I felt in the Zoo Park
swallowing sandwiches between lectures
with everyone staring amazed at me while going past
and the students envying
my satisfied-stomach state.
(They give thanks at the same time
that the lecture has finished early).

. . .

The Festival of the Birth of Christ and remembrance of the divine grace
of the Incarnation
happens to be at hand.
It must be admitted that our answer
is to give ourselves to gluttony –
Saturnalia[89] in the name of the Baby of the Manger.
Yes, the tradition is different.[90]

A similar picture emerges in 'Dewiswn Gadw Drws' ('Better to be a Doorkeeper'),[91] in which Griffiths depicts the exemplary good cheer, practicality and diligence of a Nubian concierge at a block of flats. He concludes:

Although he cares for a huge block of flats
including the secret movement of the lift,
the *Bawab*'s own cell is a narrow one.
Narrow too the space before his private door
at the bottom of the stairs,
but not too narrow to bend the long body
to all the attitudes of prayer.
The *Bawab* is busy answering a host of calls
but he is never too busy
to answer the call of heaven.[92]

Equally exemplary is the piety displayed in 'Beth yw'r mat dda?'

('What is the mat good for?'), set in a street in Cairo, and given below in full:

In the name of reason and common sense
what is the mat good for,
spread tidily on a pavement corner
and swept clean
even though everything around is untidy enough
between trash, waste paper and chips,
not forgetting the animal dung
and the traces of human defecators
where the tireless donkey brays,
where the camels and sheep walk
in the middle of the huge city?
Indeed what is the purpose of the mat,
an island of cleanliness in a sea of rubbish?

There was no need to wait long for enlightenment.
When I went back the same way
half an hour later
there was a Prayer Meeting on the mat.
Eighteen who had discarded their shoes,
standing and kneeling in three rows,
the foremost chanting quietly,
the heads bending suddenly
until every crown was as low as the floor.

Although the grave of Sheikh Hamza was opposite
(a very godly man he was)
the traffic did not halt
nor the crowd care one louse.
But on went the Prayer Meeting
addressing the One True God,
the Compassionate, the Merciful.
God is indeed great;
let all flesh know the truth.

A mat is a useful thing
but that is the first time I had seen one
forming a path
from the faeces to the firmament,
from the squalor to the stars, like a magic carpet
flying from one world to another.[93]

The poem 'Dim ond croesi' ('Just passing') tells how Griffiths and his wife shared a Nile ferry crossing with a Muslim stranger, and ends:

> *Ma salaam, habibi*!
> Farewell, friend!
> The boat slows
> and the asses and horses and the taxis
> wait on the bank.
> It has been a short wordless session of fellowship
> and we shall not meet again
> until the Great Fellowship Above.[94]

In 'Yr argae uchel yn Aswan' ('The high dam in Aswan'), prefaced by extensive quotations fom the *Qur'an*, he depicts labourers working on the Es-Sadd el-'ali dam, and finding relief in their faith:

> If Allah wills it! In the middle of the burning land
> And the exhausting toil of the host, is a refreshing sanctuary
> To flee to – a Mosque, these tired workers' House of Prayer,
> And a gentle shelter against the oppressive heat of the climate.
> In Prayer and work
> The nation longs in one act of faith
> Through the sweat and fleas for the dawn of a better day.[95]

As they are based on the same series of joint visits with Griffiths's wife, it is unsurprising that many of the poems recount the same experiences as Bosse-Griffiths's prose work. One poem, 'Y ddawns sanctaidd' ('The sacred dance'), is Griffiths's own account of the *zikr*. In this poem, as in many others in Griffiths's work, while finding comparisons between Islamic piety and Christianity, he uses terms which are not merely generalised Western Christian nomenclature but which are the forms of specifically Welsh religious fervour, thereby investing the Muslim practices with an intimacy and homeliness that instantly domesticates and authenticates them. Such is the case in 'The sacred dance' which describes the ecstatic practices of Welsh revivalism before saying that the chanting and rhythmic motions of the *zikr* are 'something similar':

> Until they reach a state beyond sense,
> an anointed hysteria,

> the enthusiasmos of the possessed.[96]

He concludes by saying that the *zikr* participants have reached such a state of ecstasy that they could swallow scorpions unharmed. While that final image is well beyond the normal range of Welsh religious categories, Griffiths's hospitable extension of Welsh terminology to Muslim devotion prior to that point is a means of collapsing the distance between the two spheres of experience, so that the exoticism of even quite alien external practices is reduced.

In 'Mosg Ibn Twlŵn' ('The Mosque of Ibn Tulun'), Griffiths gives his own view of the building whose beauty, as we have seen, had overcome his wife's initial lack of enthusiasm about the impersonality of Islamic religious decoration. He begins: 'Simplicity is the basis of the serene magnificence of the faith / and all its architectural expression.' After describing the building in its historical and architectural context, he concludes:

> It was good to take off one's shoes in order to put on
> sandals at the door;
> The blessing to the faithful soul is unfailing –
> The peace of the fair dwelling-places.[97]

With the exception of the one poem about Arab opposition to Israel examined in the previous chapter, a poem which has more to do with political attitudes than religious ones, J. Gwyn Griffiths's poems about Islam are unfailingly positive, as can be seen in the final example, 'Dau Arab yn cusanu' ('Two Arabs kissing'), in which the author, at an Arab cafe in Oxford, sees two friends greet one another with a male kiss and a hearty double embrace. He observes:

> The name Al-lah comes often to their conversation.
> Thanks be to him![98]

Also from the 1960s, it is worth mentioning in passing the work of Harry Fainlight (1935-82), an English-born writer of Jewish background who was evacuated to the Llanelli area with his sister Ruth during the Second World War, and who returned to live there and in other parts of Wales from the 1970s until his death. Fainlight was associated with the Beat movement, and was described in his obituary notice by the leading Beat poet, Allen Ginsberg, as having been, in the early 1960s, 'the most promising new consciousness poet in English tongue.'[99] Psychologically troubled and drug-damaged, Fainlight never fulfilled his promise. After years of periodic wandering, hospitalisation and reclusiveness, he was found dead from hypothermia in a field near his remote cottage in Montgomeryshire. Less a Welsh writer than a writer with a Welsh connection, Fainlight's status nonetheless merits a reference in this work which details connections between Wales and Islam, as the categories that define Welsh and English are far from impermeable. In Fainlight's case, the contact with Islam came during a visit to his sister Ruth, herself an accomplished poet, in Tangier in the 1960s:

Fugue

I

At dusk the Arab suburb manages
A few nomadic newspapers; otherwise only
Transistorised muezzins carried muffled
Beneath heavy robes. This breeze, itself
Heavy as those robes, carries music
From another quarter; muffled and then suddenly

Whirled up like newspapers. Newspapers
Circling high now like buzzards,
Circling like buzzards or like muezzins.

II

Muezzins, buzzards, newspapers – like
Circling like
Til I am heavy with their whirling.

O music without quarter! Suddenly so
Otherwise that I am carried
High now as that buzzard. Can I manage?

The breeze a transistor and this
Itself only the robe, nomadic at dusk.
The suburbs of another music.[100]

Earlier chapters have shown how powerful was religion as a motive for sending Welsh people overseas, whether as missionaries or pilgrims, and has also shown the way many other Welsh people took a profoundly faith-based perspective with them on their travels. As the twentieth century advanced, the categories of religion and imperialism which had previously provided convenient and largely unquestioned means for interpreting foreign experience, were gradually supplanted by other factors such as the general secularism of British society. In Wales also, was arising another value-system which provided its own way ot interpreting the world: a growing political consciousness, whether socialist or nationalist or both. However, while recognising the dwindling role of faith as a motive and perspective, it is still possible to find Welsh travellers in the last quarter of the twentieth century who look at the world with a religious perspective, although, as a result of wider changes in European religious thought generally during the period, the viewpoints tend to be much more liberal than in previous centuries.

One such is the Reverend. Cyril Glyndŵr Williams (1922-2004), who was a major figure in interfaith relations and a pioneer in the study of comparative religion. He was Professor of Religion at Carlton University in Ottawa, Canada, and later at Lampeter in Wales, and was honorary president of the British Association for the Study of Religions. He published extensively in Welsh and English and in 1991, he produced, directly from the Sanskrit, the only Welsh translation of a non-Abrahamic religious scripture, the *Bhagavad Gita*, published as *Y Fendigaid Gân*. In 1975, he published *Nadolig yn Calcutta* ('Christmas in Calcutta'), an account of study tour to India in the winter of 1974-75.

In Delhi, he details some of the architectural splendours of the Muslim Moghul period, and reflects on an early, although unsuccessful, attempt at ecumenism in the mid seventeenth century under the third Mughal emperor of India, Jalaluddin Muhammad Akbar, known as Akbar the Great.[101] Also in Delhi, he visits Jantar Mantar, the seventeenth-century observatory, and he wonders, given the rich heritage of Muslim science, why Arab nations and India seem now to lag behind in modern technology, and he speculates as to whether religion has hindered them.[102] At the Red Fort, a Mughal military complex of great significance in

Indian political history, in the walled city of old Delhi, Williams is impressed with the architecture, and is moved to reflection at the Diwan-i-Aam, the courtyard used for imperial audiences:

> How many beggars pleaded for their lives on the floor amid this splendour? According to Islam, the king and the beggar are on the same level on their knees in the mosque before God, but I do not suppose that many of the unfortunates of this world have worshipped in the Moti Munjid (the Pearl Mosque) which is nearby. And I wonder if the emperor was obedient to the ideal of justice in his administration. On a wall beneath one of the gates, where the colours of the decoration have been preserved exceptionally well, is an image of a pair of scales to remind all who see it, one supposes, that the throne is founded on the justice of God.[103]

In 1991, Williams also published a long and thoughtful article 'Ceisio Deall Islam' ('Trying to Understand Islam') in the *Traethodydd* magazine, in which he addressed the challenge of growing Muslim communities in the West, and of violent jihad. His solution, rooted in his Christian faith, was dialogue, love of one's neighbour and friendship: 'we will not meet Islam, but meet persons, meet Muslims.'[104]

One such example of how the essentials of religious belief can transcend cultural boundaries is given in a 1984 book, *Haul a Heli* ('Sun and Sea'), by the Montgomeryshire-born children's writer and travel author Dyddgu Owen (1906-92). In recounting a visit to Sudan, Owen depicts an incident when she was taken ill in her hotel in Khartoum. The cleaner has come to tidy her room, and Owen, exhausted by her illness, falls asleep as he goes about his duties:

> I came to myself and heard a voice above my head, and there he was with his eyes closed, praying, and the word '*Allah*' was to be heard from time to time. I hadn't the faintest idea what 'thank you' was in his language, but I ventured to say '*Salaam*'. A lovely smile came to his face, and he went out. I slept soundly, feeling safe in the firmness of this Arab's faith, and his readiness to accept me into the circle of his prayer.[105]

Later, recovering from her illness, she exempts herself from what she calls a 'pilgrimage' undertaken by the other guests to visit sites associated with Charles Gordon, the British general killed while resisting a rebellion against Anglo-Egyptian rule by the self-proclaimed Mahdi, Mohammed Ahmed, in 1885. Waiting in the hotel lounge, she is accosted by a local official who thinks she must be English. The exhausted Owen says that 'for the first time in my life I did not have the energy to disillusion him.' Assuming immediately that she must want to hear the history of General Gordon, the official embarks on a lengthy explanation. What follows is an uneasy and shifting discourse of relative cultural values, in which Owen concludes that the official must have two versions of Gordon's story: a positive one for British visitors, and an iconoclastic version for others. She suspects that the latter, which emerges due to her own initial reluctance as a Welshwoman to identify with the imperial hero, is actually the official's personal view. Ironically, in response, Owen unexpectedly finds herself warming to the British imperialist who had not even bothered to learn the language of the country he was ruling ('a burning issue for we Welsh!')[106] She adds: 'I believe that if Gordon had been a Mohamedan, he would be the perfect man, and indeed would have been the leader of this nation.'[107]

While most of the authors whose experiences of Islam are collected in this book can be grouped with other writers who travelled for similar reasons, whether of trade, education, warfare or religion, the next has claims to be genuinely unique – as it is the Welsh-language autobiography of a professional wrestler. Orig Williams (1931-2009) was a quarryman's son from the slate-mining village of Ysbyty Ifan in Conwy, and he fought in the wrestling ring under the name of 'El Bandito' – a name inspired by his impressive moustache. Williams was as famous for his personality as much as for his sporting achievements. He was a popular and familiar figure in Wales thanks to his appearances on the S4C television channel. His *Times* obituary described him well: 'a larger-than-life, wholly uninhibited, flamboyant extrovert with an innate sense of showmanship.'[108]

For nearly 50 years, he travelled the world as a wrestler and as an international promoter of wrestling. In his 1985 autobiography, *Cario'r Ddraig* ('Carrying the Dragon'), he tells of how, on one occasion, in a pioneering venture for a British wrestler, he fought in Pakistan, a country whose wrestling tradition attracts a fanatical following. Williams's encounter with Islam happens at the moment of his arrival in the country as the passport control official points at the 'religion' section of the visitor's document:

> 'What is that?' he asked.
>
> 'Well, Welsh Methodist,' I said, looking at him, surprised.
>
> 'I've never heard of that religion,' he said.
>
> 'What the heck's wrong with this guy?' I said to myself – pretty angry by this stage. Good grief, what kind of shape can this country be in if they've never heard about Calvinistic Methodism?
>
> 'Are you a Christian or a Muslim,' was the official's next question.
>
> Well, that question wasn't in *Rhodd Mam* ['Mother's Gift', a Welsh Methodist children's catechism] that's for sure.
>
> 'Uh ... um. I don't know. I am a Welsh Methodist,' I said. I bet these are cannibals, I said to myself, regretting that I hadn't given more to the Overseas Mission when I was a lad in the Sunday School in 'Sbyty,
>
> 'Do you believe in God or in Allah?' he asked further.
>
> Well, there's an odd question. I'd never heard about that other old boy.
>
> 'God, Sir, of course,' I said.
>
> 'Then, you are a Christian,' said the man, changing my card and gesturing me with his finger to get out of his sight.
>
> I went on my way astonished. What the heck was this man talking about? Hadn't I been taught that 'There is only one God?' At that moment, I thought of Mrs Davies, Bod Ifan, in the Sunday School. Hadn't this poor creature ever learned that? He'd never learned 'Calon Lân' either, I'd bet. And for certain, no-one would sing 'O Fryniau Caersalem'[109] above him when he is buried. I began to pity him...[110]

In Lahore, Williams finds himself fighting a local champion, Akram, in a giant stadium in front of a hundred thousand spectators. Williams finds that, to the crowd, he 'represented all the abomination of the British Empire, and Akbar was their saviour, avenging every wrong done to them as a nation'. The referee calls the two fighters to the centre of the ring, and warns Williams 'Akram is fighting for Allah, and he will not, as you say, submit. First he will die – or you will!'

He finds his opponent much stronger than himself, and has to rely on superior skill. 'He was a Muslim, and I was a Methodist – and I must have got strength from somewhere.'[111] He manages to floor his opponent, but Akram recovers, and Williams is finally knocked out, waking up to find chants of 'Allah Madhat! Allah

Madhat!'echoing round the stadium from 'a hundred thousand Muslims'.[112] He reflects:

> Looking at the crowd, I knew that nothing but a victory would have satisfied them that night. If I'd won, the crowd wouldn't have let me get one foot out of the ring, and the words that I had heard many times from my grandmother came back to me, now with a new meaning:
>
> 'God moves in a mysterious way
> His wonders to perform.'[113]
>
> The old lady was absolutely right – my God had won that night too![114]

For all his, possibly exaggerated, naiveté about religion, Williams, in a later passage describing a visit to Bangladesh, shows he is not insensitive to religious differences. He and his fellow British wrestlers are invited to dinner by the head man of a village near Dhaka, and Williams expresses 'great respect in my heart towards the Muslim religion', adding that it is hypocritical for British newspapers to complain when Britons who have broken Muslim laws face severe punishments, especially when Britain's imperial misdeeds are recalled. He commends the Muslim practice of deferring all fortune to God's providence, and all hopes and fears to His wisdom. He also approves Muslims' regularity in prayer and their commitment in making the pilgrimage to Mecca, and in that respect he recounts the experience of a Muslim colleague whose mother was healed of an illness while on pilgrimage there.[115] While the hard-living Williams does not pretend to have the wistful desire to emulate Muslim piety which is often expressed, but rarely acted upon, by some other Westerners, his admiration for his hosts' faith seems unfeigned.

A slightly later Welsh visitor to Bangladesh was likewise impressed with the open piety of its people. Gwenllian Jones spent many years travelling abroad, both with her husband's work and as a teacher. In 1993, she joined her husband in Bangladesh and recorded her experiences in epistolary form in a series of letters published in 1998 as *Llythyrau Bangladesh* ('Bangladesh Letters'). She commends Muslims' readiness to pray at all times and in all places and adds a typical homely Welsh comparison:

> Seeing labourers from the poor countries of the East arriving in Qatar and Kuwait to work, and seeing them unrolling their prayer mats which are an essential part of their baggage, and falling on their knees there and then, I will always think of our girls going into service with the posh people in Liverpool and Manchester, when looking for a Welsh-language chapel was one of the first things they had to do. I suppose Manchester, and London especially, was every bit as remote for a girl from Llyn or Eifionydd as is Qatar to a boy from Chittagong in the north here today.[116]

The post-imperial guilt of the Westerner confronted with the legacy of empire is examined in the work of Stewart Brown (*b.*1951), English-born, Aberystwyth-educated, and an adoptive member of the Welsh literary scene.[117] In 1989, with the Welsh press Seren, Brown published *Lugard's Bridge*, based on his experiences teaching in Nigeria. The book's long title poem, a thoughtful and trenchant commentary on the complex post-colonial condition of the country and the mixed responses of its Western residents and visitors, refers to a small suspension bridge used by the early-twentieth-century British governor of Nigeria, Frederick Lugard, to cross the Niger from his headquarters at Zungeru, and which stands as a symbol of the tenuous connection between coloniser and colonised. The following brief extract refers to Lugard's own campaigns against independent Muslim states in the north of his protectorate:

> But first the fun;
> to pacify those turbulent, ungrateful, few
> who would not see the logic
> of Colonial Rule. Emirs who swore
> they'd perish with a slave
> between their jaws before obey
> some namby-pamby white man's law;
> the Holy King of Sokoto
> avowed, 'twixt Lugard and Mohammed's sons
> no dealings except war!'
>
> No fool, Lugard declared
> he had no quarrel with the teeming folk,
> only their *alien* Emirate.

Indeed, he came, he said,
to liberate the people from oppression
fear and slavery ... and by such lights
proceeded to extinguish those
of any who demurred
as tyrants, rebels or fanatic fools.
All this, his modest wife could boast,
in service of 'The Great Ideal...
an Empire to secure the world,
ruled by its finest race.'[118]

Nigeria was also the subject of a book by Elwyn Evans, whom we first met in Chapter 7, as a British soldier in inter-war Mesopotamia, and encountered again in Chapter 8, as a return visitor to post-war Israel. In the late 1950s, this very able and under-recognised poet spent three years in Nigeria, where he worked for the BBC as director of programmes for the new Nigerian Broadcasting Corporation as the country prepared for independence. His 1995 memoir, *Cyfarfod ag Affrica* ('Meeting Africa'), gives some idea of the complexity of the country's religious make-up. He notes the jihad waged in the early nineteenth century by the Fulani group against the Hausa, whom they accused of backsliding from Islam.[119] Some Muslims and Christians oscillated between their faiths and the older traditional religions, he says, noting that Oba, the zealous Muslim local chief, had written to the Corporation saying: 'As Oba I am head of all the secret societies of Lagos.'[120]

Also visiting Nigeria shortly after independence was James Morris, later to become Jan Morris (*b.*1926), now the doyenne of all travel writers, but then a foreign correspondent for *The Times*. Morris, born in England of Welsh and English parentage, but long domiciled in and committed to Wales, served as an intelligence officer in Palestine and Italy in the Second World War, and then embarked on an adventurous career as a journalist, becoming the first person to break the news about the conquest of Everest in 1953. Morris's career, which took in many of the world's trouble spots and which involved the production of many book-length studies of foreign cities and countries, must surely make her the most travelled Welsh writer ever, as well as one of the most productive and most internationally-recognised. In 2003, she published a selection of her work in *A Writer's World:*

Travels 1950-2000, which she inscribed 'To the honour of Wales – Er Anrhydedd Cymru.' It has many passages about Muslim countries, including Egypt, Iran and Oman, in which country, in 1955, she had the extraordinary experience, in her capacity as *Times* reporter, of accompanying the Sultan of Oman and his retinue of Bedouin guides and Nubian slaves, as he attempted to establish authority over the troubled interior of his country – a project Morris describes as possessing 'agreeable possibilities of antique violence.'[121] Morris recounted this experience in her 1957 book *Sultan in Oman*, which includes descriptions of the Sultan's harem – 'but there were no henna'd houris inside, only two or three drab women who seemed to be doing the laundry'[122] – and of the institution of slavery: 'They had all the advantage of the welfare state, with one exception: they had to work.'[123] For her Nigerian journey, undertaken shortly after the country's independence in 1960, Morris travelled to the Islamic city of Kano in the north of the country:

> As the traveller wanders across the breadth of Africa, through the welter of animisms and tribal faiths, the witch-doctors and sacred stones and fetishes, the gimcrack Christian deviations, the struggling missions and occasional messiahs – as he journeys through this cauldron of devotions he finds himself upon the outer fringes of Islam; and at once the stately order of that marvellous religion brings a fresh dignity to society, and tinges the air with its ornate magic. Such an outpost of the Muslims is Kano, the principal city of northern Nigeria, where the Emir of Kano lives in state in a splendid rambling palace, and the piles of ground-nuts stand like white pyramids outside the walls.[124]

Having found 'pathos' and confusion in the deracinated condition of Westernised Africa, Morris is glad of the Islamic simplicity she finds in Kano: '...inside all is Muslim, the throaty quarter-tones of an African muezzin echo from a minaret, and there is a sense of style and latent pageantry.' The Emir's bodyguard 'wears ancient chain mail and visors, like the Muslim warriors of antiquity', and the minaret of the mosque provides a spectacular view of 'a place like Isfahan or Damascus, subtly impregnated with desert ways, with an echo of caravanserai, slave trade and pilgrimage.'

> Across the dusty plains radiate the trade routes that still link this ancient place with the Mediterranean, the Red Sea and Mecca itself. Below you lie the palaces of the great Fulani notables, still the aristocratic rulers of this city. Kano looks exceedingly old from that high eyrie, exceedingly assured, exceedingly grand.[125]

However, Morris finds this enclave threatened by progress, and by the ever-wider horizons of its citizens, whose Islamic culture itself provides a road out from isolation, whether it is through pilgrimage to Mecca, or 'as among all Muslims and speakers of Arabic, a deep interest in the doings of Egypt, at once the patriarch and the showboy of Islam.' The unique culture of Kano's people, with their 'amber prayer-beads and their pieties' should, she suggests, be appreciated while it still exists: '...what a far-flung triumph, against all the odds of the jazz age and the hucksters, for the old philosophies of Arabia![126]

For her republishing of the article in her 2003 collection, Morris appended the following suffix:

> The old philosophies of Arabia might have struck me less amiably in the Kano of a few decades later, when more severe and dogmatic forms of Islam were resurgent.[127]

While Welsh travel to Muslim countries has taken place through many centuries, such overseas ventures have largely been the preserve of those travelling by means of their profession rather than simply for pleasure. In the last quarter of the twentieth century, that changed, as cheaper air travel and increasing prosperity in Wales, as elsewhere in the United Kingdom, meant a far larger section of society could now could travel to places previously remote and inaccessible. By the end of the century, mass tourism would be the main means of contact for Welsh people with the lands of Islam.

In the work of the important English-language poet, Nigel Jenkins (*b.*1949) from Swansea, can be seen some of the beginnings of this phenomenon. In his 1989 volume *Acts of Union, Selected Poems 1974-1989*, he has two poems, 'Casbah' and 'Cafe Ahmed', which show how visits by Western tourists to Muslim-majority countries were becoming more common, and how the local people were adapting to what they thought the visitors expected:

This time of day,
    as palms and mosque
    carve an allied darkness,
you come down among the stalls
to eat. The dervish drums for an hour
have called and pipes have snaked,
    touching slivers that sleep
    in each fed man's purse.

...

Hashish, good fren? One puffa this
make him head goin sputnik –[128]

...

From States, my fren? Wales?
It's in England? Many good frens
in Glasgow, 'ippies, 'ippies, man.[129]

The increase in tourism is reflected in a 1997 collection of Welsh-language short stories set in exotic locations, *Tocyn Tramor* ('Foreign Ticket'), edited by Delyth George. It contains a short story, 'Y Mwnshi a'r Diacon' ('The Munshi and the Deacon'), by the prose writer Gwyneth Carey, winner of the National Eisteddfod's Daniel Owen Memorial Prize in 1997. The story depicts an encounter between a Welsh visitor in Malaysia being introduced to the importance of the language of respect in Malaysian Islamic culture by the 'munshi', the honorary clerk of the title. This is set in parallel with a visit to Wales by a Singaporean religious researcher, who is given a similar introduction to Welsh Nonconformist Christianity by a chapel deacon. In each case, the religious figure bemoans the fact that the younger generation seems no longer to care for the niceties of the religious culture.[130]

We saw earlier how Welsh-language television journalism, from the 1980s onwards, has become a means of sending culturally-active Welsh-speakers to Muslim countries, as to other places worldwide. The vogue for travel programmes during the same period, itself a response to mass tourism, also sent Welsh writers to Islamic countries. The first example comes from 2004, and is the work of the pop singer, actor, comedian and television presenter, Dewi Pws Morris. *Byd Pws* ('Pws's World'), edited by Lyn Ebenezer, is a travel book based on Morris's eponymous television series. While visiting Jordan, Morris approvingly describes the egalitarianism of mosque worship, but then adds, in jest:

> Remember, though, that I had reason not to like Muslims. Why? Well, next door to the place we were staying was a mosque. And at four o'clock in the morning, every morning, they were not just calling the faithful to prayer but shouting at them through microphones and huge loudspeakers. So at four o'clock every morning, I was falling out of bed. One morning I went over to the mosque with a little note saying, 'Thank you very much, but I won't need an early call tomorrow, thank you all the same,' But they did it anyway.[131]

Bethan Gwanas, novelist, columnist and television presenter, has written several books about her travels undertaken for television series. One of them, *Mwy o Fyd Bethan* ('More of Bethan's World'), from 2005, contains an account of a visit to Syria, where, touring the Umayyad mosque, she finds herself, as a blonde woman, an object of unusual interest. Afterwards, in the main street, she reflects on the different dress styles adopted by Syrian women, ranging from Western clothes to headscarves to complete covering. She herself has chosen to dress modestly, and feels annoyed at those who show a 'lack of respect' by not doing so:

> I liked the fact that women weren't going out of their way to show what they'd got, that they were keeping it a secret, sending the message: 'Look deeper first, boys.' Call me old-fashioned, but there was something that really appealed to me in that.
>
> On the other hand, I wasn't over-keen on the fact women weren't allowed to go into the coffee houses where men were puffing on their shishas (those long bottle things which bubble) and were chatting over a glass of coffee like treacle. But then, it's not so long ago that women were allowed to walk into pubs in Wales is it?[132]

The role of women within Islam is touched upon by the poet Rhian Saadat, originally from south Wales, now married to a Persian husband and domiciled in Paris. Her 2004 collection, *Window Dressing for Hermès*, contains several poems about the tensions between East and West within Iran itself and also those experienced by Iranians abroad. The question of gender roles and expectations, and their symbolic place within the tensions between Iran and the West, is examined in her poem 'Grey Raincoats', given in full, about a visit to her Iranian in-laws:

> There I am, and again, here. In the background,
> the famous gardens of Barg-i-Fin. Each of my in-laws
> is dressed in similar fashion, recognisable only
> by our headscarves. Mine came from Agnes B, Paris,
> theirs were from Chanel of Tehran. Our shapeless coats
> are indistinguishable, loose. And that's heat, rising.
>
> Mariam does not care for any external frivolity.
> She's the one in black, head to foot, but her smile
> is still the most convincing. Madia, younger, wears
> a generous helping of make-up, and, beneath the coat
> – a mini-skirt and minier t-shirt, *I Love America*!
> stretched between her breasts.
>
> Mariam had been explaining about the Ayatollah *Dot.Com*.
> He is modern, and young Iranians appear to like him.
> Madia snorts. She has just opened her own health club
> in the centre of town; sunbeds, beauty, mixed-sex hammam.
> Her sunglasses glint on the top of her head. For her,
> revolution can't come fast enough.
>
> Friday, they announced, we would visit the Bag-i-Dilgusha –
> Garden of Heart's Ease. Madia winks. She was planning
> to wear nothing, under her plain grey coat. That's me,
> there, looking wilted. Madia is the one in the orange scarf
> just slipping away from her forehead, a spiral of wild
> bottle-blonde hair escaping from beneath.[133]

The attitudes of some Muslims to women are further highlighted in a passage from one of the most attentive Welsh chroniclers of life in Islamic countries, the photographer and author Patricia Aithie. Originally from Cardiff, Aithie spent some years in the Gulf where her husband was an oil industry geologist. During that time, although a practising Christian, Aithie developed an interest in Islam, and produced numerous books about Islamic countries, particularly Yemen. Her 2005 book, *The Burning Ashes of Time*, tells of her journey to Yemen to trace the history of the contact between that rugged country on the south of the Arabian peninsula, and Wales – a contact brought about by the British navy's need for Yemeni labour in the furnaces of its steam-powered ships, and its use of the Yemeni port of Aden as a coaling station for its vessels plying the routes to the East. The relationship led to Yemeni sailors in Cardiff establishing Wales's oldest Muslim community. It also led to a legacy of widespread memories and mementoes of Wales in Yemen itself.

In the following passage, Aithie and her husband Charles, with Ahmed, a Yemeni guide, are heading to the remote western region of the country, when Aithie's desire to photograph some picturesque run-down buildings falls foul of local sensibilities, and a tribesman accosts them, telling them that photographing the house is 'against the Koran.' The uncomfortable situation is relieved by Ahmed's assertive approach as he accuses the tribesmen of un-Islamic untidiness in allowing the house to be so dilapidated. Aithie reports Ahmed's reply to a further challenge about the fact that she does not have her head covered:

> Ahmed never raised his voice but told him plainly that I had a right to wear what I wanted. 'What if someone came and asked you to veil your wife or daughter?'[134]

He goes on to require of them the respect Islam commands towards Christians, and the hospitality it commands towards strangers. To these obligations he also adds a particular Welsh-Muslim connection:

> Without faltering, Ahmed returned to the Toyota. Out of his bag came a copy of Sheikh Said's letter, from the South Wales Islamic Centre. In it Sheikh Said explained how many Yemenis had come to settle in Wales, and were happy living there, amongst the local people. Many had married in Cardiff and some of the women had converted to Islam. Of course the prophet Mohammed himself had had a Christian wife and there is a special place for 'people of the book', as the three monotheistic faiths share a common faith in one God. It is recognised that before God's revelation to Muslims via the Prophet Mohammed, God had used the Bible to reveal himself to Christians and Jews and it is part of a Muslim's mission to debate about God with them. In fact, not far from where we were standing was possibly one of the earliest venues of inter-faith dialogue. In 630 a Christian delegation from Najran – then part of Yemen, on the Saudi border – went to Medina to discuss the importance of Christians co-existing with the Muslim community.
>
> 'God be with you!' cried the man in a loud voice.
>
> As a country where just about everyone accepts that God exists, and is in control, Yemen is blessed. It is a moving experience to travel somewhere where the thought of life without God is, for most people, unthinkable.[135]

The visit ends amicably, and Aithie concedes to wear a headscarf for the remainder of the desert journey.

Gender roles in Islamic society also attract the attention of the author, radio producer and journalist Horatio Clare (*b.*1973), who was brought up on a hill farm in the Black Mountains of south Wales, and who is one of the contributors to the 2005 volume of essays, *Meetings with Remarkable Muslims*. On a visit to Morocco, he recounts how he is hustled into swift intimacy with a local family whose internal dynamics prompt his reflections on the slowly-changing attitudes to women and divorce in that particular Islamic society 'which until recently granted all men's words and whims divine and legal force'.[136] Referring to his assertive reformist hostess, Saida, he adds:

> ...though Moroccan women have decades of battles to fight, with enlightened legislation, and as long as there is no lurch back into conservatism, they will surely triumph: the strength and nous of Saida and her sisters will change their world, and ours. They are the key to a secure, prosperous and open-hearted Morocco; never mind symbolic hand-shakes with half-friendly despots: we desperately need just and tolerant Islamic societies, and Morocco is closer to that than most.[137]

Tensions between Islam and the West are also touched upon in the 2004 travelogue *Jambo Caribw*, by the librarian and author Rocet Arwel Jones, which tells the story of his charity fund-raising climb of Mount Kilimanjaro in Kenya. It includes a passage set in the Islamic district of Lamu island, where Jones is woken by the call to prayer, and is surprised to find what he suspects are two rival muezzins competing for custom, and he speculates as to whether denominationalism is as much a scourge in Lamu as in Wales, and whether Welsh chapels might not employ similarly competitive tactics. More seriously, he notices the prayer call being challenged by someone with a sound-system playing expletive-laden rap music:

> Eminem letting the *muezzin* know that he too was going to call his faithful. And that's the true clash of civilisations. Can you imagine Eminem outside Seilo, Bethania, Saron and Bethel? Is it any wonder the people of Lamu are annoyed?
>
> I got out of the hammock and wandered through the town and noticed how many of the women were wearing black, how many of

> the men were wearing beards and traditional dress. I walked past the football graffiti for the tenth time and remembered the warning – 'long live 9/11'.[138]

Elsewhere in his book, Jones recounts instances where he has had to insist on his separate cultural identity from that of the English, and where he expresses exasperation with the patronising attitudes of some of the British travellers he comes across. It would be possible to compile a substantial collection of passages in which late-twentieth-century Welsh-speaking travellers insist on being identified as Welsh rather than English – increasingly so as assertive nationalism becomes the default position of culturally-active members of that community from the 1960s onwards. Scarcely is any travelogue complete without the recounting of such a climactic moment of self-revelation, even if the travellers often have to resort to invoking the names of Ryan Giggs and Tom Jones in order to make their point. In this respect it is interesting to see how a tendency to proselytise for one's own cultural values, visible in the literature of the imperial period, is found also in the *post*-imperial period, albeit that the values displayed for the approval of the natives (and thereby, for the self-approval of the visitor) are not now those of cultural, religious or political supremacy, but are the proud badges of underdog status, of belonging to a small nation and of speaking a minority language. These Welsh travellers, few of them conventionally religious, seem as keen to share their story as a custodians of a defiant minority culture as ever their missionary forebears were to share theirs as custodians of the gospel.[139]

Such cultural assertiveness is *de rigueur* for the streetwise young travellers whose work forms the final selection in this chapter. *Blwyddyn Gap* ('Gap Year') is a 2009 collection of anonymised anecdotes from young Welsh speakers who have spent time as backpackers or volunteers in foreign countries, including Libya, Mauritania, Sudan and Morocco. The volume is indicative of how exotic international travel has become accessible for ever-greater numbers of ever-younger Westerners, the Welsh among them. Edited by Bethan Marlow and Laura Wyn, and with a foreword by Bethan Gwanas, whose work was mentioned above, the short volume includes more excessive drinking, more frank sexuality and more four-letter words than in all the previous nine-hundred years of Welsh writing collected in this study combined. Some of all those characteristics are displayed in the book's episodes involving Islamic countries. A visitor to Morocco remarks:

> It's Ramadan here which means no one can eat anything during the hours of daylight. The aim of this Muslim rule is firstly, to purify the body every year, and secondly, to ensure that everyone has the experience of being poor and hungry. How ironic that our response to it is to go for a 'Big Mac Meal' to the local McDonald's. No-one can eat, drink or smoke on the streets during Ramadan, so the city is closed during the day – apart from the McArse-place, which was still offering 'eat in, or eat out!'.[140]
>
> . . .
>
> Of course, one of the things that sets Libya apart from other Muslim countries, I suppose, is the fact that there are countless pictures of Gaddafi decorating huge walls all over the country. On the three-quarters-of-an-hour journey from the airport I counted fifteen murals of the leader. Nuts.[141]

In the following passage, a young woman on a bus journey in Nigeria takes the opportunity of a stop for the Muslim call to prayer to visit a nearby grove of sugar cane to answer the call of nature:

> I forgot to concentrate and I fell flat on my back with a devil of a racket of crunching sugar cane. And as I had flattened the sugar cane like a pancake, the world could see me with my trousers around my ankles and my cheeks flaming – all of them.
>
> The women in the taxi giggled the whole way to Bida. I hid my face in the *Nigerian Tribune*.[142]

In Libya, another Welsh woman traveller finds friendship with a young Muslim woman, Rafaa:

> She is very honest and is ready to discuss any subject – and I mean any subject! I had never expected to discuss men and sex with a girl from Libya, but that's exactly what's been on the agenda. Of course, Libya's religion and culture forbid men and women from having an open relationship before marriage. As a woman from a Western country like Wales, I find this almost impossible to imagine. Rafaa respects the rules and insists that they are there to protect women rather than to imprison them.
>
> . . .

> I respect the (alleged) self-discipline, and to a degree it has influenced how I look at things. After all, who can argue that getting to know someone before sleeping with them is a good thing? But on the other hand, I see that the sexual frustration that exists in countries like Libya causes lots of problems. For example, there's a huge sex industry here – women from Tunisia or Morocco are the prostitutes usually, but there are some Libyan women as well. And apparently there are some dodgy clinics for girls who have not 'abstained' to go to in order to be stitched back together before marriage.[143]

The Welsh traveller in Libya goes on to recount how she had her own opportunity to experience relations between the sexes in a Muslim country when she fell for an attractive young local photographer: 'I decided that moment that I believed in love at first sight.'

> This was all very innocent, of course, and him a Muslim, but this added to the sexual tension. Sometimes, when we were going for a walk or wandering around the *souk* (the market), Mohammed had to stop to pray. I loved watching him take off his shoes and set them carefully by his side before bowing to begin his prayer. If there was water available, he would throw some over his head after finishing. And even though it's wrong to think about sex when somebody's praying (is it?!), the image of him standing in the heat of the sun with the drops of water tricking through his curly black hair and on his dark skin will remain with me for ever.
>
> We were on a boat one day when I realised that Mohammed was staring at me.
>
> 'What?' I said.
>
> 'I feel like I know you forever,' he said. And no matter how totally cheesy that sounds, I agreed with him. At that moment I decided I would marry Mohammed, move to Libya and have fifteen little brown babies.
>
> So what went wrong, you ask? One word – saliva. Holding hands was the most Mohammed and I had done in Tripoli. But one night in the city of Ghadames under the stars of the Sahara, when I'd been smoking a bit too much shisha, Mohammed decided to kiss me. I had been dreaming of it for days.
>
> Unfortunately, that dream was destroyed by Mohammed's lips starting to drool over my face. Like a dog. Imagine the worst snog you have ever had and then multiply it by a thousand. Yes, it was that bad. It was disgusting. And before you suggest that I should have stuck with it and given the lad a few lessons, as he was sliming over me Mohammed said: 'I love you. Do you have a condom?'

> And that was it. A fantasy over as soon as it started. Somehow I managed to push him off and ran away, and spent the rest of the holidays trying to avoid him. And that was a difficult task with him insisting on following me everywhere and cornering me on every trip screaming: 'I know you love me! You are just afraid! Is it because I am Muslim?'
>
> Here's an e-mail I got from him shortly after I returned home, and he still sends me things like this to this day:
>
> I Hope You Received My First Message, and i hope you understand why i didn't come in the last day my angel ... i walk alone in streets last night back home, it was starry night, i was thinking about you, in that time summer breeze touch my face gently ... i knew it ... that's your breathing, it's like ambrosial and soft wind ... you far away from here, but i feel you. thank you, because you make me feel with that feelin ... one day I ill be there to see u. soon or later.
>
> (threat?)
>
> PS. I still keep your hair
>
> (Where the fuck did he get hold of my hair?)[144]

The candid, uninhibited style and unsanitised subject-matter of these first-person accounts – aided perhaps by the authors' anonymity – seem vastly different to the decorous narratives of previous generations. However, it is perhaps only in their frankness that they really differ. As has been seen, sexual interest – and some sexual contact – was evident in the exoticism of many of the writers of earlier generations; drug-taking was not unknown among British travellers and service personnel; and if the missionaries and pilgrims whose work has been examined in preceding chapters might have been expected to have set a guard upon their lips when it came to cursing, it is hard to believe that all the soldiers and seafarers were as restrained. In fact, once the difference between coyness and candour has been set aside, it is possible, in many essential respects, to see more continuity than conflict between the generations. The twenty-first-century Welsh travellers to Muslim countries, like their predecessors in previous centuries, have been journeying for their own purposes, using the opportunities opened up by the Western world, and – whatever may be their claims for national distinctiveness – have carried with them the contemporary value-system of the West, whether that be Christianity or consumerism, imperialism or post-imperialism, and they have set down their accounts in a style which conforms with the current expectations of their home society. In fundamental respects like those, therefore, it is possible to establish a clear continuum between these writers and their compatriots of earlier generations.

The question remains of whether a growth of understanding for, and sympathy with, Islam, can be discerned across the centuries of Welsh writing collected here. In this respect, while it is true that readiness to criticise Islam decreases markedly with the loss of empire following the Second World War, one must be cautious about attributing this to the positive virtue of increased appreciation rather than to the negative virtue of the inhibition of criticism caused by reduced Western confidence. In fact, as the apparent single-minded piety of Islamic belief, and the external manifestations of its culture, seem to be as intriguingly mysterious for writers in the twenty-first century as for most of those in preceding ones, it is possible that the gulf of understanding between their world and that of Islam is as wide as ever. In fact, it may even be wider. Most Welsh writers of the last fifty years are the product of an overwhelmingly secular and post-religious culture, and increasingly so. It is therefore possible that for all their globalised political and social liberalism, and for all their ever-increasing physical access to the lands of Islam, they may actually be further away from understanding the core values of an essentially spiritual world-view than were their predecessors who largely viewed the world through the eyes of faith.

Notes

1.Edward Pugh ap Fyllin, 'Cerdd o Hanes Mab i ŵr Bonheddig o Lancashire: Aeth i Drafaelio' (Oswestry, 1791). See www.e-gymraeg.org/cronfabaledi the database of eighteenth-century ballads maintained by the Schools of Welsh of the Universities of Cardiff and Bangor.
2. Siwan M. Rosser, *Y Ferch ym Myd y Faled,* (Cardiff, 2005) 65.
3. John Hanning Speke (1827-64), and James Augustus Grant (1827-92) were earlier African explorers.
4. Henry Morton Stanley, *Through the Dark Continent* (New York, 1878) 193.
5. *Ibid.* 209.
6. *Ibid.* 193.
7. J.W. Gregory, *The Foundation of British East Africa* (London, 1901) 119.

8. Siân Wyn Jones, *O Gamddwr i Gairo – Hanes y Brodyr Davies Bryan (1851-1935)* (Wrexham, 2004).
9. John Davies Bryan, *O'r Aifft* (Wrexham, 1908) vii.
10. Edward Morgan Humphreys and Robert Thomas Jenkins, 'Bryan, Robert' *Welsh Biography Online* http://yba.llgc.org.uk/cy/c-BRYA-ROB-1858.html
11. John Davies Bryan, *op. cit.* 61.
12. John Davies Bryan, 'Islam a'i Phroffwyd', *Cymru*, 42 (1912) 220.
13. *Ibid.* 257.
14. *Ibid.* 258.
15. *Ibid.*
16. *Ibid.* 259.
17. *Ibid.* 260.
18. John Davies Bryan, 'Islam a'i Phroffwyd', *Cymru*, 43 (1913) 200.
19. *Ibid.* 202.
20. *Ibid.*
21. *Ibid.* 203.
22. Robert Bryan, 'Adlais o'r Dwyrain', *Cymru*, 42 (1912) 160.
23. Robert Bryan, 'El Jihad', reprinted in Bethan Mair and R. Arwel Jones (eds.), *Cerddi'r Byd* (Llandysul, 2005) 67.
24. *Ibid.* 70.
25. Samir Rafaat, 'Davies Bryan & Co. of Emad El Din Street: Four Welshmen Who Made Good In Egypt', *Egyptian Mail* (27 May, 1995) http://www.egy.com/landmarks/95-05-27.shtml
26. Thomas Gwynn Jones, *Y Môr Canoldir a'r Aifft* (Caernarfon, 1912). See also Siân Wyn Jones, 'Yng Nghamau T. Gwynn Jones', *Taliesin*, 74 (Summer 1991) 50-6, which retraces some of Jones's footsteps in Egypt.
27. *Ibid.* 17.
28. *Ibid.* 20.
29. *Ibid.* 21.
30. *Ibid.* 23.
31. David Jenkins, *Thomas Gwynn Jones*, (Denbigh, 1973). References taken from second edition, 1994, 160.
32. Thomas Gwynn Jones *op. cit.* 24.
33. *Ibid.* 50.
34. *Ibid.* 152.
35. *Ibid.* 154.
36. *Ibid.* 156.
37. *Ibid.* 178.
38. *Ibid.*
39. *Ibid.* 179.
40. Ellis Wynne of Lasynys (1671-1734), the cleric and prose writer whose work was discussed in Chapter 3.
41. Thomas Gwynn Jones *op. cit.* 189.
42. David Jenkins, *op. cit.* 159.
43. David M. Beddoe, *The Honour of Henri de Valois* (London, 1905) 10.

44. *Ibid.* 13.
45. *Ibid.* 98.
46. *Ibid.* 105.
47. David M. Beddoe, *The Lost Mameluke* (London, 1913) 79.
48. *Ibid.* 134.
49. *Ibid.* 135.
50. *Ibid.* 85.
51. *Ibid.* 201.
52. *Ibid.* 203.
53. *Ibid.* 220.
54. *Ibid.* 317-19.
55. David Gwyn Williams, *ABC of (D)GW* (Llandysul, 1981) 190.
56. *Ibid.* 110.
57. David Gwyn Williams, *Y Ddefod Goll,* (Port Talbot, 1980) unnumbered pages.
58. Richard Poole, Introduction to Richard Hughes, *In the Lap of Atlas* (London, 1979) 7.
59. *Ibid.* 13.
60. *Ibid.* 12.
61. *Ibid.* 16.
62. Richard Hughes, 'A Woman to Talk to', *In the Lap of Atlas, op. cit.* 102.
63. *Ibid.* 102.
64. *Ibid.* 103.
65. *Ibid.* 104.
66. *Ibid.* 122.
67. *Ibid.*
68. *Ibid.* 111.
69. Rhys J. Davies, *Seneddwr ar Dramp* (Liverpool, 1934) 82.
70. *Ibid.* 86.
71. Tom Madoc Jones, *Ar Gerdded* (Liverpool, 1969) 102
72. *Ibid.* 104.
73. *Ibid.* 105.
74. William Emlyn Jones, *Tua'r Dwyrain* (Llandybïe, 1963) 37.
75. *Ibid.* 38.
76. Kate Bosse-Griffiths, *Galwad yr Aifft* (Llandybïe, 1970) 12.
77. *Ibid.* 98.
78. *Ibid.* 142.
79. *Ibid.* 146.
80. *Ibid.* 149.
81. *Ibid.* 150.
82. *Ibid.* 151.
83. *Ibid.* 153.
84. *Ibid.* 154.
85. *Ibid.* 156.
86. *Ibid.* 157.
87. *Ibid.* 159.

88. *Ibid.*
89. Ancient Roman winter festival characterised by feasting.
90.J. Gwyn Griffiths in Heini Gruffudd (ed.) *Hog dy Fwyell* (Talybont, 2007) 128.
91. Although the reference is not given by Griffiths, the title is a quotation from Psalm 84 v 10: 'Better to be a doorkeeper in the house of my God than to dwell in palaces of wickedness.'
92. J. Gwyn Griffiths. *op. cit.* 136.
93. *Ibid.* 135.
94. *Ibid.* 137.
95. *Ibid.* 153.
96. *Ibid.* 152.
97. *Ibid.* 169.
98. *Ibid.* 194. See also *Cerddi'r Byd, op cit.* 69.
99. Harry Fainlight, *Selected Poems* (London, 1986) 7.
100. *Ibid.* 60.
101. Cyril Glyndŵr Williams, *Nadolig yn Calcutta* (Llandysul, 1975) 137.
102. *Ibid.* 137.
103. *Ibid.* 139.
104. Cyril Glyndŵr Williams, 'Ceisio Deall Islam' *Y Traethodydd* 146: 618, (1991) 14-27
105. Dyddgu Owen, *Haul a Heli* (Llandybïe, 1984) 42.
106. *Ibid.* 43.
107. *Ibid.* 44.
108. 'Orig Williams, Welsh wrestler', *The Times*, 23 November, 2009 http://www.timesonline.co.uk/tol/comment/obituaries/article6927430.ece
109. Williams quotes the titles of two well-known hymns.
110. Orig Williams, *Cario'r Ddraig* (Talybont, 1985) 129.
111. *Ibid.* 134.
112. *Ibid.* 135.
113. Williams quotes the Welsh translation of the famous English hymn by William Cowper (1731-1800).
114. *Ibid.* 135.
115. *Ibid.* 145.
116. Gwenllian Jones, *Llythyrau Bangladesh* (Llanrwst, 1993) 33.
117. Peter Finch, 'Last seen in Barbados,' *Planet: The Welsh Internationalist*, 140 (April/May 2000) 108
118. Stewart Brown, *Lugard's Bridge* (Bridgend, 1989) 67.
119. Elwyn Evans, *Cyfarfod ag Affrica* (Denbigh, 1995) 39.
120. *Ibid.* 46.
121. Jan Morris, *Sultan in Oman* (London, 1983 edition) 67.
122. *Ibid.* 129.
123. *Ibid.* 130.
124. Jan Morris, *A Writer's World: Travels 1950-2000* (London, 2003) 159.
125. *Ibid.* 160.
126. *Ibid.* 161.

127. *Ibid.*
128. Nigel Jenkins, *Acts of Union, Selected Poems 1974-1989* (Llandysul, 1989) 39.
129. *Ibid.* 41.
130. Gwyneth Carey, 'Y Mwnshi a'r Diacon' in Delyth George (ed.) *Tocyn Tramor* (Talybont, 1997) 172.
131. Dewi Pws Morris, *Byd Pws* (Llanrwst, 2004) 104.
132. Bethan Gwanas, *Mwy o Fyd Bethan* (Llandysul, 2005) 22.
133. Rhian Saadat, *Window Dressing for Hermès* (Cardigan, 2004) 30.
134. Patricia Aithie, *The Burning Ashes of Time* (Bridgend, 2005) 112.
135. *Ibid.* 113.
136. Horatio Clare, 'Sisters and Brothers' in Barnaby Rogerson (ed.), *Meetings with Remarkable Muslims* (London, 2005) 16.
137. *Ibid.* 24.
138. R. Arwel Jones, *Jambo Caribw* (Talybont, 2004) 187.
139. For those who wish to maximise their opportunity to witness to their nationality while away from their nation, it is possible to buy teeshirts which declare, in various languages, 'I am not English, I am Welsh.'
140. Bethan Marlow and Laura Wyn, (eds.), *Blwyddyn Gap* (Caernarfon, 2009) 165.
141. *Ibid.* 37.
142. *Ibid.* 169.
143. *Ibid.* 52.
144. *Ibid.* 132.

'Where are you from?': Islam in Wales A Conclusion

If the questions I have been asked while researching this study are any guide, then it seems that, for Welsh people, the main object of curiosity regarding the relationship between Wales and Islam – after the burning issue of radicalism – is the experience of Muslim presence in Wales itself. Where are the main communities? Where was the first mosque? Where do most Muslims in Wales come from? And, after the quantitative questions, always, the qualitative, value-judgement inquiry: What do they think of the way they're treated? That last question is, of course, self-reflexive, barely concealing the enquirer's true anxiety to know: What do *they* think of *us*? As so often in this study, Muslims are used as a mirror: the curiosity about Islam is less a case of interest in another culture, and more a fundamental desire to know something about ourselves, namely: In relation to *them*, what kind of people do *we* find ourselves to be?

It is hoped the material reviewed in this final chapter, devoted to portrayals of Islam within Wales, and portrayals of Wales by Muslims, will go at least some way towards answering that final question, as well as giving an opportunity to show the emergent literary voices of Muslims in Wales themselves. It will also allow for a summary of the findings of the entire study. Nearly all the previous extracts have been based on Welsh people encountering Muslims outside Wales, or commenting from within Wales about Islamic matters elsewhere; as such they primarily reveal the attitudes which Welsh society exports. The literary extracts collected here will attempt to show how the two cultures have inter-reacted within the boundaries of Welsh society itself, and in so doing, may help illuminate not only the question of communal co-existence which is being asked with urgency due to contemporary political events, but also the questions of identity and belonging which many Welsh people never stop asking.

Substantial modern Muslim settlement within Wales begins

with the communities of sailors, often from Yemen, who settled in Cardiff in the mid nineteenth century as a result of the maritime coal trade. In Cardiff and the other port cities and towns of south Wales – Swansea, Newport, and Barry – those initial pioneering communities were reinforced over the decades by Somalis, Pakistanis, Bangladeshis and others according to the ever-varying forces of economic and political opportunity and necessity in those countries of origin and in Wales itself. At the time of writing, the 60,000 Muslims identified by the 2001 census account for two per cent of the population of Wales. Particularly in the cities, the number and proportion of Muslims is increasing, and the political events of recent years have made the Islamic community as a whole a focus for intense interest from the wider society. However, the current visibility and profile of these communities should not create the impression that the influence of Islam in Wales is a phenomenon of the industrial age alone. As has been shown in earlier chapters, many Welsh people have been familiar with Islam either through literary work or through first-hand encounter from as early as the Crusades. And it is not just in literature that Islam has left its mark in Wales: there is considerable evidence in the material culture of the nation as well which shows the involvement of Wales and Islamic countries over the centuries.

As an illustration of this, one might create an itinerary through Wales which takes in places demonstrating the connection between Wales and Islam. Such a journey could begin at the very northernmost tip of Wales at Llanbadrig near Cemaes on Anglesey. Here the village church[1] was restored in the late nineteenth century largely due to donations from a prominent convert to Islam, Henry Edward John Stanley (1827-1903), 3rd Baron Stanley of Alderley and 2nd Baron Eddisbury, the first Muslim member of the House of Lords. Despite his conversion in 1862, he was the main funder of the church restoration, which was completed in 1884; the decoration includes tilework and stained glass in Islamic style, in recognition of Lord Stanley's faith.[2] Moving to the mainland, then, at Llanystumdwy on the Llŷn peninsula, can be found the childhood home and adjacent burial place of David Lloyd George, whose animosity to 'The Turk', whose support of the creation of the 'Jewish National Home' in Palestine, and whose role in deciding the custody of the

Islamic holy places and the last Caliphate were shown in Chapter 6. Only a few miles to the east is the birthplace of T.E. Lawrence, who promoted Lloyd George's policy of encouraging Arab Nationalism. Heading east for another half an hour or so, the traveller comes to Ysbyty Ifan, a village whose name translates as 'John's Hospice', and whose church is built on the site of a hospice founded in the late twelfth century by the Knights of St John of Jerusalem, one of the Crusading orders. As the hospice had the right of granting sanctuary, it became a haven for criminals who terrorised the country for miles around; when they were eventually driven out, they migrated to Dinas Mawddwy where they formed the nucleus of the notorious *Gwylliaid Cochion*, the Red Bandits, who were eventually suppressed in the sixteenth century, and whose exploits formed an enduring collection of legends. About half an hour's drive away, at Cerrigydrudion, the traveller passes a public house called The Saracen's Head, with its inn-sign of a black-bearded, turbanned, scimitar-wielding warrior.

If the traveller were to head south for an hour or so, they would pass the Aleppo Merchant public house at Carno. A sweep west to Pencader would pass the Llain Arabian stud farm, legacy of the former thriving horse trade with the Ottoman empire. Turning south-east to the upper Swansea Valley, the mining village of Onllwyn has a street named after General Gordon, and a colliery spoil heap called 'Khartoum Tip', named after the city where Gordon was killed by the followers of the Mahdi. Passing through Neath, the traveller would see the remains of Neath Abbey, built by a reputedly 'Saracen' architect called Lalys, supposedly captured in Palestine by Crusaders, and employed by the Norman baron Richard de Grandville in 1129 to build his abbey. As a reward, Lalys was given a manor near Bridgend which, under the name of Laleston, still bears his name to this day. Then if the traveller headed through the Rhondda valley, they could find, in St Peter's Church, Pentre, the flag of the Khalifa, the Mahdi's successor, captured at the battle of Toski in 1889 by Francis Wallace Grenfell (1841-1925), a member of a Swansea family of industrial magnates, who commanded the Anglo-Egyptian army which finally defeated the Mahdist movement.

On the south Wales coast, then, is the former coal port of

Barry, where, in the foyer of the town's Memorial Hall can be seen, among the 1,218 entries on the roll of honour, the names of many Muslim seamen from the town who died alongside their shipmates from Britain and other nations while serving on the merchant ships which were the country's wartime lifeline of supplies. Finally, in Cardiff, as well as the numerous mosques which testify to the presence of the current Muslim community,[3] earlier Muslim influence can be seen in Cardiff Castle, which boasts a magnificent Arab Room designed and fantastically decorated in gold leaf and semi-precious jewels by the architect William Burges for his patron, the industrialist and orientalist, the Third Marquess of Bute, John Crichton-Stuart (1847-1900). Nearby, in Cathays Park, stands Cardiff's magnificent Edwardian City Hall, a monument to Cardiff's status when it was the greatest coal-exporting port of the world; there on the front of the buidling, in a relief sculpture depicting the four points of the compass, the crescent moon and star of Islam are carved into the Portland stone.[4]

Those contact-points are merely a selection of the specific Welsh locations which illustrate a relationship between wider Western culture and Islam, a relationship which, due its very age and intimacy, is often unknown or unacknowledged. That wider relationship contains such common, and essential, elements of the Western world as: the legacy of teachings from the ancient world preserved for medieval and renaissance Europe in Arabic texts; the scientific advances made by Islamic scholars and researchers; the large number of Arabic words in European languages, including English and Welsh, and the numbering system which replaced the Latin method and which greatly facilitated the advance of mathematics. The closer the subject is examined, the more numerous the connections appear until eventually it is the idea of Islam as something strange and alien that itself seems strange. Any of those brief impressionistic details could be developed much further in order to show the full extent of the material evidence for the influence of Islam in Wales. As the focus of the present study is on the literary legacy, such a task must await another researcher. However, it is hoped the above summary provides some context for the discussion of literary material which follows, and shows that the Welsh relationship with Islam exists in more than just words.

An early literary reference to the practice of Islam in Wales itself is found in a 1913 novel, *Daniel Evelyn, Heretic*, a satire on Christian chapel orthodoxy by Cadvan Rhys, a pseudonym of David Delta Evans (1866-1948), who was better known by his bardic name of Dewi Hiraddug. Evans, a native of Flintshire, was a leading figure in Unitarianism, a theology, with its roots in Christianity, which denies the divinity of Christ, and stresses the strictly monotheistic unity of God, a position which traditionally led Unitarians to be marginalised and condemned by the Trinitarian majority of Christian churches in Wales as elsewhere. Evans was an energetic promoter of Unitarianism in Wales, Liverpool and London.

In the following passage from the novel, Captain Rees, a freethinking character of whom the author clearly approves, is in conversation with a young, narrow-minded Calvinistic Methodist minister, John Assyn Llwyd, towards whom the author cannot conceal his antipathy – the character's middle name is a play on the Welsh word 'asyn', meaning 'ass'. Rees is shown to approve of the Islamic religious poet Omar Khayyam, thereby aligning himself with a non-Trinitarian monotheism in keeping with the author's own:

> 'Jesus and other great souls of history had no fear of death; nor should we, had we learned to live!'
>
> 'But death is the penalty of sin!' maintained the Pastor; 'and of course those who believe *correctly* pass through death into eternal life; but pagans and infidels and heretics and all unbelievers go to everlasting damnation, because they have not believed on the Lord Jesus Christ. The teachings of the Church make that quite plain. Nothing can be more terrible than to contemplate the terrors of an unbeliever's death!'
>
> Captain Rees was really beginning to get impatient with the puerile simplicity of this would-be eschatologist and self-constituted interpreter of the divine Mind; but again checking himself, he said, calmly –
>
> 'In the twelfth century of our era there lived in Persia a "pagan" poet whom the officially-ordained "pastors" of the land regarded as an infidel; but I don't think it was infidelity that inspired him to say that – '"Death hath no terror when the life is true; 'Tis living ill that makes us fear to die!"
>
> 'What do you think of that, Llwyd, as the utterance of a "pagan" poet? How does that kind of teaching compare with that of the

> Church of which you are an ordained pastor? Don't you think that in those two lines are summed up the whole science of life as well as the whole philosophy of death? No, my young friend, Omar Khayyam was not so much of an infidel as most of the professional theologians of this boasted Christian country of ours! What have you to say to that, Llwyd?'
>
> 'But I think I must be going now, Captain Rees,' was the answer wherewith the Pastor sought to evade the question, evidently feeling that here at all events was one too many for him, his much-vaunted education and training notwithstanding.[5]

The next passage shows William Marlès,[6] the Unitarian minister protagonist, telling his friend Dorcas about a visit to Matthew Emrys, a quarryman and former Wesleyan lay-preacher who, ostracised for his liberal views, has become a recluse, and who again incorporates elements of Islam into his personal religious practices:

> 'May I stay to form a "congregation" for you this evening?' I asked.
>
> 'Agreed!' he replied, beaming with joy at the anticipation, as I did myself.
>
> 'Well, I *did* stay, and shall never forget that beautifully devotional and most impressive service as long as I live! I felt uplifted to the very throne of God!'
>
> 'What was the order of service, Mr. Marlès?' Dorcas inquired.
>
> 'It was as follows: Short prayer, ending with a slow and reverent recital of the Lord's Prayer, in which the "congregation" joined; hymn; reading, from the Old Testament; hymn; another reading, from the New Testament, supplemented by a passage from a Persian scripture and two or three sentences from the Koran; chant; prayer; hymn; sermon; hymn; benediction. I was the only listener, humanly speaking, but a more practical, thoughtful, inspiring, and uplifting discourse it has never been my good fortune to hear. It seemed, as I have just said, to lift one to the very Throne of Heaven!'[7]

Such a private syncretistic service prefigures some of the public interfaith activities which have emerged, particularly in the field of civic life, in Wales around a hundred years later. However, in the Wales of 1913, which was still in the aftermath of the 1904-05 Christian religious revival, this was a radical scenario. Even 15 years later, in 1928, as was shown in Chapter 6, the popular minister Tom Nefyn Williams could be deprived of his duties in the Presbyterian church for doubting the divinity of Christ. David Delta Evans, of course, faced no risk of expulsion in publishing his views: Unitarians were already regarded as being beyond the Christian pale. Already a heretic, he had little to lose, therefore, in using Islam as a means of endorsing his non-Trinitarian project. It should, however, be remembered that while his depiction of the character Matthew Emrys's adoption of aspects of Islam may appear broadminded, and while this eclectic approach certainly foreshadows the syncretism of Western alternative spirituality of the twenty-first century, it is nonetheless a project conducted on Western terms for Western aims, and many adherents of the historic monotheism of Islam might well have a different view than the approving Unitarian novelist on the co-option of their holy book into a heterogeneous home-made cult.

The figure of Matthew Emrys seems to owe something to the prominent real-life Welsh mystic and sometime occultist, Arthur Machen (1864-1947), who, in his extensive and eclectic writings occasionally referenced Islamic sources, as in his successful novel *The Secret Glory*, published in 1922 but written nearly two decades earlier, where one of the characters recounts an instructive story about a learned mystical beggar who challenged Caliph Haroun to melt down all his treasure in an alchemical process which would leave 'one drop no longer than a pearl, but glorious as the sun to the moon and all the starry heavens and the wonders of the compassionate, and with this drop the Caliph Haroun might heal all the sorrows of the universe'.[8]

An early, and fragmentary, insight into life of Muslims in Wales itself comes from an unexpected source: the autobiography of the composer, musician and entertainer Donald Swann (1923-94), one half of the famous entertainment duo, Flanders and Swann. Commonly regarded as a quintessentially English performer, Swann was actually born at Llanelli in Wales, the son of Russian émigré parents: his father, Herbert, was a Russian doctor of English descent, and his mother, Naguime, was a Muslim nurse from Transcapia. Donald was given the middle name Ibrahím, and he and his family seem to have been comfortable with their exotic origins. In his 1993 autobiography *Swann's Way: A Life in Song*, the composer provides a glimpse, albeit second-hand, of life for an immigrant Muslim woman in early twentieth-century Wales:

How was this Moslem lady getting on in Llanelli? Not too well: the culture shock was enormous. The thing that finally got her down was not being able to hang out laundry on Sundays because the Sabbath was sacrosanct. Her Sunday, of course, would have been on a Friday anyway. She was indignant, and thought this the ultimate nonsense, which of course it was. I hope nowadays people can do what they like with their washing whatever the day. Another thing was the peculiar food; although she cooked her own, probably the range of food was more restricted there than in London.

. . .

Another bit of drama concerned uncle Sokolik, my mother's brother, the only member of her family to turn up, and on the day of my birth too – just like the fairy stories. He had been an officer during the war, but had managed to leave Russia after the Revolution and had roamed around Persia and Turkey until his three-week stay with us. He caused a tremendous stir in Llanelli and was certainly remembered there twenty years ago when I made enquiries. He was called 'the wild brother of Mrs Dr Swann' and his like had never been seen before. He entertained the people of the area by singing rousing songs and playing his guitar, and dancing exotic Eastern dances whilst brandishing sabres and knives. I was also told by one old chap that Sokolik had psychic powers. Evidently, he was once asked to sit down, but said, without having examined the chair, that there was a great hole under its cushion – and indeed there was. I always called him uncle Mohammed because he later changed his name in Persia.

After his visit to Llanelli in 1923, he surfaced again in 1925. I've got photographs of him with uncle Freddie taken on this visit. Then he vanished completely for thirty-five years. When he reappeared he was living in South Persia in a town called Ahwaz, about fifty miles from Abadan across the desert, and as far south as you could get from the Russian border. He was working as the director of music in the hotel Shoush. Various oilmen came to the hotel, and he asked one to try to trace his brother-in-law, Dr Herbert Swann, living in London. This oilman went back to London, found there were eight Dr Swanns listed in the Medical Directory, wrote to them all and one of the letters found Father. From then on Herbert corresponded with Sokolik, who had changed his name to Mohammed Zadek. Fascinating letters would arrive and how I'd laugh at some of the things in them. At Ramadan, he would turn his hand to interior decorating because music was frowned upon; and the fact that he tuned pianos tickled me – I mean what scale? Was it the well-tempered mode? Or some oriental Persian scale? Then one day he promised to write the whole story of the great gap between the sword dance in Llanelli and his present life. But it never arrived, and the next time we wrote, a note came back: 'deceased'. I feel deprived of his lost story to this day and ruminate on that Persian pillar box where it went missing.

There is a sequel. In 1964, I went to South Persia and took my wife and two small daughters by taxi from Abadan to Ahwaz. I started asking around about him and, after a long time of getting nowhere, someone suggested the Hollywood shoe shop. Again, we kept repeating the name Mohammed Zadek – no luck. Then I let slip the name Sokolik to the taxi-driver who was interpreting, and the shoe man said: 'Oh, we remember him; he was a musician: who used to work in this town, a nice old gentleman, then he died in hospital.' That was just eighteen months after his death.

The final part, which also touched me very much, was during an autobiographical entertainment in Cambridge. I'd been making jokes about Mohammed and sang about the camels and the desert. The professor of Persian in King's College came up to me afterwards and said: 'I was in Ahwaz and went to the hotel Shoush, and a tall gentleman came up and spoke to me. Obviously, he was your uncle.' Now, isn't that absolutely amazing? So, he's real, isn't he? This legendary uncle, in spite of the embroidery of camels, wild dances and songs, is real! And I've two framed photographs of him in my home: one playing the balalaika and another which you can see in this book. He's doing a Russian-style dance, with a big fur hat on. There he is: a professional entertainer, just like me.

We had other things in common: Moslem names were passed on to us; my sister's second name is Fatima and mine is Ibrahím. My mother opted for two popular names to remind herself of her people. There it is, on my passport, just an exoticism to which I never paid much attention. But things like that come back and joke at you from time to time. There was the moment on an El Al plane when they looked at my name and said: 'OK Mr Ibrahim – we're keeping an eye on you!' That was quite a good moment. Then, only recently, I took a Turkish bus from Salonika to Istanbul. For fun I had booked on as Mr Ibrahim and having arrived, went off to admire carpets. I let my name slip to the carpet dealer who exclaimed: 'Ibrahim Pasha, you are one of us! How about one of these?' He'd got me beaten. I had to buy one. So every now and then my Moslem name comes back. It's nice to think it's Abraham too, and I'm always cheered to think it's as much Jewish as Arabic, just the other side of the language really.

I became rather proud of the mix of religions in my family. There is the Moslem part on my mother's side; my sister is married to a Jew. My uncle Alfred became a devout Russian Orthodox; later, at school, I was plunged into high Anglicanism; and now I'm a Quaker.

> All this gives me the feeling that religion is a kaleidoscope where all these strands merge to form a beautiful pattern.[9]

Another insight, again second-hand, and brief, comes from the extensive work of Harold Ingrams (1887-1973), a senior British diplomat in Arabia from 1934 until the end of the Second World War. One of his detailed, thorough and well-regarded studies of the region, *Arabia and the Isles*, published in 1937, contains the following encounter, in a club in the town of Meshhed in what is now Yemen, an area which supplied labour for the ships of the Welsh coal export trade:

> ...it was obvious that he was the 'club bore'. 'Afif bin Abdullah al Afif,' he announced himself and sat down next to me. He was quite white with what is called white leprosy and plainly in his dotage. The conversation was left to us.
>
> 'I'm eighty-one' he said.
>
> 'Indeed,' I remarked politely, 'you must have seen much in your time.' This of course is just the remark that the club bore likes.
>
> 'Yes I have,' he said. 'I remember another Inglizi and his wife coming here.' (This must have been the Bents.) 'Do you come from London?' he went on.
>
> 'Well,' I said; 'I live most of my time in London when I'm in England, but I come from another town.'
>
> 'Cardiff?' he asked.
>
> 'No, not Cardiff' I said, 'though I've been there in the war'.
>
> 'If it wasn't London it must be Cardiff.'
>
> 'Why?' I said. 'There are lots more towns in England.' (Wales was much too difficult to explain.)
>
> 'No,' he said, 'there are only two towns in England, London and Cardiff. My son lives in Cardiff but he has been to London and he has never mentioned any other place. You must be wrong. My son says England is an island and London and Cardiff are its towns.'[10]

If the Yemeni man's geography of Britain was sketchy, it was nonetheless accurate in identifying the importance of the great coal port of Cardiff as a centre for the Arab maritime community. Indeed, in popular consciousness in Wales, Welsh-domiciled Muslims have traditionally been associated with Cardiff's docks district, an area once known by its exotic nickname 'Tiger Bay'.[11] The Muslim community is now, in fact, much more widespread geographically, but the former docks district is indeed the traditional heartland of the Welsh Muslim community; it is still an important location in Welsh Muslim life, and, with its resonant and evocative sobriquet, it still holds a nostalgic appeal. The following poem, 'Tiger Bay', by Idris Davies (1905-53), an important poet of the South Wales coalfield, is an example of the sense of exoticism and danger that attended the image of the Arab maritime community in Cardiff.

> I watched the coloured seamen in the morning mist,
> Slouching along the damp brown street,
> Cursing and laughing in the dismal dawn.
> The sea had grumbled through the night,
> Small yellow lights had flickered far and near,
> Huge chains clattered on the ice-cold quays,
> And daylight had seemed a hundred years away . . .
> But slowly the long cold night retreated
> Behind the cranes and masts and funnels,
> The sea-signals wailed beyond the harbour
> And seabirds came suddenly out of the mist.
> And six coloured seamen came slouching along
> With the laughter of the Levant in their eyes
> And contempt in their tapering hands.
> Their coffee was waiting in some smoke-laden den,
> With smooth yellow dice on the unswept table,
> And behind the dirty green window
> No lazy dream of Africa or Arabia or India,
> Nor any dreary dockland morning,
> Would mar one minute for them.[12]

As for literary portrayals of an actual Muslim character in Wales itself, an early example can be found in the work of Kate Bosse-Griffiths, the Jewish Holocaust refugee and egyptologist who became a Welsh-language author, and whose work and career were examined in greater length in Chapters 9 and 10. Her 1957 novel *Mae'r Galon Wrth y Llyw* ('The Heart Steers'), takes its title from an ancient Egyptian proverb: 'When the heart steers. / It will shipwreck its master.' The novel is set in a small Welsh town. In the following scene, two brothers – Dewi, whose Christian morality is portrayed sceptically, and Arthur, who is more liberal in his views – are discussing one of Arthur's workmates, an Egyptian, who has just announced that he is getting divorced. As in many cases, the Muslim characters are used as pawns for the purposes of an internal Christian debate, rather than being valued for their intrinsic worth. However, the novelist's depiction of the Muslim couple's dilemma, informed no doubt by her own experiences in Egypt, is unusually engaged, and foreshadows the debates about the role of women in Islam in the West which have come to wider public consciousness in recent decades:

> 'Divorced? Heaven help us! Not the one who only got married two years ago?' asked Dewi with interest.
>
> 'That's of no importance to the Mahometans. To them, marriage is just a personal agreement and they can get out of it without the courts intervening at all – at least the man can! The woman has no right to ask for a divorce.'
>
> 'Yes, but I remember you saying that this boy had gone back to Egypt especially in order to get a wife from a good family.'
>
> Arthur sank lower in his chair. Behind his cigarette smoke, he told the strange story of his friend from Egypt while his brother carried on with his work.
>
> 'My friend's particular ambition was to train his wife in the European way of life. But his wife was very conservative, religious and respectable, and she insists on keeping the old traditions like most women, I suppose. So it's not much of surprise that the two of them quarrel fiercely at home quite often. The wife insists on keeping the veil over her face when she goes out. She refuses to go shopping without it. And the result is that the poor husband has to do the shopping himself. But in order to teach his wife a lesson he'll buy bacon and pork and things which are "taboo" to those who are faithful to the old religion. And so his wife's now in a pretty pickle. She is fond enough of her husband and she has every reason to keep a hold of him, because it's she who'll suffer most if it comes to a divorce. But eating pork is an unforgivable sin according to her religion. Refusing to eat pork is a moral law for her – the same as not having two wives is a moral law for us. It's completely impossible for her to touch pork. I almost believe she'd rather die. Whatever, there have been terrible storms of fighting in the Egyptian's house. The neighbours have started to complain, and in the end the police had to come in. And the husband now is thinking seriously about divorcing his wife.'
>
> It was obvious in Arthur's way of telling the story that he was enjoying it, and possibly also exaggerating. Dewi was angered all the same.
>
> 'The woman should have her head examined,' he said. 'How can a woman in her senses endanger her entire family life just because she can't eat the same food as her husband?'

> 'I'm sorry,' said Arthur, 'but you misunderstand the problem. Your healthy common sense is an obstacle to you. It's not the question of liking or not liking food that has her worked up, but a moral law. In a word, the whole foundation of the social world is in the balance.'
>
> Arthur warmed to his topic as he spoke, and it was a pleasure to him to listen to his own smooth, musical voice as he enlarged upon his subject.
>
> 'Isn't it a beautiful and exalted thing that people can still be found who put moral standards before their little personal lives? This girl is a shining pearl who should be set in gold. She's one of the martyrs.'
>
> But this did not have the desired effect on his brother.
>
> 'I see,' said Dewi, 'what you do is intoxicate your listeners and then laugh at them at the end. This girl in reality has no culture, as is common among the pagans. Talk about moral heroism, indeed! In reality she's just motivated by superstition. The only principle I see is this, that uncultured women hinder the development of mankind.'
>
> 'If this is superstition,' said Arthur, provocatively, 'where do you think the moral order begins?'
>
> 'With Christianity of course,' answered Dewi with certainty.
>
> 'That isn't a satisfactory answer for the ethics of the Moslems.'
>
> 'Well, let me give an example. If your Egyptian was chasing other women, his wife would have the right to complain about his immorality.'
>
> 'No, not in Egypt. Every Moslem has the right to marry four wives if he wants to.'
>
> 'You and your Egyptians! They're all pagans!'
>
> 'O lovely, excellent! That's a Christian answer!,' said Arthur. 'But I'm sorry. I don't believe it goes deep enough – by a long way. This Egyptian woman's brave stand has shaken my moral faith. Perhaps they think the same about our morality as we think about their morality. Perhaps our morality is just as superstitious in their eyes, just as laughable.'[13]

The depiction of a Muslim in a setting outside that of the traditional maritime location was indicative of how the patterns of Muslim settlement in Wales were changing in the later twentieth century. This process was greatly augmented by the growth in immigration from Pakistan and India from the 1950s onwards, and from East Africa, particularly Uganda, from the 1970s, with many of the new arrivals working in industry, business and retail.[14] The spread of Muslim presence from the familiar, and in some ways safely exotic and self-contained setting of the maritime quarters of British port towns and cities, provided a new point of contact between Welsh people and Muslims, a contact that was increasingly reflected in cultural output. For instance, a song 'Ti' ('You') on the 1973 album *Hen Ffordd Gymreig o Fyw* ('Old Welsh Way of Life') by the Welsh-language rock group Edward H. Dafis, apostrophises the singer's lover with a list of the familiar and good things of life: 'You're the scent of sunshine and the tears in the waves. / You're the polly parrot that lives with Uncle John. / You're the lovely spring and the collieries in the south. / You're the Pakistani who drives the bus to town.' A satirical poem by the iconoclastic novelist and poet Eirug Wyn (1950-2004), published pseudonymously as 'Derec Tomos' in his gleefully scurrilous 1982 volume *Magnifikont* ('Magnifikunt') is entitled 'Y Pacistani Cymreig' ('The Welsh Pakistani.').[15] Eirug Wyn was himself nicknamed 'the Pakistani' due to his indefatigable entrepreneurship and his many and varied small-scale business interests, so the poem is actually an ironically vicious piece of self-satire, although, from the perspective of nearly three decades later, the use of his nickname predicated on casual stereotyping makes for rather uncomfortable reading.

The following extract from a 1973 novel by the prominent south Wales author, screenwriter and playwright, Alun Richards (1929-2004), depicts the kind of casual prejudice against the new arrivals that was common in the period. *Home to an Empty House* depicts a dysfunctional marriage between the dissatisfied Walter and his assertive, narrow-minded wife, Connie, a teacher. In the scene that follows, Walter has just been diagnosed with tuberculosis, a disease he had thought it was no longer possible to catch. Connie, who has just been discussing his case with her domineering aunt, is nursing him:

> '...You've got to be built up, Auntie said. She's coming down to talk to you in a minute. I didn't know but she lost two cousins when she was small, and five of the family next door in Telelkebir Street died of it. She only escaped herself through keeping chickens.'
>
> 'For Christ's sake!'
>
> 'She says they get very difficult. Very aggressive and self-pitying. She remembers it going through whole households. Galloping consumption, it was called then, the White Killer. She says you must have been mixing with Pakistanis and all your underclothes have got to be burnt.'
>
> I stared at her. Joey nearly came out of his hole. She put the tray

down firmly on the bed. Now, she stood well back and addressed me.

'It's much more serious than I thought. Have you had any relations with Pakistanis?'

I couldn't speak. Not a syllable, not even a glug of protest. It warmed her suspicion. She accused:

'You're always in these places!'

'What places?' At last, I got words out.

'Late night places – clubs. Have you?'

'Have I what?'

'Had relations?'

She was deadly serious and continued to stare at me with those stranger's eyes. A chilling thought was that we had gone back years to when we first met. I'd had no effect whatsoever. Five minutes in that kitchen had worked on her in a moment of panic with the effectiveness of napalm, and it was her feeling for me that fried. That I'd never forget.

'No,' I said. I knew she wanted an answer and I was too choked to say more. That she knew I knew black was beautiful goes without saying since there was nothing we didn't talk about, from my Kikuyu adventures to her music master's smelly forefinger. But now reason went out of the window like a curtain blowing in the wind.

She moved away from me, then turned, advanced again.

'You always wanted me to get a sari.'

('They undo more easily,' I'd said. Speedy Gonzalez, me.)

'What?'

'Nothing,' she said icily.

I looked for a smile, a wink, a sign that she was having me on, but there was none. There was no reason to what she said, but the effort of concentrating was beginning to fog me.

'What the hell have Pakistanis to do with it?' I shouted suddenly.

'Immigrants,' she said tartly. 'It's all very well to be liberal and educated, the intelligentsia don't have to mix with them.'

'But what has it got to do with me?'

'They're Tee Bee carriers, aren't they? They get here under false pretences and some of them must be rotten with it. That's why I'm asking. We've had smallpox, what next?'[16]

The mention of Telelkebir Street, named after a battle between the British and Egyptians in 1882, is a sly indication on the author's part that contact with eastern countries was hardly a new phenomenon, and this helps make the revelation of Connie's prejudice which follows all the more absurd.

The prejudice that fuelled Connie's attitudes in that 1973 novel is shown to be unabated in sections of Welsh Valleys society more than two decades later in the work of another writer from the region. A poem entitled 'This House, My Ghetto,' from an eponymous 1994 collection by the Merthyr Tydfil-based socialist poet Mike Jenkins, an indefatigable chronicler of social injustice; it depicts a Welsh-born Pakistani encountering communal hostility:

> It might as well be curfew here:
> the pubs I can't enter any more.
> It was 'Paki! Paki!', looks
> like jagged, cut-throat glass
> and 'You stink!' from knuckled whites of eyes.
>
> I was born in this town,
> passed the old hospital when walking home.
> I know how a woman must feel:
> every stranger a criminal,
> every sleight of hand a reach for steel.
>
> The night's no camouflage:
> I recall my uncle's shop,
> black letters of loathing
> branded across its front.
> My brother and I flung like tyres,
> our flesh slashed like rubber
> 'You don't belong ... fuck off home!'
> Their spittle slugging my face.
>
> I know how a woman must feel:
> even in daylight the enemy
> is the man who follows and a gang
> ahead sends thoughts twitching.
> Those bruises, insults, that blood
> has stained my voice so it jitters.
> Tall gate and drive, my watching window:
> this house is my ghetto.[18]

The following extract comes from the work of the hugely popular historical novelist and adopted Welshman, Alexander Cordell (1914-97). His 1994 novel *Land of Heart's Desire* is one of a long series, the most famous of which were the earliest, such as *Rape of the Fair Country* (1959), *The Hosts of Rebecca* (1960) and *Song of the Earth* (1969), in which the spirited and feisty protagonists, the Mortymer family, experience the vicissitudes of industrial and political life in nineteenth-century south Wales. *Land of Heart's Desire* follows the fortunes of the latest generation of the family, whose lives have become entangled with those of the royal house of Afghanistan. Iestyn Mortymer, deported for Chartist activism, finds himself with the British army in Afghanistan, escapes, becomes the lover of the grand-daughter of Dost Mohammed, King of Kabul, and then returns with her to Wales where, with their son Suresh, they begin a new life as farmers near Maesteg. It is there that emissaries from Dost Mohammed find them, and seek to persuade the half-Afghan, half-Welsh Suresh to return to Afghanistan to assume the throne. The Chief Vizier of the Court of Baraksai arrives 'sporting a silver headdress crowned with ostrich feathers' and, on the arm of one of his postillions, walks 'with the languid grace born of his station'[19] into Cefn-Ydfa House, which, among other evidences of the family's unusually cultured background, displays a statue of the Greek poet Sappho. The Chief Vizier begins to try to tempt Suresh to return to Afghanistan:

> '...believe me when I say that your heart will surge with joy at the prospect of such kingship!' and he waved a hand airily around the room, which doubtless, compared with his munificence, was but a hovel. 'Wealth and privilege will be yours for the asking, your every whim obeyed, and your life made free of sorcerers and incantation, such as exists here. Free, young Sire, from bedevilment and mysticism: divination is our only weakness, which is at Allah's behest for us to rule the world and make it free of the black art called Christianity.'
>
> He bent towards me, his dark eyes smiling. 'Have you the faintest idea what I am talking about?'
>
> I did not answer this, and he said, standing before Sappho's statue, 'And who might this be?'
>
> Quoting my father and speaking in the Karendeesh tongue, I replied, 'She is Sappho, one of the poets: she lived in Greece six centuries before the coming of Christ.'
>
> He made a face. 'Sappho ... Sappho ...I have never heard of her.'
>
> 'Perhaps one needs to be a student of Greek mythology.'
>
> It turned him, instantly delighted. 'Excellent! I had begun to wonder when you would cease to be a Celt, and adopt the proud role for which you were born!'
>
> I did not reply, and he said, 'This ... this Greek ... A lady poet?'
>
> 'As I have said, one of the world's great poets.'

> 'Do you not overstate? Forgive me ... I did not even know that female poets existed, even less that they should be celebrated.'
>
> 'My father will tell you more of her.'
>
> He was not satisfied. 'But a woman, Suresh! Oh, come!' and he turned away. 'Is it in the province of male propriety to grant such a status? Does that not also grant them intellectual parity, which is impossible? Women can only claim comparison with the beasts of the field – to give birth to us, true, they are excellent at that – but poets...!'
>
> I said abruptly, 'This is Wales, not Afghanistan, and my name is not Suresh!'[20]

In his use of vigorously unapologetic essentialist portrayals, the work of Cordell can be compared with that of Richard Llewellyn (see Chapter 9), in whose tradition Cordell was working. However, it should not be thought that Cordell was thoughtless in his use of the technique. His choice of Cefn Ydfa as the location for his novel recalls the widely-known eighteenth-century legend of the 'Maid of Cefn Ydfa', about a young woman, Ann Maddocks, who pines away and dies after a forced marriage. In showing that forced marriage is not merely a phenomenon of Muslim countries, and that it was previously common in Wales too, Cordell is indicating that the gulf between gender attitudes between the West and Islam is not as great as might be thought.

Also from 1994, although set in that year rather than in the past, the work of another Welsh author provides a portrayal of Muslims in Wales, although this time as long-term residents rather than exotic visitors. It is found in the work of Tom Davies (*b.*1941) a prolific novelist, journalist, travel writer, religious author and polemicist, of combative Christian beliefs. His novel *I Conker* is told from the point of view of the eponymous angel, who has been given charge of the nation of Wales. In the following passage, Conker visits Cardiff's 'Tiger Bay' docklands area. His ruminations are mixed with extracts from interviews with some of the real residents of 'this unique, multi-racial community.'

> I've enjoyed services with the Sikhs and the Moslems. I've attended the Vespers of Love with the Greeks and kneeled with chanting Buddhists. Oh they've always had the lot down here and I've enjoyed them all. Angels never lay claim to exclusive authority over forms of worship and have no truck with religious rivalry of any sort. We

understand that God's people can deal with religious truth in any way they apprehend it. A few faiths – no names, no pack drill – have gone up the pole to be sure but never too much so. Even in the most eccentric of faiths you will always find the fingerprints of the one true God if you look hard enough. The real differences are almost always in the trimmings.[21]

. . .

Ah the expression of concerned love has always been the sweetest music to my heart. There have been many grave and beautiful people in the Bay who have performed the gravest and most beautiful acts. Right here was the Rainbow Club where Shirley Bassey had her first singing date. The club for all the children of the Bay was founded by Margaret Capener who saw a rainbow forming over the city one day. She thought of the last line of D.H. Lawrence's *The Rainbow* and how it had come to represent a living, multi-coloured truth. 'There can be a rainbow,' she said.

But perhaps the real love story of the Bay, which tells everything about the great spirit of racial hope that the area came to represent, is told by Mrs Olive Salaman, a Welsh girl from the Valleys.

'I lived in the Rhymney Valley. There was no work about and I got a job in the Cardiff Royal Infirmary for one pound a month. I didn't go out for two months but one day went to the pictures in town and took a wrong turning when I came out. I ended up down in Bute Street and asked this man the way. This was A.H. Salaman, the first coloured man that I had ever met. We married when I was 16 years and three weeks old. We had twelve children who are all married now with their own children. Only one of my children married a Moslem. The rest married every race going.

'I never knew a great deal about religion but came to love the Moslem faith. Ali was a good-living man, a very religious man. He had three big warehouses in Bute Street and converted one into a Mosque. One Christmas Day these filthy tramps turned up wanting dinner. He told me to give it to them. "But Ali," I protested, "these men are filthy." But this Moslem insisted that was what Christmas was all about – giving to people like that.

'When he died everyone was there from the highest to the lowest. From the Cairo Cafe to the Empire Pool the police lined the streets and saluted his coffin. So who couldn't be a good Moslem married to a man like that? I was most fortunate in loving a man like him.'[22]

. . .

Across the road from the Pentecostal Church is the Alice Street Mosque and it has to be said that the Moslems have had more than their fair share of troubles over the years. There was the time the local kids kept pinching their shoes and throwing them over the rooftops while they were at prayer. In the Fifties there was a huge row after they began slaughtering their sheep in the street since it was upsetting the children, some locals complained, not to mention the sheep. There was also another terrific row when the cemetery people could not – or would not – dig their graves facing Mecca.

They even got into a bit of a row amongst themselves which got so bad over the years that the Moslem community split into two. This row was complicated and tied up with Middle Eastern politics although it officially began when one group claimed that the old Peel Street Mosque did not face Mecca. They imported one of the biggest set of compasses in the world to resolve that dispute but they never did.

The Moslems in this Mosque gather here every day for zawya; chanting, prayer and the settling of disputes. The Imam sits in the corner intoning prayers from the Koran – Seven times a day do I praise your righteous judgements – and incense hangs above the thick carpets as the others stretch and submit themselves to the Inscrutable and Autocratic Majesty of Allah. One member faces Mecca and stands upright, the palms of his hands raised to the level of his ears. God is greater than all else. Arms lower and the right hand is placed over the left arm. Glory and praise to thee O God. Blessed is thy name and exalted is thy majesty. Body bends forward and hands are placed on knees. Glory to my Lord, the exalted. He kneels upright, lips muttering, eyes closed. Two flies are rising up and down the window above lots of other dead flies, sometimes buzzing fiercely before turning one another over and over. Quietly does it, the Moslems are praying

. . .

Sheikh Said Hassan is the Imam here who will tell visitors: 'I've been in Wales since 1941 but was born in South Shields in the Thirties. The Moslem community was not very well organised there and we worshipped in a converted pub. My father went away to sea during the last war and he lost his life so a religious leader from Cardiff took me there to learn the faith. My mother had been born in Wales and was a Christian who converted to Islam. Eventually I settled in Cardiff so I'm a bit of everything really – part Yemeni, part Welsh and part English.'

Yes, they all talk a lot about the old days down in the Bay. In fact, I've often observed that, the stickier the present becomes, the more they talk about the old days. The young – especially the Rastafarians – are taking up increasingly alienated stances which is bringing them

> into conflict with the law. It is no longer much fun representing the long arm of the law down here but it was not always so.
>
> Sometimes I've come across an old Moslem angel when I've been down here and he also likes to talk about the old days. He's not too active any more and I've never been sure if he was ever issued with so much as a sword but I've occasionally bumped into him on the corner of Alice Street where he might be puffing on a cheroot as he talked about this and that.
>
> 'The main problem now is that the community has become ossified and there is little ambition or leadership,' he once said in the strangest of Cardiff accents. 'The old radicals are mute and the young are merely angry with their ideas becoming progressively more criminalised by a corrupt media. There is very little hope for them now and, where there is little hope, there is also a breeding ground for violence.'
>
> He's just waiting around now, he will tell anyone who passes. But he never exactly spells out what it is that he is waiting for.
>
> But, disappointingly, he wasn't on his usual spot that night since I would have loved to have discussed that ominous shadow that I had been feeling everywhere. He would have almost certainly known what I was talking about since the same angel had been around far longer than me. There was talk that he had even known Mohammed. But it was only talk.[23]

The docks district, or Butetown, to give it its more current name, is also the setting for the work of John Williams (*b.*1961), a highly-accomplished novelist and journalist who made his name with a series of Cardiff-set underworld novels. However, unlike Tom Davies, Williams's stories concentrate less on the fate of the docks residents' immortal souls, and more in their material concerns – sex, drugs and money. And it is not so much the places of worship that provide the focus for his characters, but the pubs and clubs which are their main focal points. However, in his 1999 novel, *Five Pubs, Two Bars and a Nightclub*, the roles of drinking club and place of worship collide, to comic effect. The novel is told as a series of short-stories, the first of which, 'Black Caesar's' tells of how Butetown hardman Kenny Ibadulla, who has been inspired by a chance visit to a Nation of Islam centre in London, attempts to open a branch of the sect in Cardiff.

> So Kenny had come back a bit inspired, like. He'd done his best to explain it all to the boys, and they'd gone along with it. Which wasn't surprising given that most of them were shit scared of him, but still,

most of them knew about Minister Farrakhan already, so it wasn't too difficult, once they'd customised the approach for the local conditions.

He'd thought about changing his name, calling himself El-Haji Malik or something, but then Melanie had pointed out that he already had a Muslim name. Which was true enough, of course, and his grandad had actually been a Muslim, though his dad hadn't bothered with it, specially not after he met Kenny's mum, who was a fierce bloody Baptist and the one person Kenny was not looking forward to telling about his religious conversion.[24]

Kenny decides to build his Nation of Islam mosque on the unused ground floor of his club, Black Caesar's, bribing a corrupt planning officer to approve the change of use.[25] As the day for the official opening draws closer, Kenny finds the head office of the Nation of Islam taking an uncomfortably close interest in proceedings. He has been forced to persuade his friend Mikey Thompson, a womanising shoplifter, to act the part of the minister for the occasion, when a delegation of imposing black-suited members of the Nation of Islam arrive in Cardiff for the opening.

The people parted to let through what was by now quite an impressive Muslim cortege, what with Kenny and his boys and the American's crew. But before they could enter the mosque al-Mohammed stopped, surveyed the crowd and then stared at Kenny before saying, 'This is a mixed event.'

Kenny didn't know what he was on about for a moment. Thought maybe al-Mohammed meant it ought to be a men-only event. Then he realised it was racial mixing he meant.

'Yeah,' he said, 'reaching out, you knows what I mean?'

Al-Mohammed didn't look too impressed but he carried on into the front part of the mosque where Stephanie was looking beautiful behind the counter. She should cheer the old sourface up, thought Kenny, but no, not a bit of it. Al-Mohammed took one look at her crop-top and said, 'Inappropriate dress for a Muslim woman.'

Stephanie just looked at him like she was watching something really unusual on TV. Kenny stayed silent and opened the door into the mosque proper. And he wasn't sure, but he reckoned his face probably fell a mile when the first person he saw in the room, standing by the mimbar, was Mark, looking impeccable in his suit and bow tie, his hair cropped to the bone, but obviously as white as can be.

'Mr Ibadulla,' said the American after a brief, painful silence, 'have you read any of the Nation's literature?'

Kenny nodded.

> 'Have you read perhaps our program of belief?'
> 'Uh,' said Kenny, but before he could go on the American cut in.
> 'Well, I suggest you re-read it.'[26]

Kenny's venture ends in failure as the visitors turn out to be rival gangsters, from Birmingham, who have disguised themselves as followers of Minister Farrakhan in order to gain access to Kenny's club and help themselves to the contents of his safe. When he hears of the heist, Mikey Thompson has the last word.

> 'Shit,' said Mikey, when Kenny told him what had happened. 'Don't know about you, Ken, but I don't think we're cut out for the religious life.'[27]

This is the same Cardiff docks district as that of the earlier depictions by other authors. However, its immediacy is far removed from those previous renditions. Williams's portrayal of rounded and flawed characters, seemingly affected neither by exoticism or idealism, and serving no obvious ideological project, marks a turning point in the literary depiction of Muslims by non-Muslim authors in Wales.

At around the same time as Williams's novel was published, we find an early example of portrayal of Muslim characters by a Welsh Muslim author. Afshan Malik's play *Safar* (Urdu for 'journey') is the first piece of full-length literary work produced by a Welsh Muslim in this study. It was first staged in 1996, and was published in 1998 along with two other plays by young Welsh authors in a collection entitled *New Welsh Drama*. Telling the story of a young Pakistani Muslim woman called Ismaat, brought up in Cardiff, and experiencing tension between the Western way of life and the traditional values of her community, *Safar* finally provides Welsh literature with a depiction of Welsh Muslim life from the inside. In the following extracts, Ismaat, her Welsh friend Rhiannon, and a genie they have released from a champagne bottle are, perhaps inevitably, debating identity. The italicised notes are Malik's own:

> ISMAAT: I was different. Even when I try to fit in people keep seeing me as different. Complete strangers, meet me at a party, first thing they say, where are you from?
>
> JINH: What do you say?

ISMAAT: Splott (*note – an area of Cardiff*). But they don't believe me. They don't want to know where I'm from. They want to know WHERE I'm from. My genetic history. Where were my parents born? Where were my grand parents born? What the hell am I doing in Splott they think. When I came to this country I couldn't speak a word of English. That made me feel different...

RHIANNON: Yeh, and my first language is Welsh ... I was about five before I realised that everybody didn't speak it.

ISMAAT: I ended up speaking a mish-mash of the two ... We used to call it Gulabi Urdu, pink Urdu.

RHIANNON: I still get my friends laughing when I'm on the phone to my Mum and I'm talking in Welsh and they get the occasional English word like 'camcorder'.

ISMAAT: Or 'euro-tunnel.'

RHIANNON: 'Internet'...

ISMAAT: 'Sex'...

RHIANNON: Sex is Rhyw in Welsh.

ISMAAT AND JINH: Rhyw...

RHIANNON: No, rrriiww...

ISMAAT: Do you know, there are more than 50 different words or love in Urdu. I only know a few of them...

RHIANNON: Go on then...

ISMAAT: My Urdu's so rusty ... Ishq, Muhabbat, Pyar...

JINH: Ulfat...

ISMAAT: What? Oh yes, ulfat ... What about 'love' in Welsh?

RHIANNON: Cariad. What about sex in Urdu?

ISMAAT: You know, I don't know. The only rude words I know are the ones the white kids used to shout at the Asian kids. I still don't know what they meant.

JINH: Jans. Sex is Jans...

ISMAAT: I never knew that.

JINH: It means gender...

ISMAAT: English – Angrezi...

RHIANNON: Angrezi ... English – Sais

ISMAAT: White – Gora...

RHIANNON: White? Er ... (*Whispers*) Twll din pob Sais (*note – loosely translated as 'Bugger off English git'*).

JINH: It's time to start the journey. Ismaat, tell me what is in your heart?

ISMAAT: In my heart?

JINH: The question? The meaning you've been looking for?

ISMAAT: I don't know!

JINH: I think you do...

The jinh gestures to Rhiannon. Rhiannon sits Ismaat in front of her.

RHIANNON: Close your eyes Ismaat. Close your eyes and breathe slowly. In, out, in, out. Let yourself feel relaxed. Let go and let whatever comes come into your mind.

ISMAAT: I don't know who I am. Yes. That's it. Always the same feeling. Who am I ? Who am I ? Rhiannon knows she is Welsh. She is surrounded by her own history, her own sense of identity, her family. You know you are a Jinh. But I don't know who I am. I know it sounds crazy. But I don't know who I am. Not in here. Not in my heart.

JINH: So you don't think of yourself as Welsh?

ISMAAT: No.

JINH: Pakistani?

ISMAAT: No.

JINH: English?

ISMAAT: No!

JINH: British?

ISMAAT: Oh God, I don't know!

RHIANNON: What's the confusion about Ismaat?

ISMAAT: It's a long story.[28]

Of course, it should be noted that the instinct to define an individual in relation to a community of origin is not an interrogation which Welsh people reserve only for recent arrivals. In a country where communal and familial relationships have often traditionally ranked further up the hierarchy of values than other identifiers such as profession or social class, origin is a major default mode of establishing relationships among Welsh people themselves. The questioning to which Ismaat is subjected is not in itself a sign of exclusion; it is her difficulty in providing an answer to satisfy the questioner's familiar categories that causes the discomfort. There is unease about identity within the Muslim community itself, as shown in the following scene where, Ismaat, who wants to become part of the punk-rock subculture like her white friends, is arguing with her mother Zeenat and father, Jamil:

ZEENAT: Hai Allah! What on earth have you done to your beautiful hair? What are those disgusting shameless clothes? Hai Allah! Tell me I am dreaming. Tell me I am in hell!

ISMAAT: Oh God Mum.

ZEENAT: Don't oh God mum me young lady. I am your Ammi.

ISMAAT: Oh Allah Ammi then.

JAMIL: Beti, these clothes are very unsuitable. Your hair is like a giant Tarantula. (*Laughs.*) I'm sorry darling, but you look ridiculous. (*Laughs again.*)

ISMAAT: I am not. This is fashion Dad. You're just too old to appreciate it.

ZEENAT: How will I show my face to Allah? My own daughter. Dancing, like Shaitan, with a white boy.

ISMAAT: So that's what this is really about. You are upset because I make friends with a white boy?

ZEENAT: In our people, shareef girls do not have boyfriends. And here you are, in your own home, dressed like that, with a (*With disgust in her voice*) a white man. So pale, so disgusting. Do you know, they don't even wash properly after going to the toilet? They use paper. Dirty dirty people.

ISMAAT: Mother, Ammi, there is nothing wrong with white skin, or toilet paper for that.

ZEENAT: Hai Allah (*Slaps her chest*). How will I face my family now? What will people say?

ISMAAT: You never understand, neither of you. You don't even try. Who gives a shit what other people say?

JAMIL: Calm down you two. Shouting at each other is not the answer.

ZEENAT: And you (*She points at Jamil*), it's all your fault. 'What kind of a father are you?

JAMIL: Now Ismaat, we are reasonable parents. We let you wear skirts and go out. We even said you could marry whoever you want, as long as he's a Muslim Punjabi of between 20 and 30 with a good education, preferably a doctor or an engineer, with a good family and who doesn't drink alcohol. Now, isn't that really reasonable? But this, this is going too far. Dancing with a boy in your own living room.

ISMAAT: All my friends go out and party and drink and have boyfriends. And I will if I want to.

ZEENAT: Hai Allah (*Slaps her chest*). We have raised the devil's child. She's ruined my life.[29]

Ismaat is one of the Welsh Muslim characters who suddenly become visible in the country's literature in the last years of the twentieth century. In 1998, Lewis Davies (*b.*1967), the founder of Parthian Books, published a prose piece, 'You Alright?' in which the speaker tells of his experience as the carer of a young disabled Cardiff Pakistani Muslim man called Sajid. Despite the cultural differences, the speaker and Sajid become good friends: 'His greetings of "You alright?" or "Hello, my friend" were full of smiles. Sajid always assumed you were his friend.'[30] The essay was published in Davies's 2003 collection, *as i was a boy fishing*. In the following extracts, the author is attending Sajid's funeral, after the latter's death from a hospital infection:

> On the morning of the funeral we meet in a cafe on Crwys Road. Six or seven of us. Old friends from Social Services. The mosque is a converted warehouse at the end of a scruffy street I had never noticed before. There is a respectable turn out for a big burgeoning family. Sajid's father has recently become successful with a mini-cab service. He is an employer now. Sajid's mother leads a prayer group. She is a philosopher of sorts and used to look at me sadly early on Sunday mornings when I arrived, still drunk from the night before, to get her eldest son out of bed. We have talked about God and religion. We both agree that Jesus was a man like Mohammed. Allah is another question. She thinks my body will burn in hell but likes me anyway.
>
> She calls the women in our odd group of Christians and Atheists into a room of their own. The men are segregated into a large hall that reminds me of a gym. It is full but apart from Sajid's brothers, his father and grandfather, I only recognise the people I have come with. The Imam recites a litany. I look at the community, holding each other together in a foreign culture. People on the edge of things, the divide between Pakistan, Manchester and Cardiff. Each generation pushing itself away from the last.[31]
>
> . . .
>
> We follow the funeral cars up to the cemetery at Ely. The women stay at the mosque. I can't get the translated words of the Imam out of my head. He praised Sajid's family, the strength they had shown in the long years since his first illness. I can see the eyes of the doctors at the hospital. Thinking that perhaps death would be the best way. I can't get this out of my head. I can't face the thought that I must ask myself. Did I agree with them? Was this the best way for my friend? To die scared and weak?

> The Muslim plot is on the far side of the municipal cemetery, beyond the last line of conifers. There is a line of new graves for the winter. The eldest of the first generation are beginning to die here now. The digging starts. I speak to his father for the first time since his death. I don't have much to say. He returns some of my words. Yes, he was a fine boy. I'm surprised to see his tears beyond his glasses.
>
> I leave before they can fill the grave.[32]

Also from 1998 comes the Cardiff author Othniel Smith's play *Giant Steps*, produced by the Made in Wales company and published in the 2001 collection *New Welsh Drama II*. Three characters, a public-school-educated West African called Oliver, a Welsh-born Asian called Gita, and a black Northerner called Alan, find themselves thrown together in a girls' school, which, to Alan's disappointment, is currently unoccupied:

> ALAN: Well, you never know. There might be some spare ones ligging about. You know, Mummy and Daddy too busy entertaining Lord and Lady Fartington-Smythe to have them cluttering up the house. Or maybe the odd Arab princess, who's missed her plane. Hey, do you suppose they wear suspender-belts, under those great big chador things? That's what I like about the veil. You can use your imagination. I mean, don't get me wrong, I'm all for the short skirt, the tight sweater, the figure-hugging denim trouser. But ... it's like ... the difference between listening to a pop song on the radio, and sitting and watching the video. Sometimes ... sometimes, it's just more fun to use your imagination, do you know what I mean? Rambling, aren't I? Sorry. My mind starts wandering when I think about girls.
>
> OLIVER: Yes. So does mine.
>
> ALAN: Have you got a girlfriend? I have. Well, I did. Sort of. Well, we talked a lot, anyway. I used to go in her Dad's shop. Naima, that was her name. I mean, we never actually went out or anything. We might have, though. Eventually. When she was old enough. I was even looking into converting to Islam. Just on the off-chance. But her Dad sent her off to Pakistan to get married to some geriatric goat-herder on the fucking North-West Frontier. Really pissed me off, that did. Still. Plenty more fish in the sea.[33]

The increased visibility of Islam in Cardiff, and the sense that the religion was beginning to occupy at least some of the space abandoned by Christianity, has attracted the attention of several poets. There is an example in the poem entitled 'Califfornia' in the 1995 collection *Dan Ddylanwad* ('Under the Influence') by the Welsh-language author Iwan Llwyd (1957-2010). The poem's title refers to the idea of industrial Cardiff and south Wales having attracted migrants in the same way as gold-rush California:

> ... the San Francisco of the south, where the colours melted
> from Wales, Ireland, China and the islands of the Caribbean
> in the multi-coloured cauldron of Tiger Bay.[34]

The poem concludes by showing that the area has changed since its industrial heyday, but that there is continuity with the past and hope for the future, and that Islam is occupying Christianity's vacant spaces.

> another century in the journey of Cardiff and the black valleys,
> and the cauldron still simmering,
> still melting the minerals in a multi-coloured stream,
> to pour the languages into the furnace of the present:
> where once were empty boxes casting a gloomy shade,
> today the temples of Muhammad keep the flame of faith.[35]

Another poem from a decade later, by one of the most important and influential Welsh writers of his generation, Peter Finch, (*b.*1947), also shows the way in which Islam is rivalling Christianity in twenty-first-century Cardiff. Finch, an internationally-known poet, critic, author and literary entrepreneur, is a lifelong Cardiff resident and has obsessively chronicled the changing currents of life in the Welsh capital, of which the growth in Islam is one of the latest. The poem, 'Entry of Christ Into Cardiff 2005', is written as an elided catalogue of juxtapositions, a style Finch often uses to powerful effect:

> Anointed Christos Branch of Myrhh Jesse Jesu
> Queen Street Elias Jeremias Ensign Immanuel Emmanuel
> Jesus Multifloral Carfit Melchizedek Messiah
> ObeWan Nazarene Kenobi Potentate Passover Owl
> Rabboni Tortilla Bhoona Jasu Rose of Sharon Scepter
> Isa Ibn Maryam al-Salaam Christ Shabazz Bandana
> Yasu 'Isa bin Maryam Muslim Spire Eesa Esau Yeheshua
> Rough Joshua Rahman Yoghurt Iïsous Abd of Allah

Jesus Cassanova Bute Street Sorrow Bethlehem
Llanrumney Passover Kalimatimmin Kalimaatullaah
Mary the Virgin Karate Do Splott Saviour Jesucristo come back
Kalimat'Allah (peace be upon him) Adamsdown Rasulullah
Jesu Prajapati Jehovah Lifeboat appeal Saturdays
Jesus latterday Cardiff Post Vishnu Ya Ruhullah
Enzikiriza Yaba'ddugavu Eye Nono Black Messiah
Saviour Turban Guru Gobind Singh Chapate handwrench
Blood of Ely glass and Potentate Refuge God Iesu
Diolchwch i Dduw y nefoedd Taff will baptise too late now
Bread of Heaven William Williams Cefn-y-Coed Llandovery
St Johns St Marys St Womanby fill slowly with beer[36]

A later piece, 'Fun Day', is also prompted by the growing visibility of Islamic culture in Wales, and, like the first poem, shows an interest in nomenclature as one of the methods which embody changing perceptions of identity. Again, a technique of juxtaposition is used, with the Western vocabulary of leisure set alongside images suggestive of perceived Muslim attitudes towards abstinence, modesty and gender.

The Caliphate is called off called
Britain's biggest theme park didn't work

The musselmen refusing non-musselmen they do that
the musselmen the musselmen ride without gambling
and the musselwomen they they

they enter the space time continuum they don't do this together
stipulation their atoms must pass through each other
without touching don't nudge don't touch don't look

spokesperson for the park said it had been cover up
no music halal al alcohol hij ab ab hijab

stalls selling musselmen knick knackery no pics

company had to cancel no turn out
no fun

why are you using this old-fashioned word?
it's safe

Persian pronunciation Musulman moslem based

on Urdu old fashioned transliteration today generally avoided
(why) doesn't say

can't manage this (ends)[37]

The piece echoes a long tradition of scepticism on the part of some Welsh poets towards religious prohibitions on enjoyment. Nonconformist Christianity had become a hegemony in Wales by the end of the nineteenth century, and over time there was no shortage of poets ready to satirise its joyless list of proscribed pleasures. The work of Idris Davies (1905-53), mentioned earlier in this chapter, is an example: his 'Capel Calvin' is also a list poem, and the activities that it shows fundamentalist Christianity as prohibiting are strikingly similar to those that Finch implies are forbidden by fundamentalist Islam:

There's holy holy people
They are in capel bach –
They don't like surpliced choirs,
They don't like Sospan Fach.[38]

They don't like Sunday concerts,
Or women playing ball,
They don't like Williams Parry[39] much
Or Shakespeare at all.

They don't like beer or bishops,
Or pictures without texts,
They don't like any other
Of the nonconformist sects.

And when they go to Heaven
They won't like that too well,
For the music will be sweeter
Than the music played in Hell.[40]

In ventilating the potential tensions relating to aspects of increasing Islamic influence in Welsh life, Finch is reflecting in the literary field a discourse that is taking place in public life generally as cultural practitioners, and the people of Wales and the West as a whole, work out their responses to the growth of a religion which some see not just to be replacing Christianity in terms of a positive expression of faith, but also, in some ways, and in some of its expressions, potentially as a source of censorious negativity.

Those tensions are present in the background of some of the more recent Welsh literary depictions of Muslims. The events of 9/11 and its aftermath are, inevitably, reflected in subsequent depictions of Muslims in Wales in the twenty-first century, although the focus is generally not on any currents of radicalisation or extremism within the Muslim community in Wales, but rather on the varied responses of the majority non-Muslim community to the perceived threat. A 2006 play, *Orange*, by the Pontypridd author Alan Harris, presents a scenario, inspired, according to the author's foreword,[41] by the abduction and murder of the aid worker Margaret Hassan in Iraq in 2004. In *Orange*, two violent and disaffected young white men, Viv and Chippie, abduct a peaceful Muslim called Saleem and keep him prisoner, in revenge for hostage-taking of Westerners by Islamic extremists. The two captors are depicted as almost entirely contemptible, Saleem as admirable. In the following scene, the less vicious of the captors, Viv, has been left alone with his prisoner, and, unexpectedly, gives him a copy of the *Qur'an*

> VIV: It's okay. You can take the blindfold off.
>
> SALEEM: There is no need. No need.
>
> (*Saleem caresses the book.*)
>
> SALEEM: Allahu Akbar.
>
> (*Saleem smells the book.*)
>
> . . .
>
> SALEEM: Thank you, Viv. Thank you. You'll never know what this means to me.
>
> VIV: It's only a book.
>
> (*Saleem manages a half smile.*)
>
> SALEEM: No, Viv. This is my world.[42]

Also from 2006, and dealing explicitly with the events of 9/11, is *Eleven,* a remarkable and compelling epistolary novel by David Llewellyn (*b.*1978). The novel, set on that eventful day, is told by means of a series of e-mails between a bored Welsh office worker, Martin Davies, and his various correspondents, one of whom is

Safina Aziz, a Pakistani woman who is depicted as being culturally Muslim, but as sharing, largely, the same superficial Western hedonism which is the unquestioned environment, but, ultimately, the meaningless prison, of all the characters. In between discussing hangovers, sex and arrangements for recreational drug-taking with his friends, Martin is conducting a tentative e-mail romance with Saffy, even though she is planning to leave for an arranged marriage in Pakistan. The following extracts give a flavour of the work:

> FROM: Lloyd Thomas
> (mailto: lloydt@callotech.co.uk)
> TO: martin.davies@quantumfinance.co.uk
> SENT: 09:03, Tuesday September 11, 2001
> SUBJECT: What we need is cameras
>
> I've told you before, you need to get surveillance on these laydeez, Mr Davies. Otherwise you are going to end up single for the rest of your days. Are you sat near that paki girl today?
>
> FROM: Martin Davies
> (mailto: martin.davies@quantumfinance.co.uk)
> TO: lloydt@callotech.co.uk
> SENT: 09:05, Tuesday September 11, 2001
> SUBJECT: Political Correctness?
>
> If you mean Saffy, no I'm not sat near her. She's training on another bank of desks today. And anyway, what's it got to do with you, my politically insensitive friend?
>
> . . .
>
> FROM: Safina Aziz
> TO: Martin Davies
> SENT: 09:47, Tuesday September 11, 2001
> SUBJECT: RE: We gotta get out of this place if it's the last thing we ever do
> I know. They're all w*nkers. I just had some guy on the phone trying to tell me that we over-charged him, and we didn't over-charge him. He's just being a dick. Never mind. Three more weeks of this bull$hit and I'm on holiday.

FROM: Martin Davies
TO: Safina Aziz
SENT: 09:47, Tuesday September 11, 2001
SUBJECT: RE: RE: We gotta get out of this place if it's the last thing we ever do

Holiday?

FROM: Safina Aziz
TO: Martin Davies
SENT: 09:48, Tuesday September 11, 2001
SUBJECT: RE: RE: RE: We gotta get out of this place if it's the last thing we ever do

Honeymoon, stupid. Four weeks in Pakistan with my mad aunties. You should meet them – they are SO funny. My one aunty drives this Citroen 2CV, only she can't drive at all. She's had more crashes than you've had hot dinners. My other aunty can't speak much English, so if someone's big she just calls them fat. It's SO embarrassing. You should SO meet them.

FROM: Martin Davies
TO: Safina Aziz
SENT: 09:49, Tuesday September 11, 2001
SUBJECT: RE: RE: RE: RE: We gotta get out of this place if it's the last thing we ever do

And they are SO on the other side of the planet, so I'm not going to.[45]

. . .

FROM: Safina Aziz
TO: Martin Davies
SENT: 10:37, Tuesday September 11, 2001
SUBJECT. RE: RE: RE: RE: RE: We gotta get out of this place if it's the last thing we ever do

It's not like I'm moving there for good. It's just a honeymoon.

FROM: Martin Davies
TO: Safina Aziz
SENT: 10:38, Tuesday September 11, 2001
SUBJECT. RE: RE: RE: RE: RE: RE: We gotta get out of this place,

if it's the last thing we ever do

What?

FROM: Safina Aziz
TO: Martin Davies
SENT: 10:38, Tuesday September 11, 2001
SUBJECT: RE: RE: RE: RE: RE: RE: RE: We gotta get out of this place, if it's the last thing we ever do

You sounded a bit angry, that's all. I'm only going there for a couple of weeks. Will you miss me?

FROM: martin.davies@quantumfinance.co.uk
TO:
SENT: 10:40, Tuesday September 11, 2001
SUBJECT:

You don't want to marry him. We've had this conversation. He might be a decent man and all the rest of it, but is it really what you

SAVED IN 'DRAFTS'[46]

. . .

FROM: Safina Aziz
TO: Martin Davies
SENT: 11:22, Tuesday September 11, 2001
SUBJECT: Wedding

I've given this some thought, and I've decided to ask you:
Do you want to come to my wedding? I don't mind if you say no, because it's not going to be everyone's kind of thing – that's why I haven't asked anyone from work. I mean, Saida from hotline is going, but only because she's my Mum's best friend's sister. But I didn't know whether you might want to come? No booze, I'm afraid, and there won't be a karaoke!!![47]

. . .

FROM: Safina Aziz
TO: Martin Davies
SENT: 11:54, Tuesday September 11, 2001
SUBJECT: Wedding

Did you get my email about the wedding? You've gone quiet.[48]

. . .

FROM: Safina Aziz
TO: Martin Davies
SENT: 12:07, Tuesday September 11, 2001
SUBJECT: Wedding

You don't have to come to the mosque, you can just come to the party if you like. Like I said, no booze, but some of my cousins drink, so maybe one of them will sneak a few cans in![49]

. . .

FROM: Martin Davies
TO: Safina Aziz
SENT: 13:56, Tuesday September 11, 2001
SUBJECT: Wedding

I'm thinking about it. Sorry, I'll make up my mind, honest.[50]

. . .

FROM: Safina Aziz
TO: Martin Davies
SENT: 14:38, Tuesday September 11, 2001
SUBJECT: Wedding

Have you given it any more thought? I'd love you to be there. It'll be nice not to have to speak Urdu all day, because my Urdu is rubbish. I don't know what I'm going to be like on honeymoon. I'll be asking for everything in English!![51]

. . .

FROM: Lloyd Thomas
(mailto: lloydt@callotech.co.uk)
TO: martin.davies@quantumfinance.co.uk
SENT: 15:09, Tuesday September 11, 2001
SUBJECT: Bl**dy Palestinians

According to Abu Dhabi Television there has been an anonymous call claiming responsibility for the terrorist attacks on behalf of the Democratic Front For The Liberation Of Palestine. Not very Democratic, in my book. Bl**dy typical, isn't it? We had right wing nutters, North Koreans, Iranians, the Chinese, the Russians
Didn't think of the f**king Palestinians, did we? Always with a new trick up their sleeves. Well, all bets are off.

FROM: Safina Aziz
TO: Martin Davies
SENT: 15:11, Tuesday September 11, 2001
SUBJECT: Wedding

I'll take you not saying anything as a 'no thanks' then.

FROM: martin.davies@quantumfinance.co.uk
TO:
SAVED: 15:12, Tuesday September 11, 2001
SUBJECT: RE: Wedding

It's not a 'no thanks' like you think it is. I don't know what's happening to me today.
I do know what's happening to me today.
I don't know what's going to happen to me today.
I'm sorry

SAVED IN 'DRAFTS'[52]

Although *Eleven*'s setting on the day of the Twin Towers attacks could hardly be more fraught with intercultural tension, it depicts, in its Welsh office setting, a Muslim society moving from a religious world-view to a secular one, overlapping with a post-religious Western society which has moved through secularism into something close to nihilism.

There is further evidence of convergence between Muslim and non-Muslim in the work of another young Welsh author, Catrin Dafydd. Her 2007 comic novel, *Random Deaths and Custard*, depicts a range of characters in a Valleys custard factory, with the action described in dialect from the perspective of an angst-ridden 18-year-old narrator. In the following passage, she is observing people in the works canteen, one of them a Muslim and the other a Christian fundamentalist:

> The other one sittin' there was Ahmed. He's nice enough, got brilliant English. Uses big words I've never heard of. When I hear 'im say a big word in the canteen or on lunch I try and keep it safe in my 'ead for when I get back to my desk. Sometimes I remember, sometimes I don't. Sometimes I've remembered it wrong and it's not in the dictionary how I remembered it. He's got a turban on his 'ead. I think it's really beautiful actually, 'though I'd never say that. I bet it gets bloody hot in the summer, mind. I thought it was quite funny

> how Ahmed and Malcometh-the-Day were sittin' side-by-side 'avin' a chat. There was a lesson for all the world there, I think. In a custard factory in the Rhondda.[53]

This is another example of the increasingly common use of incidental Muslim characters in Welsh fiction, and as such is evidence of the increasing representation of the Muslim community in the output of Welsh artists. It is worth noting, however, that although Dafydd's novel is a much less ambitious work than *Eleven*, and although its sketch of Ahmed is hardly intended to carry a great weight of significance, it is nonetheless the case that familiar Muslim identifiers – the character's turban, educational aspiration and interest in religion – are still routinely referenced and are allowed to define the character, as is an ironic mention of the desirability of religious tolerance.

Further meeting-points between Welsh and Muslim culture are represented in the playwright and prose author Dahlian Kirby's short story 'Aysha's Yard-Garden', collected in the 2008 anthology of writing by and about refugees and asylum seekers in Wales, *Fragments from the Dark: Women writing home and self in Wales*, edited by Jeni Williams and Latéfa Guémar. The story depicts a young Muslim girl living with her asylum-seeking family, in Cardiff and shows her preparing a surprise gift for her mother, with the help of her friends in a makeshift but supportive group of mainly-Muslim displaced people:

> Into the garden came Amina, Layla, Farima and Fatima's cousin whose name she never could remember. Shyly, behind Fatima's cousin, stood the new girl who wasn't a Muslim. She was from somewhere else, where skin was blacker and you didn't have to be a Muslim but you might be. New Girl didn't eat pork but did go and sing songs in the church where the nice lady who gave you things was. But New Girl was allowed in the gang, because really she was the same.
>
> New Girl also didn't have a dad. New Girl was also an asylum seeker. New Girl also had ragged clothes and secret stories about bad people in the night.[54]
>
> . . .
>
> As the last girls arrived with the last flowers, the back door of Ayshda's house opened and out spilled her mother, brothers and Auntie. They were followed by Mrs Jama and her baby, her husband

> and her sons. One son passed a wooden chair out to the other. The second son helped Mr Jama in to the chair. Mr Jama had been hurt by bad people in a country called Somalia in the night. Out of Mrs Jama's door came the gypsies from upstairs, followed by Yusuf and Ali from the top floor. The grownups all stood close to the door, surrounding Mr Jama in the wooden chair, as if he was a king and they his courtiers.
>
> In from the bottom of the yard, through the open gateway, came mothers of the gang, each with a bowl or plate of food. Aysha's mother hurried towards her daughter and couldn't help but exclaim: 'My daughter, what have we here?' Aysha smiled shyly and took her mother's hands. 'This is a flower festival just for you. These are our friends. This is our Garden. Croeso.'
>
> Aysha's mother looked across the filthy yard at the yellow ragged path. She looked at the wall that was crumbling, at the rusty trolley, at the sagging roof of the next house and the next house and the next. For a few moments there were no noises of traffic, this wasn't Cardiff. For a while the smell was of perfume. Transported from the decaying yard, Aysha's mother looked at the girls still placing flowers around her. And now she saw that each small girl was in blue, each girl wore a scarf. Each big sister was dressed as they would be back home. For now, Aysha's mother was safe and things were good.[55]

Given the intense ongoing debates about issues such as immigration and Islamic fundamentalism, there will inevitably be difficulty in attaining a state of affairs in which Muslim characters can routinely be portrayed without gestures to either traditional expectations or contemporary tensions. However, as has been seen in the history of the depiction in creative works of other minority groups, such as black and disabled people, the foregrounding of difference is a familiar, and probably necessary, stage in the process through which the presence of the other can gradually be normalised in literature. In their portrayal of rounded and sometimes flawed Muslim characters, works such as those of Lewis Davies, Afshan Malik, John Williams, David Llewellyn and Dahlian Kirby, examined above, demonstrate a maturing stage in the incorporation of Muslim life into the literature of Wales. They give reason to believe that a process is underway by which future portrayals will become gradually more natural, with less need for the visible triangulation of the characters' identity. The process, is, however, likely to be only a gradual one, as the negotiation of identities in Wales even in relation to the primary Welsh-English axis is still very much a work in progress, and one which it seems probable will attract the conscious attention of many authors for the foreseeable future. In a country where the politics of identity seem set to continue to be a significant factor in intellectual and artistic life, Muslims will inevitably participate in the conscious positioning within a contested cultural context that seems an inescapable condition of life in this corner of the world. This self-consciousness need not, however, be regarded as evidence of continued marginalisation. To be involved in the perpetual Welsh experience of examining, negotiating and articulating the quality of one's communal sense of attachment, or lack of it, is actually to share the majority experience in Wales, and represents the most intimate form of inclusion. Debating the degree of their belonging is how Welsh people belong.

In reviewing the history of literary portrayals of Muslims in Wales, it is apparent that, while prejudice by Welsh characters is indeed portrayed, the kind of unapologetic authorial condemnation sometimes seen in Welsh depictions of Muslims outside Wales, and detailed in earlier chapters, is largely absent. It should, of course, be noted that nearly all the extracts here are from after the Second World War, and, as such, are the product of a period where such prejudice had been widely discredited and where readiness to criticise other cultures was consequently muted. What emerges is a picture of a society applying its familiar categories of definition, whether religious, political or communal, to the Muslim other, and moving gradually through processes of exoticising, idealising, problematising and normalising.

This chapter began with the question which had seemed implicit in much Welsh curiosity about Muslims in Wales, namely: in relation to Muslims, what kind of people do the Welsh find themselves to be? The answer, as has been seen, cannot satisfy expectations for either clear reassurance or simple condemnation. Extending that question to the material covered by this entire book, we find little justification for any Welsh myth of peculiar benevolence: that consoling belief, advanced by those who, keen to stress Welsh distinctiveness, have propagated a view of the Welsh as a people singularly given to creativity, spirituality, pacifism, compassion, community and a cross-cultural appreciation driven by their own experience of marginalisation – in all of which qualities they are implied to have a moral ascendancy over the English. Despite many historians having long argued for a fuller picture, for instance, by detailing troubling incidences of anti-semitism and race riots in early twentieth-century Wales,[56] the myth persists. Most recently, it has fed a wide range of self-congratulatory post-9/11 responses to the belief that Wales is home to Britain's oldest mosque, registered in 1860, and apparently giving clear evidence of the Welsh gift for tolerance and harmony. In fact, as shown in research by Sophie Gilliat-Ray, head of Cardiff University's Centre for the Study of Islam in the U.K, this is a myth: the mosque concerned was not registered until 1991. The U.K.'s oldest mosques are in England.

The material examined in this book seems to show that Wales and England are in many respects much more alike than they are different, and to put it bluntly, even if one might have preferred the Welsh to have shown some peculiar virtue in their cross-cultural dealings, honesty demands that we acknowledge that, in the case of their literary portrayal of Islam, by and large, they have not. In fact, this study of literary records of Welsh contact with adherents of one of the world's great faiths over nearly a thousand years has found little evidence that the Welsh have shown more understanding, appreciation, tolerance or generosity towards Muslims than one would have expected from any other contemporary Briton. In the extracts from literature gathered here, Welsh people, at least as represented by their writers, are shown sharing, for good or ill, the attitudes of their island and their age: the same hostility, the same admiration; the same romanticism, the same prejudice; the same knowledge, and the same ignorance; the same human sympathy and the same human failings. This is not, therefore, a chronicle of Welsh exceptionalism, but of Welsh participation.

Those solicitous of a distinctive Welsh identity need not, however, be discouraged. The people who composed the material collected here were mostly products of Wales, most of them writing in Welsh, and most of them, whether in English or Welsh, writing for audiences in Wales. That the attitudes they expressed were largely similar to those of English, or indeed European, contemporaries makes them no less Welsh. A robust and inclusive sense of identity should be strong enough to admit what one has in common with other nations as well as stressing where one differs. It can surely only add to the fullness of one's understanding of national identity to discover that the Welsh are, and have always been, more than victims; more than tenacious resisters, more than longsuffering proponents of tolerance. They have been more culpable, more pragmatic and more prejudiced than idealism might have wished, but also more enterprising, more confident and more capable than narratives of victimhood might have allowed. Such an understanding is not reductive of identity, but expansive of it.

In conclusion, one question remains: that of the literary voice of Muslims in Wales themselves. As has been shown above, creative literature about Islam in Wales, has, almost without exception, been written by non-Muslims. Even if those portrayals move slowly to become more whole, more accurate, less exoticised and less weighted with political intent, they are still portraits of otherness. Rarely in this relationship have Welsh Muslims spoken for themselves.

The contrast with the Jewish community in Wales is marked. The Welsh Jewish community was never more than a few thousand strong, and has steadily declined numerically from its peak of 6,000 just before the First World War, until it numbers only around a thousand today,[57] but it has produced major cultural figures, often within a generation or two of immigration. They include prominent Welsh-born writers such as Lily Tobias (1887-1984), Bernice Rubens (1928-2004), and Dannie Abse (*b.*1923), the latter a one-man genre of Welsh-Jewish writing. The community has also experienced notable contributions from adopted Welsh Jewish writers such as Judith Maro (*b.*1927), whose work was examined earlier, and the painter Joseph Herman (1911-2000). Although the Welsh Muslim community, established for well over a century, now numbers well over 60,000 people, ten times the size of the Jewish population at its height nearly a century ago, and although it is still growing, it has not yet made the same literary impact. Whatever economic, educational, religious or historical factors may have contributed to this disparity in self-representation, the fact must be acknowledged that the relationship between Wales and Islam as reflected in the literatures of Wales has largely been a one-sided one.

There are, however, signs that this may change. Chapter 9 looked at the important political and cultural analysis of the

Welsh convert to Islam, Merryl Wyn Davies, and this chapter has examined the play *Safar* by Afshan Malik, as an early example of Welsh Muslim creative self-representation. Other voices are present too, and if they have not yet had a wider impact, they are evidence of literary activity among the Muslim communities of Wales which must, in due course, find a voice which will mediate Muslim identity to the wider society, and in its own words.

One Welsh Muslim never lost for words is Ali Yassine. Brought up in Cardiff, of Egyptian and Somali heritage, and a fluent learner of Welsh, he is well-known as a broadcaster and as the tannoy announcer at Cardiff City football games and Welsh international matches. In his brief 2010 autobiography, *Llais yr Adar Gleision* ('Voice of the Bluebirds'), he gives an account of when he got into trouble when, over the tannoy, he parodied the Lord's Prayer, substituting the name of Cardiff's then-chairman, the Lebanese businessman Sam Hammam, for that of God. He then led the crowd in a performance of Cardiff City fans' trade-mark gesture 'The Ayatollah', in which supporters repeatedly slap their own heads – a gesture imitating the behaviour of mourners in Iran at the funeral of Ayatollah Khomeni in 1989, an event which was widely-televised at the time.[58] Yassine reports that the club later received a complaint from a vicar, present at the game, who had been offended by the Lord's Prayer parody, and that he subsequently had to apologise, over the tannoy, to the Church, although he went on ironically include 'Muslims, Sikhs, Hindus, Tree Huggers' in his apology. While the incident recounted in Yassine's anecdote might not be quite a model of intercultural tact, it is certainly an example of an increasing organic and unofficial social integration.

As further examples of the kind of literary production taking place among Welsh Muslims, we might consider the work of Bazm e Adab, a long-established Urdu-language poetry society in Cardiff, with a mainly-Muslim membership, but one which conducts regular joint readings with Welsh-language authors under the auspices of the Academi literature promotion agency. A recent poem, 'British Muslim', by Javed Javed, a Cardiff businessman who is a member of the society, is an exhortation to the author's fellow-believers to appreciate and to be loyal to Britain. The following are extracts from Javed Javed's own translation of the Urdu original:

> Muslim of Britain, Britain is home,
> A flower filled garden, dearer than the heart and the soul.

He goes on to praise British society, and says of the non-Muslim majority:

> So what? If they don't recite Kalimah, aren't they His human beings?
> God has given freedom of choice, says the Quraan,
> Since the beginning God is unique and has no partner,
> Every one sings His praise in different tunes.

The poem was featured on the blog of the BBC Wales political correspondent Vaughan Roderick, who described it as 'a far fairer reflection of the political attitudes of British Muslims than some newspaper headlines'.[59]

Another group of Welsh Muslims who are no strangers to newspaper headlines are those who belong to the refugee and asylum-seeker community. Although these authors are more recently-arrived and less well-established than the poets represented by Bazm e Adab or by older Muslim communities in Wales, many have been given ready access to the world of Welsh literature due to a number of advocacy projects which use writing by refugees and asylum-seekers as a means of raising awareness of their presence in society. The Hafan Books project, based in Swansea, has been catalytic in producing a series of anthologies of work by and about displaced people in Wales. The extracts which follow are from some of those collections. The first poem, given in its entirety, is from Nazand Begikhani (*b.*1964), born in Iraqi Kurdistan and exiled since 1987. It is collected in the 2008 anthology *Fragments from the Dark: Women writing home and self in Wales*, mentioned above:

At a Happiness Symposium in Wales

> A psychologist said
> Graveyards may help you feel happier,
> visit a graveyard when you are depressed
>
> There is a thin line between life and death, my friend,
> and I am a graveyard

I am happy to be alive, my friend
After Halabja and Anfal,[60]
I am happy to become the voice
of a land
that contains the mass graves of our brothers.

There is a thin line between life and death, my friend.
There is a thin line between life and death.[61]

Many of the poems and prose items in the anthologies deal exclusively with the countries left behind, and are products of a condition which the anthology editors describe in their preface, in a quotation from the Egyptian writer André Aciman, as 'compulsory retrospection'.[62] Although many of those poems are strong and sometimes very moving works, emanating as they often do from experiences more intense and traumatic than those that come the way of most Welsh writers, they do not specifically address Muslim experience in Wales, and are therefore outside the scope of this study. A few, such as 'Argue with a Foreigner' by Anahita Alikhani, do, however, depict life in Wales itself. Alikhani was detained and mistreated by the regime in Iran for working with foreign television crews covering student demonstrations; she escaped to the UK in 2001, settling in south Wales. Her poem highlights some of the problems she experienced in terms of linguistic and cultural adjustment, as the extracts below show:

A: Look at this kitchen! Dog is playing, Cat is dancing!!
B: What you mean, there's no cat or dog in here.
A: I know, but if there was it didn't make any different.
B: Oh you mean it's untidy. It's 'like a war zone', that's what we say.
A: When we say something is like a war zone, we mean it actually is a war zone ... It is difficult for me to think like you; still I'm translating from my language.
B: You are living in Britain and you have to learn to talk like us!
A: You are like a grim Owl, nagging all the time.
. . .

B: I'm bored here. Why don't you ever invite me out anywhere?
A: Because women shouldn't do that.
B: Why not?
A: We don't.
B: You're living in Wales – think like us. Of course they do.

A: You mean I should think like a British?
B: Absolutely.
A: You really want me to act like one?
B: Definitely yes.[63]

In that poem, the speaker goes on to address her interrogator with a common expletive, simultaneously implicitly mocking the vulgarity of some British speech and also asserting her right to respect and to her own voice.

Muslims in Wales are finding their voice. The few examples here are indications of an embryonic Welsh Muslim writing presence which will become in time an identifiable strand within the wider existing literatures of Wales. Over nearly a thousand years, the literary relationship of Wales and Islam has been largely a monologue. However, in those those last few examples, we can identify, I believe, the beginnings of the Muslim literature of Wales. This study ends with that literature's beginnings, and with the start of the next stage of the relationship between Wales and Islam in Welsh writing, a relationship that will now, *Insha'Allah*, be increasingly a dialogue of equals.

Notes

1. Dedicated to St Patrick who is reported to have been shipwrecked there.
2. Lynn Pearson, *Tile Gazetteer: A Guide to British Tile and Architectural Ceramics Locations* (Shepton Beauchamp, 2005).
3. Sophie Gilliat-Ray, '"The first registered mosque in the UK, Cardiff, 1860": the evolution of a myth', *Contemporary Islam*, 4: 2. (2010) 179-93 http://www.springerlink.com/content/m724058668511973/.
4. The cover image for this book
5. Cadvan Rhys (Dewi Delta Evans), *Daniel Evelyn, Heretic* (London, 1913) 76.
6. The figure seems closely based on that of Gwilym Marles (1834-79), a prominent Unitarian, and the great-uncle of Dylan Thomas, whose was given the middle name, 'Marlais' in honour of his relative.
7. *Op. cit.* 265.
8. Arthur Machen, *The Secret Glory* (London, 1922). Quotation from the 1998 edition (Leyburn, 1998) 120.
9. Donald Swann, *Swann's Way: A Life in Song* (London, 1993) 42-45.
10. Harold Ingrams, *Arabia and the Isles* (London, 1937) 181.
11. For a study of Welsh-language representations of Tiger Bay, see Simon Brooks, 'Tiger Bay a'r Diwylliant Cymraeg' in *Transactions of the Honourable*

Society of Cymmrodorion, 15 (2009) 198-216.
12. Idris Davies, 'Tiger Bay' in Dafydd Johnston (ed.) *The Complete Poems of Idris Davies* (Cardiff, 1994) 73.
13. Kate Bosse-Griffiths, *Mae'r Galon Wrth y Llyw* (Aberystwyth, 1957) 16-18.
14. Muslims of Pakistani descent now form the biggest single section of the British Islamic community, accounting for 43% of the total, according to the 2001 Census.
15. Eirug Wyn, *Magnifikont* (Talybont, 1982) 20.
16. Alun Richards, *Home to an Empty House* (Llandysul, 1973). Quotations taken from the Library of Wales edition (Cardigan, 2006) 50-52.
18. Mike Jenkins, *This House, My Ghetto* (Bridgend, 1994) 61.
19. Alexander Cordell, *Land of Heart's Desire* (Sutton, 1994) 109.
20. *Ibid.* 111.
21. Tom Davies, *I, Conker* (Llandysul, 1994) 242.
22. *Ibid.* 246.
23. *Ibid.* 250-52.
24. John Williams, *Five Pubs, Two Bars and a Nightclub* (London, 1999) 3.
25. *Ibid.* 4.
26. *Ibid.* 14.
27. *Ibid.* 19.
28. Afshan Malik, *Safar*, in *New Welsh Drama* (Cardigan, 1998) 22-25.
29. *Ibid.* 54.
30. Lewis Davies, *as i was a boy fishing* (Cardigan, 2003) 46.
31. *Ibid.* 45.
32. *Ibid.* 47.
33. Othniel Smith, *Giant Steps*, in *New Welsh Drama II* (Cardigan, 1998) 185.
34. Iwan Llwyd, *Dan Ddylanwad* (Holyhead, 1995) 121.
35. *Ibid.* 122.
36. *Zen Cymru* (Bridgend, 2010) 43.
37. Unpublished.
38. A popular Welsh rugby song.
39. Robert Williams Parry, (1884-1956) a major Welsh-language poet of powerfully lyrical style and sceptical religious views.
40. Idris Davies, 'Capel Calvin', *The Collected Poems of Idris Davies*, Islwyn Jenkins (ed.) (Llandysul, 1984) 9.
41. Alan Harris, *Orange* (Cardiff, 2006) xiii.
42. *Ibid.* 71.
43. David Llewellyn, *Eleven* (Bridgend, 2006) 13.
45. *Ibid.* 23-24.
46. *Ibid.* 34-35.
47. *Ibid.* 56.
48. *Ibid.* 61.
49. *Ibid.* 63.
50. *Ibid.* 71.

51. *Ibid.* 87.
52. *Ibid.* 96.
53. Catrin Dafydd, *Random Deaths and Custard* (Llandysul, 2007) 44.
54. Dahlian Kirby, 'Aysha's Yard-Garden' in Jeni Williams and Latéfa Guémar (eds.), *Fragments from the Dark: Women writing home and self in Wales* (Swansea, 2008) 21.
55. *Ibid.* 22.
56. Pointing out, for instance, that Wales saw the only example of communal anti-Jewish violence in Britain since Jews were allowed to settle in the country again in the time of Oliver Cromwell, having been expelled in 1292 by Edward I. The so-called 'Tredegar Riots' of the Gwent Valleys in 1911 saw Jewish shops targetted for looting during a time of industrial unrest. In 1919, Cardiff, Newport and Barry saw deadly race riots against black and Chinese people as part of a wave of post-WWI race riots across Britain.
57. The estimate of Jewish communal institutions. The 2001 Census actually showed around 2,000 people identifying as Jewish.
58. Ali Yassine, *Llais yr Adar Gleision* (Talybont, 2010) 18-23. Cardiff City fans adopted the gesture in 1990, originally as an ironic comment on a poor team performance, although it quickly became a celebratory ritual.
59. *Blog Vaughan Roderick*, 14 April, 2007 http://www.bbc.co.uk/blogs/thereporters/vaughanroderick/2007/04/lincs_2.html
60. Locations of massacres of Kurdish civilians by Saddam Hussein's Ba'athist regime.
61. Nazand Begikhani, 'At a Happiness Symposium in Wales' in *Fragments from the Dark, op cit.* 124.
62. *Ibid.* 13.
63. Anahita Alikhani, 'Argue with a Foreigner' *ibid.* 44.

Bibliography

ab Ifor, Gwynfor. 'Addolwr', *Barddas,* 286 (February/March, 2006).

Abse, Dannie. *The Presence* (London, 2007).

Aithie, Patricia. *The Burning·Ashes of Time* (Bridgend, 2005).

Andrews, Rhian M. 'Ar Drywydd Pererin: Gwaith Dafydd Benfras, Cerdd 36', in *Llên Cymru,* 32 (2009).

Anon. 'Dyddiadur Cymro', *Heddiw,* 3: 6 (January 1938).

Anon. *Y Twrc wedi ei Glwyfo* (Llanerchymedd, 1827).

Ansari, Humayun. *The infidel within: Muslims in Britain since 1800* (London, 2004).

Anwyl, Edward. (ed.), *The poetry of the Gogynfeirdd from the Myvyrian archaiology of Wales. With an introd. to the study of Old Welsh poetry* (Denbigh, 1909).

ap Fyllin, Edward Pugh. 'Cerdd o Hanes Mab i ŵr Bonheddig o Lancashire: Aeth i Drafaelio' (Oswestry, 1791). See www.e-gymraeg.org/cronfabaledi

Barnes, Alison Elizabeth. 'Welsh Involvement in the Crusades, 1095-1200', MA thesis: (Cardiff University, 2002).

Beddoe, David M. *The Lost Mameluke* (London, 1913).

Beddoe, David M. *The Honour of Henri de Valois* (London, 1905).

Bell, Idris. 'Hela'r Papyrus', *Y Llenor,* 9: 1 (Spring 1930).

Bell, Idris. 'Hela'r Papyrus', *Y Llenor,* 9: 2 (Summer 1930).

Bell, Idris. 'Hela'r Papyrus', *Y Llenor,* 9: 3 (October 1930).

Bell, Idris. *Trwy Diroedd y Dwyrain* (London, 1946).

Bendon, Chris. *Jewry* (Salzburg, 1995) 96.

Blackwell, John ('Alun'). *Gwaith Alun* (Llanuwchllyn, 1909). Owen Morgan Edwards (ed).

Blythin, Islwyn. 'Islam Ddoe a Heddiw', *Cristion,* (September/October 1989).

Bosse-Griffiths, Kate. *Galwad yr Aifft* (Llandybïe, 1970).

Bosse-Griffiths, Kate. *Mae'r Galon Wrth y Llyw* (Aberystwyth, 1957).

Boyd, Matthieu. 'Celts seen as Muslims and Muslims seen as Celts', Jerold C. Frakes (ed.) *Contextualizing the Muslim Other in Medieval Judeo-Christian Discourse* (New York, forthcoming).

Boyer, William Hydwedd. *Ym Mhoethder y Tywod* (Liverpool, 1960).

Bridge, Carl and Fedorowich, Kent. (eds.) *The British World: Diaspora, Culture and Identity* (London, 2003).

Brooks, Simon. 'Tiger Bay a'r Diwylliant Cymraeg', *Transactions of the Honourable Society of Cymmrodorion,* 15 (2009).

Brooks, Simon. 'Wyneb Mohamed', *Barn,* 518 (March, 2006) 7.

Brooks, Simon. Editorial. *Barn,* 519 (April, 2006) 7.

Brown, Stewart. *Lugard's Bridge* (Bridgend, 1989).

Bryan, Robert. 'Adlais o'r Dwyrain', *Cymru,* 42 (1912).

Bryan, Robert. 'El Jihad', reprinted in Bethan Mair & R. Arwel Jones (eds.) *Cerddi'r Byd* (Llandysul, 2005).

Burgess, Anthony. *Any Old Iron* (London, 1989).

Campbell, Joseph. *The Masks of God: Creative Mythology* (London, 1977 edition) 62.

Cannon, Garland and Franklin, Michael J. 'A Cymmrodor claims kin in Calcutta: an assessment of Sir William Jones as philologer, polymath, and pluralist' *Transactions of the Honourable Society of Cymmrodorion*, ns, [11] (2004).

Carey, Gwyneth. 'Y Mwnshi a'r Diacon' in Delyth George (ed.) *Tocyn Tramor* (Talybont, 1997).

Carlyle, Thomas. *On Heroes, Hero-Worship, and The Heroic in History* (London, 1841).

Clare, Horatio. 'Sisters and Brothers' in Barnaby Rogerson (ed.) *Meetings with Remarkable Muslims* (London, 2005).

Collins, Arthur. *The English Baronetage* (London, 1741).

Cordell, Alexander. *Land of Heart's Desire* (Sutton, 1994).

Cule, Cyril Pritchard. *Cymro ar Grwydr* (Llandysul, 1941).

Curley, Michael J. 'The Miracles of St David: A New Text and its Context', *Traditio,* 62 (2007) 135-205 (184, 193-4).

Dafydd, Catrin. *Random Deaths and Custard* (Llandysul, 2007).

Dale-Jones, Don. *A.G. Prys Jones* (Cardiff, 1992).

Dale-Jones, Don. & Jones, P. Bernard (eds.) *The Complete Poems of T.H. Jones* (Cardiff, 2008).

David Gwyn Williams, *Y Ddefod Goll* (Port Talbot, 1980).

Davies Bryan, John. 'Islam a'i Phroffwyd', *Cymru,* 42 (1912).

Davies Bryan, John. 'Islam a'i Phroffwyd', *Cymru,* 43 (1913).

Davies Bryan, John. *O'r Aifft* (Wrexham, 1908) vii.

Davies, D. Ioan. 'Y Grefydd Islamaidd', *Y Cylchgrawn Efengylaidd,* 19: 2 (1980).

Davies, Glyn Gerallt. *Y Dwyrain a Cherddi Eraill 1942-1945* (Liverpool, 1945).

Davies, Grahame. *The Chosen People* (Bridgend, 2002).

Davies, Gwilym. 'Rhyddid a Chymru', *Tir Newydd,* 14 (November 1938).

Davies, Hazel Walford. 'Boundaries: the early travel books and periodicals of O.M. Edwards', in Hywel Teifi Edwards (ed.) *A Guide to Welsh Literature c.1800-1900* (Cardiff, 2000).

Davies, Idris. *The Collected Poems of Idris Davies,* Islwyn Jenkins (ed.) (Llandysul, 1984).

Davies, Idris. *The Complete Poems of Idris Davies,* Dafydd Johnston (ed.) (Cardiff, 1994).

Davies, J.E. *Crefyddau y Byd Cristionogaidd* (Scranton, 1868), trans. John Bear of Canberra, Australia. http://oldwelshbooks.net/

Davies, Lewis. *as i was a boy fishing* (Cardigan, 2003).

Davies, Merryl Wyn & Sardar, Ziauddin. *Why Do People Hate America?* (London, 2002).

Davies, Merryl Wyn. 'Wilful Imaginings', *New Internationalist,* 345 (May 2002), http://www.newint.org/features/2002/05/01/wilful-imaginings/

Davies, Rhys J. *Seneddwr ar Dramp* (Liverpool, 1934).

Davies, Stevie. 'Into Suez', advance extract published in *New Welsh Review* (Winter 2009).

Davies, Tom. *I, Conker* (Llandysul, 1994).

Donahaye, Jasmine. "'By Whom Shall She Arise? For She Is Small": The Wales-Israel Tradition in the Edwardian period,' in Eitan Bar-Yosef & Nadia Valman (eds.) *'The Jew' in Late-Victorian and Edwardian Culture: Between the East End and East Africa* (London, 2009).

Edbury, Peter. 'Preaching the Crusade in Wales', *England and Germany in the High Middle Ages,* Alfred Haverkamp & Hanna Vollrath (eds.) (Oxford, 1996).

Edwards, Bernard. *The Grey Widow-Maker* (London, 1990).

Edwards, Charles. *Hanes y Ffydd Ddi-Ffuant,* University of Wales Press edition (Cardiff, 1936).
Edwards, D. Miall. *Cristionogaeth a Chrefyddau Eraill* (Dolgellau, 1923)
Edwards, Owen Morgan. 'Arabia' *Cymru* (September 1916).
Elis, Islwyn Ffowc. *Wythnos yng Nghymru Fydd* (Cardiff, 1957).
Ellis, T.E. (Thomas Evelyn Scott-Ellis, 8th Lord Howard de Walden), *The Byzantine Plays* (Windsor, 2006).
Erbery, William. *The testimony of William Erbery, left upon record for the saints of succeeding ages* (London, 1658).
Evans, J. Gwenogvryn. (ed.) *The Black Book of Carmarthen* (Pwllheli, 1906).
Evans, Elwyn. 'Obituary: Geraint Dyfnallt Owen' *The Independent,* 22 February 1993 http://www.independent.co.uk/news/people/obituary-geraint-dyfnallt-owen-1474551.html
Evans, Elwyn. *Amser a Lle* (Llandysul, 1975).
Evans, Elwyn. *Cyfarfod ag Affrica* (Denbigh, 1995).
Evans, John. 'Dinasoedd Mahomet', *Y Traethodydd,* 74: 331 (1919).
Evans, John. 'Dinasoedd Mahomet', *Y Traethodydd,* 74: 332 (1919).
Evans, Robin. 'Cymru, Yr Yemen a'r Môr', *Cymru a'r Môr / Maritime Wales,* 17 (1995) 117-19.
Evans, Samuel. 'Y Gŵr o Fecca a'i Grefydd', *Y Traethodydd,* 45 (1890).
Fainlight, Harry. *Selected Poems* (London, 1986).
Finch, Peter. 'Last seen in Barbados', *Planet: The Welsh Internationalist,* 140, (April/May 2000).
Finch, Peter. *Zen Cymru* (Bridgend, 2010).
Forrester, Dorothy Elwyn. 'Roberts, John', *Welsh Biography Online* http://yba.llgc.org.uk/en/s-ROBE-JOH-1842.html
Franklin, Michael J. (ed.) *Sir William Jones. Selected Poetical and Prose Works* (Cardiff, 1995).
Fromkin, David. *A Peace to End All Peace* (New York, 1989).
Garlick, Raymond & Mathias, Roland (eds.) *Anglo Welsh Poetry 1480-1990* (Bridgend, 1990).
Gilliat-Ray, Sophie. *Muslims in Britain; An Introduction* (Cambridge, 2010)
Gilliat-Ray, Sophie. '"The first registered mosque in the UK, Cardiff, 1860": the evolution of a myth', *Contemporary Islam,* 4:2 (2010). http://www.springerlink.com/content/m724058668511973/
Gilmour, David. 'The Unregarded Prophet: Lord Curzon and the Palestine Question', *Journal of Palestine Studies,* 25:3 (Spring, 1996).
Giraldus Cambrensis, 'Gerald of Wales', *The Journey Through Wales/The Description of Wales,* trans. Lewis Thorpe (Harmondsworth, 1978).
Gladstone, William Ewart. *Bulgarian horrors and the question of the East* (London, 1876).
Gorlech, Dafydd. 'Ymddiddan rhwng y bardd a'r Wyddfa' in Erwain R. Rheinallt (ed.) *Gwaith Dafydd Gorlech* (Aberystwyth, 1997).
Granelli, Roger. *Crystal Spirit* (Bridgend, 1992) 165.
Graves, Alfred Perceval. (trans.) *Welsh Poetry Old and New* (London, 1912).
Greene, Emily. *Approaches to the Great Settlement* (New York, 1918).
Gregory, J.W. *The Foundation of British East Africa* (London, 1901).
Griffith, G. Penar. *Hanes bywgraffiadol o genhadon Cymreig i wledydd paganaidd* (Cardiff, 1897).
Griffith, Stephen. *Teithio'r Sahel* (Talybont, 1986).

Griffiths, Griffith Milwyn. 'Jones, Margaret', *Welsh Biography Online*; http://yba.llgc.org.uk/en/s3-JONE-MAR-1902.html
Griffiths, J. Gwyn. *Hog dy Fwyell* Heini Gruffudd (ed.) (Talybont, 2007).
Griffiths, T. Elwyn. (ed.) *Seren y Dwyrain*, (Bala, 1955).
Griffiths, Tweli. 'Yn y Drych Aneglur' in Dylan Iorwerth (ed.), *Deuddeng Mlynedd o Ohebu Tramor* (Cardiff, 1993).
Griffiths, Vivian. 'Pray Wolf,' *Sinews from Salt* (Llandybïe, 1969).
Grubb, Norman. *Rees Howells, Intercessor* (Cambridge, 1952).
Gwanas, Bethan. *Mwy o Fyd Bethan* (Llandysul, 2005).
Gwynn, Eirwen. *Dim Ond Un* (Llandysul, 1997).
Hamilton, Jill. *God, Guns and Israel* (Stroud, 2004).
Hansard. HC Deb 26 February 1920, 125, 1949-2060.
Harris, Alan. *Orange* (Cardiff, 2006).
Hicks, Raymond. *An Odyssey: From Ebbw Vale to Tyneside* (Newcastle upon Tyne, 2007).
Hiraethog, Gruffudd. 'Ateb', in D.J. Bowen (ed.) *Gwaith Gruffudd Hiraethog* (Cardiff, 1990).
Hughes, John. 'Cofiant a Llythyrau Ann Griffiths', *Y Traethodydd* (1846).
Hughes, Richard. *In the Lap of Atlas* (London, 1979).
Humphreys, Edward Morgan & Jenkins, Robert Thomas. 'Bryan, Robert' *Welsh Biography Online* http://yba.llgc.org.uk/cy/c-BRYA-ROB-1858.html
Hurlock, Kathryn. *Crusades and Crusading in the Welsh Annalistic Chronicles* (Lampeter, 2009).
Ifans, Glyn. 'Tua'r Dwyrain', *Cyfansoddiadau a Beirniadaethau Eisteddfod Genedlaethol Cymru*, Rhyl, 1953 (Liverpool, 1953).
Ifans, Glyn. *Gwynt yr Ynysoedd Bach*, (Llandysul, 1975).
Ingrams, Harold. *Arabia and the Isles* (London, 1937).
Isaac, Graham R. 'Ymddiddan Taliesin ac Ugnach: Propaganda Cymreig yn Oes y Croesgadau?' *Llên Cymru*, 25 (2002).
Iwan, Llion. *Yr Anweledig* (Llandysul, 2008).
James, Brian Ll. 'The evolution of a radical', *The Journal of Welsh Ecclesiastical History*, 3 (1986).
James, E. Wyn. (ed.) *Rhyfeddaf Fyth, Emynau a Llythyrau Ann Griffiths Ynghyd â'r Byrgofiant Iddi gan John Hughes, Pontrobert, a Rhai Llythyrau gan Gyfeillion* (Newtown, 1998).
James, E. Wyn. 'The New Birth of a People': Welsh Language and Identity and the Welsh Methodists, *c*.1740–182' in Robert Pope (ed.) *Religion and National Identity: Wales and Scotland c.1700-2000* (Cardiff, 2001).
James, E. Wyn. 'Williams Pantycelyn a Gwawr y Mudiad Cenhadol' *Cof Cenedl*, 17 (Llandysul, 2002).
James, E. Wyn. '"Seren Wib Olau": Gweledigaeth a Chenhadaeth Morgan John Rhys (1760-1804)', *Trafodion Cymdeithas Hanes y Bedyddwyr*, 5 (2007).
Jarman, A.O.H. (ed.) *Chwedlau Cymraeg Canol* (Cardiff, 1957).
Jarman, A.O.H. (ed.) *Llyfr Du Caerfyrddin* (Cardiff, 1982).
Jenkins, David. *Thomas Gwynn Jones* (Denbigh, 1973). References from second edition, 1994.
Jenkins, Mike. *This House, My Ghetto* (Bridgend, 1994).
Jenkins, Nigel. *Gwalia in Khasia* (Llandysul, 1995).
Jenkins, Nigel. *Acts of Union, Selected Poems 1974-1989* (Llandysul, 1989).
Jenkins, Robert Thomas. 'Lewis, Sir Henry', *Welsh Biography Online*, http://yba.llgc.

org.uk/en/s-LEWI-HEN-1847.html
Jobbins, Siôn. 'Llanistan', *Cambria* (August/September, 2006) 28.
Johnston, Dafydd. (ed.) *Gwaith Iolo Goch* (Cardiff, 1988).
Johnston, Dafydd. (ed.) *Gwaith Lewys Glyn Cothi* (Cardiff, 1995).
Johnston, Dafydd. (ed.) *Iolo Goch: Poems* (Llandysul, 1993) Poem I, line 55.
Jones, Bobi. *Casgliad o Gerddi* (Aberystwyth, 1989).
Jones, D. Rhagfyr. *I'r Aifft ac Yn Ôl* (Wrecsam, 1904).
Jones, Dafydd Gwilym Merfyn. *Blwyddyn y Newyn* (Caernarfon, 1981).
Jones, Dafydd Gwilym Merfyn. *Y Popty Poeth a'i Gyffiniau* (Caernarfon, 1990).
Jones, David James. ('Gwenallt'), 'Mosg Al-Agsa', in Christine James (ed.) *Cerddi Gwenallt: Y Casgliad Cyflawn* (Llandysul, 2001) 332.
Jones, Dyfrig. 'Cenhadon Casineb', *Barn,* 518 (March, 2006) 5.
Jones, Elias Henry. *The Road to En-Dor* (London, 1919).
Jones, Elizabeth J. *Y Drysorfa,* 88 (May 1918).
Jones, Gareth Lloyd. *Yng Ngwlad yr Addewid* (Caernarfon, 1966).
Jones, Geraint Vaughan. *Omega* (Llanrwst, 2000).
Jones, Gerallt. (ed.) *Y Capten Jac Alun* (Llandysul, 1984).
Jones, Griffith Hartwell. *Celtic Britain and the Pilgrim Movement* (London, 1912).
Jones, Gruffydd Aled. 'Meddylier am India': Tair Taith y Genhadaeth Gymreig yn Sylhet 1887-1947', *Trafodion Anrhydeddus Gymdeithas y Cymmrodorion,* 4 (1997).
Jones, Gwenllian. *Llythyrau Bangladesh* (Llanrwst, 1993).
Jones, Huw. *Hanes y Capten Ffactor* in A. Cynfael Lake (ed.) *Anterliwtiau Huw Jones o Langwm* (Swansea, 2000).
Jones, J. Graham & Owen, Goronwy Wyn (eds.) *Gweithiau Morgan Llwyd o Wynedd,* I (Cardiff 1993).
Jones, John & Daniel (eds.) *Cofiant ynghyd â gweddillion caniadau Edward Jones o Faes y Plwm* (Mold, 1839).
Jones, John. 'Mynydd Sinai' *Y Traethodydd,* 60: 264 (1905).
Jones, John. 'Traethawd ar Dwrci, a Hanes Bywyd Nicholas o Rwsia' (Llanidloes, 1855).
Jones, Margaret. *Llythyrau Cymraes o Wlad Canaan* (Liverpool, 1869).
Jones, Michael D. 'Y Cymry ac Ymfudaeth', *Yr Amserau* (3 December, 1856).
Jones, Morgan. *Gogoniant y Byd Hwn, neu ddesgrifiad o'r Dinasoedd mwyaf, godidocal, a rhyfeddaf yn y Byd* (Carmarthen, 1813).
Jones, Owen. *Y Cyniweirydd* (Mold, 1834).
Jones, Patrick. *darkness is where the stars are* (Blaenau Ffestiniog, 2008).
Jones, R. Arwel. *Jambo Caribw* (Talybont, 2004).
Jones, Siân Wyn. 'Yng Nghamau T. Gwynn Jones', *Taliesin,* 74 (Summer 1991).
Jones, Siân Wyn. *O Gamddwr i Gairo - Hanes y Brodyr Davies Bryan (1851-1935)* (Wrexham, 2004).
Jones, Thomas Gwynn. *Y Môr Canoldir a'r Aifft* (Caernarfon, 1912).
Jones, Thomas. (ed.) *Brut y Tywysogion or The Chronicle of the Princes, Peniarth MS 20 Version* (Cardiff, 1952)
Jones, Tom Madoc. *Ar Gerdded* (Liverpool, 1969).
Jones, Tom Madoc. *O'r Aifft i Baghdad* (Liverpool, 1953).
Jones, W. Hughes. 'On Translating Omar', in *At the Foot of Eryri* (Bangor, 1912).
Jones, William Emlyn. *Tua'r Dwyrain* (Llandybïe, 1963).
Jones, William Emlyn. *Y Saith Ganhwyllbren Aur* (Llandybïe, 1969).
Kirby, Dahlian. 'Aysha's Yard-Garden' in Williams, Jeni & Guémar, Latéfa (eds.) *Fragments from the Dark: Women writing home and self in Wale*s (Swansea, 2008).

Lane, Tony. *The Merchant Seaman's War* (Manchester, 1991).
Lansdown, Gwenllian. 'Y Gwir yn Erbyn y Byd?', *Barn,* 519 (April, 2006).
Laqueur, Walter. *A History of Zionism* (London, 1972).
Lawrence, T.E. *Seven Pillars of Wisdom* (private edition Oxford, 1922, public edition London 1926) References to 1940 edition (London).
Lewis, Alun. Gweno Lewis (ed.) *Letters to my Wife* (Bridgend, 1989).
Lewis, Barry. 'St Margaret of Llanfaches'in *Poems for Saints and Shrines* (Dublin, forthcoming).
Lewis, Caryl. *Naw Mis* (Talybont, 2010).
Lewis, Evan. *Hanes chwech o benboethiaid crefyddol, sef Joseph Smith, Mahomet, Richard Brothers, Jemimah Wilson, Ann Lee, a Joanna Southcotte* (Merthyr Tydfil, 1849).
Lewis, Gwyneth. 'Imaginary Walks in Istanbul,' *New Writing Partnership* website: http://www.newwritingpartnership.org.uk/nwp/site/page2-5.html
Lewis, Hywel David. *Hen a Newydd* (Caernarfon, 1971)
Lewis, R. John. 'Iesu Grist: yr Unig Ffordd?', *Y Cylchgrawn Efengylaidd,* 24:5 (1987).
Lewis, R. John. 'Islâm', *Y Cylchgrawn Efengylaidd,* 24:6 (1987).
Llewellyn, David. *Eleven* (Bridgend, 2006).
Llewellyn, Richard. *I Stood on a Quiet Shore* (London, 1982).
Lloyd George, David. *British War Aims, Statement by the Right Honourable David Lloyd George* (New York, 1918).
Lloyd George, David. *The Great Crusade Extracts from Speeches Delivered During The War* (New York, 1918).
Lloyd George, David. *War Memoirs of David Lloyd George,* 3 (London, 1938).
Lloyd, D. Myrddin. *Rhai Agweddau ar Ddysg y Gogynfeirdd,* (Cardiff, 1977).
Lloyd, Elizabeth M. *Hanes Assam* (Caernarfon, 1916).
Lloyd, Rhiannon. *Llwybr Gobaith* (Caernarfon, 2004).
Lloyd, Simon. *Amseryddiaeth Ysgrythurol,* second edition (Bala, 1842).
Llwyd, Iwan. *Dan Ddylanwad* (Holyhead, 1995).
Llywelyn, Robin. *Un Diwrnod yn yr Eisteddfod* (Llandysul, 2004).
Lowe, Walter Bezant. *The Heart of Northern Wales, I* (Llanfairfechan, 1912) 357.
Machen, Arthur. *The Secret Glory* (London, 1922). Quotation from the 1998 edition (Leyburn, 1998).
MacMillan, Margaret. *Paris 1919: Six Months That Changed the World* (London, 2001).
Mair, Bethan & Jones, R. Arwel. (eds.) *Cerddi'r Byd* (Llandysul, 2005).
Malik, Afshan. *Safar,* in *New Welsh Drama* (Cardigan, 1998).
Malik, Norah A. 'Y Ffordd i Feca', *Cristion* (July / August, 1993).
Marlow, Bethan & Wyn, Laura. (eds.) *Blwyddyn Gap* (Caernarfon, 2009).
Maro, Judith. *Atgofion Haganah* (Liverpool, 1972).
Maro, Judith. *The Remembered Gate* (Liverpool, 1974).
Martin, C.T. (ed.) *Registrum Epistolarum Johannis Peckham* 2: 359 (London, 1884).
Matar, Nabil I. *Islam in Britain 1558-1685* (Cambridge, 1998).
Megan, Siân. *Gwaith Ann Griffiths* (Llandybïe, 1982).
Messamah, Siân. 'Yn enw Duw; y mwyaf grasol, y mwyaf trugarog', *Cristion* (January-February, 1998).
Mills, John. *Palestina* (Llanidloes, 1858).
Milton, Giles. *White Gold* (London, 2004).
Minhinnick, Robert. *After the Hurricane* (Manchester, 2002).
Minhinnick, Robert. *To Babel and Back* (Bridgend, 2005).
Môn, Lewys. Eurys I. Rowlands (ed.) *Gwaith Lewys Môn* (Cardiff, 1975).

Morgan, D. Densil. 'Crefydd ar ôl 9/11', *Y Traethodydd,* 161: 679 (October, 2006).
Morgan, D. J. 'Gair o Ogledd Affrica', *Detholiad o Ysgrifau* (Aberystwyth, 1953).
Morgan, Derec Llwyd. 'Morgan Llwyd a'r Iddewon', *Ysgrifau Beirniadol,* 21 (Denbigh, 1996).
Morgan, Derec Llwyd. *Adnabod Deg* (Denbigh, 1977).
Morgan, Eluned. *Ar Dir a Môr* (Abergavenny, 1913).
Morgannwg, Lewys. 'Moliant Wiliam, Arglwydd Herbert', in A. Cynfael Lake (ed.) *Gwaith Lewys Morgannwg* I (Aberystwyth, 2004).
Morris, Dewi Pws. *Byd Pws* (Llanrwst, 2004).
Morris, James. *Farewell The Trumpets: An Imperial Retreat,* (Harmondsworth, 1978).
Morris, Jan. *A Writer's World: Travels 1950-2000* (London, 2003).
Morris, Jan. *Sultan in Oman* (London, 1983 edition).
Morris-Jones, John. *Caniadau* (Oxford, 1907).
Nasr, Vali. *The Shia Revival: How Conflicts within Islam Will Shape the Future* (New York, 2006).
'Obituary: The Rev D.G. Merfyn Jones': http://www.independent.co.uk/news/obituaries/obituary-the-rev-d-g-merfyn-jones-1143992.html
'Orig Williams, Welsh wrestler', *The Times,* 23 November, 2009 http://www.timesonline.co.uk/tol/comment/obituaries/article6927430.ece
Owen, Dyddgu. *Haul a Heli* (Llandybïe, 1984).
Owen, Geraint Dyfnallt. *Aeth Deugain Mlynedd Heibio: Dyddiadur Rhyfel* (Caernarfon, 1985).
Owen, Morfydd E. 'Cwyn y Pererin', in R. Geraint Gruffydd (ed.) *Gwaith Dafydd Benfras ac Eraill* (Cardiff, 1995).
Parry, John. *Gwyddoniadur,* 10 (Denbigh, 1879).
Parry-Williams, T.H. 'Y Groes Naid', *Y Llinyn Arian* (Aberystwyth, 1947).
Pearson, Lynn. *Tile Gazetteer: A Guide to British Tile and Architectural Ceramics Locations* (Shepton Beauchamp, 2005).
Peate, Iorwerth Cyfeiliog. 'Tua Granada', *Y Llenor,* 8:4 (Winter, 1929).
Peate, Iorwerth Cyfeiliog. *Plu'r Gweunydd* (Liverpool, 1933).
Penman, Sharon. *Falls the Shadow* (London, 1988).
Penri Davies, John. *Blas y Môr* (Denbigh, 1976) 75.
Phillips, Edgar. *Trysor o Gân i'r Plant* (Cardiff, 1931).
Phillips, Eluned. *Cerddi Glyn y Mêl* (Llandysul, 1985).
Phillips, Rhiain M. *Cefndir* (Denbigh, 1986).
'Poet "stirred up" storm over book.' BBC News Online, 15 November, 2008: http://news.bbc.co.uk/1/hi/wales/7730396.stm
Powys, Betsan. 'Bosnia', in Gwyn Erfyl (ed.) *Y Teithiwr Talog* (Llanrwst, 1998).
Powys, John Cowper. *Obstinate Cymric* (Carmarthen, 1947).
Price, Angharad. '"O! Tyn y Gorchudd": Golwg ar fywyd a gwaith Hugh Jones, Maesglasau', *Transactions of the Honourable Society of Cymmrodorion,* 10 (London, 2003).
Prosser, Alwyn. 'Diddordebau Lleyg Williams Pantycelyn', *Llên Cymru,* 4:4 (1955).
Pugh, Sheenagh. *Beware Falling Tortoises* (Bridgend, 1987).
Pugh, Sheenagh. *Id's Hospit* (Bridgend, 1997).
Pugh, Sheenagh. *Selected Poems* (Bridgend, 1990).
Pugh, Sheenagh. *Sing for the Taxman* (Bridgend, 1993).
Pugh, Sheenagh. *Stonelight* (Bridgend, 1999).
Raafat, Samir. 'Four Welshmen Who Made Good In Egypt', *Egyptian Mail,* 27 May 1995. http://www.egy.com/landmarks/95-05-27.shtml See also Edward Morgan

Humphreys , 'Evans, Samuel', in *Welsh Biography Online* http://yba.llgc.org.uk/en/s-EVAN-SAM-1859.html

Rees, D. Ben. 'Cyril Cule' *The Guardian*, 23 April 2002, http://www.guardian.co.uk/news/2002/apr/23/guardianobituaries2

Rees, Evan ('Dyfed'). *Gwlad yr Addewid* (Caernarfon, 1900) 2nd edition.

Rees, Evan. ('Dyfed'), *Gwaith Barddonol Dyfed* (Cardiff, 1907).

Rhys, Cadvan. (Dewi Delta Evans), *Daniel Evelyn, Heretic* (London, 1913).

Rhys, Gethin. 'Ymateb i Rushdie', *Cristion* (January/February, 1993).

Rhys, James Ednyfed. 'Rees, Evan', *Welsh Biography Online*, http://yba.llgc.org.uk/en/s-REES-EVA-1850.html

Rice, David. Hanes *Brwydr Naverino* (Swansea, 1828).

Richard of Devizes, *Richard of Holy Trinity, Itinerary of Richard I and others to the Holy Land* (Ontario, 2001) 70.

Richards, Alun. *Home to an Empty House* (Llandysul, 1973). Quotations from the Library of Wales edition (Cardigan, 2006).

Richards, Morgan. *Hanes bywyd a chrefydd y gau-brophwyd Mahomet, yn nghyda rhagdraith ar Arabia* (Bangor, 1855).

Roberts, John John. 'Cymeriadau Mawrion', *Y Traethodydd*, 63: 285 (1908).

Roberts, O. Trevor. *Ar Dir a Môr* (Ruthin, 1987).

Roberts, R. 'Dysgeidiaeth Muhammed am Grist' *Y Traethodydd,* 64: 290 (1909).

Roberts, Selyf. *Hel Meddyliau* (Denbigh, 1982).

Roberts, Thomas E. *Jerusalem: Y Ddinas Sanctaidd* (Caernarfon, 1904).

Roberts, Thomas E. *Palesteina Hen a Newydd* (London, 1933).

Roberts, William Owen. *Pestilence*, trans. Elisabeth Roberts (London 1991).

Roderick, Vaughan. *Blog Vaughan Roderick*, 14 April, 2007 http://www.bbc.co.uk/blogs/thereporters/vaughanroderick/2007/04/lincs_2.html

Rosser, Siwan M. *Y Ferch ym Myd y Faled* (Cardiff, 2005).

Rowlands, Gwyddno. 'Islâm', *Y Cylchgrawn Efengylaidd*, 28:2 (1991).

Saadat, Rhian. *Window Dressing for Hermès* (Cardigan, 2004).

Salter, H.E. & Lobel, Mary D. *'Jesus College', A History of the County of Oxford: 3: The University of Oxford* (Oxford, 1954).

Smith, Othniel. *Giant Steps*, in *New Welsh Drama II* (Cardigan, 1998).

St Jerome, 'Letter XLVI. Paula and Eustochium to Marcella', Philip Schaff & Henry Wace (eds.) T*he Principal Works of St. Jerome* (Grand Rapids, 1889).

Stanley, Henry Morton. *Through the Dark Continent* (New York, 1878) 193.

Stephens, Meic (ed. & trans.). *Illuminations: an anthology of Welsh short prose* (Cardiff, 1998).

Stephens, Meic (ed.) *The New Companion to the Literature of Wales* (Cardiff, 1998).

Stephens, Meic. 'Obituary: Eirwen Gwynn, Welsh nationalist and writer,' *The Independent*, 30 January, 2007: http://www.independent.co.uk/news/obituaries/eirwen-gwynn-434251.html

Stephens, Meic. 'Robin Williams: Sophisticated Welsh-language essayist' *The Independent,* 23 December 2003. http://www.independent.co.uk/news/obituaries/robin-williams-549141.html

Swann, Donald. *Swann's Way: A Life in Song* (London, 1993).

Teignmouth, Lord. *The Work of Sir William Jones* (London, 1807).

Temperley, H.W.V. (ed.) *A History of the Peace Conference of Paris*, 6 (Oxford 1969).

The Holy Qur'an, trans. Abdullah Yusuf Ali, (Lahore, 1938). Quotations from 10th edition, (Beltsville, Maryland, 1997).

The Islamic Review, April 1920.

Thomas, Gwyn. 'Y Mae'r Tyrau Mawr yn Torri', *Barddas,* 303 (April/May/June, 2009).

Thomas, Gwyn. *Apocalups Yfory* (Swansea, 2005).

Thornton, Tim. 'The battle of Sandeford: Henry Tudor's understanding of the meaning of Bosworth Field,' in *Historical Research,* 78: 201 (August 2005) 436.

Tobias, Lily. *The Samaritan* (London, 1939).

Tomos, Angharad. *Rhagom* (Llanrwst, 2004).

Tri Brenin o Gwlen (ms. 1552) British Library Additional 14986, 37. *A Historical Corpus of the Welsh Language 1500-1850*: http://people.pwf.cam.ac.uk/dwew2/hcwl/menu.htm

Tudor Jones, John ('John Eilian'). 'Ym Maghdad', *Y Llenor,* 9:3 (October 1930).

Walker, David. *Medieval Wales* (Cambridge, 1990) 108.

Walters, John. *An English and Welsh Dictionary* (Denbigh, 1770-94).

Watkins-Thomas, M. 'Our Asian Crews', *About Ourselves* (September 1955) http://www.lascars.co.uk/crew.html

Wiliam, Urien. *Tu Hwnt i'r Mynydd Du* (Swansea, 1976).

Wiliams, Gerwyn. 'Mab yr Archdderwydd yn Hyrwyddo Achos Islâm – y pennawd na fu!', *Barddas,* 273 (June/July/August 2003).

Wiliams, Gerwyn. *Tir Newydd* (Cardiff, 2005)

Williams, Cyril Glyndŵr. 'Ceisio Deall Islam' *Y Traethodydd,* 146: 618 (1991).

Williams, Cyril Glyndŵr. 'The Unfeigned Faith and an Eighteenth Century Pantheologia' *Numen,* 15: 3 (Nov, 1968).

Williams, Cyril Glyndwr. *Nadolig yn Calcutta* (Llandysul, 975).

Williams, David Edmund. *Hwylio'r Moroedd* (Denbigh, 1945).

Williams, David Gwyn. (ed.) *Flyting in Egypt* (Port Talbot, 1991).

Williams, David Gwyn. 'Durrell in Egypt' *Twentieth Century Literature,* 33:3, Lawrence Durrell Issue, Part I (Autumn, 1987).

Williams, David Gwyn. *Y Cloc Tywod* (Talybont, 1984).

Williams, David Gwyn.*ABC of (D)GW* (Llandysul, 1981).

Williams, J.E. Caerwyn. Lynch, Peredur I. & Gruffydd, R. Geraint. (eds.) *Gwaith Meilyr Brydydd a'i Ddisgynyddion* (Cardiff, 1994).

Williams, J. Griffith. *Omar* (Denbigh, 1981).

Mathew Williams *Hanes holl grefyddau'r byd* (Carmarthen, 1799).

Williams, John Jones. *Llongwr o Ros-Lan* (Pen-y-groes, 1983).

Williams, John. *Five Pubs, Two Bars and a Nightclub* (London, 1999).

Williams, John Roberts. *Chwarter Canrif Fesul Pum Munud* (Caernarfon, 2001).

Williams, Mathew. *Hanes Holl Grefyddau'r Byd* (Carmarthen, 1799).

Williams, Llewelyn. *Rheng o Dri* (Llandybïe, 1964).

Williams, Orig. *Cario'r Ddraig* (Talybont, 1985).

Williams, R.J. *Y Parchedig John Roberts, D.D. Khasia* (Caernarfon, 1923).

Williams, R.R. *Be Di Be Mewn Diwinyddiaeth* (Caernarfon, 1965).

Williams, R.R. *Breuddwyd Cymro Mewn Dillad Benthyg* (Liverpool, 1964).

Williams, Rhydwen. *Barddoniaeth Rhydwen Williams:Y Casgliad Cyflawn 1941-1991* (Llandybïe, 1991).

Williams, Robin. *Hoelion Wyth* (Llandysul, 1986).

Williams, Robin. 'Muhammad Ali', *Colofn Bapur* (Llandysul, 1992).

Williams, Robin.*Tynnu Llwch* (Llandysul, 1991).

Williams, Tom Nefyn. *Yr Ymchwil* (Denbigh, 1949).

Williams, W.D. *Cerddi'r Hogiau* (Llandybïe, 1943).

Williams, W.E. *Llyncu'r Angor* (Denbigh, 1977).

Williams, William ('Caledfryn'). *Caniadau Caledfryn* (Llanrwst, 1856).
Williams, William ('Pantycelyn'). *Pantheologia* (Carmarthen, 1762).
Williams, William Philip. *Heli yn y Gwaed* (Caernarfon, 1969).
Wilson, Jeremy. Lawrence of Arabia (London, 1989).
Wyn, Eirug. *Magnifikont* (Talybont, 1982).
Wynne, Ellis. *Gweledigaetheu y bardd cwsc, The Visions of the Sleeping Bard* trans. Robert Gwyneddon Davies (Caernarfon, 1897).
Wynne, Ernest Edward. 'Jones, Huw', *Welsh Biography Online*, National Library of Wales, http://yba.llgc.org.uk/en/s-JONE-HUW-1700.html
Y Dioddefaint (ms. 1552) British Library Additional 14986, 10v-33v. 13. *A Historical Corpus of the Welsh Language 1500-1850.*
Yassine, Ali. *Llais yr Adar Gleision* (Talybont, 2010)

THANKS AND ACKNOWLEDGEMENTS.

In preparing this work I am greatly indebted to the many friends and colleagues who have generously provided vital information, assistance and advice.

Firstly, *diolch o galon* to Dr E. Wyn James of the School of Welsh at Cardiff University, who read the typescript and to whom I owe a deep debt of gratitude for his generous assistance. Prof. Peter Edbury of the Centre for the Crusades at Cardiff University's School of History, Archaeology and Religion, and Dr Barry Lewis of the University of Wales Centre for Advanced Welsh and Celtic Studies at Aberystwyth kindly read the chapter on the Crusades and I am very grateful to them for sharing with me so readily the benefit of their expertise in the period. Vaughan Roderick, Political Correspondent for BBC Wales, read the typescript, and I am indebted to him likewise for his comments and guidance.

To Cardiff University's School of History, Archaeology and Religion, and particularly to Dr Sophie Gilliat-Ray, Director of the University's Centre for the Study of Islam in the U.K, I am grateful for the Honorary Research Fellowship in the department, and also for much help and advice.

For the opportunity of lecturing on the subject of Wales and Islam at Harvard University, my gratitude goes to: Dr Aled Llion; Prof. William Granara of the Center for Middle Eastern Studies; Catherine McKenna, Margaret Brooks Robinson Professor and Chair of Celtic Languages and Literatures, and Tomás Ó Cathasaigh, Henry L. Shattuck Professor of Irish Studies and Director of Graduate Studies.

For guidance, assistance, additional information, or for permission to use material, I would like to thank, among others: Patricia Aithie, whose photograph is used for the cover of this book; Geoff Ballinger; Dr Matthieu Boyd; Dr Simon Brooks; Dr Tom Cheesman; Dr Jasmine Donahaye; Peter Finch; Jon Gower; Keith Greenway for assistance with research into the *S.S. Trevessa*; Havard Gregory; Dr David Jenkins; Prof. Dafydd Johnston, Director of the University of Wales Centre for Advanced Welsh and Celtic Studies; Dr Iwan Russell Jones; Dwynwen Kovacs; Dr Jody Mellor; Dr Gwyneth Lewis; Alan

Llwyd; Gareth Miles; Giles Milton, and Sheenagh Pugh.

Among members of the Islamic community, I am very grateful to Sheikh Shahid Khan, his family and members of the Naqshbandi Haqqani tariqah for sharing their hospitality and the experience of the *zikr*; to Safiya Sayed Baharun, and to Cardiff's Bazm e Adab poetry society for sharing fellowship and Urdu poetry.

I would like to record my thanks to Academi, the national literature promotion agency for Wales, for the award of a writer's bursary which made this work possible.

My thanks go to Mick Felton and the staff at Seren Books for their faith in this project and for their customary hard work.

The research for this study was carried out mainly at: Cardiff University's Arts and Social Studies Library; Cardiff Central Library; the National Library of Wales, Aberystwyth, and the British Library, London, and I am very grateful to the dedicated staff of those institutions for their ready assistance and efficiency. I am grateful also to all the people around the world who digitised Welsh or other relevant texts, whether as academic projects or as labours of love.

While I am indebted to all those mentioned above, and to others not named here, any errors or omissions in this work, are, of course, my sole responsibility.

Finally, this book is dedicated to the memory of my father, Oswald Davies (1929-2010), whose lecturing work in Sudan first brought me into contact with the world of Islam. *Gŵr gorwelion eang, gŵr ei filltir sgwâr.*

Publisher's Acknowledgements.

The publisher is grateful to the following for permission to quote: Nazand Beginkhani for 'At a Happiness Symposium in Wales' from *Fragments from the Dark: Women writing home and self in Wales* (Hafan Books, 2008); Stewart Brown for the extract from 'Lugard's Bridge', taken from *Lugard's Bridge* (Seren 1989); The Estate of Glynne Gerallt Davies for Y Balmwydden' from *Y Dwyrain a Cherddi Eraill 1942-1945* (1945), translated here by Grahame Davies; The Estate of Idris Davies for 'Tiger Bay' and the extract from 'Capel Calvin', from *The Collected Poems of Idris Davies* (Gomer, 1984); Stevie Davies for the excerpt from *Into Suez* (Parthian, 2010); Tom Davies for the extract from *I Conker* (Gomer, 1994); The Estate of Harry Fainlight for 'Fugue', from *Selected Poems* (Turret Bookshop, 1986); Peter Finch for 'Entry of Christ Into Cardiff' from *Zen Cymru* (Seren, 2010) and 'Fun Day' (unpublished); Gwynfor ab Ifor for 'Addolwr', published in *Barddas* magazine, 2006 and translated here by Grahame Davies; Mike Jenkins for 'This House, My Ghetto' from *This House, My Ghetto* (Seren, 1995); Nigel Jenkins for excerpts from *Acts of Union* (Gomer, 1990) and *Gwalia in Khasia* (Gomer, 1996); The Estate of Albert Evans-Jones for 'Salaam' from *Cerddi Cynan* (Gomer, 1987) translated here by Grahame Davies; The Estate of David James Jones for 'Mosg Al Asga' and 'Gabriel', from *Cerddi Gwenallt: Y Casgliad Cyflawn* (Gomer, 2002), translated here by Grahame Davies; The Estate of J Gwyn Griffiths for 'Flam Casineb' and 'Beth yw'r mat dda?' from *Hog dy Fwyell* (Talybont, 2007), translated here by Grahame Davies; Patrick Jones for 'moment of light' and the extract from 'hymn', from *darkness is where the stars* are (Cinnamon Press, 2008); The Estate of T. Harri Jones for 'Djinn Master Solomon', from *The Complete Poems of T.H. Jones* (University of Wales Press, 2008); Gwyneth Lewis and New Writing Partnership for 'Imaginary Walks in Istanbul', published: http://www.newwritingpartnership.org.uk/nwp/site/page2-5.html; The Estate of Eluned Phillips for 'Gwario' from *Cerddi Glyn y Mêl* (Gomer, 1985), translated her by Grahame Davies; Sheenagh Pugh for 'The Embarkation of the Pigs' from *Id's Hospit* (Seren, 1997) and 'The Tormented Censor' from *Later Selected Poems* (Seren, 2009), and for extracts from 'Crusaders', from *Beware Falling Tortoises* (Poetry Wales Press, 1987) and 'M.S.A.' from *Selected Poems* (Seren, 1990); Rhian Saadat for 'Grey Raincoats' from *Window Dressing for Hermes* (Parthian, 2004)

INDEX